Learning Aid for use with

basic marketing

A GLOBAL-MANAGERIAL APPROACH

ELEVENTH CANADIAN EDITION

KENNETH B. WONG
Queen's School of Business
Queen's University

STANLEY J. SHAPIRO
Simon Fraser University
(Professor Emeritus)

WILLIAM D. PERREAULT
University of North Carolina

E. JEROME McCARTHY
Michigan State University

Prepared by
ALGIS JUZUKONIS
Seneca College of Applied Arts and Technology

 **McGraw-Hill Ryerson**

Toronto Montréal Boston Burr Ridge, IL Dubuque, IA Madison, WI New York
San Francisco St. Louis Bangkok Bogotá Caracas Kuala Lumpur Lisbon London Madrid
Mexico City Milan New Delhi Santiago Seoul Singapore Sydney Taipei

McGraw-Hill Ryerson

Learning Aid for use with
Basic Marketing: A Global-Managerial Approach
Eleventh Canadian Edition

ISBN: 0-07-095233-7

1 2 3 4 5 6 7 8 9 10 TRI 0 9 8 7 6 5

Printed and bound in Canada.

Vice President, Editorial and Media Technology: Patrick Ferrier
Sponsoring Editor: Kim Brewster
Developmental Editor: Darren Hick
Marketing Manager: Kim Verhaeghe
Supervising Editor: Joanne Murray
Senior Production Coordinator: Jennifer Wilkie
Printer: Tri-Graphic Printing

Contents

III

Introduction

This *Learning Aid* is designed to help you organize, learn and apply the concepts that are presented in *Basic Marketing, Eleventh Canadian Edition*. Over the years marketing instructors and students have confirmed that students who regularly use the *Learning Aid*, understand and apply the concepts better, and also tend to do better on tests and examinations.

The Learning Aid is used together with the text book. It is not a substitute for reading and carefully studying the textbook.

How the Learning Aid is Organized

The Learning Aid is divided into 19 chapters – one chapter for each corresponding chapter in *Basic Marketing, Eleventh Canadian Edition*. Each chapter in the Learning Aid contains the following five sections:

- *Chapter Summary:* Each chapter has a number of different learning outcomes or goals. The chapter summary lists, explains and summarizes each of the learning outcomes. You should read the chapter summary over before reading the chapter.

- *Important Terms:* Each chapter of *Basic Marketing, Eleventh Canadian Edition* introduces important terms. This section lists the terms and gives you page references to locate them.

- *True/False Questions:* This is the first self-testing section. True/False will test your ability to remember and understand various concepts presented in the chapter. Try this test after reading the text book chapter and reviewing the important terms. Answer all of the questions before looking up the answers at the end of the test.

- *Multiple-Choice Questions:* The second self-testing section, tests your understanding and comprehension of the materials presented. Multiple Choice questions require a greater understanding and comprehension of the terms and concepts, so you should try them after completing the True/False questions. The answers to the questions are at the end of the test.

- *Additional Questions to Test Your Understanding:* The third self-testing section demands an even greater knowledge and understanding of the key concepts. There a variety of different questions, ranging from matching terms to the correct definition, to providing short answers that describe or explain a particular concept.

- *Exercises:* This section helps you apply the concepts that you have learned in typical marketing situations. This section is more of an opportunity to not only review, but to integrate and apply the concepts. Each exercise is designed to illustrate and apply some of the more important concepts and analytical approaches in the text. There is one question which is based on the computer-aided problem found at the end of each chapter. (except Chapter 18)

Remember that the self-testing True/False, Multiple-Choice and Additional Questions are just a sample of what you might expect on a test or examination. They do not cover every single concept discussed in the text, and they do not cover every possible type of question that might be asked on an exam. Just answering the questions is not enough to prepare for tests and exams. You must also read and study the text, and attend classes!

How to Study for Examinations

No single study style and organization works best for everyone, however the following suggestions are based on proven learning principles and should be of benefit to most students. For every chapter your instructor assigns in *Basic Marketing, Eleventh Canadian Edition*:

1. Read the Chapter Summary section in the *Learning Aid*.

2. Study the Important Terms section in the *Learning Aid*, and their definitions in the glossary.

3. Read the chapter from beginning to end without any interruptions and without doing any underlining or note taking. (Underlining key points while you read interrupts your flow of thought and tends to reduce reading comprehension.)

4. Read the chapter again, this time underlining key points and/or writing notes in the page margins. Look at the exhibits and illustrations and think about how they relate to the text material.

5. Review the Important Terms section in the *Learning Aid* and make sure you can define each term.

6. Take the self-testing True/False test in the *Learning Aid* and review the text to study any questions you answered incorrectly.

7. Take the self-testing Multiple Choice test in the *Learning Aid* and review the text to study any questions you answered incorrectly.

8. Take the self-testing Additional Questions test in the *Learning Aid* and review the text to study any questions you answered incorrectly.

9. Take detailed classroom lecture notes and review them immediately after class to make sure they are complete and that you understand everything your instructor said.

10. Do any Exercises in the *Learning Aid* that your instructor assigns.

11. *Optional: Do the Exercises that were not assigned by your instructor.*

12. Just before the test or examination review:
    a. the points you underlined in the text and/or your notes in the page margins.
    b. the Important Terms in the Learning Aid.
    c. the self-testing True/False, Multiple Choice, and Additional Questions in the Learning Aid, particularly the questions you answered wrong the first time.
    d. any Exercises in the Learning Aid assigned by your instructor.
    e. your lecture notes.

Chapter 1

The Nature of Marketing

Chapter Summary

- **Know what marketing is.**

  Marketing is a set of activities done by organizations for some benefit and a social process. Marketing creates time, place, and possession utility and should guide decisions as to what types of goods and services a company should produce to provide form and task utility.

  The American Marketing Association defines marketing as the process of planning and executing the conception, pricing, promotion and distribution of ideas, goods and services to create exchanges that satisfy individual and organizational objectives.

- **Know what the marketing concept is.**

  This is an important and simple idea that states that all of the actions and functions of a company or organization should satisfy customers at a profit. A firm should not invest its resources such as money and time in producing products and then trying to convince customers to buy them (production orientation); instead companies should produce what customers already want or need. Finally, the company needs profit or some other way to measure success.

- **Understand how the marketing concept relates to customer value.**

  A customer will likely consider buying a product or service in one of two ways: either in terms of the benefits they will get, or by what they have to give up (money, etc.) to get those benefits. The more benefits gotten and the less that has to be sacrificed means that customer satisfaction will increase. This also means that if in the mind of the consumer the costs are greater than the benefits, the consumer will probably not become a customer.

Important Terms

production, p. 7
customer satisfaction, p. 6
utility, p. 7
form utility, p. 7
task utility, p. 7
time utility, p. 7
place utility, p. 7
possession utility, p. 9

marketing concept, p. 9
production concept, p. 9
marketing orientation, p. 10
market-oriented firm, p. 10
customer value, p. 13
social responsibility, p. 19
marketing ethics, p.19

True-False Questions

_____ 1. According to the text, marketing means "selling" or "advertising."

_____ 2. Actually, making goods or performing services is called marketing.

_____ 3. Marketing plays an essential role in creating customer satisfaction.

_____ 4. Production is a more important economic activity than marketing.

_____ 5. Form and task utility are provided by production with the guidance of marketing.

_____ 6. Marketing provides time, place, and possession utility.

_____ 7. The internet contributes to form and task utility.

_____ 8. Marketing is both a set of activities performed by organizations and a social process.

_____ 9. Companies should eliminate costs that do not contribute to customer value.

_____ 10. Marketing takes place whenever a person needs something of value.

_____ 11. The term marketing comes from the word market—which is a group of potential customers with similar needs who are willing to exchange something of value with sellers offering various ways of satisfying those needs.

_____ 12. Responsibility for performing the marketing functions can be shifted and shared in a variety of ways, but no function can be completely eliminated.

_____ 13. The term "marketing orientation" means making products that are easy to produce and then trying to sell them.

_____ 14. The marketing concept says that a company should aim all its efforts at satisfying customers, even if this proves unprofitable.

_____ 15. The three basic ideas included in the definition of the marketing concept are: a customer orientation, a total company effort, and sales as an objective.

_____ 16. Large corporations like General Electric and Procter & Gamble were one of the last to accept the marketing concept.

_____ 17. Low price and high customer value are the same thing.

_____ 18. Building mutually beneficial relationships with customers requires that everyone in an organization work together to provide customer value before and after each purchase.

___ 19. A company will only have one functional department if they have adopted the marketing concept.

___ 20. Profit is not the bottom line measurement of a company's success.

___ 21. The marketing concept allows a company to ignore competition.

___ 22. Companies define product or service value and then market it to consumers.

___ 23. Because they do not try to earn a profit, the marketing concept is not very useful for nonprofit organizations.

___ 24. A nonprofit organization does not measure profit in the same way as a for profit corporation.

___ 25. A company's obligation to improve its positive effects on society and reduce its negative effects is called fiscal responsibility

___ 26. The moral standards that guide marketing decisions and actions are called marketing ethics.

Answers to True-False Questions

1. F, p. 5	10. F, p. 10	19. F, p. 11
2. F, p. 6	11. T, p. 10	20. F, p. 13
3. T, p. 6	12. T, p. 10	21. F, p. 14
4. F, p. 6	13. T, p. 10	22. F, p. 14
5. T, p. 7	14. F, p. 9	23. F, p. 17
6. T, p. 7	15. F, p. 9	24. T, p. 17
7. F, p. 8	16. F, p. 10	25. F, p. 17
8. T, p. 8	17. F, p. 13	26. T, p. 18
9. T, p. 11	18. T, p. 11	

Multiple-Choice Questions (Circle the correct response)

1. According to the text:
   a. marketing is much more than selling or advertising.
   b. the cost of marketing is about 25 percent of the consumer's dollar.
   c. production is a more essential economic activity than marketing.
   d. only marketing creates economic utility.
   e. all of the above are true statements.

2. When a "fruit seller" drives his truck through residential neighbourhoods and sells fruits and vegetables grown by farmers, he is creating:
   a. form utility.
   b. time and place utility.
   c. possession utility.
   d. all of the above.
   e. all of the above, *except* a.

3. Tam Furniture Stores recently purchased several rail carloads of dining room tables. The tables were distributed to retail outlets in the Northeast, where they sold rapidly to customers. In this situation, Tam Furniture Stores created:
   a. both task and possession utility.
   b. both place and time utility.
   c. place, time, and possession utility.
   d. only place utility.
   e. both form and place utility.

4. The text stresses that:
   a. advertising and selling are not really part of marketing.
   b. marketing is nothing more than a set of business activities performed by individual firms.
   c. marketing techniques have no application for nonprofit organizations.
   d. marketing is a social process and a set of activities performed by organizations.
   e. a good product usually sells itself.

5. *Customer Satisfaction*:
   a. is concerned with need-satisfying goods, but not with services.
   b. involves an attempt to anticipate customer or client needs.
   c. is primarily concerned with efficient use of resources and fair allocation of output.
   d. includes activities such as accounting, production, and financial management.
   e. is the process of selling and distributing manufactured goods.

6. *Customer Satisfaction*:
   a. is not concerned with the flow of goods and services from producers to consumers.
   b. seeks to match homogeneous supply capabilities with homogeneous demands for goods and services.
   c. refers with the extent to which customer needs, desires and expectations are met be the company.
   d. focuses on the objectives of society.

e.   All of the above are true statements.

7.   A company that focuses its attention primarily on "selling" its present products in order to meet or beat competition is using the following approach:
    a.   a free market-directed concept.
    b.   the production orientation.
    c.   market-oriented approach.
    d.   planned economic approach.
    e.   market concept approach.

8.   The marketing concept means that consumers:
    a.   are free to do anything they want.
    b.   who smoke cigarettes should be able to determine where and in what form they can buy them.
    c.   needs and wants should be understood by companies.
    d.   decide whether a product is safe and/or beneficial.
    e.   will only buy if there are low prices.

9.   Marketing cannot occur unless:
    a.   an economy is market-directed rather than planned.
    b.   producers and consumers can enter into face-to-face negotiations at some physical location.
    c.   an economy has a money system.
    d.   there are two or more parties who each have something of value they want to exchange for something else.
    e.   middlemen are present to facilitate exchange.

10.   The internet has helped to develop new types of intermediaries that connect buyers and sellers because:
    a.   Setting up online stores is relatively inexpensive and there are no need for intermediaries.
    b.   intermediaries reduce the total number of buyer-seller transactions
    c.   there is an increase place utility and a decrease in time utility.
    d.   becomes less advantageous as the number of producers and consumers, their distance apart, and the number and variety of products increase.
    e.   online malls and VertMarkets make it easier to buyers to find sellers.

11.   Based on the following company statements, which company is most likely to practice a marketing orientation approach:
    a.   Our sales force was able to sell intermediaries more of our new product than they can resell in all of this year."
    b.   Our marketing manager is coordinating pricing, product decisions, promotion, and distribution to help us show a profit at the end of this year."
    c.   "The whole company is in good shape – demand exceeds what we can produce."
    d.   "Our long-range plan – developed by our marketing manager – is to expand so that we can profitably meet the long-range needs of our customers."
    e.   "Our new President previously led our marketing effort as Vice President of Sales."

12.   Which of the following is best explains what the *"marketing concept"* means?
    a.   Companies should spend more money on marketing than they have in the past.

b. A company should only worry about the efficient utilization of its resources
c. All of the company's efforts and resources should be organized to satisfy the needs of its customers at a profit.
d. A company's President should always consult his marketing manager.
e. A company should produce what customer's want regardless of the cost.

13. Which of the following is a *true* statement?
a. Since marketing is concerned with many thousands of different products, there is no one set of marketing functions that applies to all products.
b. Responsibility for performing marketing functions can be shifted and shared, but no function can be completely eliminated.
c. From a micro viewpoint, every firm must perform all of the marketing functions.
d. Marketing functions should be performed only by marketing middlemen or facilitators.
e. Many marketing functions are not necessary in planned economies.

14. Which of the following statements best explains the concepts of customer value?
a. It is a standard policy to set prices as low as possible in order to provide good value for customers.
b. It means the same as customer satisfaction.
c. It is a bonus points or coupon program to increase a product's value to customers.
d. It is only a method used to defeat the competition.
e. It is the difference between the benefits a customer sees from a marketing offering and the costs of obtaining those benefits.

15. For a company to be profitable, which conditions should be met?
a. Satisfaction of all customer needs.
b. A positive balance when total costs are subtracted from total revenues.
c. Efficient production processes
d. A marketing orientation throughout the entire organization.
e. A competitive business environment.

16. Which of the following statements about nonprofits is false?
a. Marketing is being more widely accepted by nonprofit organizations.
b. The marketing concept is as important for nonprofit organizations as it is for business firms.
c. In business firms and in nonprofit organizations, support comes from satisfied customers.
d. A nonprofit organization does not measure profit in the same way as a for profit firm.
e. The marketing concept provides focus in both business firms and nonprofit organizations.

Answers to Multiple-Choice Questions

1. a, p. 5	7. b, p. 9	13. b, p. 13
2. e, p. 7	8. c, p. 10-12	14. e, p. 13
3. c, p. 7	9. d, p. 7-9	15. b, p. 12-13
4. d, p. 7	10. e, p. 8	16. c, p. 16-18

Additional Questions to Test Your Understanding (Fill in the Blanks)

1. Name the appropriate kind of economic utility for each statement listed below:

   a. _____ mean obtaining a good or service and having the right to use or consume it.

   b. _____ is provided when someone produces something tangible (e.g. running shoes).

   c. _____ means having the product available when the customer wants it.

   d. _____ is provided when someone performs a task for someone else (e.g., when a bank handles financial transactions).

   e. _____ means having a product available where the customer wants it.

2. Which of the five kinds of economic utility are provided by marketing?

   a. _____

   b. _____

   c. _____

3. What are the three basic ideas included in the definition of the "marketing concept"?

   a. _____

   b. _____

   c. _____

4. Briefly explain why marketing managers should be concerned with social responsibility.

   _____

   _____

   _____

   _____

Answers to Additional Questions

1.

   a. Possession utility (p. 8)

     b. Form utility (p. 7)
     c. Time utility (p. 7)
     d. Task utility (p. 7)
     e. Place utility (p. 6)

2.

     i. Time utility
    ii. Place utility
   iii. Time utility

     (see Exhibit 1-1, p. 7)

3.

     a. Customer satisfaction
     b. A total company effort
     c. Profit - not just – sales as an objective.

     (p. 10)

4. see discussion of social responsibility, pp. 18-20

Exercise 1-1

What is marketing?

Introduction

Society ignored or even criticized the contributions of marketing until the beginning of the 20th century. At that time, economies once marked by a scarcity of goods began to enjoy an abundance of goods. Marketing skills were needed to solve the distribution problems that resulted. Thus, it was not until the early 1900s that the importance of marketing was realized—and that marketing was accepted as a separate academic subject in schools and colleges.

Today, countries that operate with market-directed economies have achieved genuine improvements in standards of living—while most planned economies have collapsed or are "on the ropes." Even today, however, many people do not have a very clear understanding of marketing. No one single definition of marketing will satisfy everyone. Many people—including some students and business managers—tend to think of marketing as just "selling" or "advertising." Others see marketing as an all-inclusive social process that can solve all the world's problems. Some critics, meanwhile, seem to blame marketing for most of society's ills!

This exercise is intended to help you see more clearly what marketing is all about. One way to learn about marketing is to study the definitions in the text. Another way is to use these definitions. This is the approach you will follow in this exercise.

Assignment

Listed below are some commonly asked questions about marketing. Answer each of these questions in a way that shows your understanding of marketing.

1.   What activities does marketing involve besides selling?

2.   How would you respond to the criticism "Marketing just adds unnecessary costs to the price of everything we buy"?

3.   Is marketing useful for nonprofit organizations? Explain.

4.   How does marketing relate to the five kinds of economic utility?

5.   What are the key components of customer value?

6.   Why is effective marketing needed in an advanced economy? Is not mass production—with its economies of scale—the real key to meeting consumer needs at the lowest cost?

7.   What is involved in building mutually beneficial relationships with customers?

8.   Can a company that sells hazardous products like handguns ever be considered "socially responsible"? Why or why not? What about cigarette manufacturers?

Question for Discussion

Should marketing be viewed as a set of activities performed by business and nonprofit organizations, or alternately as a social process? Why is it important to make this distinction?

Exercise 1-2

Marketing-oriented vs. production-oriented firms

Introduction

Business firms can be classified as either "production-oriented" or marketing-oriented" depending on whether they have adopted the "marketing concept." The marketing concept is a modern idea that simply states that a firm should aim all its efforts at satisfying its customers – at a profit. This approach implies a total management commitment to (1) a customer orientation, (2) a total company effort, and (3) profit not just sales, as a goal of the company. The same idea applies to nonprofits, but some measure of long-term success other than profit may serve as a goal for nonprofits.

In general, a production-oriented company tries to get customers to buy what the firm has produced, while a marketing-oriented firm tries to produce and sell what the customer need. Actually, the two terms can be thought as on opposite ends of a scale and a company's approach can be located anywhere in between the two. Many times a company is identified as being mainly production oriented or mainly marketing-oriented.

In practice, however, there is no simple way of identifying the two types of firms. Instead, one must look for "clues" to help determine what type of approach has more influence within a company. These "clues" can take many forms, such as the attitudes of management toward customers, the company's organizational structure, and its methods and procedures.

Assignment

This exercise gives you some practice in identifying production-oriented and marketing-oriented companies. You will be given a pair of companies – and a "clue" about each firm. Based on these clues, you must decide which one of the two companies is more marketing-oriented or more production-oriented. For each pair of companies, print an *M* before the company you think is marketing-oriented and a *P* before the company that is production-oriented – and than briefly explain your choice. (Note: each set should have an *M* and a *P* – you must make a choice.) The first pair is answered for you as an example.)

Orientation	Clues
1. *P*__Firm A: *M*__Firm B:	"Our goal is to run at full capacity and sell everything we make." "Our goal is to build customer loyalty by designing products that they want to buy." *Firm A is interested in production and costs, than in what customers want.* *Firm B has focused on producing what customers want and need.*

1.		Firm A	"Sure our inventory costs are high, but how many customers would we lose if we were frequently unable to fill orders immediately?"
		Firm B	"Our inventory costs are too high. We'll have to reduce our inventory, even if it means that it will take longer for customers to get their order."
		Explanation	

2.		Firm A	"We've given the people in this city one of the finest theatres in the world, where many stars have begun their careers, but it seems that people don't appreciate it. The people in this city must be just too socially ignorant and unsophisticated to appreciate great theatre.
		Firm B	"We've got to find out what it is about our shows that isn't bringing people in. We have to do a better job of understanding and meeting people's needs. We can't just sit back and wait for people to see the light."
		Explanation	

3.		Firm A	"As sales manager, my job is to hire salespeople who can "move" as many units as we can produce. After all, the higher the sales the higher the profits."
		Firm B	As Finance manager, my job is to determine how many units it will be profitable for us to sell at the price customers are willing to pay."
		Explanation	

4.		Firm A	"Our sales have dropped. Let's ask our intermediaries why customers have stopped buying our product."
		Firm B	Our sales are too low. Perhaps we could use our most persuasive salespeople to recruit some intermediaries."
		Explanation	

5.		Firm A	"We're getting killed by foreign competitors. We need to improve our quality control and do a better job of meeting customer" expectations."

		Firm B	"Foreign producers compete unfairly with cheap labour. We need to have our public relations department lobby the government for tighter import quotas so that we can make a profit."
		Explanation	
6.		Firm A	"Our profits have been declining. Perhaps we should search for new opportunities to satisfy unfulfilled needs."
		Firm B	"Our profits have been declining. Perhaps we should search for ways to cut costs and become more efficient."
		Explanation	
7.		Firm A	"How would the new product better meet customer needs as compared to our competitor?"
		Firm B	"Our competitor's new product is great. Let's see if we can produce and sell it a t a lower cost."
		Explanation	
8.		Firm A	"People today want the convenience of one-stop shopping and we've got to go where the customers are. It will cost us more to rent space for our bank in the shopping centre, but we will attract more regular customers and that's the key to profit for the bank."
		Firm B	"It would cost us too much to rent a space for our bank in the shopping centre. We will locate our bank a few blocks away where the land is cheaper. We can depend on our low prices and good selection to bring the customers to us."
		Explanation	
9.		Firm A	"It helps to have an accountant as President. When she took over the company, she found that it was too expensive for a salesperson to visit many of our smaller customers, and now our sales force concentrates its efforts on serving the larger accounts that contribute most to profits."

		Firm B	"Our sales have nearly doubled since the sales manager was promoted to President. She's tripled the amount we spend on personal selling and advertising, and told the accountants to stick to balancing the books and leave the marketing budget to him."
		Explanation	
10.		Firm A	"How much will it improve our customer service and enhance repeat sales if we buy an additional delivery truck?"
		Firm B	How much money will we save if we wait a year before buying an additional delivery truck? Customers won't mind waiting an extra day for their deliveries."
		Explanation	
		Firm A	"Our goal is to exceed customer expectations. Profits will follow."
		Firm B	"We need to do a cost-benefit analysis before implementing any new customer service programs."
		Explanation	

Question for Discussion

If, as the text emphasizes, it is so important for a company to be market-oriented, why are many production-oriented companies not only surviving but also earning profits?

Exercise 1-3

How marketing functions create economic utility

Introduction

Marketing has been defined as the "creation and delivery of a standard of living." In economic terms, marketing contributes to the consumer welfare through the creation of three of the five basic kinds of economic utility—time, *place,* and *possession* utility. Further, marketing may also guide development of *form* and *task* utility.

The marketing process does not take place automatically. It requires that certain marketing functions or activities be performed by various marketing institutions—and by *consumers* themselves. The following eight functions are essential to the marketing of all goods: buying, selling, transporting, storing, grading, financing, risk-taking, and market information. No matter how simple or complex the marketing process is, these functions must be performed. Some functions may be performed several times to facilitate the marketing of a given product, while others may be performed only once. At times, the performance of a function may be shifted from one member of a marketing system to another. For example, some modern wholesalers and retailers shift the burden of storing goods back to manufacturers. However, the fact remains that each of the eight functions must be performed by someone at least once before any good can be marketed—none can be eliminated.

Assignment

This assignment illustrates how the performance of marketing functions creates economic utility. Read the following case carefully and then answer the questions that follow in the space provided.

HARMONY MARKET

Don and Julie Langlois are a young couple that work in Montreal and live in a small apartment downtown. They shop for most of their food—including meat—at Harmony Market, a small grocery store located near their apartment. The Warrens inspect the packages of meat and select the amount and type of meat they want for their meals that week. They have always been happy with the quality and selection of meat at Harmony Market—and they like the store's "satisfaction or your money back" guarantee.

The Harmony Market is too small to have a full butcher department and meat freezer. Instead, the owner, Jose Perez, buys fresh meat from The Meat Shoppe, a wholesale butcher. The wholesaler keeps a large quantity of bulk meat in cold storage—and then cuts grade-A stew beef, steaks, roasts, hamburger, and other selections to fill orders from the Harmony Market and its other grocery store customers. The wholesaler delivers the meat to Perez each morning before the store opens. At the end of the month the wholesaler bills Harmony Market for its purchases.

This arrangement seems to work well. Although Perez does not keep computerized records, he knows his customers' preferences and he orders carefully. He knows that steaks sell well when the weather allows even apartment dwellers to barbecue on their balconies, but he cuts back on big steaks as soon as cooler weather hits. He packages the meat in convenient serving sizes and makes up more small packages than most grocery stores because many apartment dwellers live alone. With a day or two's notice, he can also handle special requests. As a result, Harmony Market can offer a selection that meets most customers' needs. If Perez orders too much of a certain type of meat and it has not sold within a few days, he marks down the price— to prompt a quicker sale.

Based on your analysis of this description, answer the following questions.

1. What kind(s) of economic utility is created by Harmony Market for its customers?

_____

_____

_____

2. Does the Harmony Market help to resolve the difference between how much producers produce and how much and where consumers will buy? Briefly, explain your answer.

_____

_____

_____

3. The eight basic marketing functions are listed below. Check Yes or No whether each function is performed by someone in this description. If "Yes, " explain *when* and *by whom* each function was performed. If "No," explain why not.

a) Buying: Yes _____ No _____ Explain.

_____

_____

_____

b) Selling: Yes _____ No _____ Explain.

_____

_____

_____

c) Grading: Yes _____ No _____ Explain.

_____

_____

_____

    d)   Transporting: Yes _____ No _____ Explain.

_____

_____

_____

    e)   Storing: Yes _____ No _____ Explain.

_____

_____

_____

    f)   Financing: Yes _____ No _____ Explain.

_____

_____

_____

    g)   Market information: Yes _____ No _____ Explain.

_____

_____

_____

    h)   Risk-taking: Yes _____ No _____ Explain.

_____

_____

_____

Like most young couples, Don and Julie Langlois are always interested in ways to make their budget stretch further. An article in the Sunday newspaper on cutting grocery costs suggests buying meat directly from downtown wholesalers. According to the article, some meat wholesalers will sell direct to consumers—if the consumer buys a whole side of beef. The article described it this way. The customer calls the meat company and agrees on a price and time to pick up the purchase. The meat packing plant then cuts the side of beef into large pieces and wraps them in freezer paper. The wholesaler requires customers to pay with cash when they pick up the meat. The newspaper article says that on a per pound basis the price is about 25 percent cheaper than the same selection of meat would be at a grocery store.

4. If the Langlois' were to buy meat directly from the wholesaler, they would probably need to perform some of the basic marketing functions themselves. Each of the basic marketing functions is listed below. For each function, check Yes or No to indicate if the Langlois' would need to perform this function. In addition, briefly explain any difficulties you think they might face in trying to perform the function.

a) Buying: Yes _____ No _____ Explain.

_____

_____

_____

b) Selling: Yes _____ No _____ Explain.

_____

_____

_____

c) Grading: Yes _____ No _____ Explain.

_____

_____

_____

d) Transporting: Yes _____ No _____ Explain.

_____

_____

_____

e) Storing: Yes _____ No _____ Explain.

_____

_____

_____

f)   Financing: Yes _____ No _____ Explain.

_____

_____

_____

g)   Market information: Yes _____ No _____ Explain.

_____

_____

_____

h)   Risk-taking: Yes _____ No _____ Explain.

_____

_____

_____

Question for Discussion

Name a product for which all eight marketing functions do *not* need to be performed by someone somewhere in the marketing system. Explain your thinking about what functions do not need to be performed.

Exercise 1-4

Ethical challenges in marketing

Introduction

Marketing managers face many challenges—including difficult decisions in areas of social responsibility and ethics. Some guidelines in these areas are provided by the laws of our society. Clearly, a marketing manager must know and obey laws that govern marketing actions. However, there are many decision areas in marketing where laws do not exist, and where the question of what is "right" or "wrong" is not so clear-cut. Usually, these are decision areas where the marketing manager must deal with trade-offs or conflicts—situations where what is good for some customers, stockholders, employees, other channel members, or society in general is not good for someone else. These are situations where the marketing manager must weigh all of the facts—and make a personal judgment about what to do.

Throughout the text, you will be alerted to many of the decision areas where a marketing manager must be sensitive to ethical decisions. This exercise provides an opportunity for you to start thinking about some of these issues. Later in the course you may want to look at your answers again—to see if you have changed your mind about any of them.

Assignment

Listed below are short descriptions of situations that *might* be classified as "ethical" dilemmas. For each situation, identify which person or group has the ethical dilemma and state what action you would recommend in their position—and why. Be sure to write down any assumptions you are making. Keep in mind that different people might have a very different reaction to what is a "correct" or "incorrect" answer for most of the situations in this exercise. Therefore, the objective is for you to analyze the situation—and think about what *you* would do.

1.   Affordable Rubber Products has for many years made strong rubber tie-down straps. The straps are very useful for securing loads on large commercial trucks and they are sold directly to large trucking companies and through cash-and-carry wholesalers to smaller firms. Last summer, sales of the straps picked up suddenly and Affordable Rubber found from newspaper articles that they were being used by inner-city youths for a game of "bungee jumping" from overpasses and railroad bridges. Concerned about the possibility of being held liable if any accidents occurred, Affordable Rubber sent a memo to all its customers asking them not to sell the straps to youngsters and the president of the company appeared on TV interview shows expressing his disapproval of using the tie-down straps for anything other than securing loads on trucks. The media attention has only heightened the craze and an influential consumer rights group has written to Affordable Rubber to ask them to withdraw the tie-down straps from the market.

Recommendation (and reason):

2. Matt Navarette is very flattered to be invited for a second round of interviews for a job as assistant marketing manager with Spence Designers and Builders. Spence is a company that designs and builds higher end houses. As a new graduate, he is eager to get a position with Spence, which has done well developing new designs for houses aimed at the "executive" market. Navarette has some background in the business because he has worked each summer as a junior salesperson for similar housing developments run by his uncle's company. In fact, on several occasions he has been in direct competition with Spence to sell customers a home. The managers at Spence know about his family connection and Navarette has told them that he wants to be hired on his own merits. In the last interview of the day, the president of Spence asks Navarette: "So what do you think are going to be the "hot" trends in high-end homes this coming year?" Navarette thinks that this is a great opportunity to demonstrate his knowledge, but also worries that the whole interview process may be part of an effort to get inside information about his uncle's marketing plans.

    Recommendation (and reason):

3. Two different advertising agencies were doing the advertising planning work for two competing computer manufacturers—Advanced Digital Computers and Blue Sky Computing. However, the larger of the two advertising agencies, Genesis Advertising, recently bought out the other agency. The acquired agency had been doing the work for Blue Sky Computing. The president of the newly merged agency wrote a letter to the marketing manager at Blue Sky and said, "Because there may be the appearance of a conflict of interest in our handling both your account and Advanced Digital Computers, the most ethical thing for us to do is resign from your account." The marketing manager at Blue Sky immediately telephoned to say: "Ethical? You're going to leave me high and dry looking for a new agency and in the meantime all the people who used to work on my account will be telling Advanced Digital Computers the details about my marketing plans."

    Recommendation (and reason):

4.   Cathy Markham has been shopping for a new leather reclining chair for her family room and is very impressed with the price quoted by Recliners 'n More for a brand-name reclining chair she has seen advertised in a decorating magazine. Recliners 'n More is able to offer customers deeply discounted prices on brand-name leather furniture because it sells by phone. It has no warehouse or showroom and has eliminated those costs. Instead, telephone orders are passed along to manufacturers who ship furniture directly to consumers by contract truck carriers. Although the price is good, Ms. Markham is reluctant to order the reclining chair because it might not be as comfortable as it looks. To help close the sale, the Recliners 'n More telephone salesman tells Ms. Markham the name of a retailer in Markham's area that carries the same chair—and suggests "Why don't you go over there and try the reclining chair and then call me back to order it if it's what you want."

Recommendation (and reason):

5.   A company that sells bottled "pure mineral water" has just found that a problem in its filtering process has resulted in trace amounts of chemicals in some of the bottles it has already shipped. The small levels of chemicals involved are not a health hazard, and no law has been violated. Further, it is very unlikely that anyone else would detect the problem. On the other hand, the company has always promoted its product as "pure and of the highest quality." The only way to correct the problem is to recall all of the bottles that are already in retailer and wholesaler inventories—which would be very costly and also generate bad publicity in a very competitive market. What should the company do?

Recommendation (and reason):

6.   A manufacturer that sells telecommunications equipment to foreign governments is working on an important sale in a developing nation. The company's local agent middleman in the country has explained that competitor firms from other countries are paying influential local citizens to serve as "consultants." The agent has pointed out that "this is how business is done here—it's who you know that counts. Without consultants, someone else will definitely get the business." The agent has asked for $50,000 to hire consultants. As director of international sales, Clere Neyhart worries that some of the money paid to consultants might be used to bribe the foreign government officials involved in the purchase. On the other hand, she believes that the company will miss the sale if it does not have the help of the local consultants who know how decisions will be made—and by whom.

Recommendation (and reason):

7.   A large chain of retail stores is considering opening a store in a small city. The chain's low prices will almost certainly drive many of the existing local retailers out of business. They simply cannot buy in large enough quantities to be cost competitive. There are equally profitable opportunities for new stores in other, more competitive markets. On the other hand, if the chain does not move into the small city it is likely that eventually some other competitor will—and the market is not large enough for two chains.

Recommendation (and reason):

8.   Doctors at Riverdale Medical Centre were awarded a very large contract to conduct research on the weight-loss effects of a diet supplement. Because the doctors are on the staff of the medical school, all the money from the study goes to a special fund to provide scholarships for needy medical students. When the physicians agreed to the contract, they were pretty sure that sooner or later they'd see their results in an advertisement which would begin: "Doctors at a major research hospital proved that significant weight-loss . . . " So, they were especially careful in their research and set up a controlled study in which the researchers did not know which patients were taking the supplement and which weren't. The results were clear-cut and showed that most patients taking the supplement lost more than 10 pounds during the study. In the final report, the researchers noted that almost all of the patients regained their excess weight when they stopped using the supplement. However, advertisements for the supplement do not mention the weight regain.

Recommendation (and reason):

Question for Discussion

Are the ethical challenges faced by a marketing manager any different—in a basic way—than the challenges faced by businesspeople in other types of jobs? Why or why not?

Exercise 1-5

Revenue, cost, and profit relationships

This exercise is based on computer-aided problem number 1--Revenue, Cost, and Profit Relationships. A complete description of the problem appears on pages 21-22 of Wong/Shapiro, 11th edition.

This is a practice problem—to get you started with the PLUS computer program and help you see how spreadsheet analysis will help you with more complicated problems.

Sue Cline is interested in increasing profits from the notebook line. She knows that she can do this by increasing revenue, by decreasing costs—or, more generally, developing a marketing mix that results in a greater difference between revenue and cost.

1.   Write down the selling price, quantity sold, revenue, cost, and profit as they appear in the notebook column of the initial spreadsheet.

> Price: _____   Cost: _____
> Quantity: _____   Profit: _____
> Revenue _____
> :

2.   Revenue will increase if a higher price can be charged and the quantity sold remains unchanged. Change the price for a notebook to $2.20 and record the resulting profit.

> Profit: _____

3.   Revenue will increase if a larger quantity can be sold at the same price. Change the price on the spreadsheet back to $2.00, and increase the quantity sold to 6,600. Record the resulting profit.
> Profit: _____

   b.   Profit will increase if the same revenue can be achieved at lower cost. Change the quantity sold back to 6,000 and decrease the total cost amount to $7,800. Record the resulting profit.

> Profit: _____

5.   Another possible approach for increasing profits would be to lower prices—if it results in a larger quantity sold. Cline thinks that she might sell 6,500 notebooks at a price of $1.85, 7,200 notebooks at $1.70, or 7,500 notebooks at $1.55. If she is right about these price-quantity relationships, what price would you recommend? Why? (For simplicity here, we will assume that the total cost is $9,000 regardless of the quantity sold).

6.   As another alternative, Cline is thinking of improving the product and charging a higher price—about $2.25 a unit. To improve the product, she will need to use a different supplier who uses better materials—and who would charge $12,250 for a minimum order of 7,000 notebooks. Assuming that she could sell all 7,000 notebooks, approximately what price would she have to be able to charge to make at least as much profit as in the best alternative from the question above. (Hint: change the quantity sold and total cost values on the spreadsheet, and then do a What If analysis. In the What If analysis, select the notebook selling price as the variable to vary and vary it between a minimum of $2.18 and a maximum of $2.28. Select revenue and profit as the values to display. Study the results and compare them to your answer to Question 5.)

Approximate price she would have to charge: _____, which would result in a profit of _____.

7   If Cline decided that customers would only pay $2.15 for the improved notebook, approximately how many would she have to sell to make some profit (that is, profit greater than O) given a total cost of $12,250? (Hint: change the notebook selling price to $2.15 on the spreadsheet, and then do a What If analysis—selecting quantity as the value to vary and revenue and profit as the values to display; or, try different prices on the spreadsheet until you zero in on the correct answer. If the first What If analysis does not provide an answer, continue with the What If analysis using a large or smaller minimum or maximum value until you get closer to the answer.)

Quantity she would have to sell: _____ units.

Chapter 2

Marketing's role within the firm or nonprofit organization

Chapter Summary

- **Understand what a marketing manager does.**
  The marketing manager's job includes (1) planning marketing activities, (2) directing the implementation of the plans, and (3) controlling these plans. Each task is related to the others and they are all in constant flux due to the dynamic attributes of the market.
  The marketing manager works with top management in identifying and developing attractive marketing plans, which helps to ensure that all of the company's departments are working towards common goals.

- **Know what strategic planning is.**
  Strategic market planning means finding and developing profitable marketing strategies. These strategies involve identifying a target market and developing a marketing mix to satisfy the target market.

- **Understand target marketing.**
  Under the target marketing approach, the marketer realizes that there are many consumer groups, each with its own distinct set of characteristics and likes and dislikes. Using a target marketing approach, a particular defined consumer group is chosen and the marketing mix is developed to address the target consumer profile. This approach is different from mass marketing, because mass marketing assumes that all consumers are the same, and all are treated as potential customers.

- **Be familiar with the four Ps in a marketing mix.**
  Although there are many variables to any given marketing mix, it is useful to reduce them to four basic ones. These are Product, Place, Promotion and Price. A *product* is developed to satisfy the target customer's needs. *Place* is how a company locates its product or service where and when the customer wants to buy it. *Promotion* is used to inform the target customers of the product. The *price* is set based on market factors, costs and finally on the consumers response to the customer value offering. Note that the customer is not a part of the marketing mix.

- **Know the difference between a marketing strategy, a marketing plan, and a marketing program.**
  A marketing strategy is the big picture. It defines who the target customer is and lays out a marketing mix to satisfy the target customer. A marketing *plan* takes the process one step further by including time-related details, projected costs, and expected results. The plan also includes control procedures to indicate successes and failures. A marketing program incorporates all of a firm's marketing plans into one big plan. This plan should fit the overall company strategy.

Important Terms

marketing management process, p. 27
strategic (management) planning, p. 28
marketing strategy, p. 28
target market, p. 28
marketing mix, p. 28
target marketing, p. 29
mass marketing, p. 29
product, p. 30
price, p. 30
place, p. 30
promotion, p. 30

channel of distribution, p. 31
personal selling, p. 32
mass selling, p. 32
advertising, p. 32
publicity or public relations, p. 32
direct marketing, p. 32
sales promotion, p. 32
marketing plan, p. 35
tactical or operational decisions, p. 35
marketing program, p. 36

True-False Questions

_____ 1. The marketing management process consists of (1) planning marketing activities, (2) directing the implementation of the plans and (3) controlling these plans.

_____ 2. Strategic (management) planning is a managerial process of developing and maintaining a match between the resources of the production department and its product opportunities.

_____ 3. Strategic market planning is the process of deciding how best to sell the products the company produces.

_____ 4. A marketing strategy specifies a target market and a related marketing mix.

_____ 5. A target market consists of a group of consumers who are usually quite different.

_____ 6. A marketing mix consists of the uncontrollable variables that a company puts together to satisfy a target market.

_____ 7. Target marketing limits an organization's profit potential.

_____ 8. Target marketing aims a marketing mix at some specific target customers.

_____ 9. The mass marketing approach is more production-oriented than marketing-oriented.

_____ 10. "Mass marketing" and "mass marketer" mean the same thing.

_____ 11. The problem with target marketing is that it limits the firm to small market segments.

_____ 12. The four "Ps" are: Product, Promotion, Price, and Profit.

_____ 13. The customer should not be considered part of a "marketing mix".

_____ 14. The "product" area is concerned with developing the right physical good, service, or blend of both for the target market.

_____ 15. Personal selling, mass selling, and advertising are all forms of sales promotion.

_____ 16. A channel of distribution must include several kinds of intermediaries and specialists.

_____ 17. Price is the most important of the four Ps.

_____ 18. The marketing mix should be set before the best target market is selected.

_____ 19. A marketing plan and a marketing strategy mean the same thing.

_____ 20. Implementation means putting the marketing plan into operation.

_____ 21. Short-run decisions that stay within the overall guidelines set during strategy planning are called implementation decisions.

_____ 22. A marketing program may consist of several marketing plans.

_____ 23. An extremely good marketing plan may be carried out badly and still be profitable, while a poor but well-implemented plan can lose money.

_____ 24. The watch industry has become much more marketing-oriented.

_____ 25. Toddler university, a company specializing in sales of shoes to toddlers, identified one target market as traditionalists. Traditionalists preferred basic colours.

_____ 26. IBM's target market for its Lotus Notes product are corporate and institutional buyers.

Answers to True-False Questions

1. T, p. 27	10. F, p. 29	19. F, p. 36
2. F, p. 28	11. F, p. 29	20. T, p. 35
3. F, p. 28	12. F, p. 30	21, F. p. 35
4. T, p. 28	13. T, p. 30	22. F, p. 36
5. F, p. 29	14. T, p. 31	23. T, p. 36
6. F, p. 28	15. F, p. 32	24. T. p. 37
7. F, p. 30	16. F, p. 31	25. F, p. 33
8. T, p. 28	17, F. p. 33	26. T, p. 29
9. T, p. 29	18. F, p. 33	

Multiple-Choice Questions (Circle the correct response)

1. Spin Master Toys, Canada's largest toy maker has chosen as it target markets:
    a. fathers of boys between the ages of 6 and 11
    b. college students
    c. pre-teens and teens
    d. infants and preschoolers
    e. none of the above

2. Mass marketing assumes that:
    a. everyone is different
    b. most people are similar but there are differences
    c. different age groups think alike
    d. gender differences are the most important
    e. everyone is the same

3. Place, a part of the marketing mix is concerned with decisions involved in:
    a. channel type
    b. Types of intermediaries
    c. kinds and locations of stores
    d. transportation and storage
    e. all of the above

4. Direct marketing is becoming more popular, especially because of the opportunities that media such as _____ give to marketers in developing relationships that are more personal with customers.
    a. telemarketing and television
    b. telephones and call forwarding
    c. internet and cell phones
    d. direct mail
    e. outdoor animated billboards

5. In the Toddler University case, four different target markets were identified. Three of the target markets were well served by existing shoe manufacturers, however the attentive parents target market was not. What four customer value(s) did TU use to help them develop a marketing mix for this target market.
    a. fit, function, fun and fashion
    b. fun, fashionable, functional, and prestigious
    c. fashion, colourful, and fit
    d. fit, quality
    e. inexpensive

6. The Internet has become a vital part of marketing and fundraising activities for nonprofit organizations. These organizations have found that the most effective online marketing tool in soliciting contributions is:
    a. Interactive web sites with colourful graphics
    b. Video and audio examples of how contributions are used
    c. Direct marketing using emails
    d. Requests that are combined with videos
    e. None of the above.

7. Which of the following is one of three basic marketing management jobs?
    a. To direct the implementation of plans
    b. To control the plans in actual operation
    c. To plan marketing activities
    d. All of the above

8. The marketing management process:
    a. includes the on-going job of planning marketing activities.
    b. is mainly concerned with obtaining continuous customer feedback.
    c. involves finding opportunities and planning marketing strategies, but does not include the management tasks of implementing and control.
    d. is called "strategic planning."
    e. Both a and d are true statements.

9. A marketing strategy consists of two interrelated parts. These are:
    a. selection of a target market and implementing the plan.
    b. selection of a target market and development of a marketing mix.
    c. selection and development of a marketing mix.
    d. finding attractive opportunities and developing a marketing mix.
    e. finding attractive opportunities and selecting a target market.

10. Strategic market planners should recognize that:
    a. target markets should not be large and spread out.
    b. mass marketing is often very effective and desirable.
    c. firms like General Electric, Sears, and Procter & Gamble are too large to aim at clearly defined markets.
    d. target marketing is not limited to small market segments.
    e. the terms "mass marketing" and "mass marketers" mean essentially the same thing.

11. A marketing mix consists of:
    a. policies, procedures, plans, and personnel.
    b. the customer and the "four Ps."
    c. all variables, controllable and uncontrollable.
    d. product, price, promotion, and place.
    e. none of the above.

12. Which of the following statements about marketing mix variables is *false?*
    a. "Promotion" includes personal selling, mass selling, and sales promotion.
    b. The term "Product" refers to services as well as physical goods.
    c. A channel of distribution does not have to include any middlemen.
    d. Generally speaking, "Price" is more important than "Place."
    e. The needs of a target market virtually determine the nature of an appropriate marketing mix.

13. A "marketing plan":
    a. is just another term for "marketing strategy."
    b. consists of several "marketing programs."
    c. includes the time-related details for carrying out a marketing strategy.
    d. is a strategy without all the operational decisions.
    e. ignores implementation and control details.

14. Which of the following would NOT require an operational decision for a leading hair colour

    manufacturer?
    a. Solicit orders from any new, financially attractive, salons.
    b. Drop colours that are losing appeal.
    c. Create a fresh ad for each Sunday newspaper.
    d. Set a competitive price if a primary competitor offers a special discount.
    e. Promote the fair price and satisfactory quality of the product.

15. A "marketing program":
    a. is another name for a particular marketing mix.
    b. blends several different marketing plans.
    c. consists of a target market and the marketing mix.
    d. is primarily concerned with all of the details of implementing a marketing plan.
    e. must be set before a target market can be selected.

16. The watch industry example in the text serves to illustrate that:
    a. good implementation and control is usually more important than good planning.
    b. there are a limited number of potential target markets.
    c. an effective marketing strategy guarantees future success.
    d. consumers want only high-quality products.
    e. creative strategy planning is needed for survival.

Answers to Multiple-Choice Questions

1. c, p. 28	7. d, p. 27	13. c, p. 35
2. e. p. 29	8. a, p. 27	14. e, p. 35
3. e. p. 31	9. b, p. 28	15. b, p.36
4. c. p. 33	10. d, p. 29	16. e, p. 37
5. a. p. 33	11. d, p. 30	
6. c. p. 38	12. d, p. 31	

Additional Questions to Test Your Understanding

1. After determining the target market, what four sets of management decisions make up the marketing task?

    _____

    _____

    _____

    _____

2. Give two examples of how target marketing helps profitability.

    _____

    _____

    _____

    _____

3. Briefly explain the difference between "mass marketing" and "mass selling"

    _____

    _____

    _____

    _____

4. Define the term "marketing plan"

    _____

    _____

    _____

    _____

5. What are the components of a "marketing plan"?

    a. _____

       _____

    b. _____

       _____

c. _____

_____

d. _____

_____

Answers to the Additional Questions

1. The marketing task can be thought of as four sets of decisions to be made by managers (p. 30)

   Product: everything the target group receives.
   Price: everything the target group gives up to receive it.
   Place: everything that is done to give the customer possession.
   Promotion: everything the customer hears about the other three Ps.

2. See pages 28-29 and Toddler University case pages 33-34.

3. See the definition of "mass marketing" and "mass selling" on pages 29 and 33

4. A "marketing plan" is a written statement of a marketing strategy and the time-related details (schedule) for carrying out the strategy (p. 28).

5. a. "What marketing mix will be offered, to whom (that is, the target market), and for how long.

   b. What company resources (shown as costs) will be needed and when (month by month)

   c. What results are expected (sales and profits, perhaps monthly or quarterly)

   d. Control procedures. e.g. comparing actual sales to expected sales.

See the discussion on page 35

Exercise 2-1

Mass marketing vs. target marketing

Introduction

A marketing manager's planning job is to find attractive market opportunities and develop effective marketing strategies. A "marketing strategy" consists of two interrelated parts: (1) a *target market--a* fairly homogeneous group of customers to whom a company wishes to appeal, and (2) a *marketing mix*--the controllable variables which the company puts together to satisfy this target group.

Here, it is important to see the difference between *mass marketing* and *target marketing* in planning marketing strategies.

Production-oriented firms typically assume that everyone's needs are the same. They try to build universal appeals into a marketing mix that--it is hoped--will attract "everyone. " This approach we will call "mass marketing." Marketing-oriented firms, on the other hand, recognize that different customers usually have different needs-so they try to satisfy the needs of some particular group of customers--whose needs are fairly similar--rather than trying to appeal to everyone. This "target marketing" approach--a logical application of the marketing concept--simply means that a marketing strategy should aim at *some* target market.

Assignment

This exercise is designed to illustrate the difference between mass marketing and target marketing. Read each of the following cases carefully, and then (1) indicate in the space provided whether each firm is following a mass-marketing or a target-marketing approach and (2) briefly explain your answers.

1.   Lawn Products Corp. has just introduced a new type of revolving lawn sprinkler called the "Summer Shower Sprinkler" and it is being promoted as the "ultimate lawn sprinkler-- better than rain." According to Lawn Products' president, the sprinkler is "absolutely guaranteed" not to leak, rust, or break. Moreover, "it has a unique mechanical timer so that it turns itself off automatically after a set period of time--and when it is on, the water pressure makes it 'crawl' around the lawn, so that different areas get watered without having to touch or move the sprinkler." Available in several models ranging in price from $40 to $70, the "Summer Shower Sprinkler" is expected to sell "in the millions." "This product is so superior," say company officials, "that no household in Canada will want to be without one."

      a)   Mass marketing _____   Target marketing _____

b)   Comments:

_____

_____

_____

_____

_____

_____

2.   Sani Ahmad recently retired after 20 years of service as a chef for a luxury cruise line. During his career, he worked on ships that took him to almost every part of the world. In the process, he learned to prepare the favourite dishes of many different countries. Sani and his wife--also an outstanding cook--have decided to use their savings to open an "ethnic" restaurant in Toronto, but with a difference. Each week they will feature the cuisine of a different area of the world. Sani is sure that their restaurant will be an outstanding success. "We want to be a destination restaurant," he says, "a place where adventurous folks want to come for special meals and service to celebrate special occasions. Our prices won't be cheap, but that will help us pay for special promotional mailings to the upscale professionals who live within driving distance of the restaurant."

a)   Mass marketing _____   Target marketing _____

b)   Comments:

_____

_____

_____

_____

_____

3.   "Personalized" cable TV channels--with shows that are tailored to each individual viewer's interests in both entertainment and advertising content are starting to become available to consumers. These personalized channels use digital interactive technology. By using detailed consumer survey information collected from Prime Time, Inc.'s customers, producers of news, comedy, and other types of shows may be able to create personalized broadcasts. Every show and ad in these personalized broadcasts will appeal to each reader's self-identified interests. Thus, people who drink beer will see shows with beer ads, but non-beer drinkers never will. And antique collectors can look forward to special shows on antiques, while bicycle racers can look forward to documentaries about the sport. But because of equipment limitations, for the next four or

five years the "personalized" broadcasts will be limited to markets with no more than 300,000-500,000 potential viewers.

a) Mass marketing _____   Target marketing _____

b) Comments:

_____

_____

_____

_____

_____

_____

4.   Kyna Electronics markets personal computers (PCs) in the U.S. and Canada. The company started out selling fast, sophisticated machines to scientists and enthusiasts. Machines were only assembled on order and were distributed through the company's regional branches. But, recently the company decided to take a different approach after the company had two years of losses. The company's founder made the following announcement: "PCs are now a commodity. From now on, Kyna will buy computers from whoever can make them cheapest—whether they are in Korea, Singapore, or wherever--and distribute them through any retail store that wants to sell them. We already have contracts with department stores like Sears, electronics stores like Best Buy, office supply stores like Office Depot, and even discount stores like Wal-Mart. We plan to become the country's leading volume supplier."

a) Mass marketing _____   Target marketing _____

b) Comments:

_____

_____

_____

_____

_____

_____

Question for Discussion

A marketing strategy should aim at some target market. But does "target marketing" guarantee that a firm's marketing strategy will be successful?

Exercise 2-2

Developing a unique marketing mix for each target market

Introduction

Developing a marketing strategy consists of two *interrelated* tasks: (1) selecting a target market and (2) developing the best marketing mix for that target market.

Marketing-oriented firms recognize that not all potential customers have the same needs. Thus, rather than first developing a marketing mix and *then* looking for a market to sell that mix to, marketing-oriented firms first try to determine what kind of mix each possible target market may require. Then they select a target market based on their ability to offer a good marketing mix at a profit.

Assignment

This exercise assumes that different groups of customers in a general market area may have different needs and therefore may require different marketing mixes. Three possible target markets and alternative marketing mixes are described below for each of four different product types. For each product type, select the marketing mix which would be best for each target market. *(All alternatives must be used, i.e., you cannot use one alternative for two target markets.)* Indicate your selection by writing the letter of the marketing mix in front of the target market you select.

Note: To make it easier for you, each target market consists of only one individual or family, but it should be clear that each individual or family really represents a larger group of potential customers who have similar needs.

I.   Product type: Automobile

Possible Target Markets	*Alternative Marketing Mixes*
_____ (1) Middle-aged couple with two children who have just purchased a mountain cabin for use as a family "retreat."	(a) A five-year-old, "for sale by owner" Honda Civic listed in the classified ads of a local newspaper.
_____ (2) A manager of a real estate firm who uses his company car to show clients the community--and demonstrate a successful business image.	(b) A Lincoln Continental with luxury features--on an one-year lease from the Ford/Lincoln dealer in a nearby city.

_____ (3) A student who needs a car to commute to the college campus--and to get to her part time job at the mall.

(c) A Jeep Grand Cherokee purchased with financing arranged by the salesman at a local car dealer--and backed with an extended service warranty.

II. Product type: Food

Possible Target Markets

Alternative Marketing Mixes

_____ (1) Airline pilot who has just arrived from an out-of-town flight at 8:30 p.m.

(a) A large pepperoni pizza and some Cokes delivered to the house-- purchased at "2.00 off the regular price" with a coupon from an insert in the newspaper.

_____ (2) Middle-aged low-income housewife concerned with feeding her large family a well-balanced meal, while operating on a tight budget.

(b) Nationally advertised brand of frozen "gourmet" dinner on display in the frozen-food case of a "7-Eleven" convenience food store.

_____ (3) Young mother who has spent the day at the office and has to rush to get her children dinner before going to a business dinner.

(c) "Market basket" of spaghetti sauce, pasta, and garlic bread loaf purchased at a large supermarket that advertises "low everyday prices."

III. Product type: Computer

Possible Target Markets

Alternative Marketing Mixes

_____ (1) Young working couple that wants their child to learn about computers by using educational game programs.

(a) A laptop computer from Dell with pre-loaded software—sold with an "on-site or on-the-road" service agreement.

2-14

_____ (2)   Sales rep that wants to keep records of his sales calls and prepare short reports for the home office while he travels.

(b)   Powerful mini-computer leased from a manufacturer--such as Sun Micro-systems--that uses knowledgeable salespeople to help the customer decide on the right equipment.

_____ (3)   A local Savings and Loan that has to constantly update deposit and withdrawal information--and prepare a variety of company records and reports.

(c)   Inexpensive Acer computer sold by a mass-merchandiser that advertises its discount prices.

IV.   Product type: Clothing for Vacations

Possible Target Markets

Alternative Marketing Mixes

_____ (1)   Wealthy couple planning to go on a winter cruise in the Mediterranean.

(a)   Discount clothier that spends most of its advertising budget on radio spots and features "final markdowns" on last season's fashions.

_____ (2)   Young college student planning to go to Florida for Spring Break.

(b)   Mail-order catalog sent to subscribers of "Architectural Digest" which features high-priced "resort wear" in exotic prints.

_____ (3)   Middle-income, family planning to go to Disney World for a week with their two young children.

(c)   Department store with women's, men's and children's clothing departments with moderate prices that advertises through inserts in the local paper.

V.   Product type: Sound Systems

Possible Target Markets

_____ (1)   Middle-class married couple that are looking for a system that will blend in with their living room furniture.

(a)   Popular brand of a console system with an attractive wood cabinet purchased on credit at a large department store.

_____ (2)   Affluent young executive who wants to install a system in her penthouse, but does not know much about equipment.

(b)   Expensive component sound system manufactured by a firm with a reputation for high quality and sold by a dealer who specializes in high-end equipment.

_____ (3)   Do-it-yourself enthusiast who wants to add a system to the basement recreation room he has just built.

(c)   Build-it-yourself component sound system kit featured in a catalog published by a large mail-order distributor of electronic equipment.

Question for Discussion

If a firm cannot satisfy all the needs of all potential customers, what factors should a marketing manager consider before selecting a target market?

Exercise 2-3

Target marketing

This exercise is based on computer-aided problem number 2--Target Marketing. A complete description of the problem appears on page 41 of Wong/Shapiro, 11th edition.

1.   Marko's marketing manager is interested in ways to reduce distribution cost--to increase profits. Marko knows that many customers in the target market want products quickly once they decide to buy. And at present, no competitor provides really fast delivery. Marko could switch to air transportation--and that would get products delivered faster and increase the percent of purchasers who would buy its product. But better delivery service would also increase distribution cost per unit sold to $2.50. If Marko were to change to the new distribution system, approximately what share of the target market's purchases would it need to get to earn a total profit of $41,800? (Hint: Set the distribution cost per unit to $2.50 on the spreadsheet, and then do a What If analysis--varying the firm's share of purchases and displaying profit.)

Firm's Percent (share) of target market purchases
required to earn a profit of $41,800: _____

2.   If Marko won this share of the target market's purchases, how many units would it expect to sell? What would its total cost be? What would its total revenue be?

Quantity Sold (units)   _____

Total Cost at this quantity $_____

Total Revenue at this cost $_____

3.   If Marko implemented this strategy, but only won a share of the purchases that was 5 percent less than the percent needed to earn $41,800, what would happen to total profit?

Profit: _____

4.   If Marko were to use air transportation with the mass marketing approach and this added $0.50 a unit to distribution cost--resulting in a unit distribution cost of $3.00--approximately what share of purchases would Marko have to win to earn a profit of $41,800? (Hint: change the unit distribution cost on the spreadsheet, and then do a "What If" analysis as described above. If the first What If analysis does not provide an answer to the question, continue with the What If Analysis using a larger or smaller minimum and maximum value for the share value until you get closer to the answer. In other words, use the "What If" analysis to help "search" for the answer you need.)

Firm's Percent (share) of target market purchases

required to earn a profit of $41,800: _____

5. If Marko implemented this approach, but only won a share of purchases that was 5 percent less than the percent needed to earn about $41,800, what profit would be earned?

    Profit: _____

6. Marko is thinking about doing additional marketing research to help "fine tune" the promotion it is thinking about using with its target marketing strategy. The marketing research will add $4,000 to the total promotion cost, but Marko thinks that the more precisely targeted promotion might increase its share of purchases to 55 percent. If Marko's estimates are correct, would it make sense to spend the extra money on marketing research? Briefly, explain the reason for your answer. (Note: do your analysis assuming that distribution cost will be $2.00 per unit, and that other values are as originally planned--that is, as they appeared on the original spreadsheet.)

    _____

    _____

7. If the marketing research above cost $10,000 and Marko managers estimated that the improved promotion might increase their share of market to as much as 56 percent of the market, would it make sense to spend the money on the additional marketing research? Why?

    _____

    _____

8. Marko thinks that it would have to charge an even lower price of $13.75 a unit to win a larger share of the "mass market. " If it charged a price $13.75 and its share of purchases in the mass market increased to 25 percent, what profit would be earned?

    Profit: $_____

9. If other competitors reacted to Marko's price cut with price cuts of their own, and Marko's share of purchases in the mass market fell back to 20 percent, what profit would be earned?

    Profit: $_____

10. Briefly, discuss the profit implications of firms trying to compete with each other in the mass market by offering lower and lower prices?

    _____

    _____

Chapter 3

Focusing marketing strategy with segmentation and positioning

Chapter Summary

- **Know about the different kinds of marketing opportunities.**
  There are four basic types of marketing opportunities. Market penetration means trying to increase sales of a firm's present products in its present markets. Market development means trying to increase sales by selling in new markets. Product development means offering new or improved products for present markets. Diversification means moving into totally different lines of business. An attractive opportunity will be one that matches the firm's resources and objectives.

- **Understand why opportunities in international markets should be considered.**
  With barriers to trade collapsing and the rapid progression of communication technology (such as the internet) and transportation (jet plane, containerization), international markets are more accessible today than ever before. These markets contain consumers with many of the same needs as domestic consumers, and they have money to spend. Targeting international markets may allow the firm to take advantages of areas with less competition or to take advantage of increased economies of scale.

- **Know how to screen and evaluate marketing opportunities, including international opportunities.**
  The firm must first screen out obvious mismatches to the overall strategic plan of the company. Once opportunities have been narrowed down, an in-depth screening and evaluation should take place. There are many criteria that could be used, including *total profit* and *return–on-investment (ROI)* approaches. Planning grids such as GE's strategic planning grid are also useful. International markets can be more risky depending on the political, legal, cultural, economic and business environments. A thorough analysis should be taken before entering any foreign market.

- **Know about defining generic markets and product markets.**
  A generic market is a market with broadly similar needs and sellers offering *various, and often diverse ways*, of satisfying those needs. Any product that satisfies the customer's needs can compete in this generic market. A generic market definition includes a three-part definition made up of (1) customer needs (2) customer types, and (3) geographic area.
  In contrast, a product market is a market is a market with very similar needs and sellers offering various *close* substitutes ways of satisfying those needs. A product market definition also includes customer needs, customer types, and geographic area, along with a fourth element: product type.

- **Know what market segmentation is and how to segment product-markets into submarkets.**

Market segmentation is a two-step process of (1) naming broad product-markets and (2) segmenting these broad product-markets to select target markets and develop suitable marketing mixes. Since no one firm can satisfy every need, it must identify various generic needs and broad markets in which it has the resources and experience to compete successfully and earn a profit. The idea behind market segmentation is to cluster individuals into individuals into homogenous segments that will respond to a marketing mix in a similar way.

Four criteria are used to segment a broad product-market into submarkets: (1) the submarket should be homogenous (alike) within a given submarket, consisting of customers who are likely to respond to marketing mix variables in similar fashion; (2) it should be heterogeneous(different) between different submarkets, making the different segments as different as possible with regard to their likely response to marketing mix variables; (3) the submarket should be large enough to be profitable; (4) it should be actionable, and useful for identifying customers and marketing mix variables.

- **Know three approaches to choosing the target segment.**
  1. The *single* target market approach. This approach involves segmenting the market and picking one of the homogenous segments as the firm's target.
  2. The *multiple* target approach. The market is segmented and two or more of these segments are chosen and treated as separate target markets, each requiring a unique (different) marketing mix.
  3. The *combined* target marketing approach. This combines two or more submarkets, into one larger target market as the basis for a single strategy.

  Marketers who follow the first two approaches are known as *segmenters*, while those who follow the third approach are known as *combiners*. *Segmenters* try to satisfy their target market "*very well*", while *combiners* try to satisfy "*pretty well*".

- **Know the dimensions that may be useful for segmenting target markets.**
  There are many qualifying and determining dimensions to consider when segmenting markets. Qualifying dimensions are those that are relevant to including a customer type in a product-market. Determining dimensions are those that actually affect the customer's purchase of a specific product or brand in a product-market. Exhibits 3-9, 3-10, 3-11, 3-12 and 3-13 (pp. 63-67) all contain useful information and are worth a second look.

- **Know what positioning is, and why it is useful.**
  Positioning shows how customers locate (perceive) proposed and/or present brands in a market. The results are usually presented in a graph, such as Exhibit 3-14 (p. 71), to show how customers locate (perceive) competing products. The product positions are typically related to two or three product features.

  Positioning is useful because it allows a manager to make informed decisions as to whether to make changes to the marketing mix or to reposition the product to gain an advantage over the competition. It may also come as a shock to many product managers that many consumers do not view a product in the same way that the manager does. This fact leads to many other important positioning decisions.

Important Terms

breakthrough opportunities, p. 49	segmenting, p. 58
competitive advantage, p. 49	market segment, p. 58
differentiation, p. 53	single target market approach, p. 61

____ 1. Attractive opportunities are those that the firm has some chance of doing something about given its resources and objectives.

____ 2. "Breakthrough opportunities" are ones that help innovators develop hard-to-copy marketing strategies that will be very profitable for a long time.

____ 3. A firm with a "competitive advantage" has a marketing mix that the target market sees as better than a competitor's mix.

____ 4. It is useful to think of the marketing strategy planning process as a narrowing-down process.

____ 5. Segmentation is the process a manager goes through to decide which subgroups of customers to select.

____ 6. Differentiation means that the firm's marketing mix is similar to its competitors' mixes.

____ 7. There are usually more different strategy possibilities than a firm can pursue.

____ 8. A S.W.O.T. analysis is one way to zero in on a marketing strategy that is well-suited to the firm.

____ 9. Marketing opportunities involving present markets and present products are called "market penetration" opportunities.

____ 10. A "market development" opportunity would involve a firm offering new or improved products to its present markets.

____ 11. When it comes to choosing among different types of opportunities, most firms tend to be production-oriented and usually think first of diversification.

____ 12. Often, attractive opportunities are fairly close to markets the firm already knows.

____ 13. A market consists of a group of potential customers with similar needs.

____ 14. A generic market is a market with broadly similar needs and sellers offering various and often diverse ways of satisfying those needs.

____ 15. A product-market is a market with very similar needs and sellers offering various close substitute ways of satisfying those needs.

____ 16. A generic market description looks at markets narrowly--and from a producer's viewpoint.

____ 17. A firm's "relevant market for finding opportunities" should be bigger than its present product-market--but not so big that the firm could not expand and be an important competitor in this market.

_____ 18. Just identifying the geographic boundaries of a firm's present market can suggest new marketing opportunities.

_____ 19. A generic market description should include both customer-related and product-related terms.

_____ 20. Effective market segmentation requires a two-step process: (1) naming broad product-markets and (2) segmenting these broad product-markets into more homogeneous submarkets--also called product-markets--for the purpose of selecting target markets and developing suitable marketing mixes.

_____ 21. The first step in segmenting product-markets is to name the broad product-market area to be segmented.

_____ 22. Naming markets is a disaggregating process.

_____ 23. Segmenting is an aggregating process.

_____ 24. When segmenting markets, "good" market segments are ones that are heterogeneous within, homogeneous between, substantial, and operational.

_____ 25. The multiple target market approach combines two or more homogeneous submarkets into one larger target market as a basis for one strategy.

_____ 26. A segmenter is usually attempting to satisfy a submarket with its own unique demand curve--and therefore must settle for a smaller sales potential than a combiner.

_____ 27. Demographic segmenting dimensions are always more effective than behavioural dimensions (such as needs, benefits sought, and rate of use).

_____ 28. Determining dimensions rarely change.

_____ 29. The determining dimensions may help identify the "core features" which will have to be offered to everyone in the broad product-market.

_____ 30. Segmenting international markets is usually easy because so much good data is available.

_____ 31. The first step in segmenting international markets is to segment by country or region.

_____ 32. Segmenting approaches cannot be used for business markets.

_____ 33. Clustering techniques try to find similar patterns within sets of customer-related data.

_____ 34. Customer relationship management (CRM) is a variation of the clustering approach.

___ 35. "Positioning" refers to a packaged goods manufacturer's efforts to obtain the best possible shelf or display location in retail stores.

___ 36. The only way to "reposition" a product is to make some physical change to it.

___ 37. Positioning analysis is useful for combining but not for segmenting.

___ 38. Both a firm's manager and its customers are likely to view its marketing mix alike.

39. One of the alternatives that can be used to express a unique selling proposition is End-use application

Answers to True-False Questions

1. T, p. 45	14. T, p. 55	27. F, p. 64
2. T, p. 49	15. T, p. 55	28. F, p. 64
3. T, p. 49	16. F, p. 55	29. F, p. 64
4. T, p. 50	17. T, p. 49	30. F, p. 67
5. T, p. 68	18. T, p. 49	31. T, p. 67
6. F, p. 53	19. F, p. 55	32. F, p. 67
7. T, p. 49	20. T, p. 55	33. T, p. 68
8. T, p. 53	21. T, p. 55	34. T, p. 70
9. T, p. 46	22. T, p. 58	35. F, p. 71
10. F. p. 46	23. T, p. 58	36. F, p. 71
11. F, p. 48	24. F, p. 60	37. F, p. 72
12. T, p. 48	25. F, p. 61	38. F, p. 72
13. F, p. 54	26. F, p. 61	39. T, p. 73

Multiple-Choice Questions (Circle the correct response)

1. Breakthrough opportunities:
    a.   are so rare that they should be pursued even when they do not match the firm's resources and objectives.
    b.   seldom occur within or close to a firm's present markets.
    c.   are especially important in our increasingly competitive markets.
    d.   are those, which a firm's competitors can copy quickly.
    e.   are best achieved by trying to hold onto a firm's current market share.

2. A S.W.O.T. analysis includes:
    a.   strengths.
    b.   weaknesses.
    c.   opportunities.
    d.   threats.
    e.   all of the above.

3. When a firm tries to increase sales by selling its present products in new markets, this is called:
    a.   market penetration.
    b.   market development.
    c.   product development.
    d.   diversification.
    e.   market integration.

4. A market consists of:
    a.   a group of potential customers with similar needs who are willing to exchange something of value.
    b.   various kinds of products with similar characteristics.
    c.   sellers offering substitute ways of satisfying needs.
    d.   all the firms within a particular industry.
    e.   both a end c.

5. A market in which sellers offer various close substitute ways of satisfying the market's needs is called a:
    a.   generic market.
    b.   relevant market.
    c   product-market.
    d.   central market.
    e.   homogeneous market.

6. Which of the following is the best example of a "generic market"?
    a.   The expensive ten-speed bicycle market
    b.   The U.S. college student creative expression market
    c.   The photographic market
    d.   The pet food market
    e.   The teenage market

7. A generic market
    a.   competitor might have only a tiny market share in the generic market but a large share in its product-market.

b.   often includes consumers who will satisfy the same need in quite different ways.

c.   often involves sellers who compete in different product-markets.

d.   All of the above are true.

e.   None of the above are true.

8.   A firm's "relevant market for finding opportunities":
   a.   should be as large as possible.
   b.   should have no geographic limits.
   c.   should be no larger than its present product-market.
   d.   should always be named in product-related terms.
   e.   None of the above is a true statement.

9.   Market segmentation:
   a.   tries to find heterogeneous submarkets within a market.
   b.   means the same thing as marketing strategy planning.
   c.   assumes that most submarkets can be satisfied by the same marketing mix.
   d.   assumes that any market is likely to consist of submarkets.
   e.   All of the above are true statements.

10.   Naming broad product-markets is:
   a.   an assorting process
   b.   a disaggregating process
   c.   a segmenting process
   d.   an accumulating process
   e.   an aggregating process

11.   Segmenting:
   a.   is essentially a disaggregating or "break it down" process.
   b.   assumes that all customers can be grouped into homogeneous and profitable market segments.
   c.   tries to aggregate together individuals who have similar needs and characteristics.
   d.   usually results in firms aiming at smaller and less profitable markets.
   e.   assumes that each individual should be treated as a separate target market.

12.   "Good" market segments are those, which are:
   a.   heterogeneous within.
   b.   operational.
   c.   homogeneous between.
   d.   substantial--meaning large enough to minimize operating costs.
   e.   all of the above.

13.   Having segmented its market, the Stuart Corp. has decided to treat each of two submarkets as a separate target market requiring a different marketing mix. Apparently, Stuart is following the _____ target market approach.
   a.   single
   b.   combined
   c.   multiple
   d.   separate
   e.   general

14. Segmenting and combining are two alternate approaches to developing market-oriented strategies. Which of the following statements concerning these approaches is *true*?
    a. Combiners treat each submarket as a separate target market.
    b. Segmenters try to develop a marketing mix that will have general appeal to several market segments.
    c. A combiner looks at various submarkets for similarities rather than differences.
    d. A segmenter assumes that the whole market consists of a fairly homogeneous group of customers.
    e. Both segmenters and combiners try to satisfy some people very well rather than a lot of people fairly well.

15. Which of the following types of dimensions would be the most important if one were particularly interested in why some target market was likely to buy a particular brand within a product-market?
    a. Primary dimensions
    b. Secondary dimensions
    c. Qualifying dimensions
    d. Determining dimensions
    e. Both a and c above.

16. Behavioural segmenting dimensions do not include:
    a. benefits offered.
    b. kind of shopping involved.
    c. brand familiarity.
    d. family life cycle.
    e. type of problem-solving.

17. International marketing:
    a. requires more segmenting dimensions than domestic marketing.
    b. adds just one step to other segmenting approaches.
    c. requires segmenting by country or region first.
    d. usually involves working with data that is less available and less dependable.
    e. All of the above are true statements.

18. Which of the following statements about clustering techniques is *true?*
    a. Clustering techniques try to find dissimilar patterns within sets of customer-related data.
    b. Computers are usually needed to search among all of the data for homogeneous groups of people.
    c. Computers identify the relevant dimensions and do the analysis.
    d. A cluster analysis of the toothpaste market indicated that most consumers seek the same benefits.
    e. All of the above are true.

19. Which of the following statements about customer relationship marketing (CRM) is *true?*
    a. Instead of segmenting information, CRM uses information on a customer's past purchases.
    b. Amazon.com is a good example of a firm that uses CRM.
    c. Firms that operate on the Internet may be able to communicate with their customers faster than other firms, but the costs of doing so are higher.
    d. CRM is a variation of the positioning approach.

e.   All of the above are true.

20.   "Positioning":
    a.   involves a packaged-goods manufacturer's attempt to obtain the best possible shelf space for its products in retail outlets.
    b.   is useful for segmenting but not combining.
    c.   helps strategy planners understand how customers think about various brands or products in relation to each other.
    d.   applies only to existing products, not new products.
    e.   eliminates the need for subjective decision making in product planning.

21.   "Positioning" is concerned with
    a.   how current target customers think about the products available from one company.
    b.   how customers think about the competing brands in a market.
    c.   an analysis of the design strengths and weaknesses of products in a market
    d.   the economic factors that affect consumer choices among alternative brands.
    e.   None of the above is true.

Answers to Multiple-Choice Questions

1. c, p. 49
2. e, p. 53
3. b, p. 46
4. e, p. 54
5. c, p. 55
6. b, p. 55
7. d, p. 55

8. e, p. 49
9. d, p. 57
10. b, p. 56
11. c, p. 57
12. b, p. 60
13. c, p. 61
14. c, p. 61

15. d, p. 64
16. d, p. 64
17. e, p. 67
18. b, p. 68
19. b, p. 70
20. c, p. 71
21. b, p. 71

Additional Questions to Test Your Understanding

1. a. What are the four components included in a complete product-market definition?

    1) _____

    2) _____

    3) _____

    4) _____

    b. Match each of these four components with appropriate definition listed below:

    1) _____   Where a firm competes, or plans to compete for customers

    2) _____   The final consumers or users of a product type.

    3) _____   The goods and/or services customers want.

    4) _____   The needs the product type satisfies for the customer.

2. Which of the three basic ways of developing market-oriented strategies in a broad product-market are used by segmenters?

    1) _____

    2) _____

3. Which of the three basic ways of developing market-oriented strategies in a broad product-market are used by "combiners"?

    1) _____

    2) _____

4. Generally, should a firm be a segmenter or a combiner"? Provide reasons for your answer.

    _____

    _____

    _____

    _____

Answers to Additional Questions.

1. a.
    1) product type
    2) customer (user) needs
    3) customer types
    4) geographic area

    See page 56

   b.
    1) geographic area p. 57
    2) customer type p. 56
    3) product type p. 56
    4) customer needs p. 56

2.
    1) single target market approach p. 61
    2) multiple target market approach p. 61

3. combined target market approach p. 61

4. See discussion pp. 61-63

Exercise 3-1

Product-markets vs. generic markets

Introduction

A practical first step in searching for breakthrough opportunities is to define the firm's present (or potential) markets. Markets consist of potential customers with similar needs and sellers offering various ways of satisfying those needs.

Markets can be defined very broadly or very narrowly--with either extreme being a potential threat to effective strategy planning. For example, defining its market too broadly as "transportation" could result in General Motors seeing itself in direct competition with manufacturers of airplanes, ships, elevators, bicycles, little red wagons, and perhaps even spaceships! On the other hand, a definition such as "the market for six-passenger motor vehicles with gasoline-powered internal-combustion engines" would be too narrow--and does not even identify "potential customers."

While there is no simple and automatic way to define a firm's *relevant* market, marketers should start by defining the relevant generic market and product-market using the 3 and 4 part definitions discussed on pages 55-57 of the text and shown below:

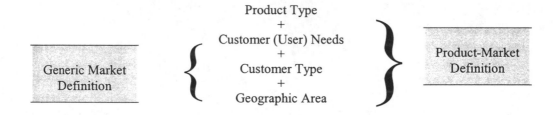

It often requires a lot of creativity to think in terms of generic markets and product-markets--but failure to do so can cause strategy planners to overlook breakthrough opportunities--and leave themselves exposed to new forms of competition. Just ask the manufacturers of kerosene lamps, buggy whips, and mathematical slide rules!

Assignment

This exercise will give you some practice in naming product-markets and generic markets. It will also require you to be creative and apply your marketing intuition.

Listed below are several generic markets and brand-name products. Using the 3 and 4 part definitions of generic markets and product-markets, suggest possible market names in the blanks. Note: There are no "right answers," but they should be logical and consistent. Generic markets should *not* include any product-related terms. A generic market can have several related product-markets. In addition, a product is offered to a product-market that is a part of a larger generic market. Question 1 is answered to help you get started.

1.　　Generic market: Security for families in the world

　　　a) Product-market: *Homeowner's insurance for financial security for home-owning families in the Ontario.*
　　　b) Product-market: *Guards for physical security for wealthy families in the world*
　　　c) Product-market: *Smoke alarms for mental security for families in the developed countries.*

2.　　Generic market: Duncan Hines chewy chocolate-chip cookies.

　　　a)　　Product-market:

_____

　　　b)　　Product-market:

_____

　　　c)　　Product-market:

_____

3.　　Generic market: Communication systems.

　　　a)　　Product-market:

_____

　　　b)　　Product-market:

_____

　　　c)　　Product-market:

_____

4.　　Generic market: Family entertainment for lower income people in Canada.

　　　a)　　Product-market:

_____

　　　b)　　Product-market:

_____

　　　c)　　Product-market:

_____

5.　　Product: Calvin Klein (label on back pocket) jeans

　　　a)　　Product-market:

_____

b)   Generic market:
_____

6.   Product: Ben and Jerry's Chocolate Fudge Brownie Low-Fat Frozen Yogurt

    a)   Product-market:
_____

    b)   Generic market:
_____

7.   Product: Sony Handycam digital video camera-recorder

    a)   Product-market:
_____

    b)   Generic market:
_____

Questions for Discussion

1.   How can a firm decide *which* and *how many* markets to enter?

2.   With the use of the product-market grid illustrated below, explain what strategies gourmet cookie companies in major cities might undertake due to problems of increased competition and decreased sales.

	Present Products	New Products
Present Markets	Market Penetration	Product Development
New Markets	Market Development	Diversification

Exercise 3-2

Applying marketing segmentation concepts

Introduction

The development of successful marketing strategies depends to a large extent on the planner's ability to segment markets. Unfortunately, this is not a simple process. Segmenting usually requires considerable management judgment and skill. Those marketers who have the necessary judgment and skill will have a real advantage over their competitors in finding profitable opportunities.

Segmenting is basically a process of gathering individuals into homogeneous market segments based on similar customer needs and characteristics. Although segmenting is often helped by the use of marketing research and computer techniques, such techniques are not always necessary--or economically practical. Further, even if formal research is to be conducted, it may be necessary for a manager to first sharpen the problem-solving focus by developing some preliminary ideas about what market segments might be of particular interest.

Although market segmentation is critically important, too many managers do not really know how to get started-because they have not practiced applying the concepts discussed in Chapter 3. Yet, by using these concepts as part of an organized, integrative approach, the strategy planner can often identify useful segments. This exercise takes you step-by-step through such an approach. It is workable and has been used in the development of successful marketing strategies. *It is especially useful when looking for new market opportunities.*

Thus, in this exercise you will be asked to segment a market and then to think of what products (and whole marketing mixes) might be most appropriate for each segment. Practice this approach by applying the same ideas to other product-markets.

Assignment

Assume you have been asked to segment the following broad product-market: automotive vehicles for transporting families or small groups in the world. Think about the many product offerings in this market and the people who buy them. Then, answer the following questions.

1. *List potential customers needs.* In the space below, list all the needs you can think of that potential customers may have in this product-market area. Be sure to focus on needs rather than product features. (Note: do not limit the list just to needs that might apply to most people-also include needs that may only apply to certain types of people. For example, some people may want a "prestige" image, and for others that may be totally irrelevant-or even a big negative.)

2. *Form "homogeneous submarkets"- i.e. "narrow" product-markets.* Recognizing that some people have different needs than others, on a piece of scratch paper "rough out" at least four different submarkets based on needs. Start by forming one submarket around some typical type of customer-perhaps even yourself. (You want to be able to aggregate similar people into this segment as long as they can be satisfied by the same marketing mix.) For this submarket, write down the most important need dimensions and customer-related characteristics (including demographic dimensions). Continue this process by identifying another "distinct" submarket (that is, one that would be composed of people who are not similar to the first submarket in terms of needs, characteristics, and the type of marketing mix they would want). Continue this process until you have identified the needs and characteristics of at least four submarkets.

    Still working on your scratch paper, review the list of need dimensions for each possible submarket and identify the determining dimensions by putting an asterisk beside them. Although the qualifying dimensions are important-perhaps reflecting "core needs" that must be satisfied well-they are not the determining dimensions we are seeking now. To help identify the determining dimensions, think carefully about the needs and attitudes of the people in each possible submarket. At first, those dimensions may not seem very important from market to market, but if they are determining to those people then they *are* determining!

    Once you are satisfied that you have identified at least four distinct submarkets, name ("nickname") the product-markets involved. You will probably want to select names by thinking about which of the determining dimensions you have identified as most important for each submarket-perhaps aided by your descriptions of customer characteristics.

Now, review the notes on your scratch paper and make any refinements that help to clarify the ways in which the different submarkets might be dissimilar (and how they might be similar).

3. Summarize the work you did in Question 2 by using the diagram below to draw a picture of the product-market and the subproduct-markets you identified. Vary the size of the submarkets to show what you think might be their estimated market potential. Give each submarket a name.

A diagram of the broad product-market
for automotive vehicles for transporting
families or small groups in the world

4. Now, for the product-markets that you identified in Question 2, show:

    a) the name of each submarket.
    b) each submarket's important needs.
    c) other customer characteristics for each submarket--especially demographic or lifestyle dimensions.
    d) the type of products that would appeal to each submarket.

Product-Market 1

a)   Name:

_____

b)   Needs:

_____

_____

c)   Characteristics:

_____

_____

_____

d)   Products:

_____

_____

_____

_____

Product-Market 2

a)   Name:

_____

b)   Needs:

_____

_____

c)   Characteristics:

_____

_____

_____

d)   Products:

_____

_____

_____

_____

Product-Market 3

a)	Name:

_____

b)	Needs:

_____

_____

c)	Characteristics:

_____

_____

_____

d)	Products:

_____

_____

_____

_____

Product-Market 4

a)	Name:

_____

b)	Needs:

_____

_____

c)	Characteristics:

_____

_____

_____

d)	Products:

_____

_____

_____

_____

Question for Discussion

If you were a marketing manager, what else would you like to know about possible product-markets before selecting a target market?

Exercise 3-3

Using positioning to evaluate marketing opportunities

Introduction

Finding target market opportunities is a continuing challenge for all marketers. Understanding how customers view current or proposed market offerings is often a crucial part of this challenge. In addition, understanding customer perceptions is more difficult when different segments of the market have different needs and different views of how well current or proposed products meet those needs. Developing insights requires that you try to answer questions such as: Are there customer segments with needs which no existing products are satisfying very well? Could our existing product be modified to do a better job of satisfying the needs of some segment? Could promotion be used to communicate to consumers about aspects of the product--so that target customers would "see" it in a different way?

There are no easy answers to such questions, but *positioning* approaches can help. As explained in the text (pages 70-73), positioning uses marketing research techniques, which measure customer views of products or brands according to several product features (e.g., do consumers think of a brand of detergent as "gentle" or "strong" relative to other brands?). Usually, customers are also asked to decide the amount of each feature than would be "ideal" (e.g., how strong a detergent do you want?)

The results are plotted on a two- or three-dimensional diagram--called a "product space. " Each dimension represents a product feature that the customers feel is important. The diagram shows how each product or brand was rated on each of the dimensions. In other words, it shows how the various products or brands are "positioned" relative to each other--and relative to the "ideal" products or brands of different segments of customers. Usually, circles are used to show segments of customers with similar "ideal points" along the dimensions.

The mechanics of how all this is done are beyond the scope of this course. However, you should know that positioning research techniques produce a very useful graphic aid to help marketing managers do their job better. Looking at a product space for a market, a marketing planner may see opportunities to "reposition" existing products or brands through product and/or promotion changes. Alternatively, he may spot an empty space, which calls for the introduction of a new product. Often, he may be quite surprised to see that customer views of market offerings differ a great deal from his own ideas.

Assignment

Figure 3-3 is a fictional "product space" diagram for ready-to-eat breakfast cereal. The diagram shows how target customers rated several brands of cereal along two product dimensions which have been identified only as Dimension A and Dimension B. respectively. The diagram also shows 8 segments of customers grouped together on the basis of similar "ideal points. " For example, customers in segment #8 desire a lot of both attribute A and B.

Study Figure 3-3 carefully and then answer the following questions.

FIGURE 3-3
Product Space for Ready-to-Eat Breakfast Cereal

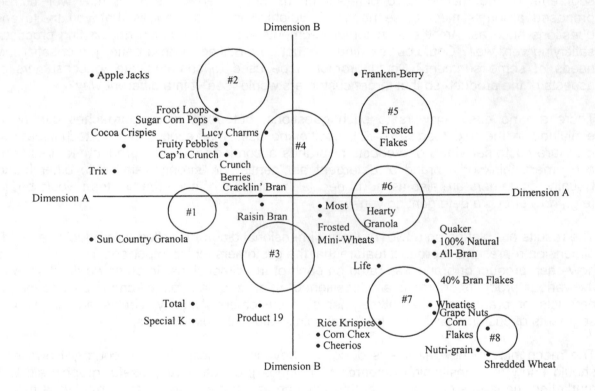

1. a) Based on your interpretation of Figure 3-3, what product feature does Dimension A appear to represent?

   b) Based on your interpretation of Figure 3-3, what product feature does Dimension B appear to represent?

2.   What opportunities for "repositioning" *existing* products do you see in Figure 3-3? Be specific, and indicate the segment(s) to which you want to target your appeal(s).

3.   What opportunities for introducing *new* products do you see in Figure 3-3? Be specific, and indicate the segment(s) whose needs you would want to satisfy.

4.   If you were interested in targeting customers in segment #6, which existing brands would be your most direct competitors?

5.   If you were the marketing manager for Raisin Bran cereal and you were thinking about using the combined target market approach to appeal to two different segments, which segments would be the likely target for your marketing strategy? Briefly explain your choice.

6. In Figure 3-3 there are already many competing product offerings in the upper left and lower right quadrants. Why does not an innovative producer offer a new product to the far left and bottom of the space--where there is currently no product?

7. Are the two product dimensions shown in Figure 3-3 the two most important dimensions in choosing a brand of breakfast cereal? If not, what dimensions are most important?

8. Do all potential customers agree as to which two dimensions are the most important dimensions in choosing a brand of breakfast cereal? If not, what are the implications for using "positioning" as an aid in evaluating market opportunities?

Question for Discussion

Is positioning an art or a science? Why?

Exercise 3-4

Segmenting multidimensional markets

Introduction

Marketing-oriented business managers realize that what is often considered as the mass market may actually consist of many smaller more homogeneous market segments. Thus, market segmentation becomes a crucial step in the development of a successful marketing strategy.

Market segmentation can be illustrated graphically using "market grids". The grid approach pictures a market as a large box that is divided up into smaller boxes based on relevant needs and characteristics of potential customers. Each smaller box within the larger box represents a smaller more homogeneous market segment – and a potential target market.

For example, a watch manufacturer who believed that gender and social class were the most relevant customer dimensions for his product-market might construct the market grid shown in Figure 3-4-1.

Figure 3-4-1
Market Grid for the Watch Market

Male			
Female			
	Upper-Class	Middle-Class	Lower-Class

In looking at Figure 3-4, however you should keep in mind that gender and social class are only two of many possible dimensions that might be used to segment the watch market. As discussed in the text, possible segmenting dimensions include geographic dimensions, geographic dimensions, need or attitude dimensions, lifestyle dimensions, benefit dimensions, usage patterns, brand familiarity, and buying situations.

In other words, market segmentation is complicated by the fact that markets can be defined in many different ways. In keeping with the marketing concept, markets should be defined I terms of the needs and characteristics of potential customers. However, this remains a difficult task because customers are *multi-dimensional* and typically display many similarities and differences – only some of which may be relevant for a particular market situation.

The task of deciding which dimensions are relevant for segmenting a particular market is further complicated by the need to distinguish between qualifying and determining dimensions. *Qualifying dimensions* include *any factors which qualify one as potential customer*, while *determining dimensions* include only those factors which *determine which type of product or even which brand* may be purchased.

For example, any person who needs to know the correct time and can afford the price of a watch presumably would qualify as a potential customer. However, these dimensions would not be sufficient to determine which type of watch (e.g. calendar watch, digital watch, sports watch, etc.) or which brand a person might purchase.

This exercise is designed to familiarize you with some of the different types of dimensions that are often used to segment markets – and to emphasize the need for considerable management judgment in deciding which dimension are most relevant for a particular market.

Figure 3-4-2
Alternative Dimensions for the Canadian Instant Breakfast Food Market

a. Based on family income levels of potential customers	b. Geographic location of potential customers	
Under $10,000	Atlantic Provinces - Urban	Rural
$10,000 - $19,999	Ontario - Urban	Rural
$20,000 - $29,999	Quebec - Urban	Rural
$30,000 - $39,999	West - Urban	Rural
$40,000 – $49,999		
Over $50,000		

c. Based on "brand loyalty" of potential customers.
Strong Brand Loyalty
Weak Brand Loyalty
No Brand Loyalty

d. Based on personality traits of potential customers.	
Extroverted Conformists	Extroverted Nonconformists
Introverted Conformists	Introverted Nonconformists

e. Based on potential customers needs and benefits sought (see definitions below)	
Harried Commuters	Working Mothers
Snack Servers	Calorie Counters

- **Harried commuters** – busy career people who need a source of energy or nutrition – but who do not have time to prepare and eat a complete breakfast.
- **Working mothers** – The women whose work schedules prevent them from making sure their children eat a full and nutritious breakfast.
- **Snack servers** – Homemakers who see to it that their children eat a full and balanced breakfast – but who also want to provide them with nutritious and good-tasting snacks.

- **Calorie counters** – Dieters looking for tasty, filling and nutritious meal substitutes.

Assignment

Assume you are the marketing manager for a company that has decided to enter the instant breakfast market. The firm feels that an opportunity exists to introduce a new product that is superior to anything already on the market in terms of taste and convenience.

As marketing manager, it is your job to develop a successful marketing strategy for the new product – starting with the selection of a target market. Therefore, you have asked your marketing research staff to analyze breakfast food market and describe the various market segments that make up the overall market. However, as it turned out there was considerable disagreement among the researchers as to which dimension should be used to segment the market. Unable to reach agreement among themselves, they therefore submitted five different dimensions for the instant breakfast food market as shown in Figure 3-4-2.

1. Of the five dimensions shown in Figure 3-4-2, which two do you think would be most relevant and effective for segmenting the instant breakfast food market? Why?

2. Draw a grid based on the two dimensions you selected in question 1. Based on your grid, which of the following approaches would you recommend in selecting a target market for the instant breakfast food market: (a) the single target market approach, (b) the multiple market approach, or (c) the combined target market approach. In answering this question, specify your recommended target market and explain why you selected it.

3. Assume your company was able to acquire the rights for an instant breakfast food product from another country. This product comes in a relatively expensive multiple-unit package, looks and tastes like chocolate cake, requires no preparation, and can be used as either a nutritious meal substitute, a snack, or a diet food. Would this product meet the needs of your recommended target market? If not, how would it have to be changed?

Question for Discussion

What criteria should marketing managers use to judge whether the segmenting dimension they are using are relevant and effective for strategic market planning.

Exercise 3-5

Segmenting customers

This exercise is based on computer-aided problem number 3--Segmenting Customers. A complete description of the problem appears on pages 75-76 of Wong/Shapiro, 11th edition.

1.   Audiotronics Software's marketing manager is thinking about the possibility of combining two of the segments into a single target market. He is not certain which segments to combine. However, he thinks he will be more successful if the two segments are as similar as possible.

   It occurred to him that the same spreadsheet he used to cluster customers could be used to compute a score showing how similar the segments are to each other. All that would be needed would be to enter the "summary" importance ratings for a segment in the spreadsheet, and then record how similar that segment is to each of the other segments. Complete this analysis for each of the segments and fill in the table below. (Remember that the spreadsheet computes "how far" customers are from the typical segment member, so a *lower* score is more *similar.)*

Summary Importance Rating				Overall Similarity		
No. of features	*Easy to Use*	*Easy to Learn*	**Segment**	Fearful Typists	Power Users	Prof. Specialists
3	8	9	Fearful			
9	2	2	Power			
7	5	6	Specialist			

2.   Based on this analysis, which pair of segments seems to be most similar (homogeneous) with respect to the importance of different software features?

   _____

   _____

3.   Based on this analysis, which pair of segments seems to be least similar (homogeneous) with respect to the importance of different software features?

4. The marketing manager is thinking about developing a product that could be "positioned" to satisfy each of the two most similar segments "pretty well." He thinks that the summary importance ratings for each segment are a good indicator of what each segment's "ideal" product would be like. Therefore, he decided to average the importance ratings for the *two most similar* segments and develop a product that matched that "average need. " However, he wants to see how well such a product would meet the needs of the individual segments. To further evaluate this idea, complete the table below.

Importance Factor	Importance First Segment	Importance Second Segment	Sum of Ratings	Average Rating
Features				
Easy to Use				
Easy to Learn				

5. If a product could be developed to match the average ratings above, how well do you think it would satisfy each of the segments? Briefly, explain your answer. (Hint: enter the "average" ratings in the spreadsheet, and see how similar the needs met by this "average" product are with the needs of each of the different segments.)

Similarity Score for the "average product"	Fearful Typists	Power Users	Prof. Specialists

Explanation:

_____

_____

_____

6. A computer programmer at the company has suggested that they just try to produce a product based on the average needs of all three segments. Use the same approach you used above to evaluate how similar a product based on the average of all three segments would be to the needs of each of the individual segments.

Factor	Fearful	Power	Specialist	Sum	Average
Features					
Easy to Use					
Easy to Learn					

Similarity Score for the "average product"	Fearful Typists		Power Users		Prof. Specialists	

7. Based on the "average product similarity scores" you computed in Question 6 above, does it appear that the programmer's idea would provide a good basis for developing a product that would appeal to "the whole market" (i.e., all three segments)? Briefly, explain your answer.

_____

_____

_____

Chapter 4

The Changing Marketing Environment

Chapter Summary

- **Know the variables that shape the environment of marketing strategy planning.**
  These variables include the objectives and resources of the company, the competitive environment, the economic and technological environment, the political and legal environment and, lastly, the social and cultural environment. However, each firm must do its own scan of the environment to identify those changes and developments of particular relevance to its product offerings and the markets it serves.

- **Know why company objectives are important in guiding strategic market planning**
  The basic objectives of any company mentioned in your text are just a starting point for strategic planning. A company's mission statement sets out the organization's basic purpose for being. Such a statement, while essential, is not a substitute for more specific objectives that can provide guidance in screening possible market opportunities. The likely consequences of pursuing each identified opportunity must be measured against specific objectives like "earn 25-per cent annual return on investment (ROI)" or "become the market-share leader in each of our product markets."

- **See how the resources of a company affect the search for opportunities.**
  Most companies have unique resources that set it apart from other companies. Breakthrough opportunities – or at least some competitive advantage – come from making use of these strengths while avoiding direct competition with firms having similar strengths. By analyzing past successes and failures in pursuing identified marketing opportunities, management can discover not only why it succeeded or failed but also, as the Harley-Davidson example (p. 84) shows, how it might be more successful in the future.

- **Know how the different kinds of competitive situations affect strategic planning.**
  Economists refer to four basic kinds of market (competitive) situations: pure competition, oligopoly, monopolistic competition, and monopoly. In a world of pure competition, the company's marketers would have failed to differentiate their marketing mix from that of competing firms. Ideally, every firm would like to monopolize the market segments in which it has chosen to compete. However, a monopoly is both difficult to achieve and, more often then not, leads to government regulation. In monopolistic competition, some degree of differentiation has been achieved, providing the firm with its own downward sloping demand curve. However, the shape and elasticity of that demand curve depends on how successful the firm has been in developing a marketing mix that sets its product offering apart from that of its competitors.

- **Understand how the economic and technological environments can affect strategic planning.**

The economies of the world are becoming increasingly interconnected. Economic conditions elsewhere – especially in the U.S., which is five times as important a trading partner for Canada as the rest of the world combined – can have a tremendous effect on the Canadian economy. As the softwood lumber controversy and the Canadian beef import bans shows, tariffs, quotas, and trade disputes can have a marked impact on the Canadian industries affected. Other factors that managers must consider include the development of trading blocs such as NAFTA and the European Union and the growing importance of the WTO.

- **Know why the marketing manager must carefully monitor the legal environment.**
Every Canadian business operates within a framework established by the Competition Act, other federal legislation, many provincial laws, and municipal (local) laws and regulations. In recent years, the legal and regulatory emphasis has switched from "let the buyer beware" to " let the seller beware". The courts are placing a steadily increasing degree of responsibility on manufacturers. With increasing frequency, consumers are being directly protected with specific legislation. Those making the laws are no longer convinced that legislation designed to preserve a competitive market provides all the protection that consumers need.

- **Understand how to screen and evaluate marketing strategy opportunities**
A firm cannot possibly pursue all of the opportunities available. Using quantitative and qualitative criteria, a firm will evaluate possible opportunities to determine whether there is a match with their resources and objectives. Two approaches that are used are the total-profit (how much profit will an opportunity earn) and an ROI analysis (what percentage return will the firm get on an investment in an opportunity). Another method is to use strategic-planning grids such as the one that GE has developed. Screening is particularly complicated for multiproduct firms, using either a strategic business unit (SBU) or a portfolio management approach.

Important Terms

competitive environment, p. 85
competitor analysis, p. 88
competitive rivals, p. 88
competitive barriers, p. 89
consumerism, p. 97
cultural and social environment, p. 102
economic and technological
environment, p. 92
environmentalism, p. 98
exchange rate p. 93
internet, p. 95

legal environment, p. 99
mission statement, p. 82
nationalism, p. 96
North American Free Trade Agreement
(NAFTA), p. 96
political environment, p. 96
portfolio management, p. 109
quotas, p. 93
tariffs, p. 93
technology, p. 94
strategic business unit (SBU), p. 109

True-False Questions

____ 1. A business firm's only objective should be to earn enough profit to survive.

____ 2. Trying to maximize short-run return on investment may not be good in the long run.

____ 3. A mission statement should focus on just the key goals for the organization.

____ 4. Winning a larger market share necessarily leads to greater profitability.

____ 5. Company objectives should lead to a hierarchy of marketing objectives.

____ 6. Attractive opportunities should make use of a firm's resources and its unique strengths.

____ 7. A large producer with economies of scale always has a competitive advantage over smaller firms.

____ 8. A patent owner in Canada has a 20-year monopoly to develop and use its new product, process, or material.

____ 9. Although the marketing manager cannot control the competitive environment, he can choose strategies that will avoid head-on situations.

____ 10. In a competitor analysis, a current (or planned) target market and marketing mix is compared with what competitors are currently doing (or are likely to do).

____ 11. Competitive rivals are always easy to identify.

____ 12. Competitive barriers are the conditions that make it possible for a firm to compete in a market.

____ 13. The inflation rate experienced by the Canada in recent years was just about the highest in the world.

____ 14. When the Canadian dollar is strong in international exchange, it is easier to sell our products in overseas markets.

____ 15. Technology is the application of magic to convert an economy's resources to output.

____ 16. The Internet is a system for linking computers around the world.

____ 17. Changes in the technological environment could be rejected by the cultural and social environment--through the political and legal environment--even though such changes might help the economic environment.

____ 18. Nationalism may affect marketing strategy planning by determining to whom and how much a firm may sell.

_____ 19. Many countries in Europe have moved to the euro, a new unified money system for the European Union.

_____ 20. Because NAFTA is a short-term proposition, its economic impact has already been significant.

_____ 21. The political environment may either block or promote new marketing opportunities.

_____ 22. Consumerism is a social movement seeking to give sellers as much power and legal rights as buyers and consumers.

_____ 23. Businesses and individual managers are subject to both criminal and civil laws.

_____ 24. The Competition Act deals with tying contracts, exclusive dealing contracts, and price-fixing conspiracies.

_____ 25. Laws such as the Food and Drugs Act were passed because pro-competition legislation did not protect consumers very well in some areas.

_____ 26. The Canadian Standards Association (CSA) tries to encourage safe product design, but the commission has almost no power to deal with unsafe products.

_____ 27. Recent trends indicate a major shift in traditional thinking about buyer-seller relations from "let the seller beware" to "let the buyer beware."

_____ 28. Because the cultural and social environment tends to change slowly, firms should try to identify and work with cultural attitudes rather than trying to encourage big changes in the short run.

_____ 29. Product-market screening criteria should be mainly quantitative in nature, because qualitative criteria are too subjective.

_____ 30. Forecasts of the probable results of implementing whole strategic plans are needed to apply quantitative screening criteria.

_____ 31. The profit potentials of alternative strategic plans can be evaluated at the same time only if the plans are very similar.

_____ 32. The General Electric "strategic planning grid" forces company managers to make three-part judgments (high, medium, and low) about the business strengths and industry attractiveness of all proposed or existing product-market plans.

_____ 33. The G.E. "stop-light" evaluation method is a very objective approach because G.E. feels there are too many possible errors if it tries to use subjective criteria for judging "attractiveness" or "strength."

_____ 34. SBUs are small businesses that try to compete with major divisions of larger multiproduct companies.

____ 35. Portfolio management tends to emphasize current profitability and return on investment, often neglecting the long run.

____ 36. Most industrial products tend to be near the "insensitive" end of the continuum of environmental sensitivity.

____ 37. If the risks of getting into international marketing are difficult to evaluate, it usually is best to start with a joint venture.

Answers to True-False Questions

1. F, p. 82	14. F, p. 93	26. F, p. 101
2. T, p. 82	15. F, p. 94	27. F, p. 102
3. T, p. 82	16. T, p. 95	28. T, p. 102
4. F, p. 83	17. T, p. 102	29. F, p. 105
5. T, p. 83	18. T, p. 96	30. T, p. 105
6. T, p. 84	19. T, p. 97	31. F, p. 105
7. F. p. 84	20. F, p. 97	32. T, p. 107
8. T, p. 85	21. T, p. 96	33. F, p. 107
9. T, p. 85	22. F, p. 97	34. F, p. 109
10. T, p. 88	23. T, p. 99	35. T, p. 109
11. F, p. 88	24. F, p. 99	36. T, p. 109
12. F, p. 89	25. T, p. 100	37. F, p. 109
13. F, p. 92		

Multiple-Choice Questions (Circle the correct response)

1. Which of the following objectives of a business is the *most* important?
    a. To engage in some specific business activity, which will perform a socially and economically useful function.
    b. To develop an organization to carry on the business and implement its strategies.
    c. To earn enough profit to survive.
    d. All three of the above are equally important, because a failure in any one could lead to a total failure of the business.
    e. Both b and c are more important than a.

2. Of the following, the *last* objectives that a firm should specify are its:
    a. company objectives.
    b. marketing objectives.
    c. promotion objectives.
    d. advertising objectives.
    e. price objectives.

3. A first step in evaluating marketing opportunities is to:
    a. decide which markets the firm wishes to enter.
    b. consider the objectives and resources of the firm.
    c. hire a "futurist" as a marketing consultant.
    d. estimate market and sales potentials.
    e. find out if potential competitors are larger.

4. Which of the following statements about the competitive environment is *false?*
    a. Competition-free environments are rare.
    b. Marketing managers should choose strategies that avoid head-on competition.
    c. A firm that has a marketing mix that its target market sees as better than its competitors' has a competitive advantage.
    d. Over the long run, most product-markets tend toward monopolistic competition.
    e. In a competitor analysis, the firm's first step should be to identify all potential competitors.

5. Which of the following is *not* an example of how the economic and technological environment may affect marketing strategy planning?
    a. The price of bicycles is rising because of inflation.
    b. Bicycle manufacturers are finding it difficult to keep up with the growing demand for bicycles because of raw material shortages.
    c. Because of exchange rates, imported bikes are cheaper than those made in the United States.
    d. Computer-controlled assembly lines can turn out a new bike every three and one-half seconds.
    e. The demand for bikes is increasing because consumers are becoming more health conscious.

6. With the "unification of Europe":

a. many of the taxes and rules that have limited trade among member countries of the European Community were eliminated.
b. the need to adjust strategies to reach submarkets of European consumers disappeared.
c. firms operating in Europe have harder access to large markets.
d. consumer prices rose.
e. All of the above are true statements.

7. NAFTA is:
a. a free-trade pact between the U.S., Canada, and Mexico.
b. a short-term proposition.
c. trying to eliminate most trade barriers with Mexico in the next five years.
d. all of the above.
e. none of the above.

8. Bill C-6, the Personal Information Protection and Electronic Documents Act. a privacy commissioner was established under the Canadian Human Rights Act, gives Canadians:
a. a clean and safe environment.
b. protection form unnecessary and intrusive emails.
c. a set of private sector ground rules governing the collection and use of consumer information.
d. protection from door-to-door salespeople
e. access to personal credit reports and ratings and the right to legally dispute them.

9. A unique aspect of Quebec's Consumer Protection Act is::
a. prevention monopolies or conspiracies in restraint of trade.
b. stopping the flow of foreign products into Quebec.
c. prevents unfair or deceptive acts or practices in commerce.
d. a virtual ban on all advertising targeting children.
e. elimination of deceptive selling practices.

10. The Food and Drugs Act is primarily concerned with:
a. quality standards, packaging, labeling, and advertising.
b. price-fixing agreements.
c. conspiracies in restraint of trade.
d. mergers, which might substantially lessen competition.
e. unfair methods of competition.

11. The Competition Act is *most* concerned with:
a. product warranties.
b. price discrimination by manufacturers.
c. exclusive dealing contracts.
d. tying contracts.
e. preventing anticompetitive behaviour.

12. A firm that discriminates in price on goods of "like grade and quality" may be in violation of the _____ Act.
a. Sherman
b. Robinson-Patman
c. Wheeler-Lea

d. Competition Act
e. Food and Drugs Act

13. The Canadian Standards Council is **not** responsible for:
    a. developing technical standards for products.
    b. developing technical terminology for products, services and systems.
    c. preventing the distribution and sale of adulterated or misbranded foods, drugs, and cosmetics.
    d. representing Canada at international standards conferences.
    e. reporting to parliament on Canadian standards issues..

14. Some companies have established their own:
    a. product standards and terminology.
    b. consumer regulations that are not as demanding as government rules.
    c. corporate privacy code and a corporate privacy officer.
    d. anticompetition rules so as to avoid government interference.
    e. Links to their competitors to ensure everybody is charging a fair price..

15. The recent interest in physical fitness has forced producers of food, clothing, and other products to reconsider their marketing strategies. Which of the following does this trend illustrate?
    a. economic and technological environment.
    b. cultural and social environment.
    c. existing business situation.
    d. political and legal environment.
    e. resources and objectives of the firm.

16. In the short run at least, which of the following is usually *beyond* the control of the marketing manager?
    a. political and legal environment.
    b. economic and technological environment.
    c. cultural and social environment.
    d. competitive environment.
    e. All of the above.

17. Product-market screening criteria should be:
    a. quantitative.
    b. qualitative.
    c. realistic and achievable.
    d. all of the above.
    e. all of the above *except* b.

18. Which of the following is a quantitative screening criteria?
    a. increase sales by $100,000.
    b. earn 25 percent return on investment.
    c. break even within one year.
    d. all of the above are quantitative criteria.
    e. all of the above are qualitative criteria.

19. General Electric's "strategic planning grid":

a. substitutes precise quantitative estimates for management judgment and intuition.

b. places too much emphasis on industry attractiveness, almost ignoring the firm's own business strengths.

c. emphasizes market share and market growth rate.

d. is oversimplified in that it assumes all opportunities must be either "good" or "bad."

e. None of the above is a true statement.

20. GE's Planning Grid approach to evaluating proposed and existing plans and businesses:
a. considers how profitable opportunities are likely to be.
b. reflects the corporation's objectives.
c. helps managers see why some ideas are supported and others are not
d. can use quantitative data but it is basically a qualitative approach.
e. All of the above are true.

21. Organizational units within a larger company which focus their efforts on selected product-markets and are treated as separate profit centres are called:
a. portfolios.
b. strategic business units.
c. BTUs.
d. functional departments.
e. basing points.

22. According to the "continuum of environmental sensitivity":
a. industrial products need to be adapted to foreign markets more than consumer products.
b. faddy or high-style consumer products are easily adaptable to foreign markets and thus involve very little risk in international marketing.
c. it is extremely risky to market basic commodities in international markets.
d. some products are more adaptable to foreign markets than others--and thus may be less risky.
e. All of the above are true statements.

Answers to Multiple-Choice Questions

1. d, p. 82	9. d, p. 102	17. d, p. 105
2. d, p. 82	10. a, p. 100	18. d, p. 105
3. b, p. 82	11. e, p. 99	19. e, p. 107
4. d, p. 92	12. e, p. 99	20. e, p. 107
5. e, p. 97	13. c, p. 101, http://www.scc.ca/	21. b, p. 109
6. a, p. 97	14. c, p. 99	22. d, p. 109-110
7. a, p. 97	15. b, p. 102	
8. c, p. 99	16. e, p. 81	

Exercise 4-1

How marketing environment variables
affect strategy planning

Introduction

Marketing managers are not free to choose *any* marketing strategy they please. On the contrary, their choice of strategies is usually affected by variables related to the:

1. Objectives and resources of the firm
2. Competitive environment
3. Economic and technological environment
4 Political and legal environment
5. Cultural and social environment

These variables are sometimes called "uncontrollable" because, in the short run, they are beyond the control of marketing managers--although in the long run, marketing managers may be able to influence some or all of these variables.

In the short run, at least, these marketing environment variables may force marketing managers to change their present strategies--or even to choose less-than-ideal strategies. On the other hand, trends in the marketing environments often create new opportunities for alert marketing strategy planners.

Assignment

This exercise is intended to stimulate your thinking about how the marketing environment variables *might* affect marketing strategy planning. Read each of the following situations carefully and answer the questions that follow each situation.

1. In recent years, various federal and local agencies, environmental groups, and consumer advocates have been promoting greater concern for the environmental impact of solid waste, especially disposable products and packaging. Consequently, many communities now have active "recycling" programs, and some consumers have begun to switch from products or packages that are not biodegradable. What effect do you think these trends might have on the marketing efforts of a consumer packaged goods company like Unilever?

_____

_____

_____

2. The rapid growth of ethnic groups--including Asians, Hispanics, Blacks, and Eastern Europeans--and the increasing share of income going to these consumers is influencing the marketing strategy of many firms, especially in geographic areas where ethnic subgroups are most concentrated. How would this increasing cultural diversity affect a manufacturer of children's clothing that is interested in increasing its market share among Chinese consumers who live in The GTA?

_____

_____

_____

3. The North American Free Trade Agreement has spurred North American and Japanese auto companies to build new assembly plants and parts factories in Mexico. The market in Mexico is growing but in addition, many of the cars that are produced in Mexico will be exported to other Latin American countries. How do these free trade changes affect marketing opportunities for Ford? For Honda?

_____

_____

_____

4. The three major TV networks, CBC, CTV, and Global, used to split almost all the audience for "prime time" TV. However, the wide penetration of cable television means that viewers can now tune in a wide variety of cable shows--ranging from sports and comedy to news and weather. In addition, advertisers can select from more channels too. The result is a very large number of TV advertising outlets each of which delivers a smaller number of viewers. How do these changes in the competitive, economic, and technological environments affect the marketing strategies of the major networks?

_____

_____

_____

5. Computerized scanners at checkout counters can provide retailers, wholesalers, and producers with instant data on the sales on a wide variety of packaged goods. How would this technological advance affect a retailer such as Loblaws stores?

_____

_____

_____

6.   For years, Intel enjoyed explosive growth in the demand for its Pentium processors as the demand for PCs grew. Although other companies offered processors at lower prices, they took only a small share of the market because their processors operated at a slower speed. Intel continues to lead the market with the fastest processors, but recently the fastest growth in demand for personal computers has been for units intended for home use--and almost every manufacturer has introduced home models with price tags under $1,000. Because home computers typically do not require as much processing speed, and because the price of the processor is the most expensive part of a low price computer, Intel's competitors have very rapidly taken away market share. How do you think the competition Intel faces has affected its marketing strategy for its current and new chips.

_____

_____

_____

Question for Discussion

How can marketers deal effectively with changing trends and developments in their marketing environments?

Exercise 4-2

Analyzing competitors' strategies

Introduction

The competitive environment affects the number and types of competitors a marketing manager must face--and how the competitors may behave. Although a marketing manager usually cannot control what a competitor does, it is possible to plan for competition--and where possible to avoid head-on competition by finding new or better ways to satisfy customers' needs. Thus, the search for a breakthrough opportunity--and some sustainable competitive advantage--requires an understanding not only of customers but also of competitors. That is why marketing managers often turn to competitor analysis to evaluate the strengths or weaknesses of competitors' marketing strategies.

As discussed on pages 88-89 of the text, competitor analysis is simply a logical extension of the marketing strategy planning framework that focuses on identifying a target market and the marketing mix to meet that market's needs. It also considers competitive barriers--conditions that may make it difficult or impossible for a firm to compete in a market. A careful competitor analysis may help a marketing manager see opportunities to serve new markets--ones, which play to a firm's strengths while avoiding its weaknesses, including competitive weaknesses.

Doing a complete competitor analysis is a real challenge. You will be better equipped to take on that challenge at the end of the course when you know more of the details of marketing strategy planning. However, this exercise gets you started with this type of thinking.

Assignment

The following case describes a retail hardware store and its competitive environment. Read and analyze the case carefully--to better understand the company's marketing strategy strengths and weaknesses. Then, complete the competitor analysis table and answer the questions--being sure to support your ideas with facts from the case.

Bonlee's Home Hardware

Bonlee's Home Hardware is located in an affluent suburb of a medium-sized city. The store is in a neighbourhood shopping centre that also includes a grocery store, drugstore, dry cleaners and a pet store. It is between two of the city's largest private schools--and the area is favoured as a place to live by doctors, lawyers, and other high-income families.

Kari Bonlee bought the store five years ago in partnership with her brother, Trent Bonlee. Kari quit her job as a financial advisor with RBC to try her hand at retailing, and Trent had taken early retirement from his city job. When the Bonlees took it over, the store had been in business for ten years. At first, they made few changes except that Karl used acquired skills to computerize inventory and ordering.

Bonlee's is a typical Home Hardware with more than 15,000 items kept regularly in stock. Almost all the stock is ordered through the regional Ace Hardware warehouse, which is about three hours away. With computer links and Xpresspost delivery, most items can be restocked within two days to a week. Because the store is small, Bonlee's often orders in small quantities.

To meet customers' needs, Bonlee's has added more decorating items than many similar stores. One employee is regularly assigned to a van that will go to customers' houses to measure and install blinds and match existing paint colours. Over the years, the Bonlees have also added locksmithing, glass cutting, and lawnmower engine repair to the services they offer.

The Bonlees found that most customers tend to come to the store at the beginning or end of the day and that mid-day business is very slow. Two full-time employees operate cash registers at the front of the store but most of the sales staff are part-timers. The Bonlees hired several retired tradesmen to work a three-hour shift in the morning. In the afternoon and on week-ends, high-school students assist customers. The Bonlees try to have enough salespeople "on the floor" to greet almost all customers as soon as they enter the store and help them find and select what they need.

Until recently, Bonlee's competition came from Everwood, a builders' supply house and lumber yard, and from another neighbourhood hardware store, Chatham Sentry Hardware, which is on a country road about three miles away. Last year, however, Home Depot--a subsidiary of a national retailer--opened a large big box store. It is located on an abandoned railroad switching yard two miles towards the centre of town. The Home Depot store is huge--more than 5 times the size of the local builder's supply and more than 20 times the size of Bonlee's.

When Home Depot opened, Trent Bonlee said: "This'll probably be the end of us. There is hardly an item that we sell that the big box store does not sell--and at a deep discount too. There is no way we can match their prices! When they sell lawnmowers, they bring in a truckload." However, after a year, Karl was not so pessimistic. As she said to Trent, "We've had our best year ever. I wish I understood it. I hear that the Sentry Hardware is about to close its doors--and one of our part-timers says that Everwood Builders Supply is like a ghost town."

Concisely complete the table on the following page--with specific emphasis on aspects of Bonlee's strategy that is different from its competitors. Some of the blanks have been filled in for you.

	Bonlee's Home Hardware	Everwood Builders' Supply	Home Depot
Target Market (Who are the customers; how do they shop)		Builders and contractors; some walk-in homeowner business; most customers are probably knowledgeable and know specifically what they want	
Product (focus of product line, including service; branding; guarantees			Very broad product line of hardware and lumber; Some well-known brands; Mainly self-service with some help available at front-desk
Place (channel relationships with suppliers; transportation and storing considerations	Tied to Regional Ace Hardware Wholesaler		National purchasing; truck-load direct deliveries from manufacturers
Price (price level; credit terms; special sales; etc.)	High compared to competition	Discounts to big customers or on large orders, and free delivery for large items	Very low everyday prices; delivery available at extra cost; modest discounts and credit to contractors who are regular customers
Promotion		Ads in newspaper & in local real estate mag.; Yellow pages; some telemarketing and personal selling (out of store) to big developers and contractors	National TV ads and local newspaper inserts; special sales desk for contractors to place special orders
Competitive Barriers			Chain's large volume purchases give it a cost advantage; large facility supports product availability

1.   What are some of the key ways that the Home Hardware wholesaler might help Bonlee's to compete with the other competitors?

2.   Do you think that Bonlee's competes most directly with Everwood or with Home Depot? Explain your reasons.

3.   Why do you think that Bonlee's could have a profitable year even when Chatham Sentry Hardware and EverWood are having real problems?

4.   Is there anything that Bonlee's could do if another local hardware store were to open nearby (or if Chatham Sentry Hardware were to make changes) and offer a similar marketing mix designed to serve the same target customers?

Question for Discussion

If head-on competition makes it more difficult to develop a successful marketing strategy, why do so many firms continue to compete in markets that are characterized by pure (or nearly pure) competition?

Exercise 4-3

How the legal environment affects marketing strategy planning

Introduction

Even in a "free enterprise" economy like the one in Canada, a marketing strategy planner faces many legal constraints. These laws are often confusing--and may even appear contradictory. Further, the laws are frequently written vaguely by legislators--to allow the courts to interpret and apply them. However, the interpretation may vary depending on the current political environment. In spite of these problems, it is critical that marketing managers make every effort to understand the political-legal environments--because business must operate and develop its marketing strategies within these environments.

Assignment

The following cases describe marketing activities that might be judged illegal. Study each case carefully and determine the law (or laws), which appear to be *most relevant* to each situation. Then state why you answered as you did. You should refer to the following list of laws in completing this exercise:

Competition Act   Food and Drugs Act
Personal Information Protection and   Provincial Trade Practices
Electronics Document Act   Legislation

Note: Most of these laws are discussed in this chapter and summarized on pages 99 -102 of the text--and this is the depth of understanding expected here. Most are discussed later--see subject index--but here we want to get a "big picture" feel for the likely impact of legislation.

The first case is answered for you as an example--but try to answer it yourself before looking at the suggested answer! [Note: You do not have to decide on legality, but merely indicate what law(s) *might* be involved or be most relevant in the situation.]

1.   Industrial Drill Press (IDP)--a large manufacturer of industrial drill presses with an estimated 45 percent share of the Canadian market--wanted to diversify its product line. After investigating several possibilities, IDP decided to enter the rapidly growing market for industrial band saws--which are used to cut metal bars and tubes. The company felt it would take too long to develop its own manufacturing and distribution facilities, and therefore chose to diversify by buying firms already in the band-saw business.

Over a two-year period, IDP bought out three leading producers of band saws. Some observers have predicted that IDP will dominate the market for industrial band saws within another three years.

a)   Competition Act

b)   Reason: *The firm is engaged in mergers, which may tend to substantially lessen competition in the band-saw industry.*

2.   Edyie Ianni purchased a "boom box"--a portable cassette and CD player--from a mail-order retailer after seeing the retailer's ad in the Calgary Herald. Edyie was attracted by the low price-- and was assured by the "full one-year warranty" highlighted in the ad. Three months after the unit arrived, the cassette unit stopped working. Edyie called the retailer's toll-free number to find out how to get warranty service. The salesperson who answered Edyie's call said that he would send her a copy of the written warranty issued by the manufacturer--and all Edyie needed to do was follow the instructions. To Edyie's surprise, the manufacturer's "full one-year warranty" read as follows:

"The manufacturer warranties this high quality stereo unit against all possible defects for a period of one full year, except for the motors on the cassette and CD players, which are covered for 30 days, and except for all plastic parts, which are not covered at all. Should this set fail to operate during this period, it should be shipped at the purchaser's expense in the original carton to: Repair Depot, 1716 Portage Ave. Winnipeg, Manitoba. A certified check for $49.95 should be enclosed to cover handling charges. This is the only warranty provided by the manufacturer, and all other express or implied warranties are hereby excluded. This warranty does not cover damage caused by improper handling or abuse. The manufacturer shall be the sole judge of whether any parts are defective or whether they were damaged through improper handling or abuse."

a)   Federal/Provincial legislation:

_____

b)   Reason:

_____

_____

_____

_____

_____

3. Ski Products, Inc. has just discovered that some of its high performance fibreglass water skis were manufactured with a faulty fastener which could cause the adjustable rubber "shoe" on the ski to pop off under stress--such as might occur when skiing at high speed or performing spins or other tricks. Company officials estimate that no more than 5 percent of the 10,000 pairs of skis manufactured and sold during the past year were defective. Rather than engage in an expensive recall, Ski Products, Inc. has notified its retailers to repair the skis at no cost to the owner whenever a defective model is discovered.

    a) Federal/Provincial legislation:

    _____

    b) Reason:

    _____

    _____

    _____

    _____

    _____

4. At-Home Exercise Corporation, a firm located in Markham, Ontario, advertised *its Body Shaper,* "an amazing new isometric exercise device" in the *Halifax Chronicle Herald.* According to the ad, "individual results vary, but through only 5 minutes a day of effortless exercise you can expect to add up to 2 inches to your biceps and up to 3 inches to your chest while losing up to 4 inches from your waistline and up to 10 pounds from your present weight during an average 14-day period." The ad stated that the body shaper could be purchased by mail for only $14.95 and added "Try the Body-Shaper risk free. If you are not completely satisfied, return the Body Shaper within 30 days and the purchase price will be promptly refunded."

    The ad caught Michael Colombo's eye and he ordered the exerciser--enclosing a money order for the specified amount. About a month later, he received a package containing a hard rubber cable about 2 feet long, and a small pamphlet describing various diet plans. Believing he had been cheated, he demanded that his money be refunded as advertised. Shortly afterwards, he received a form letter from the firm stating that his request for a refund had been denied on the grounds that "more than thirty days has passed since you placed your order."

    a) Federal/Provincial legislation:

    _____

    b) Reason:

    _____

    _____

_____

_____

_____

5.   Garrett Paint Co. has been selling its products only through paint and hardware retailers, but recently the company decided to try to sell its spray paints through supermarket chains. To encourage the food chains to purchase in large quantities, Garrett offered them a special 12 percent quantity discount. Garrett does not plan to offer quantity discounts to its paint and hardware retailers. Several food chains have already agreed to carry the spray paints, but one large national chain--whose business Garrett really wants--has refused to stock the paints unless Garrett agrees to give the chain an additional 3 percent "advertising allowance."

a)   Federal/Provincial legislation:

_____

b)   Reason:

_____

_____

_____

_____

6.   Fuel-oil producers were caught by surprise when December temperatures dropped unexpectedly. Because of inadequate fuel-oil reserves, most producers had trouble quickly filling orders from their distributors across the country. In a number of areas across the country, fuel-oil prices shot up by as much as 60 percent more than normal. During the shortage, the three fuel-oil distributors in Summit, a mountain area on the British Columbia and Alberta border, kept their delivery trucks running 24 hours a day to ensure that customers did not find themselves without heat. By mid-January, the shortages had begun to let up. About that time, the owners of the three distributorships saw each other at a monthly civic club luncheon. As they were discussing the added costs of all of the "overtime" deliveries, one of the men suggested that they all keep their prices at the current level "until the February peak demand period is over. " The other two agreed that this would help improve profits.

a)   Federal/Provincial legislation:

_____

b)   Reason:

_____

_____

_____

_____

_____

Question for Discussion

Marketing-related legislation has often had different objectives and varying degrees of interpretation and enforcement. Why? What is the current trend? In which direction does the political and legal environment appear to be moving?

Exercise 4-4

Competitor analysis

This exercise is based on computer-aided problem number 4--Competitor Analysis. A complete description of the problem appears on page 112 of Wong/Shapiro, 11th edition.

1. Mediquip has focused on lowering costs because the market appears to be price-sensitive. However, Mediquip sees that there may be other ways to take advantage of its company strengths. Laser Tech already has parts it could use in producing the laser scalpel, but that may reduce its flexibility. Mediquip product designers think they can develop a product that better meets a doctor's needs if Mediquip spends $50,000 for front-end design costs, but they wonder if a profit can still be earned with a product that costs $7,400 to produce. Mediquip's marketing manager thinks that the firm could get a 70 percent share of the market--leaving only a 30 percent share for Laser Tech--if it could develop this product and still set a price to meet what Laser Tech will have to charge. Based on this situation, what would Mediquip's average cost per machine be, and what price would it have to charge to earn a $1,000 profit per machine? Based on these estimates, would you recommend that Mediquip move ahead with the idea of improving the product? Why?

    Average cost per machine: $ _____   Price: $ _____

    _____

    _____

    _____

    _____

    _____

2. Mediquip can keep its product development plans secret until it enters the market. However, Mediquip is wondering about what Laser Tech might do if Mediquip does keep its plans secret. For example, Laser Tech might think that it would be able to capture 70 percent share of the market and set its price to cover its costs based on that quantity. In this case, what would Laser Tech estimate as its likely average cost per machine? What price would it set if it expected each unit to contribute $1,000 to profit?

    For Laser Tech:

    Average cost per machine: $ _____

    Price (at 70 percent share): $ _____

3. If these events occur, each firm would enter the market with a price that had been set assuming that it would win 70 percent of the market. Clearly, it is not possible for each firm to have 70 percent share of the market. If Mediquip developed the improved product but only captured 40 percent of the market, its sales, costs, and profits might look quite different than it had planned. Assume Mediquip spent the extra money on product design and unit product costs, but then only won 40 % of the market. For this case, fill in the information requested below.

For Mediquip:

Price (at 70 percent share) $ _____

Less, Average Total Cost per Machine
      (at 40 percent share,) $ _____

= Profit (or Loss) per Machine $ _____

4. In the space provided below, calculate what profit (or loss) Mediquip would earn in this situation:

Actual total revenue = quantity actually sold X price set

Quantity sold (at 40 percent share)   _____

Price set (assuming 70 percent share) $ _____

Actual total revenue $ _____

Less, Total Design, Production
      and Selling Costs (at 40%) $ _____

= Total Profit (or Loss) Contribution $ _____

5. Drawing on this analysis, briefly explain several important reasons why a marketing manager should understand the competitive environment when planning a marketing strategy.

Reason number 1:

_____

Explanation:

_____

_____

_____

Reason number 2:

_____

Explanation:
_____

_____

_____

Chapter 5

Demographic Dimensions of Canadian and Global Consumer Markets

Chapter Summary

- **Know about population and income trends in global markets and how they affect marketers.**

  Canada's exports more than 60% of what it produces. Canadian companies are always looking for new foreign markets, or ways to expand sales to existing markets. Population trends, income growth and other demographic factors provide the marketer insight into potential success within a particular market. This is true for both domestic and global markets.

- **Understand how population growth is shifting in different areas and for different age groups.**

  Certain provinces (such as British Columbia and Ontario) and some CMAs (Census Metropolitan Areas – p. 131) are growing much faster than the average for Canada as a whole or for CMAs as a group. Also, the 65+ age group has recently grown – and will continue to grow – much faster than any other age group. Big-picture information like this is useful for getting a sense of how demography shapes the future. However, marketers must also use much more detailed data on small areas and on the spending patterns of different age groups.

- **Know about the distribution of income in Canada**

  Noteworthy differences exist between the provinces in per capita (per unit – the unit can be a person or some other such as a family/household) individual or household income. Within a province, higher average incomes are likely found in urban areas. However, much more significant differences are revealed when one examines the percentage of Canada's national income received, on average, by members of the various income quintiles. For example, the 20% of Canadians with the lowest income (lowest income quintile) receive a smaller disproportionate share of the total amount received by all Canadians. In contrast, the 20% of Canadians (top income quintile) who receive the highest income receive a disproportionately larger share of the total amount received by all Canadians.

- **Know how consumer spending is related to family life cycle and other demographic dimensions**

  Statistics Canada regularly provides detailed information on household spending patterns, both by province and by income quintile. Information is also available on the distribution of income by province, CMA, and smaller geographic areas. Taken together, this information makes it possible for marketers to come up with a reasonable estimate of the size of the market for a given category of product. To do this, one first multiplies the number of households within each income quintile (grouping) living in a given geographic area (e.g. Ottawa) by the average amount spent by that quintile on a product category (e.g. women's shoes). The final step involves adding together the total amount spent by the members of each income quintile.

- **Know why ethnic markets are important – and why increasingly they are the focus of multicultural marketing strategies.**
  7.6 million Canadians or 25% of the total population of Canada stated that they were members of an ethnic heritage that was not Canadian, English or French. These Canadians have consumer preferences that may be quite different from other Canadians. Marketers understand that both ethnic origin and mother tongue (the language first spoken and still understood) are both important. Marketers also must remember that ethnic markets are fast changing. Finally, marketers should avoid the stereotyping these markets. For example, there is not every black person is from the Caribbean, Chinese can be from Taiwan, Hong Kong or Mainland China.

Important Terms

demographics, p.118
birthrate, p. 127
gross domestic product (GDP), p. 122
gross national product (GNP), p. 122
Census Metropolitan Area (CMA), p. 131
discretionary income, p. 135
disposable income, p. 135
metropolitan area, p. 132

True-False Questions

____   1.   Global population growth has slowed to 1.3% over the past 30 years.

____   2.   The population of the Canada is about 0.5 percent of the world's population.

____   3.   Widely spread out populations is attractive to marketers, because there is less competition.

____   4.   One widely used measure of national income is gross national product (GNP).

____   5.   The gross national product is a limited measure of the output of the economy since it considers the total market value of goods, but not services, produced in a year.

____   6.   The gross domestic product (GDP) does not include foreign income earned in a country.

____   7.   An analysis of literacy in various countries shows that only one tenth of the world's population can read and write.

8.   Based on population alone, California looks like a more attractive market than Canada.

9.   Ontario, Alberta and British Columbia experienced large increases in population in the 1980s and 1990s, while other provinces experienced only small increases or even in some cases, declines.

10. In spite of declining birthrates, it seems certain that the Canadian population will continue to grow because of increased immigration.

11. The birthrate--the number of babies born per 1,000 people--has continued to decline for the last fifty years.

12. Despite a declining birthrate, the average age of the population will continue to decrease for some time due to the effects of the post-World War II baby boom.

13. During the 1990s, there were big increases in the 45-64 age group and that growth is continuing in this decade.

14. The decline in the number of teenagers continues in this decade.

15. Over 60 percent of all households consist of married couples with children under 18.

16. Single-adult households account for over 25 percent of all households in the Canada.

17. Over the last 50 years, more and more Canadians have moved from cities to suburban centres.

18. A Census Metropolitan Area (CMA) is an integrated economic and social unit having a population nucleus of at least one hundred thousand people.

19. Metropolitan Areas, are attractive to marketers because of their large concentrated populations.

20. The 2001 census found that over 40% of Canadians moved between 1996 and 2001.

21. Some economists believe that the decline in the manufacturing sector threatens the Canadian middle class standard of living.

22. More than 40 percent of the total Canadian income goes to families who are in the top or fifth quintile (top 20%).

23. Disposable income is the income remaining after taxes and savings have been subtracted.

24. Most discretionary income is spent on necessities.

_____ 25. While income has a direct bearing on spending patterns, other demographic dimensions--such as age and stage in family life cycle--may be just as important to marketers.

_____ 26. "Empty nesters" are an important group of highly mobile individuals who do not maintain a regular place of residence and thus are a very difficult group to track.

_____ 27. Many firms cater to the senior citizen market--although about half of these older people are below the poverty level.

_____ 28. In Canada, about 1 in 10 families speak a language other than English or French at home.

_____ 29. More than 90% of the French Canadian market lives in Quebec..

_____ 30. Nearly 80% of Canada's entire ethnic population lives in Toronto, Vancouver, and Montreal.

Answers to True-False Questions

1. F, p. 119	11. T, p. 127	21. T, p. 133
2. F, p. 119	12. F, p. 127	22. T, p. 133
3. F, p. 119	13. T, p. 127	23. F, p. 135
4. T, p. 122	14. F, p. 127	24. F, p. 135
5. F, p. 122	15. F, p. 129	25. T, p. 136
6. F, p. 122	16. T, p. 129	26. F, p. 137
7. F, p. 124	17. T, p. 130	27. F, p. 137
8. T, p. 125	18. T, p. 131	28. T, p. 138
9. T, p. 126	19. T, p. 132	29. F, p. 141
10. T, p. 126	20. T, p. 132	30. T, p. 138

Multiple-Choice Questions (Circle the correct response)

1. Which of the following statements are true?
    a. Canada makes up less than 0.5 percent of the total world population.
    b. In general, less-developed countries experience a faster rate of growth than developed countries.
    c. There is a worldwide trend toward urbanization.
    d. This book considers GNP to be a better measure of national income than GDP.
    e. All of the above are true.

2. In 1999, Canada had an average GNP (USD) per capita of:
    a. $12,599
    b. $35,600
    c. $17, 800
    d. $19,300
    e. $23, 550

3. Which of the following countries had the *lowest* GNP per capita in 1999?
    a. India
    b. Kuwait
    c. Italy
    d. Mozambique
    e. Brazil

4. The province with the largest percentage increase in population between 1982 and 2002 was:
    a. British Columbia
    b. Ontario
    c. Manitoba
    d. Alberta
    e. Quebec

5. Canadian population trends suggest that:
    a. Canada will grow at a faster rate during the next 25 years than it did during the last 50 years.
    b. the Canadian population has started to decline because the birthrate has been declining for the past 50 years.
    c. the dominant population will continue to be senior citizens.
    d. Canada has finally reached "zero population growth."
    e. the average age of the Canadian population will continue to rise for many years.

6. Which of the following is *not* an accurate statement about consumer markets in Canada?
    a. There are already over 31 million people in Canada.
    b. The average age of the Canadian population is rising.
    c. The number of people in the 45-64 age group will decline very substantially in this decade.
    d. Single-adult households account for about 25 percent of all households.
    e. About 20 percent of the people who move are moving to a different community.

7. Which of the following statements about Canada's population is *true?*
    a. Between 1982 and the present, the population doubled in every province.

b.   The Canadian population will stop growing by the year 2004.
c.   Our population is getting younger despite decreasing birthrates.
d.   50% of Canada's population lives in the 19 largest CMA's.
e.   All of the above are true statements.

8.   Which of the following statements is *true?*
   a.   A Census Metropolitan Area (CMA) generally centres on a continuously built up area of 100,000 or more in population.
   b.   Some national marketers sell only in the largest CMAs.
   c.   Census Metropolitan Areas are a more useful classification method for marketers than political boundaries.
   d.   All of the above are true statements.
   e.   None of the above are true statements.

9.   Mobility has an important bearing on marketing planning. Approximately what percent of Canadians move every five years?
   a.   6 percent
   b.   16 percent
   c.   26 percent
   d.   42 percent
   e.   50 percent

10.   The income distribution in Canada:
   a.   makes little difference to marketing decisions, since it cannot be controlled by the marketing manager.
   b.   has stayed about the same for 50 years.
   c.   now has a larger percent of people at the lower levels.
   d.   shows that higher income people still receive a very large share of the total income.
   e.   none of the above are true.

11.   With respect to income, government data indicate that:
   a.   the top 20 percent get more than 40 percent of total income.
   b.   most Canadians are still at the bottom of the income pyramid.
   c.   middle-income families are enjoying huge increases in real income.
   d.   there are only a few families in Canada with incomes over $50,000.
   e.   None of the above is a true statement.

12.   Disposable income is defined as:
   a.   total market value of goods and services produced.
   b.   gross national product per capita.
   c.   income available after taxes.
   d.   income available before taxes.
   e.   income available after taxes and "necessities."

13.   Salina Chu's base salary as a sales rep for a computer software firm was $25,000 last year. She earned an additional $10,000 in sales commissions. Her tax bill was $9,000 and bills covering other necessities such as food, housing, and transportation amounted to $10,000. What was John's disposable income last year?
   a. $35,000.
   b. $26,000.

c. $25,000.
d. $19,000.
e. $16,000.

14. Which of the following statements is true?
    a.   Most senior citizens have money to spend.
    b.   Singles and young couples are more willing to try new products.
    c.   Empty nesters are frequently big spenders.
    d.   Divorced spend a larger percentage of their income on necessities..
    e.   All of the above are true statements.

15. Which of the following is *not* an accurate statement about ethnic groups in Canada?
    a.   People from different ethnic groups may be influenced by different cultural variables.
    b.   One in five families speaks a language other than English at home.
    c.   Chinese are the largest minority group.
    d.   Four million Canadians or about 12% 0f Canada's total population identified themselves as visible minorities.
    e.   6.8 million Canadians or about 21% of Canada's total population identified. French as their mother tongue.

Answers to Multiple-Choice Questions

1. e, p. 119
2. e, p. 120
3. d, p. 121
4. a, p. 126
5. e, p. 127-128

6. c, p. 125-132
7. d, p. 125-132
8. d, p. 131
9. d, p. 132
10. d, p. 133

11. a, p. 133
12. c, p. 135
13. b, p. 135
14. d, p. 136-138
15. b, p. 138-141

Additional Questions to Test Your Understanding (Fill in the blanks)

1. Match each of the following terms with correct definition.

   Birthrate   Megalopolis   CMA   Lifestages

   b. _____ - A concept developed for promotional campaigns that focuses on the very different stages that a person passes through from birth to death.

   c. _____ - A continuous city such as the 1200 kilometre strip of land that runs approximately from Windsor in the west to Quebec city in the east.

   d. _____ - The number of live births per thousand of population.

   e. _____ - A separate population classification developed by Statistics Canada for the "main labour market area" of each continuous built up area having a population of 100,000 or more.

2. Briefly, describe two marketing choices that are made before targeting visible minorities.

   b. _____

   _____

   _____

   c. _____

   _____

   _____

3. Match each of the following lifestages with the correct spending behaviour.

   Singles and Young Couples   Divorced Parents   Teenagers   Empty Nesters

   b. _____ They eat more, want expensive clothes and have expensive tastes when it comes to recreation.

   c. _____ They are more interested in travel, small sport cars and other luxury items.

   d. _____ They spend more of their total income on necessities and have little left over for discretionary items.

   e. _____ They are more willing to try new products and brands, and they have more discretionary income.

4. (a) Briefly, describe the difference between discretionary and disposable income.
   (b) What categories of products would be bought by each type of income.

   (a) _____

   _____

_____

_____

(b) _____

_____

_____

_____

Answers to Additional Questions

1. a. lifestages, p. 136
   b. megalopolis, p. 131
   c. birthrate, p. 127
   d. CMA, p. 131

2. a. Mainstream advertising that includes visible minorities. (p. 140)
   b. Use mother tongue languages for newspaper, radio and television advertising campaigns. (p. 140)

3.
   a. Teenagers, p. 137
   b. Singles and young couples, p. 137
   c. Divorced parents, p. 137
   d. Empty nesters, p. 137

4.
   a. Disposable income is the income you have left after paying your taxes, while discretionary income is your disposable income minus your necessities. The problem with discretionary income is what does each of us define as our necessities. (p. 135)
   b. Disposable income would first be used to purchase necessities like food, clothing and shelter. Discretionary income would be used to buy luxuries like sport cars, entertainment, and fine wines. (p. 135)

Exercise 5-1

Strategy planning for international markets: Consumer products

Introduction

Many brand names are recognized worldwide and firms with successful products in their domestic markets frequently turn to international markets for rapid growth and new profit opportunities. Marketing strategy planning is, in essence, no different for international markets than for domestic markets. The firm should choose a target market and develop a marketing mix to satisfy the needs of that target market.

But in practice, international marketing strategy planning can be much more difficult, however. Strategy planners often must deal with unfamiliar marketing environment variables. And there may be big differences in language, customs, beliefs, religion and race, and even income distribution from one country to another. Even identical products may differ in terms of which needs they satisfy, the conditions under which they are used, and people's ability to buy them. In addition, new and unfamiliar competitors are likely to be encountered.

Also, reliable data for market analysis may be harder to obtain when a firm moves into international markets. The wealth of published data which American marketers tend to take for granted may not exist at all. And consumers in some countries are far less willing to take part in market research studies than most Americans.

This exercise shows how some market analysis might be done for international markets—and shows some of the common pitfalls a marketer is likely to make in planning international marketing strategies.

Assignment

Read the following case and answer the questions that follow:

BEVERAGES TO GO CORPORATION

The Beverages to Go Corporation recently developed a new beverage named "Mocha Magic," a chocolate-coffee flavoured drink targeted to people who take their lunch to work. The flavourful combination is packaged in "drink boxes" which have a long shelf life and don't require refrigeration. Mocha Magic met with success when introduced for sale in Canada a year ago. The product had originally been formulated to be consumed cold. However, research showed a very large market for people who drink Mocha Magic warm, after microwaving it in its original carton. A majority of lunchrooms and cafeterias have one or more microwave ovens available.

When Beverages to Go commissioned extensive survey data in Canada, the company found that the new drink appealed to different groups of consumers, depending on their previous lunchtime drink habit. According to the survey, Mocha Magic had a favourable rating with 40 percent of the Canadian coffee drinkers, a 30 percent favourable rating with those who usually drank soft drinks, and a 10 percent favourable rating with those whose typical lunchtime drink was tea. Sales and survey data show that among those that like the taste, about 10 percent of purchasers actually switch to Mocha Magic. Little acceptance was achieved among wine, milk, and water drinkers.

Encouraged by the success of Mocha Magic, Beverages to Go Corporation decided to expand its market coverage overseas. The following four countries are being considered as potential new markets: United Kingdom, France, Spain, and Germany. Because limited funds for expansion are available, only *one* of these countries will be selected for the first international market for Mocha Magic. The marketing manager of Beverages to Go was asked to decide which of the four countries would offer the highest dollar sales potential.

As a start, the manager obtained the market data shown in Table 5-1 by looking up the populations of the four countries (use the population figures from Exhibit 5-1 on pages 120-121 of the text), and then asking a market research firm to estimate the average per capita expenditures in these countries for tea, coffee, and soft drinks.

TABLE 5-1
Estimated Average Annual per Capita Expenditures on
Selected Meal-Time Beverages in Four Countries

Country	Population	Per Capita Beverage Expenditures		
		Coffee	Soft Drink	Tea
United Kingdom	59,508,000	$40	$12	$80
France	59,330,000	$20	$40	$15
Spain	39,997,000	$15	$40	$30
Germany	82,797,000	$60	$80	$25

The manager got an initial estimate of dollar sales potential for Mocha Magic in each country based on the experience in Canada with each of the three segments identified by the present drink choice. For example, based on Canadian experience, 40 percent of the coffee drinkers in a country can be expected to like Mocha Magic, and of those, 10 percent are likely to switch their beverage purchases to Mocha Magic. So Mocha Magic can be expected to pick up 4 percent (that is, 40 percent times 10 percent) of coffee drinkers' per capita beverage purchases. Looking at Table 5-1, we see that in the U.K., per capita coffee purchases were $40, so Mocha Magic could expect $1 .60 (that is 4 percent of $40) expenditure. This result is entered into the table that follows, and the calculations for the U.K. have been completed.

1.   a.   Determine the per capita dollar sales potential for Mocha Magic in France, Spain, and Germany by completing the table.

Canadian Experience				
Percent who like taste of Mocha Magic	**Former Drink Preference**			**Total Potential per Capita Expenditure for Mocha Magic**
	Coffee	**Soft Drink**	**Tea**	
	40	30	10	
Country	**Per Capita Potential Expenditure On Mocha Magic, by Segment**			
	Coffee	**Soft Drink**	**Tea**	
United Kingdom	$1.60	$0.36	$0.80	$2.76
France				
Spain				
Germany				

    b.   Now calculate the total sales potential by country. Again, the U.K. has been completed as an example.

Country	Population	Calculated per capita sales of Mocha Magic	Total Sales Potential
United Kingdom	59,508,000	$2.76	$164,242,080
France	59,330,000		
Spain	39,997,000		
Germany	82,797,000		

2.   Based on your estimates in the table above, which one of the four countries would offer the highest dollar sales potential for Mocha Magic?

3.   What do the above calculations assume about the Beverages to Go Corporation's potential target markets for Mocha Magic?

4.   Will Beverages to Go Corporation have to change its marketing mix when it expands overseas? Why or why not?

Question for Discussion

The per capita beverage expenditures shown in Table 5-1 are just imaginary--but an actual market research study would no doubt show that beverage expenditures do in fact vary considerably among these and other countries. Should a firm's marketing strategy planning be based solely on such data and Canadian experience--or would further study or even test marketing be desirable.

Exercise 5-2

How demographic trends affect marketing strategy planning

Introduction

A common approach to identifying markets uses "demographic" characteristics of customers--such as age, sex, race, education, occupation, geographical location, income, marital status, and family size. The popularity of demographics is due to the fact that such characteristics are easily measured, easily understood, and readily available in published form. Demographic characteristics are very useful for identifying market segments, planning appropriate marketing mixes and estimating market potential.

This exercise will stress another major use of demographics--to monitor changes and trends in the uncontrollable cultural and social environments to help find new marketing opportunities.

We will focus on three major demographic trends:
1. People in the "baby boom" generation are entering their peak earning--and saving--years.
2. The increasing life spans of senior citizens.
3. The trend toward smaller family units and a larger number of "single adult" households.

You will be asked to evaluate the likely positive or negative effects of these three trends on three major industries.

Assignment

Listed below are three major industries in Canada. In the space provided, discuss the likely positive and/or negative effects of the above-mentioned demographic bends on *each* of the three industries. Base your answers on the text discussion and your general knowledge--**DO NOT DO ANY LIBRARY OR FIELD RESEARCH**. Use your head instead--to apply what you already know!

Industries

Leisure Time	Cosmetics	Restaurants

1. Industry: Leisure Time

   a) Effects of baby boom generation's peak earnings and saving years.

   b) Effects of longer life span of senior citizens.

   c) Effects of smaller family units and more "single adult" households.

2.   Industry: Cosmetics

    a)   Effects of baby boom generation's peak earnings and saving years.

    b)   Effects of longer life span of senior citizens.

    c)   Effects of smaller family units and more "single adult" households.

3.   Industry: Restaurants

   a)   Effects of baby boom generation's peak earnings and saving years.

   b)   Effects of longer life span of senior citizens.

   c)   Effects of smaller family units and more "single adult" households.

Question for Discussion

Name some other important demographic trends. How might these trends affect the three industries discussed in the exercise?

Exercise 5-3

Marketers must know their markets

Introduction

The "golden rule" of marketing is: "Know thy market!" Firms that live by this rule are generally more successful than those that do not. And the fact that *most* new businesses and products fail is ample proof that many firms do *not* know their markets.

Some marketers pay close attention to government statistics--anxious to take advantage of any new opportunities such data may reveal. Surprisingly, however, many marketers seem to be almost totally unaware of how much valuable demographic data is already available.

This exercise has a twofold purpose. First, it will help you see how much you know about the Canadian market. If you are like most people, some of your views will be grossly inaccurate. That explains our other purpose--to familiarize you with the kinds of demographic data that are usually available in published form.

Every marketer should be an expert on sources of marketing information. We will look in depth at just one source, census data available form Statistics Canada at http://www.statcan.ca/english/Pgdb/. Census data is collected every five years and includes demographic, social, cultural and economic information. The *Census is* probably the best starting point for locating statistical data--and an invaluable reference book for any marketer who wishes to keep informed of demographic trends. Keep in mind that some government statistics are published with a considerable "lag" and some figures are estimates.

Assignment

The following list of questions is designed to compare your "best guess" about the Canadian market with actual government statistics. First of all, look at the questions and write down your estimate for the demographic data in question. *Do not try to look up the correct answer in any reference source until you have completed this part!* There is no penalty for being wrong!

After you have completed the first column, go to the site http://www.statcan.ca/english/Pgdb/ and click through to Canadian Statistics. Look up the correct answers to each question and write the answers in the adjacent column. Note the date of the most recent data available and the units of measurement. The answers to all of these questions can be found in the *site*. Take the opportunity to browse through the other kinds of information available and remember that the *site is* constructed from a very large number of Canadian government reports and the census.

Q.	Date of *Abstract* used _____	Your Estimate	Answer from Abstract, /units (date)
1.	What is the total population of the Canada?		
2.	What is the Canadian birthrate?		
3.	What is the median age of the Canadian population?		

4.	What percentage of all people over 25 years old in the Canada,
	    a. Did not finish high school?
	    b. Have completed at least 4 years of college?		

5.	What is the median income of married-couple families,
	    a. Wife in paid labour-force?
	    b. Wife not in paid labour-force?
	    c. Male householder, no wife present?
	    d. Female householder, no husband present?		

6.	What are the annual expenditures (for the province or territory you are living in) by household in the following categories:
	    a. Food
	    b. Shelter?
	    c. Clothing?
	    d. Transportation?
	    e. Health care?
	    f. Recreation?
	    g. Education
	    h. Tobacco products and alcoholic beverages?		

7.	What is the Canadian annual *per capita* consumption of the following:
	    a. Sugars and syrups?
	    b. Red Meat?
	    c. Cheese?
	    d. Fresh fruits?
	    e. Fresh vegetable?
	    f. Soft drinks?
	    g. Coffee?
	    h. Tea?
	    i. Fruit juices?
	    j. Bottled water		

8.	What percentage of Canadian households have: a. access to the Internet at home?		
9.	How many Canadians subscribe to basic cable television services		
10.	How many First Nations members are there in your province?		
11.	How many Canadians with a West Indian heritage are there in your province?		

Question for Discussion

Identify which of your estimates was closest to the mark, and which was farthest away from the data; what are the implications for marketing strategy planning?

Exercise 5-4

Demographic analysis

This exercise is based on computer-aided problem number 5--Demographic Analysis. A complete description of the problem appears on page 152-53 of Wong/Shapiro, 11th edition.

1.   a.   The estimate of the growth rate for the 45-59 age segment in part depends on guessing the number of people who will move into or out of the areas served by Stylco's retailers. That may vary considerably due to regional shifts, employment trends, and other social factors. However, Naomi Davis realizes that her marketing mix will be more profitable if she has good distribution in areas where her target market is living. If she can realign distribution so that she is represented in boutiques in retail markets serving 75 percent of her 45-59 year-old target market (rather than the current boutiques, that reach only 60 percent of that market), what would happen to total profits by the year 2005?

Total profit from 45-59 age group in year 2005 with 75 % penetration _____

b.   If Davis works on building distribution in the wrong retail markets, she might end up with stores that serve a smaller--rather than larger--percent of her target market. If she made changes and the percentage of Black population (age 45-59) served by the retailers fell from 60 percent to 40 percent, what would happen to profits?

c.   What are the implications of this pattern of results?

2.   Davis is also considering another type of change in her approach for reaching consumers in the 45-59 age group. Currently, her retailers are in markets that include about 60 percent of the Black consumers in that age range. However, a chain that is doing a very good job of attracting consumers with the highest incomes has approached Davis about carrying her lines. The chain's stores are in markets that include about 35 percent of Black consumers in the 45-59 age range, but most of the consumers it reaches are in the higher income range and they are willing to spend more on clothes. Therefore, the chain would like to be the *exclusive* distributor of a higher priced line of styles for the 45-59 age group. Davis figures that the profit per unit on the new line would be $15, in part because of lower selling costs and in part because of higher prices. Further, the chain is expanding rapidly and it is estimated that by the year 2005 it will reach 35 percent more customers than it did in 2000. Finally, because the chain enjoys such strong loyalty from its target market, Davis believes that the ratio of unit sales to market size might increase to .010.

If Davis decides to make the required changes and to work exclusively with the retail chain to reach the 45-59 age target customers, would she earn greater profits?

2005 Profit from the line for the 45-59 age range customers using the chain

_____

2005 Total profit from both lines

_____

Would working with the chain increase profits?

_____

3. Davis is concerned that if she gives the chain store an exclusive on the line for the 45-59 age group then the boutiques that have been carrying her products will switch to another supplier for the 35-44 age range line. In other words, the profit contribution from the 35-44 age range product line would drop to 0 by the year 2005. If that were to happen, what would be the impact on total profits?

   Total profit from both lines in year 2005   _____

   less Profit contribution expected in 2005   − _____
         from the 35-44 product line

   Profit without the 35-44 line: _____

4. What do you think about the proposition of going with the chain store? Give your reasons.

Chapter 6

Behavioural dimensions of the consumer market

Chapter Summary

- **Understand the economic buyer model of buyer behaviour**
  An economic buyer is a person who knows all of the facts and logically compares choices in terms of cost and value received to get the greatest satisfaction from spending their time and money. Since economic needs guide most consumer behaviour, consumers look for the lowest price, convenience, quality, or best overall value. Exhibit 6-1 page 148 shows that psychological variables, social influences, and the purchase situation all affect a person's buying behaviour.

- **Understand how psychological variables affect an individual's buying behaviour.**
  Psychological variables are *needs, wants and drives*. A *need* is a basic force that motivates a person to do something (see Exhibit 6-2, page 149, for examples of different types of needs). *Wants* are needs that have been learned during a person's life. A *drive* is a strong stimulus (motivation) that encourages actions to reduce a *need*. Perceptions and attitudes are also important aspects that help determine an individual's buying behaviour.

- **Understand how social influences affect an individual's and household's buying behaviour.**
  Many social influences have change buying behaviour. The influences include a person's relationships with friends and family, social class, and culture. For example, a family may purchase a new luxury automobile as a symbol of status, or an Indian family may choose to eat only authentic Indian foods.

- **See why the purchase situation has an effect on consumer behaviour.**
  The reason of a purchase, the time available to make the purchase, and the surroundings where the purchase is to be made all have an effect on consumer behaviour. Even the needs of consumers and the benefits they seek may change under different purchase situations. This combination of factors may result in changes being made to the marketing mix.

- **Know how consumers use problem solving processes.**
  Most consumers use a five step problem solving process to select particular products. They (1) become aware of the problem, (2) recall and gather information about possible solutions, (3) evaluate alternative solutions, (4) decide on the appropriate solution, and (5) evaluate the decision. The amount of problem solving can be very little as in routinized response behaviour, where there is little risk, low cost and low involvement. It can be very high as for example in extensive problem solving, which has a high risk, a high cost and a high involvement.

- **Have some feel for how a consumer handles the behavioural variables of incoming stimuli.**

Consumers go through an adoption process, which is similar to the problem solving process, although learning and promotion play a much more important role. Some marketing managers use a grid (like Exhibit 6-10, on p. 168) to decide which criteria consumers consider most important and what consumer attitudes are toward their product (or marketing mix) and how consumers combine criteria to reach a final decision.

Important Terms

economic buyers, p. 147
economic needs, p. 148
drive, p. 149
needs, p. 149
wants, p. 149
social needs, p. 150
personal needs, p. 150
physiological needs, p. 150
safety needs, p. 150
perception, p. 151
selective exposure, p. 151
selective perception, p. 151
selective retention, p. 151
cues, p. 152
learning, p. 152

positive reinforcement, p. 152
response, p. 152
attitude, p. 153
belief, p. 154
expectation, p. 154
psychographics, p. 157
social class, p. 158
opinion leader, p. 160
reference group, p. 160
culture, p. 161
dissonance, p. 164
extensive problem solving, p. 165
limited problem solving, p. 166
routinized response behaviour, p. 166
adoption process, p. 168

True-False Questions

_____ 1. Because demographic analysis isn't of much value in predicting which specific products and brands will be purchased, many marketers have turned to the behavioural sciences for insight and help.

_____ 2. Economic needs affect many buying decisions, but for some purchases, the behavioural influences are more important.

_____ 3. Economic needs include things such as convenience, efficiency in operation or use, dependability in use, and economy of purchase or use.

_____ 4. A drive is a strong need that is learned during a person's life.

_____ 5. The PSSP needs are power, security, social acceptance, and prestige.

_____ 6. Motivation theory suggests that people have hierarchies of needs, and that they never reach a state of complete satisfaction.

_____ 7. Consumers select varying ways to meet their needs because of differences in perception.

_____ 8. Selective perception refers to a person's ability to screen out or modify ideas, messages, or information that conflict with previously learned attitudes and beliefs.

_____ 9. Learning is a change in a person's thought processes caused by prior experience.

_____ 10. Reinforcement of the learning process occurs when a cue follows a response and leads to a reduction in the drive tension.

_____ 11. An attitude is a person's point of view towards something.

_____ 12. Advertising is so powerful that changing consumers' negative attitudes is usually the easiest part of the marketing manager's job.

_____ 13. An expectation is an outcome or belief that a person likes to remember.

_____ 14. Personality traits have been very useful to marketers in predicting which products or brands target customers will choose.

_____ 15. Lifestyle analysis refers to the analysis of a person's day-to-day pattern of living--as expressed in his activities, interests, and opinions.

_____ 16. Social influences are concerned with how an individual interacts with family, social class, and other groups who may have influence on the buying process.

_____ 17. Buying responsibility and influence within a family vary greatly--depending on the product and the family.

___ 18. The social class system in Canada is usually measured in terms of occupation, education, and type and location of housing.

___ 19. More than half of our society is *not* middle class.

___ 20. Middle-class consumers tend to be more future-oriented and self-confident than lower-class consumers.

___ 21. A person normally has several reference groups.

___ 22. "Opinion leaders" are generally higher income people and better educated.

___ 23. The attitudes and beliefs that we usually associate with culture tend to change slowly.

___ 24. Different purchase situations may require different marketing mixes--even when the same target market is involved.

___ 25. A grid of evaluative criteria can be used to help managers think about what criteria are important to their target customers.

___ 26. A homemaker doing weekly grocery shopping is more likely to use extensive problem solving than limited problem-solving or routinized response behaviour.

___ 27. Low involvement products are products that are seldom purchased by the target market.

___ 28. In the adoption process, the evaluation step usually comes before the trial step.

___ 29. Dissonance might cause a consumer to pay more attention to automobile advertisements after a new car is purchased than before the purchase.

___ 30. Knowing how a target market handles the problem-solving process, the adoption process, and learning can aid marketing strategy planning

___ 31. Using your intuition in developing marketing mixes for international markets is generally a safe way to proceed.

Answers to True-False Questions

1. T, p. 148	12. F, p. 154	23. T, p. 161
2. T, p. 148	13. F, p. 154	24. T, p. 162
3. T, p. 148	14. F, p. 156	25. T, p. 168
4. F, p. 149	15. T, p. 157	26. F, p. 165-166
5. F, p. 151	16. T, p. 157	27. F, p. 166
6. T, p. 150	17. T, p. 157-158	28. T, p. 170
7. T, p. 151	18. T, p. 159	29. T, p. 164

Multiple-Choice Questions (Circle the correct response)

1. According to the text, the economic-buyer theory:
   a. says that the economic value of a purchase is the most important factor in a purchase decision.
   b. explains why people behave the way they do.
   c. includes psychological variables and social influences.
   d. is too simplistic to explain consumer behaviour.
   e. assumes that consumers always buy the lowest price alternative.

2. Which of the following is *not* a psychological variable?
   a. Social class
   b. Motivation
   c. Perception
   d. Attitudes
   e. Learning

3. A good marketing manager
   a. knows that only a few basic needs explain almost all consumer product choices.
   b. doesn't have to understand consumer needs if his product has some design improvements over his competitor's product.
   c. should find ways to create internal drives in consumers.
   d. knows that consumer needs in product-markets are probably much more specific than those in a related generic market.
   e. will make fewer strategy planning mistakes if he uses the economic-buyer theory.

4. According to motivation theory, the *last* needs a family would usually seek to satisfy would be:
   a. safety needs.
   b. personal needs.
   c. physiological needs.
   d. social needs.

5. Motivation theory suggests that:
   a. lower-level needs must be completely satisfied before higher-level needs become important.
   b. a particular good or service might satisfy different levels of needs at the same time.
   c. all consumers satisfy needs in the same order.
   d. self-esteem is an example of a social need.
   e. All of the above are true statements.

6. When consumers screen out or modify ideas, messages, and information that conflict with previously learned attitudes and beliefs, this is called:
   a. selective retention.
   b. selective exposure.
   c. selective perception.
   d. selective dissonance.
   e. selective cognition.

7. A change in a person's thought processes caused by prior experience is called:

a. learning
b. attitude change
c. belief change
d. response
e. reinforcement

8. Which of the following is not a major element in the learning process?
   a. Drive
   b. Cues
   c. Dissonance
   d. Reinforcement
   e. Response

9. An attitude:
   a. is easily changed.
   b. is a person's point of view toward something.
   c. is the same as opinion and belief.
   d. is a reliable indication of intention to buy.
   e. All of the above are true statements.

10. The AIO items used in lifestyle analysis include:
    a. activities, interests, and opinions.
    b. attitudes, interests, and opinions.
    c. activities, intentions, and opinions.
    d. attitudes, intentions, and opinions.
    e. attitudes, income, and opinions.

11. Which of the following is *not* a social influence?
    a. Culture
    b. Social class
    c. Family
    d. Reference group
    e. Personality

12. According to the text, social class is usually measured in terms of:
    a. income.
    b. occupation, education, and housing arrangements.
    c. income, occupation, and education.
    d. race, religion, and occupation.
    e. income, occupation, and religion.

13. Matt Kerr, now an account representative responsible for selling computer systems to some of ABC Corporation's major accounts--has been with ABC since graduating from Simon Fraser University in 1992. Matt's father was a plumber, but Matt is a professional--one of ABC's top five salespeople--and earns about $70,000 a year in salary and commissions. Matt is a member of the _____ social class.
    a. upper, lower-upper
    b. upper-middle
    c. middle
    d. working
    e. lower

14. Which of the following statements about social class is NOT true?
    a.   The various classes tend to shop in different stores.
    b.   The upper class tends to avoid shopping at mass-merchandisers.
    c.   Upper-middle class consumers tend to buy quality products that will serve as symbols of their success.
    c.   Lower-class buyers often want guidance from a salesperson about what choice to make.
    e.   Lower-class consumers are more likely to save and plan for the future than middle class consumers.

15. For which of the following products would reference group influence probably be *least important?*
    a.   Clothing
    b.   Cigarettes
    c.   Furniture
    d.   Canned peaches
    e.   Wine

16. Opinion leaders are:
    a.   usually better educated.
    b.   usually reference group leaders.
    c.   not necessarily opinion leaders on all subjects.
    d.   usually wealthy, middle- or upper-class people.
    e.   All of the above are true statements.

17. Behavioural scientists recognize different *levels* of consumer problem solving. Which of the following is *not* one of these levels?
    a.   Routinized response behaviour
    b.   Limited problem solving
    c.   Rational problem solving
    d.   Extensive problem solving
    e.   All of the above are recognized levels of problem solving.

18. Which of the following gives the proper *ordering* of the stages in the "adoption process"?
    a.   Awareness, interest, trial, evaluation, decision, dissonance
    b.   Awareness, interest, trial, decision, evaluation, confirmation
    c.   Awareness, interest, evaluation, trial, decision, confirmation
    d.   Interest, awareness, trial, decision, evaluation, dissonance
    e.   Awareness, interest, evaluation, decision, trial, confirmation

19. Dissonance is:
    a.   a type of cue.
    b.   a form of laziness commonly observed among low-income consumers.
    c.   a type of positive reinforcement.
    d.   tension caused by uncertainty about the rightness of a decision.
    e.   none of the above.

20. In developing marketing mixes for consumers in international markets, marketing managers should:
    a.   generalize from one culture to another.

b.   use their intuition.
c.   know about the specific social and intrapersonal variables.
d.   follow their beliefs.
e.   all of the above.

21.   The present state of our knowledge about consumer behaviour is such that:
a.   the behavioural sciences provide the marketing manager with a complete explanation of the "whys" of consumer behaviour.
b.   we still must rely heavily on intuition and judgment to explain and predict consumer behaviour.
c.   relevant market dimensions can be easily identified and measured using "psychographics."
d.   marketing research can't tell us much more about specific aspects of consumer behaviour.
e.   All of the above are true statements.

Answers to Multiple-Choice Questions

1. d, p. 147
2. a, p. 149
3. d, p. 150-151
4. b, p. 150-151
5. b, p. 150-151
6. c, p. 151
7. a, p. 152

8. c, p. 152
9. b, p. 153
10. a, p. 157
11. e, p. 157-158
12. b, p. 159
13. b, p. 159
14. e, p. 159

15. d, p. 160
16. c, p. 160-161
17. c, p. 165-166
18. c, p. 170
19. d, p. 164
20. c, p. 171
21. b, p. 172

Additional Questions to Test Your Understanding (Fill in the Blanks)

1. Match each of the following terms with the appropriate definition below:

   Wants   Selective Exposure   Response   Expectation
   Cues   Needs

   a. _____ - Our eyes and minds seek out and notice only information that interests us.

   b. _____ - Needs that are learned during a person's lifetime

   c. _____ - Products, signs, ads, and other stimuli in the environment.

   d. _____ - An effort to satisfy a need

   e. _____ - The basic forces that motivate a person to do something

   f. _____ - An outcome or event that a person anticipates or looks forward to.

2. Consumer buying behaviour can be affected by the "purchase situation". Give three examples of "purchase situations".

   a. _____

   _____

   _____

   b. _____

   _____

   _____

   c. _____

   _____

   _____

3. List and briefly describe the three levels of problem solving most often used by consumers.

   a. _____ -

   _____

   _____

   _____

   b. _____ -

   _____

   _____

   _____

c. _____-____

_____

_____

_____

Answers to Additional Questions

1.
    a. selective exposure, p 151
    b. wants, p. 149
    c. cues, p. 152
    d. response, p. 152
    e. needs, p. 149
    f. expectation, p. 154

2.
    a. The reason for the purchase, for example if you are buying it as a gift for a very close friend or just for yourself. p. 162
    b. The time factor of the purchase, how much time do you have to make the purchase. p. 162
    c. The place or surroundings of the purchase, is it in a supermarket or at a used car auction. p. 162

3.
    a. Extensive problem solving – used by consumers for a completely new or important need – when they put much effort in to solving it. P. 165
    b. Limited problem solving – when they are willing to put some effort into deciding the best way to satisfy a need and when they have some previous experience in solving the problem. p. 166
    c. Routinized problem solving – when they regularly select a specific way of satisfying a need when it occurs. Usually used when the consumer has considerable experience in how to satisfy the need and does not require additional information. p. 166

Exercise 6-1

Psychological variables and social influences affect consumer buying behaviour

Introduction

To plan good marketing strategies, marketing managers must try to improve their understanding of buying behaviour. Ideally, marketers would like to know *how* and *why* individual consumers buy the way they do. Then it might be possible to group individual consumers with similar needs and buying behaviour into homogeneous market segments for which suitable marketing mixes could be developed.

This is easier said than done, however, because human behaviour is very complex. Traditional demographic analysis, for example, can be used to study basic trends in consumer spending patterns, but it is of little use in explaining *why* people like, choose, buy, and use the products and brands they do.

For this reason, many marketers have turned to the behavioural sciences for help in understanding how and why consumers behave as they do. However, there is no "grand theory" available right now, which ties together all the behavioural theories and concepts in a way, which will explain and predict all aspects of human behaviour. Therefore, marketers must try to understand the various behavioural theories and concepts. Then they can put them together into a model of consumer behaviour that works in their own particular situation.

Hopefully, the complex decision-making processes that take place within the buyer behaviour model are clearer to you after reading Chapter 6 of the text. Although the model presented in the text can't explain or predict consumer behaviour, it does provide a useful framework that identifies the major variables that influence consumer behaviour.

This exercise should improve your understanding of various psychological (*intra*personal) variables and social (*inter*personal) influences that may affect a consumer's behaviour. You will recall from Chapter 6 that psychological variables focus on the individual while social influences involve relations with others.

Assignment

In the short cases that follow, a variety of psychological variables and social influences are operating to influence a consumer's response. For each case, identify the relevant psychological variables and social influences and briefly explain how each item is illustrated in the case. The first case has been completed for you as an example.

1. Ross and Jan Pfaff and their two children are considering the purchase of a recreational vehicle. Ross is enthusiastic because, he argues, the RV would be perfect for family camping trips, as well as fishing trips with his friends. Jan is less in favour of the purchase. She is nervous about camping in remote locations--and wonders how they would get help in emergencies. She also remembers a report that RVs get low gas mileage and are, therefore, expensive to run. Ross is quick to point out that the same report described the large potential savings of a weeklong vacation in an RV compared to staying at a hotel or motel.

   a. Psychological variables
      1) *PSSP hierarchy*   Explanation: *Jan is afraid of being isolated--safety needs.*

      2) *Selective Processes*   Explanation: *Jan only remembers the part of the report that supports her viewpoint.*

   b. Social influences
      1) *Family*   Explanation: *Ross wants to take family on camping vacations, but Jan is concerned about the family's safety.*

      2) *Reference Group*   Explanation: *Ross wants to take his friends on a fishing trip in "his" RV.*

2. Wendy Yee has had a cold--and all of the typical symptoms that come with it--for almost a week. At first she hadn't taken any medicine. She had always felt that there wasn't anything you could do about a cold. However, while she was playing cards at the home of some friends they kidded her about her runny, red nose. When they offered her a Benadryl cold tablet, she figured it wouldn't hurt to try it. To her surprise, she felt much better after taking the tablet. The next morning, she stopped at a drugstore on her way to work and bought a package of the medicine. Wendy had never heard of Benadryl before, but while driving home from work that evening she noticed a large billboard for Benadryl.

   a. Psychological variables

      1) _____   Explanation: _____

      _____

      _____

      _____

      2) _____   Explanation: _____

      _____

      _____

      _____

      3) _____   Explanation: _____

_____

_____

_____

b.   Social Influences

1) _____ Explanation: _____

_____

_____

_____

2) _____ Explanation: _____

_____

_____

_____

3.   Greg Lorek just returned from a year in Japan as an exchange student. To see his old friends, he is planning a dinner party with a traditional Japanese menu. As he is grocery shopping, he recalls his first experience with sushi--a raw fish delicacy he plans to serve at his party. When his host family first served it to him, he was not sure he would be able to eat it. Nothing in his American upbringing had prepared him to eat raw fish. However, he did not want to offend his hosts, so he smiled bravely and downed the sushi. To his amazement it was delicious, and he now enjoys sushi frequently. He is sure he will have a lot of fun persuading his friends to try it too.

a.   Psychological variables

1) _____ Explanation: _____

_____

_____

_____

2) _____ Explanation: _____

_____

_____

_____

3) _____ Explanation: _____

_____

_____

_____

b.   Social Influences

1) _____ Explanation: _____

_____

_____

_____

2) _____ Explanation: _____

_____

_____

_____

4.   Valentina Zaric is planning to buy a VCR, but is unsure where she wants to shop or what brand she wants to buy. She has asked her boss, who is an "electronics nut," for his advice, and she has started noticing magazine ads about the various features. She is most interested in a Sony brand unit that has a 7 day timer--since she is often away from home during the week on business trips and the timer would allow her to tape her favourite programs while she is gone. It also comes with a remote control unit that makes it easy to speed past commercials. An added plus is that the VCR's remote control unit would also work with her Sony brand TV, which she has had for a year and found very satisfactory. In addition, her boyfriend thinks that the Sony offers "a good value for the price," although it is more expensive than what she had originally expected to spend.

a.   Psychological variables

1) _____ Explanation: _____

_____

_____

_____

2) _____ Explanation: _____

_____

_____

_____

3) _____ Explanation: _____

_____

_____

_____

b. Social Influences

1) _____ Explanation: _____

_____

_____

_____

2) _____ Explanation: _____

_____

_____

_____

5. Steve and Renee Segal are trying to decide where to go on a vacation trip. Steve had been interested in going to Florida, but they rejected that alternative based on reports from friends that it wasn't that interesting. They briefly considered a trip to Aruba, but Renee didn't like the idea of "leaving Canada." Two very expensive resorts in Thailand were also considered, but rejected because both Steve and Renee were afraid they would feel out of place at such "fancy" accommodations. Finally, they settled on a moderate-priced motel in Prince Edward Island, where they have previously enjoyed relaxing visits.

a. Psychological variables

1) _____ Explanation: _____

_____

_____

_____

2) _____ Explanation: _____

_____

_____

_____

3) _____ Explanation: _____

_____
_____
_____

b.   Social Influences

1) _____ Explanation: _____

_____

_____

_____

2) _____ Explanation: _____

_____

_____

_____

Question for Discussion

Which items--psychological variables or social influences--have the most influence over consumer behaviour and thus are more important for the marketing strategy planner?

Exercise 6-2

Consumer behaviour is a problem-solving process

Introduction

While consumer behaviour may often appear to be quite irrational to the casual observer, most behavioural scientists agree that consumers are *problem solvers* seeking to relieve tension caused by their unsatisfied needs. How an individual consumer goes about solving problems depends on the intrapersonal and interpersonal variables that affect that individual. In general, however, most consumers tend to follow a five-step problem-solving process:

1. Becoming aware of--or interested in--the problem.
2. Gathering information about possible solutions.
3. Evaluating alternative solutions--perhaps trying some out.
4. Deciding on the appropriate solution.
5. Evaluating the decision.

The length of time it takes to complete the problem-solving process and how much attention is given to each of the five steps depends, of course, on the nature of the problem and how much experience an individual has had in trying to solve this particular kind of problem. To understand the process better, it helps to recognize three levels of problem solving: *extensive problem solving, limited problem solving,* and *routinized response behaviour.*

The purpose of this exercise is to illustrate the three levels of consumer problem solving by relating the problem-solving process to *your* problem-solving experiences in the marketplace.

Assignment

Think of *three* recent purchases that *you* made that involved extensive problem solving, limited problem solving, and routinized response behaviour. For each of these purchases, outline the problem-solving process that you used. You may wish to follow the five-step process listed above, indicating how you went about performing each of the five steps.

1.   Routinized response behaviour:

Product: _____

Explanation:

2.   Limited problem-solving:

Product _____

Explanation:

3.   Extensive problem-solving:

Product _____

Explanation:

Question for Discussion

Which of the three levels of problem solving offers marketers the most opportunity? The least opportunity? Why?

Exercise 6-3

Selective processes

This exercise is based on computer-aided problem number 6--Selective Processes. A complete description of the problem appears on pages 175 of Wong/Shapiro, 11th edition.

1.   Submag's marketing manager analyzed the response of a previous mailing to customers on the first mailing list. She found that 3,105 subscriptions were received from a total mailing of 25,000 promotion pieces.

   What percent of the people who received the initial mailing subscribed?

   _____

2.   By analyzing subscription orders from the first list by zip code area, she found that the orders from people who lived in large cities averaged $4.00, substantially higher than their "country cousins." She concluded that city residents were more interested in her magazines. The company that provided the first mailing list said that it could use a computer to sort future lists so that Submag only got names and addresses of people who live in large cities. This service would cost an extra $.02 per name (mailing). Would it make sense for Submag to target its promotion at people who live in large cities and spend more (i.e., by using the sorted mailing list)? Explain your answer.

   _____

   _____

   _____

3.   Submag's marketing manager thinks that people who live in large cities are also less likely to miss the point of the ads. This would result in losing fewer potential customers due to selective perception. Assuming 25,000 mailings, do an analysis that shows how the number of subscribers and expected profit change as the percent of consumers lost due to selective perception varies between 50 percent to 70 percent, and then answer the questions below. (Note: remember that city dwellers are likely to spend an average of $4.00 per subscription, and that it will cost $.34 per mailing).

   In this situation, how many subscribers would be required to earn a profit of $8,060?

   _____ number of subscribers

   At a profit of $8,060, what percent of potential customers would be lost due to selective perception?

   _____ percent

If the percentage of customers lost due to selective perception were reduced from the above percent to 52 percent, what would the difference in expected profits be?

$ _____.00 profit at 52 percent lost due to selective perception

- 8.060.00

$_____ difference in profit if selective perception is reduced

4. The supplier of the first list has told Submag's marketing manager that other direct mail marketers have found that people in large cities are more likely to open the envelope and read a mailing if the name is printed directly on the envelope (instead of on an adhesive mailing label) or if the name and address is printed on the letter itself. It would cost Submag an extra 2 cents per mailing to add this personalizing. This would probably reduce the number of people who threw out the mailings without opening them. If using the sorted mailing list and personalizing the letters reduced the percentage of potential customers lost due to selective exposure to 4 percent, would it make sense for Submag to go to the extra expense of personalizing the letters? Explain your answer.

_____

_____

_____

_____

_____

Chapter 7

Business and Organizational Customers and Their Buying Behaviour

Chapter Summary

- **Know who the business and organizational customers are.**
  Business and organizational customers are any buyers who buy for resale or to produce other goods and services. These customers are also referred to as "industrial buyers" or "intermediate buyers". The basic purchasing needs are largely economic (as opposed to psychological or physiological), and buyers try to consider the total cost of selecting a supplier, not just the initial unit price. Other factors may include service, speed of delivery, dependability, and general cooperativeness.

- **See why multiple influence is common in business and organizational purchase decision**
  The large dollar value of many organizational purchases often generates both an opportunity and an economic justification for formalizing parts of the buying process. This may involve analysis that is more rigourous, formal processes, or even the assignment of specific tasks to different people in the organization. More people are involved in the purchase and each brings a particular set of concerns to the task. Therefore, in selling to an organization, marketers must be certain that they are not only saying the right things but also addressing the right audiences.

- **Understand the problem-solving behaviour of organizational buyers.**
  New task buying occurs when an organization has a new need. This involves setting up product specifications, evaluating sources of supply, and establishing an ordering procedure. A straight rebuy is a routine repurchase involving little or no effort in getting product specifications or searching for suppliers. The modified rebuy is the in-between process where some re-evaluation of the buying situation is done.

- **Know the basic methods used in organizational buyers.**
  The four basic approaches used by organizational buyers for evaluating and purchasing products are (1) inspection, (2) sampling, (3) description, and negotiated contracts.

- **Understand the different types of buyer seller relationships and their benefits and limitations.**
  Closer relationships between firms are being established and the companies realize the cost saving benefits of working together. The customer also benefits from a guaranteed, dependable source of supply. These benefits may mean less flexibility in terms of delivery times, specifications, price, etc. The various types of relationships are information sharing, operational linkages, co-operation, legal bonds, and relationship specific adaptations, as seen in Exhibit 7-8. (p.188)

- **Know the basic e-commerce methods used in organizational buying.**

The more efficient flow of information between suppliers and buyers has lowered the cost of searches and in most cases the cost of transactions. The business buyer or seller can use (1) *community sites*, where the sharing of ideas and experiences among members of the same industry can take place: (2) *catalogue sites* are digital catalogues; (3) *exchanges*, which operate similarly to stock or commodity exchanges, except buyers and sellers are exchanging products and services; (4) *procurement hubs* unite buyers and sellers from a particular industry, who use an interactive system to get competitive bids; (5) *auction sites* are popular for used equipment, excess inventory and perishable products; (6) *collaboration hubs* allows buyers and sellers to coordinate design, manufacturing and distribution.

- **Know about the number and distribution of manufacturers and why they are an important customer group.**
  NAICS, the North American Industry Classification system helps marketers identify manufacturers, financial institutions, health care providers and entertainment companies. The code structure for any given company: (1) identifies the broad industry to which they belong; (2) than the sub-industry; (3) finally a further subdivision by specific function.

- **Know how buying by service firms, retailers, wholesalers, and governments is similar to** – and different from – buying by manufacturers.
  Because organizations buy products and services for use in the creation of other products or services, we need to understand something about how these customers operate if we hope to adjust our marketing mix to meet their needs. Each of these sectors has distinctive characteristics that set the context within which marketing operates.

Important Terms

business and organizational customers, p. 179
purchasing managers, p. 179
purchasing specifications, p. 179
deciders, p. 180
influencers (gatekeepers) p. 180
initiators, p. 180
buyers, p. 182
ISO 9000, p. 183
modified rebuy, p. 184

new-task buying, p. 184
straight rebuy, p. 184
users, p. 182
vendor analysis, p. 185
just-in-time delivery, p. 189
negotiated contract buying, p. 189
reciprocity, p. 191
competitive bids, p. 192

True-False Questions

____ 1. Business and organizational customers are wholesalers or retailers, but not buyers who buy to produce other goods and services.

____ 2. Since sellers usually approach each business or organizational customer directly through a sales representative, it is possible that there can be a special marketing strategy for each individual customer.

____ 3. Specific business customs vary little from country to country.

____ 4. ISO 9000 assures a customer that the supplier has effective quality checks in place.

____ 5. A salesperson usually must see the organizational buyer or purchasing manager first, before any other employee in the firm is contacted.

____ 6. Multiple buying influences make the promotion job easier.

____ 7. A buying centre consists of all the people who participate in or influence a purchase.

____ 8. "Vendor analysis" involves a formal rating of suppliers on all relevant areas of performance.

____ 9. Emotional needs are often quite relevant for the different people involved in the purchase decision, and therefore a marketing mix should satisfy both the needs of the customer company and the individual needs of those who influence the purchase.

____ 10. A purchasing specification is just a request to buy something.

____ 11. Strong multiple buying influence is most likely to be involved when there is new-task buying.

____ 12. When the majority of a company's purchases involve straight rebuy buying, these purchases occupy most of an effective buyer's time.

____ 13. Many firms are increasing the number of suppliers with whom they work—and expecting less cooperation from them.

____ 14. "Just-in-time" delivery means reliably getting products there before or very soon after they are needed.

____ 15. Negotiated contracts commonly are used for products that can be described sufficiently well that suppliers know what is wanted and can submit definite prices or bids.

____ 16. Even if a supplier has developed the best marketing mix possible and cultivated a close relationship with the customer, that customer may not give all of its business to that one supplier.

_____ 17. Purchasing managers tend to resist reciprocity, but it may be forced on them by their sales departments.

_____ 18. Basic e-commerce website resources include: community sites, catalog sites, exchanges, procurement hubs, auction sites, and collaboration hubs.

_____ 19. Competitive bids are the terms of sale offered by different suppliers in response to the purchase specifications posted by the buyer.

_____ 20. Competitive bidding over the Internet is becoming much more common.

_____ 21. Purchasing managers often use Internet (ro)bots to search for products by description.

_____ 22. Business customers are usually more interested in the total costs of working with a supplier—rather than the cost of a particular order.

_____ 23. Organizational buyers typically do not even see a sales rep for straight rebuys since e-commerce order systems now automatically handle those orders.

_____ 24. Buyers who delegate routine buying to a computer often will be more impressed by a new company's offer of an attractive marketing mix, perhaps for a whole line of products, rather than just one individual product.

_____ 25. Manufacturers tend to be concentrated by geographic location and industry, and the majority of them are quite small.

_____ 26. Two-digit NAICS code breakdowns start with broad industry categories, but more detailed data may be available for three-digit and four-digit industries.

_____ 27. The government market is the largest customer group in Canada.

_____ 28. All government customers are required by law to use a mandatory bidding procedure that is open to public review.

_____ 29. Government buyers avoid the use of negotiated contracts whenever there are many intangible factors.

_____ 30. The Internet is not a very effective way to locate information on potential government target markets.

Answers to True-False Questions

1. F, p. 179
2. T, p. 179-180
3. F, p. 183
4. T, p. 180

12. F, p. 184
13. F, p. 187
14. F, p. 189
15. F, p. 189

23. T, p. 197
24. T, p. 197
25. T, p. 200
26. T, p. 201

5. T, p. 180
6. F. p. 180
7. T, p. 181
8. T, p. 185
9. T, p. 185
10. T, p. 183
11. T, p. 184

16. T, p. 191
17. T, p. 191
18. T, p. 192-193
19. T, p. 192
20. T, p. 192
21. T, p. 195
22. T, p. 195

27. T, p. 200
28. T, p. 200
29. F, p. 199
30. F, p. 199
31. F, p. 199-200

Multiple-Choice Questions (Circle the correct response)

1. The bulk of all buying done in Canada is not by final consumers--but rather by business and organizational customers. Which of the following is a business or organizational customer?
    a. a manufacturer.
    b. a retailer.
    c. a wholesaler.
    d. a government agency.
    e. All of the above are business and organizational customers.

2. In comparison to the buying of final consumers, the purchasing of organizational buyers:
    a. is strictly economic and not at all emotional.
    b. is always based on bids from multiple suppliers.
    c. leans toward economy, quality, and dependability.
    d. is even less predictable.
    e. None of the above is true.

3. Today, many agricultural commodities and manufactured items are subject to rigid control or grading. As a result, organizational buyers often buy based on:
    a. purchasing specifications.
    b. negotiated contracts.
    c. competitive bids.

4. A large manufacturer is about to purchase a large supply of an unfamiliar chemical that will be used in the production of an important new product. What kind of buying is the company most likely to do?
    a. New-task buying
    b. Straight rebuy buying
    c. Modified rebuy buying

5. An automobile manufacturer's practice of buying some of its raw materials from other manufacturers who in turn buy from it is an example of:
    a. tying contracts.
    b. vendor analysis.
    c. buying by description.
    d. being "open to buy."
    e. reciprocity.

6. A plastic manufacturer is selecting a new supplier. People from sales, production, quality control, and finance are working with the purchasing department on the decision. The sales manager wants to select a supplier that is also a customer for some of the firm's own products. The sales manager
    a. is a gatekeeper.
    b. is more likely to get his way if his company is located in Japan instead of Canada.
    c. is trying to use vendor analysis to his advantage.
    d. is not a member of the buying centre, so he can be ignored.
    e. none of the above.

7. Basic e-commerce website resources include:
   a. community sites.
   b. catalog sites.
   c. exchanges.
   d. procurement hubs.
   e. all of the above.

8. Which of the following NAICS codes would provide the most specific information about a subcategory of an industry?
   a. 31
   b. 315
   c. 3152
   d. Cannot be determined without additional information.

9. If you obtain a customer's four digit NAICS code, you should know that:
   a. this firm might be manufacturing quite different products than other firms with the same number.
   b. the firm may also have a five-digit code.
   c. a number of other firms probably have the same code.
   d. the firm may also have a six-digit code.
   e. All of the above are true.

10. As contrasted with manufacturers, producers of services are:
    a. more geographically spread out.
    b. growing fast domestically and internationally.
    c. more numerous.
    d. All of the above.
    e. None of the above.

11. Which of the following statements about buying is *false?*
    a. In most business operations, a "buyer" runs their own department--and their decision is final.
    b. Buyers may be responsible for supervising the salesclerks who sell the merchandise they buy.
    c. Buyers make most purchases as straight rebuys.
    d. A buyer is usually "open to buy" only when they has not spent all of his budgeted funds.
    e. None of the above.

12. Which of the following statements about bidding for government business is *true?*
    a. Government buying needs are hard to identify--and their primary concern is with finding the lowest price.
    b. Government buyers avoid using negotiated contracts since they must purchase at a pre-set price.
    c. A government buyer may be forced to accept the lowest bid whether he wants the goods or not.
    d. The biggest job of the government buyer is to locate enough potential suppliers so the bidding procedure works effectively.
    e. All of the above are true statements.

13. The roles that make up a buying centre are:
   a. initiator, influencer, decider, buyer, user
   b. initiator, opener, decider, buyer, user
   c. sales representative, gatekeeper, decider, buyer, user
   d. initiator, influencer, decider, user, owner
   e. None of the above

Answers to Multiple-Choice Questions

1. e, p. 178
2. c, p. 182
3. a, p. 183
4. a, p. 184
5. e, p. 191

6. b, p. 191
7. e, p. 192-193
8. c, p. 201
9. e, p. 201
10. d, p. 208

11. e, p. 183-185
12. c, p. 198-199
13. a, p. 181-182

Additional Questions to Test Your Understanding (Fill in the Blanks)

1. Match each of the following terms with the correct definition listed below:

    purchasing managers   NAICS   vendor analysis
    deciders   competitive bids   users

    a. _____ - A formal rating of suppliers on all relevant areas of
        performance.

    b. _____ - Company buying specialists.

    c. _____ - The people who actually employ the product or service being
        bought.

    d. _____ - Terms of sale offered by different suppliers in reply to the
        buyer's purchase specification.

    e. _____ - An internationally accepted version of the SIC system

    f. _____ - They evaluate the choices that are identified by the
        gatekeepers.

2. List and briefly describe three kinds of buying processes used by organizational
    customers:

    a. _____ -

    _____

    _____

    _____

    b. _____ -

    _____

    _____

    _____

    c. _____ -

    _____

    _____

    _____

3. The following are five key dimensions that help to characterize most buyer-seller
    relationships in business markets. Briefly describe each of these key dimensions.

a.   Cooperation -

_____

_____

_____

b.   Information sharing -

_____

_____

_____

c.   Legal bonds -

_____

_____

_____

d.   Operational linkages -

_____

_____

_____

e.   Adaptive relationships -

_____

_____

_____

Answers to Additional Questions

1.
a. vendor analysis, p. 185
b. purchasing managers, p. 179
c. Users, p. 182
d. Competitive bids, p. 192
e. NAICS, p. 200
f. Deciders, p. 180

2.
a. new-task buying – occurs when an organization has a new need and wants a great deal of information (p. 184)
b. straight rebuy – a routine purchase that may have been made many times before. Buyers probably don't look for new information or new sources of supply. (p. 184)
c. modified rebuy – the in-between process where some review of the buying situation is done – though not as much as in new-task buying. (p. 184)

(Also look at Exhibit 7-5, p. 184)

3.
a. Cooperation – The buyer and seller work together to achieve mutual and individual objectives. Problems are treated as a joint responsibility. (p. 187-188)
b. Sharing information – Open sharing of information that is useful to both the buyer and the seller. This might include the exchange of proprietary cost data, discussion of demand forecasts, and joint work on new product design. (p. 188)
c. Legal bonds – the responsibilities of the buyer and seller are spelled out in a detailed legal agreement (contract). (p. 189)
d. Operational linkages – Direct ties between the internal operations of the buyer and seller firms, which usually involve formal arrangements and ongoing coordination of activities. (p. 188-189)
e. Adaptive relationships – Changes in a firm's product or procedures that are specific to the needs or capabilities of a relationship partner. (. 190)

Exercise 7-1

Analyzing organizational buying behaviour

Introduction

Some people see organizational buying and consumer buying as two very different processes. Organizational buying is thought of as "economic," while consumer buying is seen as "emotional." In fact, closer study of buying processes suggests that organizational and consumer buying may be quite similar in many ways. For example, like consumers, organizational buyers are *problem solvers.* And while their problems may be very different, both consumer and organizational buyers seem to use three levels of problem solving. In Chapter 6, we saw that consumer buyers do extended, limited, and routinized problem solving. Similarly, organizational buyers do *new-task, straight rebuy, and modified rebuy buying.*

Recognition of the three levels of problem solving by organizational buyers *and* the different problem solving steps they pass through has important implications for market analysis. It suggests that organizational markets can be segmented not only in terms of product-related needs, industry categories, and geographic location--but also in terms of similarities and differences in buying behaviour. *Each level of problem solving may require a different marketing mix*--especially in regard to the promotion variable--even when identical goods or services are involved. Knowing the nature of buying behaviour at each level helps to determine the proper ingredients for a marketing mix.

This exercise shows how knowledge of organizational buying behaviour can improve marketing strategy planning--in three "case" situations. You will be asked to identify the problem-solving level for a business product. Then you will discuss likely buying behaviour and how this might affect a firm's marketing strategy planning.

Assignment

Assume the role of marketing manager for a large firm that produces stain-resistant fabrics that are used by furniture companies to upholster chairs, sofas, and love seats. Similar fabrics are typically available to the furniture producers from several competing suppliers, including some larger and some smaller firms. While some slight differences in patterns and colours may exist, all of the suppliers produce fashionable fabrics that meet the quality and style standards set by the customers' production and marketing departments. In fact, most of the competing suppliers use the exact same method to treat fabrics so that they will resist stains. And, with few exceptions, the prices charged by all suppliers tend to be almost identical.

Recently, you learned--from your sales force--of three potential customers whose needs might be satisfied by the fabric you sell. Read each of the three buying situations described below, and then:

a)   Determine which level of problem solving--new-task buying, straight rebuy, or modified rebuy--applies to each situation.

b)   Discuss in detail the probable nature of the firm's buying behaviour in each situation. Which of the five problem solving steps used by consumers described in Chapter 6 (page 163) would be most important in each situation? Why? Which is the next most important? Why? How important would multiple buying influence be in each situation?

c)   Explain how your firm might vary its marketing mix to satisfy the potential customer's needs in each situation.

Situation 1:

The potential customer has been selling a very successful line of upholstered furniture for a number of years. The company has not been using a stain-resistant fabric. But, furniture retailers have recently been complaining that the furniture is soiled very easily. The potential customer thinks that your stain-resistant fabric could possibly be used instead of the fabric it gets from its current supplier.

a)   Level of problem solving:

_____

b)   Nature of buying behaviour:

c)   Marketing mix:

Situation 2:

The customer has been purchasing a similar fabric from one of your firm's competitors for several years, but is dissatisfied with its present supplier's delivery service and technical support.

a)   Level of problem solving:

_____

b)   Nature of buying behaviour:

c)   Marketing mix:

Situation 3:

The customer has been purchasing all of its fabric from one of your competitors on a regular basis for several years. No change in this procedure is expected.

a)   Level of problem solving:

_____

b)   Nature of buying behaviour:

c)   Marketing mix:

Question for Discussion

In which of the three buying situations would emotional needs be most important? Least important? To what extent does this depend on the overlap between individual buyer needs and company needs?

Exercise 7-2

Using NAICS codes to analyze business markets

Introduction

Compared to the final consumer market, business markets have a smaller number of customers and much of the buying potential is concentrated among a relatively few large firms. Further, firms within the same industry often cluster together by geographic location. For these reasons, it may be less difficult to analyze business markets than consumer markets.

Much published data is available to help the marketing manager analyze business markets. The most important source of information is the federal government--that regularly collects data on the number of establishments, their sales volumes, and number of employees for a large number of industry groups. The data is reported for North American Industry Classification System (NAICS) code industries. NAICS is a unique, all-new system for classifying business establishments. It is the first economic classification system that groups together economic units that use like processes to produce goods or services. NAICS includes some 350 new industries being separately recognized for the first time. NAICS replaces the old SIC system and reflects the structure of today's economy in Canada, the U.S., and Mexico, including the emergence and growth of the service sector and new and advanced technologies. It is a flexible system that allows each country to recognize important industries in more detail.

NAICS groups the economy into 20 broad sectors, up from the 10 divisions of the old SIC system. NAICS industries are identified by a 6-digit code, in contrast to the 4-digit SIC code. The first two digits designates a major Economic Sector (such as Manufacturing, 33, in this exercise). The third digit designates an Economic Subsector (such as Electrical Manufacturing, Equipment, and Supplies, 335, in this exercise). The fourth digit designates an Industry Group and the fifth digit the NAICS Industry. The international NAICS agreement fixes only the 1st five digits of the code. The sixth digit identifies subdivisions in individual countries. Thus, six-digit Canadian codes may differ from counterparts in the U.S. or Mexico, but at the five-digit level they are standardized.

Assignment

Electricom Manufacturing Company produces a line of electrical products for business markets. Electricom's recently-appointed marketing manager is currently in the process of reevaluating the firm's marketing strategy for an important product, "electric widgets," which he suspects may not be realizing its full sales potential. In particular, he feels that Electricom has been following a "mass-marketing" approach for this product and has neglected to identify which markets the product appeals to and their relative importance.

The marketing manager began his analysis by attempting to determine which six-digit NAICS industries may have some need for electric widgets. First, he analyzed past sales records for the product and assigned NAICS codes to previous and present customers. Next, he asked his sales manager to go through the NAICS manual and check off the six-digit industries that he believed would be relevant for the product. Finally, to make sure that other potential customers were not being overlooked, he conducted a survey of companies falling under other NAICS categories to find out whether they might have any possible use for the product. As a result of this analysis, a total of 12 industries were identified as potential target markets for electric widgets. These industries are listed in columns 1 and 2 of Table 7-1.

Having identified 12 potential target markets for electric widgets, the marketing manager then conducted another survey of a sample of firms belonging to each industry to determine the market potential for each industry. Included in the data he collected were the amount of each firm's annual dollar purchases for the product and the number of production workers employed. This data is summarized in columns 3 and 4 of Table 7-1. From the sample data for each NAICS industry, the marketing manager then calculated the average dollar purchases per production worker. The results are shown in column 5.

1.   Complete column 5 of Table 7-1 by calculating the average dollar purchases per worker for NAICS industry #335311- transformers. Show your calculations below.

In order to project the sample data to the entire Canadian market, Electricom's marketing manager turned to *Statistics Canada* to estimate the national market potential for each NAICS industry. These estimates are shown in column 7.

2.   Complete column 7 of Table 7-1 by calculating the national market potential for NAICS industry #335311. Show your calculations below.

Finally, because Electricom's sales territories were aligned according to provinces, the marketing manager proceeded to estimate the market potential for each industry in each state. For example, he again turned to the *Statistics Canada* to determine the number of production workers employed in the state of Illinois for those industries that operated in Ontario. From this data, shown in column 8, he was then able to estimate the market potential for each NAICS industry within Ontario. The results, computed by multiplying column 8 by column 5, are shown in column 9.

3.   Complete column 9 of Table 7-1 by calculating the market potential in Ontario for NAICS industry #335311. Show your calculations below.

TABLE 7-1
Calculation of Market Potential for "Electric Widgets" Using Market Survey Approach for National and Ontario Markets

NAICS Code	Manufacturing Potential "Industry" Target Markets	Market Survey Results		Average Purchases per Worker	National Market Number of Production Workers (1,000)	Estimated National Market Potential ($1,000)	Ontario Market Number of Production Workers ($1,000)	Estimated Ontario Market Potential ($1,000)
		Product Purchases	Number of Production Workers					
(1)	(2)	(3)	(4)	(5)	(6)	(7)	(8)	(9)
334513	Electric measuring instruments	$11,250	3,700	$3.04	45.1	$137.1	3.1	$9.4
335311	Transformers	50,150	4,616	$___	37.6	$___	3.8	$___
335312	Motors and generators	28,400	10,896	2.61	78.3	204.4	3.0	7.8
335314	Industrial controls	40,100	4,678	8.57	30.8	264.0	3.2	27.4
335221	Household cooking appliances	2,600	2,104	1.24	16.9	21.0	3.9	4.8
335222	Household refrigerators and home freezers	149,600	5,215	28.69	40.2	1,153.3	–	–
335224	Household laundry equipment	35,200	3,497	10.07	17.8	179.2	–	–
335211	Electric housewares and fans	1,200	3,208	0.37	40.3	14.9	3.7	1.4
335212	Household vacuum cleaners	1,875	402	4.66	7.5	35.0	–	–
335228	Other appliances	600	912	0.66	4.9	3.2	–	–
335121	Residential lighting	65,500	6,451	10.15	101.6	1,031.2	–	–
334111	Computers	132,100	6,889	19.18	185.7	3.561.7	7.5	143.8
	TOTAL	$518,575				$7,013.3		$235.9

Column:

(1),(2) Six-digit NAICS industries making up the industrial market for "electric widgets."

(3) Dollar value, classified by industries, of purchases of electric widgets as reported by those firms included in the survey.

(4) Number of production workers as reported by those firms included in the survey.

(5) Average dollar value of "electric widget" purchases per production worker for each NAICS industry. Computed by dividing column 3 by column

(6) Number of production workers for the entire Canadian market for the given NAICS industries.

(7) The resultant estimated national market potential for the total market. Computed by multiplying column 6 by column 5.

(8) Number of production workers for Ontario trading area for the given NAICS industries. Note: Blanks in column 8 indicate either that there are no firms in Ontario for a particular NAICS industry, or that there are only a few firms and the Statistics Canada has deleted the information to avoid disclosure.

(9) The resultant estimated Ontario are market potential. Computed by multiplying column 8 by column 5.

4. a) *For all industries combined,* what percentage of the total national market potential for electric widgets is represented by the state of Ontario? Show your work below.

   b) *For NAICS industry #335311 only,* what percentage of the national market potential for electric widgets is represented by the state of Ontario? Show your work below.

5. Suppose Electricom's marketing manager learned that actual sales of his firm's electric widgets to NAICS industry #335312 amounted to about 20 percent of its national market potential for that industry--while sales to the other 11 industries ranged from 5-10 percent. Suppose further that he then decided that the firm should aim at achieving 20 percent of its national market potential in *each* of the 12 NAICS industries--and set his sales quotas accordingly. Is it likely that Electricom could achieve these sales quotas? Why or why not? Comment on this approach to marketing strategy planning.

   Which of the 12 NAICS industries would you select as your target market(s) for the electric widgets if you were Electricom's marketing manager? Why?

   a) For the national market:

   b) For the Ontario market:

Question for Discussion

After selecting its target market(s), how could Electricom then go about identifying and reaching those firms that make up the target market(s)? What other information would be needed and how could the information be obtained?

Exercise 7-3

Vendor analysis

This exercise is based on computer-aided problem number 7--Vendor Analysis. A complete description of the problem appears on page 214 of Wong/Shapiro, 11th edition.

1.   Supplier 2 is thinking about adding U.S. wholesalers to its channel of distribution. The supplier would ship in large, economical quantities to the wholesaler and the wholesaler would keep a stock of chips on hand. The wholesaler would charge CompuTech a higher price--$1.90 a chip. But with the chips available from a reliable wholesaler CompuTech's inventory cost as a percent of its total order would only be 2 percent. In addition, the cost of transportation would only be $.01 per chip. Assuming CompuTech planned to buy 84,500 chips, what would its total costs be with and without the wholesaler? Should CompuTech encourage the supplier to add a wholesaler to the channel?

Total Costs for Vendor Supplier 2, buying direct   _____

Total Costs for Vendor Supplier 2, using wholesaler _____

_____

_____

_____

2.   Supplier 2 has explored the idea of adding wholesalers to the channel, but has found that it will take at least another year to find suitable wholesalers and develop relationships. As a result, if CompuTech deals with Supplier 2 its inventory cost as a percent of the total order would remain at 5.4 percent, and transportation cost would remain at $.03 per chip. But the supplier is still interested in improving its marketing mix now--so it can develop a strong relationship with CompuTech. Based on an analysis of CompuTech's needs, Supplier 2 has developed a new design for the electronic memory chips.

The redesigned chips would have a built-in connector, so CompuTech would not have to buy separate connectors. In addition, the new design would make it faster and easier to replace a defective chip. The supplier estimates that with the new design it would cost CompuTech only $1.00 to replace a bad chip.

The supplier has not yet priced the new chip, but it would cost the supplier an additional $.06 to produce each chip. If the supplier set the price of the chip at $1.93 each (the old price of $1.87 plus the additional $.06), how much would the new design cost CompuTech on an order of 84,500 chips. (Hint: compute CompuTech's total cost for the current design based on an order quantity of 84,500 chips, and then compute the total cost assuming the new price, the reduced cost of replacing a defective chip, and no cost for a connector.)

For Supplier 2:

Total Cost for Vendor, old version of chip   _____

Total Cost for Vendor, redesigned chip   _____

Change in total cost   _____

3.   The supplier is thinking about pricing the new design at a price higher than $1.93--so it can make more profit than it would have made with the old design. But the supplier also wants CompuTech's total cost to be lower than it would have been with the old design. What price would you recommend? Explain the reason for your recommendation. (Hint: set the values on the spreadsheet to correspond to CompuTech's costs if it buys the new design, but vary its cost--the supplier's price--for the chips and display CompuTech's total vendor cost.)

Price Supplier 2 should charge for the new chips   _____

Explanation:

_____

_____

_____

_____

_____

_____

Chapter 8

Improving decisions with marketing information

Chapter Summary

- **Know about marketing information systems (MIS).**
  A marketing manager could get lost in the amount and clutter of information available. That's where a marketing information system (MIS) is useful. An MIS is an organized way of continually gathering, accessing, and analyzing information that managers need to make decisions. With the rapid developments in information technology, MIS has become an increasingly powerful research tool. In addition, the Internet means that corporate databases are now available worldwide, regardless of physical location, allowing sales people and company personnel to make educated decisions on the move.

- **Understand the scientific approach to marketing research**
  The scientific approach is a systematic process for conducting research studies. (1) The problem is defined. (2) A hypothesis (assumption) is developed that is based on the manager's intuition, observations and experiences. (3) The hypothesis is tested to see whether it is true or not. (4) Based on the results of step two a final decision to solve the problem is made. This scientific approach forces managers to work in a consistent, defensible and orderly way, which increases the usefulness of a study's findings.

- **Know how to define and solve marketing problems.**
  Defining the problem is the most important - and often the most difficult – step in the marketing research process. Knowing who the target consumer is, and what needs they have, is essential. Furthermore, the marketing manager must determine how sensitive the target group of consumers is to changes in the marketing mix. It is important not to confuse symptoms with the real problem, because valuable time and resources may be spent answering unimportant questions.

  In the problem-solving step, managers use the information gathered from the market research to make decisions. The research should help guide decisions on the choice of a target market or the mix of the four Ps.

- **Know about getting secondary and primary data.**
  Secondary data is information that has already been collected. It may be found in the local library, government agencies, periodicals, on the Internet, or even within the company's MIS. Many private research firms sell data that has already been collected. This means a lower cost, but it can also mean that the information can also be used by your competitors.

  Primary Data is information that is not available elsewhere and must be obtained by conducting an experiment, survey or observation.

  Secondary data are often less specific to the matter in question than primary data, though the cost of secondary data is much less. Secondary and primary data can be either qualitative or quantitative.

- **Understand the role of questioning, observing, and using experimental methods in marketing research.**

  Questioning can be performed in many ways, whether through focus groups or mail, telephone, or in-person interviews. *Focus groups* are the most common form of qualitative questioning because they are relatively fast and cheap; however, it is sometimes difficult to measure the results objectively. *Mail surveys,* because of their low cost, are useful when extensive questioning is needed. The problem is the low return rate and long wait time. *Telephone surveys* are fast and effective; though it is difficult to obtain confidential information. The *personal interview* is easiest for obtaining and keeping the respondent's attention, but it is more expensive than either mail or telephone surveys.

  Much research is done by informally observing what customers do naturally. This method allows the firm to obtain information that is potentially more objective than information obtained through questioning or formal observation (when the customer knows he is being observed).

  Experimental methods involve dividing a group of participants into smaller groups based on specific characteristics. Questions or observations are then developed or made based on groups with similar qualities, and decisions are based on the results.

Important Terms

data warehouse, p. 207
marketing information system (MIS), p. 207
primary data, p. 207
decision support system (DSS), p. 208
marketing model, p. 208
search engine, p. 208
intranet, p. 209
marketing research, p. 209
hypotheses, p. 211
scientific method, p. 211
marketing research process, p. 213
research proposal, p. 215
situation analysis, p. 215

population, p. 216
random sampling, p. 216
sample, p. 216
statistical packages, p. 217
confidence intervals, p. 218
validity, p. 218
focus group interview, p. 227
qualitative research, p. 227
quantitative research, p. 228
response rate, p. 230
consumer panels, p. 233
experimental method, p. 235

True-False Questions

_____ 1. The key advantage in using an MIS is that it makes available information readily accessible.

_____ 2. A marketing information system is an organized way of using "one-shot" research projects to gather, access, and analyze information that will help marketing managers make better decisions.

_____ 3. Intranets are becoming common in firms of all sizes.

_____ 4. A decision support system (DSS) is a computer program that makes it easy for a marketing manager to get and use information as he or she is making decisions.

____ 5. Marketing managers who have decision support systems probably don't need search engines also.

____ 6. Decision support systems that include marketing models allow the manager to see how answers to questions might change in various situations.

____ 7. Marketing research is best defined as a set of techniques applied by specialists in survey design or statistical methods.

____ 8. Unethical practices among researchers make consumers unwilling to participate in any research.

____ 9. Marketing research details may be handled by staff or outside specialists, but the marketing manager must know how to plan and evaluate research projects.

____ 10. The scientific method is a decision-making approach that focuses on being objective and orderly in testing ideas before accepting them.

____ 11. Hypotheses are statements of fact about relationships between things or what will happen in the future.

____ 12. The marketing research process is a five-step application of the scientific method that includes: defining the problem, analyzing the situation, getting problem-specific data, interpreting the data, and solving the problem.

____ 13. Defining the problem is usually the easiest job of the marketing researcher.

____ 14. Developing a list that includes all possible problem areas is a sensible start to the situation analysis step.

____ 15. Gathering primary data about the problem area is part of analyzing the situation.

____ 16. Secondary data is information that is already collected or published.

____ 17. Much secondary data can be found on the Internet.

____ 18. Even though there's a lot of secondary data on the Internet, there are no good tools for finding it.

____ 19. Most computerized database services are now available on the Internet.

____ 20. Both Dow Jones and ProQuest Direct provide powerful indexes for researching articles on the Internet.

____ 21. The *Statistics Canada* is a good source of primary data.

____ 22. The *Statistics Canada* is an excellent source of secondary data in print form, but unfortunately, it is not yet available on the Internet.

___ 23. A written research proposal is a plan that specifies what marketing research information will be obtained and how.

___ 24. Misunderstandings between marketing managers and technical experts can be avoided by using written research proposals.

___ 25. The two basic methods for obtaining information about customers are questioning and observing.

___ 26. Qualitative research seeks in-depth, open-ended responses.

___ 27. A focus group interview involves interviewing 6 to 10 people in an informal group setting.

___ 28. Focus groups are now being held online as well as in person.

___ 29. Focus groups are a way to gather primary data quickly and at a relatively low cost.

___ 30. Focus groups are a way to gather secondary data quickly and cheaply.

___ 31. It is typical to use quantitative research in preparation for doing qualitative research.

___ 32. Quantitative research seeks structured responses that can be summarized in numbers --like percentages, averages, or other statistics.

___ 33. A common quantitative research approach to summarize consumers' opinions and preferences is to have respondents indicate how much they agree or disagree with a questionnaire statement.

___ 34. The response rate is the percent of people contacted who complete a questionnaire.

___ 35. Mail, e-mail, and online surveys are economical per questionnaire--if a large number of people respond.

___ 36. A mail survey is the best research approach if you want respondents to expand on particular points and give in-depth information.

___ 37. With the observation method, the researcher avoids talking to the subject.

___ 38. Customers' use of online shopping services on the Internet allows retailers to observe customers' behaviour without talking to them.

___ 39. A device called the "people metre" provides observation of television audiences.

___ 40. The use of computer scanners to observe what customers actually do is changing research methods for many firms.

___ 41. A consumer panel is a group of consumers who provide information occasionally --whenever a meeting of the group is called.

___ 42. With the experimental method, the responses of groups that are similar, except on the characteristic being tested, are compared.

___ 43. The experimental method is the most widely used marketing research method because managers want and need quantitative information to make better decisions.

___ 44. Syndicated research is an economical approach for collecting research data needed by many different firms.

___ 45. Statistical packages are easy-to-use computer programs that help analyze data.

___ 46. In regard to marketing research, *population* means the total group that responds to a survey.

___ 47. In most marketing research studies, only a sample--a part of the relevant population--is surveyed.

___ 48. Random sampling is sampling in which each member of the population does not have the same chance of being included in the sample.

___ 49. With random samples, researchers can narrow confidence intervals by increasing sample sizes.

___ 50. Validity concerns the extent to which data measures what it is intended to measure.

___ 51. Conducting and interpreting a marketing research project should be left entirely to the researcher because most marketing managers have no training in this area.

___ 52. Marketing managers are of less importance in international marketing research efforts because of the greater need for local experts.

___ 53. One should always seek to obtain as much marketing information as possible before making a decision.

1. T, p. 207
2. F, p. 207
3. T, p. 209
4. T, p. 207
5. F, p. 208
6. T, p. 208
7. F, p. 209
8. T, p. 212
9. T, p. 211
10. T, p. 211-212
11. F, p. 211
12. T, p. 213
13. F, p. 213
14. T, p. 215
15. F, p. 215
16. T, p. 207
17. T, p. 223
18. F, p. 223

19. T, p. 223
20. T, p. 224
21. F, p. 224
22. F, p. 224
23. T, p. 215
24. T, p. 215
25. T, p. 226
26. T, p. 227
27. T, p. 227
28. T, p. 227
29. T, p. 227-228
30. F, p. 227
31. F, p. 228
32. T, p. 228
33. T, p. 229
34. T, p. 230
35. T, p. 230
36. F, p. 230

37. T, p. 232
38. T, p. 234
39. T, p. 233
40. T, p. 233
41. F, p. 233
42. T, p. 235
43. F, p. 238
44. T, p. 235
45. T, p. 217
46. F, p. 216
47. T, p. 216
48. F, p. 216
49. T, p. 216
50. T, p. 218
51. F, p. 219
52. F, p. 219
53. F, p. 221

Multiple-Choice Questions (Circle the correct response)

1. Which of the following statements about marketing information systems is *true?*
   a. Marketing information systems are used to gather, access, and analyze data from intracompany sources, while marketing research deals with external sources.
   b. Decision support systems allow managers to see how answers to questions might change in different situations.
   c. Computerized marketing information systems tend to increase the quantity of information available for decision making but not without some corresponding decrease in quality.
   d. The value of decision support systems is limited because the manager can't use them while he is actually making his decisions.
   e. All of the above are true statements.

2. Marketing research:
   a. requires a market research department in the company.
   b. consists mainly of survey design and statistical techniques.
   c. should be planned by research specialists.
   d. is needed to keep isolated marketing planners in touch with their markets.
   e. All of the above are true.

3. In small companies,
   a. there is no need for marketing research.
   b. there should be a marketing research department--or there will be no one to do marketing research.
   c. the emphasis of marketing research should be on customer surveys.
   d. salespeople often do what marketing research gets done.
   e. specialized marketing consultants should be called in to do marketing research.

4. The scientific method is important in marketing research because it:
   a. forces the researcher to follow certain procedures, thereby reducing the need to rely on intuition.
   b. develops hypotheses and then tests them.
   c. specifies a marketing strategy, which is almost bound to succeed.
   d. Both a and b are correct.
   e. All of the above are correct.

5. The most difficult step of the marketing research process is:
   a. analyzing the situation.
   b. collecting data.
   c. observation.
   d. defining the problem.
   e. interpreting the data.

6. A small manufacturing firm has just experienced a rapid drop in sales. The marketing manager thinks that he knows what the problem is and has been carefully analyzing secondary data to check his thinking. His next step should be to:
   a. conduct an experiment.
   b. develop a formal research project to gather primary data.

c. conduct informal discussion with outsiders, including middlemen, to see if he has correctly defined the problem.
d. develop a hypothesis and predict the future behaviour of sales.
e. initiate corrective action before sales drop any further.

7. When analyzing the situation, the marketing analyst:
a. sizes up the situation by talking with executives in competitive companies.
b. searches the Internet for information that is already available in the problem area.
c. begins to talk informally to a random sample of customers.
d. talks to experts in data analysis at trade association meetings.
e. All of the above.

8. Popular search engines for locating secondary data on the Internet can be found at the websites for:
a. Yahoo.
b. Altavista.
c. Northern Light.
d. Google
e. All of the above.

9. Which of the following is a good source for locating secondary data:
a. a focus group interview.
b. personal interviews with customers.
c. *Statistics Canada.*
d. a marketing research survey.
e. none of the above.

10. A research proposal
a. should be written by the marketing manager--not the researcher--since the manager knows what needs to be done.
b. usually can't provide much information about how data will be collected, since it is hard to tell until the research is started.
c. might lead a marketing manager to decide that the proposed research will cost more than it is worth.
d. is a plan developed during the problem definition stage of research.
e. All of the above are true.

11. A marketing analyst would *not* use which of the following research methods when gathering primary data?
a. Observation
b. Experiment
c. Mail survey
d. Library search
e. Personal interviews

12. With regard to getting problem-specific data:
a. the observation method involves asking consumers direct questions about their observations.
b. telephone surveys are declining in popularity.
c. focus group interviews are usually more representative than a set of personal interviews.

d.   mail surveys are limited to short, simple questions--extensive questioning cannot be done.

e.   None of the above is a true statement.

13.   To be effective, marketing research should be:

a.   quantitative.

b.   qualitative.

c.   either or both--depending on the situation.

14.   A marketing researcher wants to do a survey to probe in-depth consumer attitudes about their experiences with the company's products. He is **LEAST** likely to get what he wants if he uses

a.   personal interviews.

b.   the focus group approach.

c.   a telephone interview approach.

d.   a mail survey.

e.   None of the above is very useful for getting in-depth information about consumer attitudes.

15.   Experimental method research:

a.   is often hard to use in "real world" markets.

b.   can use either questioning or observing.

c.   is less popular than focus group interviews.

d.   is used to compare groups for differences.

e.   all of the above.

16.   A statistical package is most likely to be used for a marketing research project that:

a.   used focus group interviews.

b.   relied on secondary data.

c.   included a mail, e-mail, or online survey.

d.   consisted of open-ended questions in a personal interview.

e.   was based on qualitative research.

17.   Using random samples:

a.   guarantees that the findings will be valid.

b.   is stressed by theoretical statisticians--but usually is unnecessary in marketing research.

c.   guarantees that the sample will have the same characteristics as the population.

d.   allows the researcher to use confidence intervals to evaluate estimates from the sample data.

e.   All of the above are true statements.

18.   At the step when data are interpreted, a marketing manager should:

a.   leave it to the technical specialists to draw the correct conclusions.

b.   realize that statistical summaries from a sample may not be precise for the whole population.

c.   know that quantitative survey responses are valid, but qualitative research may not be valid.

d.   be satisfied with the sample used as long as it is large.

e.   All of the above are correct.

19. Which of the following statements about marketing research is *false?*
    a. A low response rate may affect the accuracy of results.
    b. Managers never get all the information they would like to have.
    c. Getting more or better information is not always worth the cost.
    d. Because of the risks involved, marketing managers should never base their decision on incomplete information.
    e. A marketing manager should evaluate *beforehand* whether research findings will be relevant.

Answers to Multiple-Choice Questions

1. b, p. 207
2. d, p. 209
3. d, p. 209
4. d, p. 211
5. d, p. 213
6. c, p. 213
7. b, p. 215

8. d, p. 223
9. c, p. 221-226
10. c, p. 215
11. d, p. 226
12. e, p. 227-237
13. c, p. 227-228
14. d, p. 227

15. e, p. 235
16. c, p. 217
17. d, p. 217
18. b, p. 217
19. d, p. 237

Additional Questions to Test Your Understanding (Fill in the blanks)

1. What are the five steps in the Marketing Research process?

    a. _____

    b. _____

    c. _____

    d. _____

    e. _____

2. Step 3 of the five-step approach to marketing research is getting problem specific data, which involves getting primary data. What is the researcher's objective with respect to step 3?

    _____

    _____

    _____

    _____

    _____

3. Match each of the following terms with the correct definition listed below:

Intranet	Consumer Panels	Statistical Package	Marketing Model
Validity	Population	Focus Group Interview	Quantitative Data

    a. _____ - Easy-to-use computer programs that analyze data

    b. _____ - The total group that marketers are interested in.

    c. _____ - Involves interviewing 6 to 10 people in an informal group setting.

    d. _____ - Can be summarized in numbers like percentages, averages, or other statistics.

    e. _____ - Groups of consumers who provide information on a continuing basis.

    f. _____ - A system for linking computers within a company.

    g. _____ - A statement of relationship among marketing variables.

    h. _____ - Is concerned with how well the data actually measures what the researcher wants to measure.

Answers to Additional Questions

1.

a. Defining the problem
b. Analyzing the situation
c. Getting problem-specific data.
d. Interpreting the data
e. Solving the problem.
   See Exhibit 8-2 on p. 214, also p. 213

2   In most primary data collection the researcher tries to learn what customers think about some topic – or how they behave under some conditions. (p. 216-217)

3.

a. Statistical Package, p. 217
b. Population, p. 216
c. Focus group Interview, p. 227
d. Quantitative Data, p. 228
e. Consumer Panel, p. 233
f. Intranet, p. 209
g. Marketing Model, p. 208
h. Validity, p. 218

Exercise 8-1

Controlling an Internet or intranet search for secondary data

Introduction

Marketing managers often fail to take full advantage of all the information that is available to help them make effective decisions. While time and cost factors usually prevent a manager from obtaining perfect information, there is often much more information--already collected and readily available--than managers actually use.

On the other hand, too many marketers tend to be "survey researchers" who feel they must always rush out to gather original data--i.e., *primary data*--whenever some problem arises. They tend to overlook the large amount of *secondary data* that is already available for free-or for a fee that is usually far less than the cost of a "start from scratch" effort to obtain primary data. Information that is relevant to a problem or decision often is available in the firm's internal records, in various published sources, or from a variety of on-line sources that often can be tapped from a manager's desktop computer.

In the past few years many managers have turned to "search engines" to help them find information available from web sites on the Internet or from their firms' own intranets. Using a search engine can really help to speed up a search and zero in on the right information. With a search engine, the manager types in a word or phrase and the search engine returns a list of links to documents where that search term appears. However, sometimes a search for a simple term will return hundreds or even thousands of links-many of which are not directly relevant to the manager's interest but which take time to review.

Most search engines allow the user to control the search and make it more specific-by entering the search term using special formats. Knowing how to use this sort of feature helps the user zero in on the right information-and screen out information that is not useful-more quickly and efficiently. Therefore, the purpose of this exercise is to give you a feel for the different ways that you can control a search. For this exercise, we will focus on the search term formats used by Google (www.google.ca)-because it is one of the best and most widely used Internet search engines. However, many other search engines offer the same features and often they are based on exactly the same formatting approaches ("search syntax"). This is a pencil and paper exercise and you do NOT need to have an Internet connection or use Google to complete it. However, you'll immediately see the advantages of what you're learning if you try a search (on a topic of interest to you) and experiment with the different search formats discussed below.

Assignment

In this assignment, several different marketing management decision-making situations are briefly described. In each case, there is a description of the type of information that is of interest to the manager. Your job is to provide search terms that would help the search engine focus the search on finding links to information that is most relevant to the manager's problem. You are also asked to provide a brief explanation of what you are trying to accomplish with each search term. Table 8-1 (below) summarizes some of the special formatting approaches that you can use to focus a search, and gives an example of how each of them might be used. Study the table and then use it as a guide to developing the search terms and explanations you provide for each case. The first case is completed for you as an example.

Table 8-1
Tips for Better Searching with the Google Search Engine*

What You Are Trying to Do, and How To Do It	Example	Search Term You Would Enter
Get a list of links to web pages where a particular word is found: *Simply type the word*	Search for references to the allergy drug, *Allegra*	Allegra
Get a list of links to web pages where *any* of several words are found: *Type one search word, then a space, then the next word, and continue for as many words as you want.*	Search for references to the allergy drug *Allegra* or for the allergy drug *Claritin*	Allegra Claritin
Search for words that are part of a phrase: *Put quote marks around the whole phrase*	Search for references to the phrase *allergy symptoms*	"allergy symptoms"
Get a list of links to web page3s that must include certain words: *Attach a + in front of words that must appear in the results document*	Search for references that include both the word *allergy* and the word *symptoms*, but not necessarily together as a phrase.	+allergy +symptoms
Specify a word that must *not* appear in the results list: *Attach a – in front of word that must not appear in the results*	Find references to the allergy drug *Allegra* but exclude references to the rock band, *Allegra Rocks*	Allegra -Rocks
Combine any of the above into a single request: *Type one formatted term and then a space and then the next formatted term and so on until they are all entered*	Find references to the term *allergy symptoms* and the allergy drug *Allegra* but no the rock band, *Allegra Rocks*	+ "allergy symptoms" +Allegra -Rocks

1.   Marnie Miguel has just been appointed product manager at Lubricant Technology, Inc. after a number of years in field sales and customer support positions. She is now responsible for strategy planning for the firm's SiLube brand of silicon-based machine lubricants. However, because the previous product manager left the company before she was appointed, she feels that she needs a lot more background on her new brand and her new job responsibilities. Her first thought is to do a search on her firm's intranet to see what she can find that's relevant.

Search term: _SiLube "marketing plan"_

Explanation: _This search should find all pages on the firm's intranet that reference the word SiLube or the phrase marketing plan (but not pages that just include a reference the word marketing or the word plan by themselves)._

2.   Ms. Miguel tried the searches given in the example above, but each search has returned a report with hundreds of links. To help narrow things down for an initial look, she has decided to try to find only marketing plans that actually reference the SiLube brand.

Search term:

_____

Explanation:

_____

_____

_____

3.   Ms. Miguel was talking with another manager about trying to improve the new-product development process for SiLube brands. Her colleague said, "I got a flyer on a new-product development conference that's going to be held in Calgary, or maybe it was Edmonton, next month-it might be a good place to get ideas. But, I don't remember the details about the conference and unfortunately I threw the flyer away."

Search term:

_____

Explanation:

_____

_____

_____

4.   Jock Ratner is the marketing manager for a biotech startup firm that is developing a new medicine for treatment of respiratory disorders. Its first product is showing promising results in first stage clinical trials with patients, but it will be some time before the firm will be able to get approval from the Food and Drugs Act to release the drug. Ratner has learned from a contact at the Canadian Lung Association that another firm, United Therapeutics, is working on several products in the same area. Ratner is interested in finding out anything he can about United Therapeutics or its LungRx subsidiary.

Search term:

_____

Explanation:

_____

_____

_____

5. Val Parker is evaluating the market for various types of household appliances and wants to see if there is *Statistics Canada* data available on the Internet for how many households have microwave ovens, air conditioners, trash compactors, and dishwashers.

Search term:

_____

Explanation:

_____

_____

_____

6. James Staelin is the sales manager for Western Canada Ford, a large Ford dealership with facilities in a number of cities. In the past, the Ford Taurus was one of the firm's best selling models, but since the Taurus was redesigned and the list price was raised, sales have been slow. Staelin's salespeople have complained that they keep losing sales to the Toyota Camry. Staelin wants to prepare a sales kit to give his sales reps a lot more information about the Taurus, including information based on what favourable product reviews have said. He did an initial search of the Internet to look for automobile reviews. His search on the word Taurus produced many thousands of links, but as he started reviewing the links in detail he found that most of them were to web pages concerned with astrology (where Taurus was usually referenced as one of the astrological "signs.")

Search term:

_____

Explanation:

_____

_____

_____

7. Staelin (case above) has decided to refine his search to see if he can find web pages that discuss both the Taurus and the Camry and that discuss crash tests.

Search term:

_____

Explanation:

_____

_____

_____

Question for Discussion

With so much *secondary* data readily available from the Internet and from other sources, why is there ever a need for a marketing manager to gather *primary* data?

Exercise 8-2

Evaluating marketing research

Introduction

Marketing managers need good information to develop effective marketing strategies. They need to know about the marketing environment variables, about possible target customers, and about the marketing mix decisions they can make.

Sometimes the only way to get needed information is with marketing research. When this is the case, the manager can sometimes get help--perhaps from marketing research specialists in the firm or from outside specialists. However, marketing managers must be able to explain what their problems are--and what kinds of information they need. They should also know about some of the basic decisions made during the research process--so they know the limitations of the research. They need to be able to see if the results of a research project will really solve the problem!

It is true that marketing research can involve many technical details--that is why specialists are often involved. However, often a marketing manager can use "common sense" --and knowledge of marketing strategy planning--to improve marketing research.

Assignment

In this exercise you are presented with short cases that involve marketing research. You are asked to identify and comment about the possible limitations of the research. The cases are accompanied by questions that will help to get your thinking started.

You will need to know about the marketing research ideas discussed in Chapter 8 to evaluate the cases. Nevertheless, remember that the idea here is *not* just to memorize the points from the text. Rather, you should really think about the *problem,* and use common sense along with the information in the book to evaluate the case situation.

A sample answer is provided to the first case--to give you an example of the type of thinking that might be helpful. But--before you read the answer--think about how you would answer the question yourself.

1. A marketing manager for a big industrial equipment company wanted to get ideas about new products he should develop. A salesman suggested that they conduct a few focus group interviews with a few "friendly" customers--to get some ideas. This seemed like a good idea, so an outside marketing specialist was hired to set up and videotape two focus group sessions.

After the sessions, the specialist presented a short summary report. His main conclusion was that 40 percent of the participants wanted a certain type of machine, and urged the company to develop one quickly "since the market will be large." He also said that from watching the tapes he was certain that the customers were unhappy with the products they had been getting from the firm. This left the marketing manager quite concerned and wondering what to do.

a) Is a focus group interview a good basis for drawing the type of conclusions offered by the outside researcher? Why or why not?

Sample Answer: The conclusion probably is not justified. A focus group interview includes relatively few customers, and they may not be representative. In addition, trying to provide quantitative summaries of the qualitative results might be really misleading. The new product might be a good idea, but just because a few people in a focus group mentioned it does not mean that there will be a large market. That will require more study.

b) Should the manager hire the marketing research firm to do a large survey to see if customers are really unhappy, as he suggests based on the focus groups? Why or why not?

Sample Answer: It is too early to be thinking about rushing out to do a big expensive survey. After all, conclusions reached by watching a focus group interview can vary a lot depending on who watches it. As a start, the marketing manager might watch the tapes of the focus groups and see if he draws the same conclusions. Other views might be sought as well. Even if the conclusion seems correct, it would be best to define the problem more specifically, and do a situation analysis to get a better idea about what research is needed.

2. A marketing manager for a Volvo dealership is trying to decide how many cars to order during the coming year--to be sure to have enough on hand to meet demand. He decides that it would be useful to do a survey of customers to whom he has sold this brand in the last year. He wants to know how satisfied they are with their current car, and he wants to know how many want to buy another Volvo from him in the coming year. He would also like to know if they could afford another expensive car so soon. He decides to have salesmen call the customers and ask the following questions:

(1) How do you feel about the car you bought from us? Are you very satisfied, or only moderately satisfied?

(2) Do you plan to buy another Volvo from us during the coming year? Yes, you plan to buy; or no, you don't plan to buy.

(3) I have one final question, and your response will be strictly confidential and used only in statistical summaries with answers from other respondents. Would you please tell us your annual income?

$_____

a) Do you think that customers will give a valid response to the second question? Why or why not?

b) Do you think that customers will give a valid response to the last question? Why or why not?

c) What is there about the way that the first question is worded that might keep the manager from getting valid information about how satisfied a customer really is? (*Hint:* Read the whole question several times carefully from the point-of-view of different customers.)

3. A marketing manager for TD Bank wants to survey potential customers to see if they know about the bank's new investment services. An outside marketing research specialist tells the manager that for $5,000 the research firm can send out a mail survey to 500 people, tabulate the results, and present a report. He explains that the bank will need to provide a computer mailing list of people who have accounts at the bank--to save costs in developing the sample. He concludes by pointing out that the research will be quite inexpensive: "We will give you results from a representative sample of 500 people, at only $10 per respondent. And you can be confident with a sample of 500 that the statistics are accurate."

a) Is the proposed sample well-suited to the manager's problem? Why or why not?

b) Is the researcher's concluding statement misleading? (*Hint:* Think about the response rate issue.) Why or why not?

4. A marketing manager for Holt Renfrew's, an expensive men's clothing store, is concerned that profits have dropped, and he has noticed that many customers who once were "regulars" are not coming back anymore. He decides to send out a questionnaire to a sample of old customers, using addresses from his mailing list. He wrote a letter asking customers to respond to his questionnaire. He also provided a postage paid envelope for return of the completed forms. The instructions on the short questionnaire were:

(1) Please discuss the things you liked most about this store the last time you purchased clothing here?

(2) Please explain what you like least about this store. Please discuss anything that bothers you.

(3) Please tell us at what other men's clothing stores you shop, and what it is about each store that you like?

a) Is a mail survey useful for questions like these? Why or why not?

b) What would you recommend if the manager asked you for ideas on how to get better information about his problem?

Question for Discussion

How do the limitations of qualitative research differ from the limitations of quantitative research?

Exercise 8-3

Marketing research

This exercise is based on computer-aided problem - Marketing Research. A complete description of the problem appears on page 239 of Wong/Shapiro, 11th edition.

1. Texmac asked firms that had the old machine if they would replace it with their new product if it were priced at $10,000. Forty percent said that they would buy the new equipment. Texmac asked another question of the respondents who said that they would not buy the new equipment at $10,000. Specifically it asked if they would buy the new machine if it were priced at $9,750. Another 25 firms said that they would buy the new machine at the lower price. Texmac figures that those who said that they would buy the machine at the higher price would also buy it at the lower price.

    Based on this information and information from the spreadsheet for the problem (assuming that there are 5,000 firms), calculate what percent of the sample would buy the machine at the lower price:

    _____ percent that would buy only at the $9,750 price.

    plus _____ percent that would buy at either price.

    equals _____ total percent that would buy at lower price.

2. Now, use the spreadsheet to compute what results the firm would expect based on the lower price ($9,750) and the total percent that would buy at the lower price. Fill in the table below to compare these results with the results that would be expected at the higher price ($10,000).

	Price $10,000	Price $9,750
Expected quantity of replacements:	_____	_____
Total expected revenue:	_____	_____
Expected contribution to profit:	_____	_____
Recommended price	_____	

Explanation:

_____

_____

_____

3. The marketing manager at Texmac wants more detail about what might happen at the price you are recommending. He knows that the number of "old machines" reported by the 500 sample firms may not be exactly representative of the total population. But, marketing research specialists at the firm say that he can be 95 percent confident that the estimate of the number of old machines per 500 firms is probably accurate within a confidence interval of plus or minus 20 machines. Thus, the marketing manager wants to know how your estimate of contribution to profit might change if the actual number of old machines per 500 in the market varies over the range of the confidence interval. To provide this information, do a "What If" analysis and complete the table below. (Note: use the price and percent that would buy based on your recommendation from the previous page).

Estimated Number of Old Machines	Expected Profit
200 (minimum)	_____
204	_____
208	_____
212	_____
216	_____
220	_____
224	_____
228	_____
232	_____
236	_____
240 (maximum)	_____

4. Texmac's marketing manager says that the market opportunity will be less attractive than it looks if the actual number of textile producers in the population is smaller than the company thinks. Indicate if you agree or disagree with his statement. Briefly discuss why.

_____

_____

_____

Chapter 9

Elements of Product Planning for Goods and Services

Chapter Summary

- **Understand what "product" really means.**

  A product is really the need satisfying offering of a firm. It is often thought of in terms of the total satisfaction it provides. It may be made up of a combination of the right service, a physical good with the right features, instructions on use, convenient packaging, warranties and the like.

- **Know the key differences between *goods* and services.**

  A good is a tangible, physical item that can be touched and seen. On the other hand, a service is an action performed by one party for another. Services are used, consumed, experienced and intangible.

  While goods are typically produced in advanced in advance of the purchase, services cannot be. This makes it difficult to balance the supply with the demand for a service, and to achieve any economies of scale.

- **Know the differences between the various consumer and business product classes.**

  Consumer product classes are convenience products, shopping products, specialty products, and unsought products.

  Business product classes are installations; accessory equipment; raw materials; component parts and materials; maintenance, repair and operating supplies (MRO); and professional services.

- **Understand how the product classes can help a marketing manager plan marketing strategies.**

  Product classes help the manager plan marketing strategies by understanding the nature of a buyer's involvement and search process. This knowledge provides insights into the appropriate marketing mix. See Exhibit 9-5 (p. 249) for marketing mix considerations and consumer behaviour buying behaviour for consumer product classes. See Exhibit 9-6 (p. 249) for marketing mix considerations and buying behaviour for business product classes.

- **Understand what branding is and how to use it in strategy planning.**

  Branding means using a name, term, symbol, or design, or a combination of these, to identify a product. Good, recognized brands reduce the marketer's selling time and effort, improve the company's image, and even speed up the acceptance of new products. Achieving a high level of brand familiarity is often difficult and requires a good product with regular promotion. Five levels of brand familiarity are useful for strategic planning: (1) rejection, (2) nonrecognition, (3) recognition, (4) preference, and (5) insistence.

When branding more than one product, the brander must decide whether to use a family brand, or individual brands for each product. Family brands are useful for products that are similar in both type and quality. In this case, efforts to promote the brand help all of the family brand products. An individual brand is necessary when each product must have its own identity because of differences in type and qualities. Individual brands help avoid confusion among consumers.

- **Understand the importance of packaging in strategy planning.**
  Packaging involves promoting and protecting the product. A well designed package can make the product more convenient to use, prevent spoilage or damage, and identify and promote the brand. Because of increasingly cluttered store shelves, a good package can be the difference when a customer is making a purchase decision. Other considerations to remember regarding packaging are possible savings in shipping costs and various federal laws regulating packaging and labeling of certain products.

- **Understand the role of warranties in strategic planning.**
  The marketing manager must decide whether to give a specific warranty and what will the warranty cover. Warranties can be used to improve the attractiveness of a firm's marketing mix by offering a guarantee that the product is up to reasonable standards. Service warranties are becoming increasingly popular in an attempt to keep customers happy. Similarly, it is common to see optional extended warranty contracts available for an additional fee to keep price down for those who do not want the full warranty coverage.

Important Terms

product, p. 243
quality, p. 244
relative quality, p. 245
service, p. 245
product assortment, p. 247
individual product, p. 248
product line, p. 247
business products, p. 249
consumer product, p. 249
convenience products, p. 249
emergency products, p. 250
heterogeneous shopping products, p. 250
homogeneous shopping products, p. 250
impulse products, p. 250
shopping products, p. 250
specialty products, p. 250
staples, p. 250
unsought products, p. 250
capital item, p. 252
derived demand, p. 252
expense item, p. 252
installations, p. 252
accessories, p. 253

supplies, p. 254
professional services, p. 255
brand name, p. 256
branding, p. 256
service mark, p. 256
trademark, p. 256
brand familiarity, p. 257
brand rejection, p. 257
new unsought products, p. 257
regularly unsought products, p. 257
brand insistence, (brand loyalty) p. 259
brand nonrecognition, p. 259
brand preference, p. 259
brand equity, p. 260
brand recognition, p. 262
family brand, p. 262
individual brands, p. 262
licensed brand, p. 262
battle of the brands, p. 263
co-branding, p. 263
dealer brands, (private brand) p. 263
generic products, p. 263
manufacturer brand, p. 263

farm products, p. 253

natural products, p. 253

raw materials, p. 253

components, p. 254

packaging, p. 265

universal product code (UPC), p. 266

unit-pricing, p. 267

warranty, p. 267

True-False Questions

___ 1. A "product" may not include a physical good at all.

___ 2. Quality refers to the ability of a product to satisfy a customer's need.

___ 3. The more features a product has the higher-quality product it is.

___ 4. It is usually harder to balance supply and demand for services than for physical goods.

___ 5. It is usually easier to achieve economies of scale when the product emphasis is on a service rather than a good.

___ 6. A product line should be thought of as a firm's product assortment.

___ 7. An individual product is a particular product within a product line and is usually differentiated by brand, level of service, size, price, or some other characteristic.

___ 8. Consumer product classes are based on how consumers think about and shop for a product.

___ 9. Convenience products are products a consumer needs but is not willing to spend much time or effort to shop for.

___ 10. Because customers are not willing to spend much time or effort shopping for staples, they are not bought very often.

___ 11. Impulse products are items that the customer decides to purchase on sight, may have bought the same way many times before, and wants "right now."

___ 12. The distinctive aspect of emergency products is that they are only purchased when the consumer is in danger.

___ 13. Shopping products are those products that a customer feels are worth the time and effort to compare with competing products.

___ 14. If customers see a product as a homogeneous shopping product, they will base their purchase decisions on the one variable they feel is or can be different--price.

___ 15. Price is considered irrelevant for products that the customer sees as heterogeneous shopping products.

16. Specialty products are expensive and unusual products that customers insist upon having and generally have to travel far to find.

17. Unsought products are those products that have no potential value for customers.

18. A consumer product must be either a convenience product, a shopping product, or a specialty product--it cannot be all three.

19. In times of recession, a good marketing mix aimed at business and organizational customers may not be very effective unless it has some impact on final consumer demand, because the demand for final consumer products derive from the demand for business products.

20. The fact that the demand for most business products is derived means that industry demand will be fairly elastic, although the demand facing individual firms may be extremely inelastic.

21. For tax purposes, the cost of a business expense item is spread over a number of years.

22. Since business products buyers do relatively little shopping compared to consumer products buyers, the business products classification system is determined by how buyers see the products and how they will be used.

23. Installations include only buildings and land rights--such as factories, farms, stores, office buildings, mining deposits, and timber rights.

24. If a customer purchases an installation, it is a capital item.

25. Although accessory equipment are capital items, purchasing agents usually have more say in buying accessories than in buying installations.

26. Raw materials become part of a physical good--and they are expense items.

27. Component parts and materials are capital items that have had more processing than raw materials.

28. Unlike farm products, components are usually bought using purchasing specifications.

29. A product originally considered a component part when it was sold in the OEM market might become a consumer product for the replacement market--and probably would require a different marketing mix.

30. Supplies are commonly described as MRO items, meaning that "More Rational Ordering" procedures are normally followed for them.

31. High-level executives may negotiate contracts for some important operating supplies that are needed regularly and cost a lot.

32. Maintenance supplies are similar to consumers' convenience products--and branding may become important for such products.

33. Professional services are expense items, and often the cost of buying them outside the firm is compared with the cost of having company personnel do them.

34. The terms branding, brand name, and trademark all mean about the same thing—and can be used interchangeably.

35. Service mark is a legal term that refers to a service offering.

36. Branding is advantageous to producers--but not to customers.

37. Despite the many advantages of branding, a marketing manager would probably be wise to avoid spending large amounts on branding unless the quality can be easily maintained.

38. A firm whose products have reached the brand insistence stage will enjoy a more inelastic demand curve than a firm whose products have achieved brand preference.

39. A respected brand name lowers brand equity.

40. The Trademarks Act specifies what types of trademarks can be protected by law and makes provisions for registration records--but it does not force registration.

41. Counterfeiting is illegal everywhere in the world.

42. A licensed brand is a well-known brand that different sellers pay a fee to use.

43. Generic products are products, which have no brand at all other than identification of their contents and the manufacturer or middleman.

44. The major disadvantage of manufacturer brands is that manufacturers normally offer lower gross margins than the middleman might be able to earn with his own brands.

45. Eventually, dealer-branded products may win the "battle of the brands," perhaps because dealers are closer to customers and they can control shelf space.

46. While packing is concerned with protecting the product, packaging refers only to promotion.

47. Packaging plays no role when the product emphasis is on service.

48. Better protective packaging is more important to final consumers than to manufacturers and middlemen.

___ 49. A firm should adopt a more expensive package only when the overall effect will be to reduce the total distribution cost for its product.

___ 50. Large supermarket chains have been eager to use the universal product code system—to speed the checkout process and eliminate the need for marking the price on every item.

___ 51. The Consumer Packaging and Labeling Act, requires bilingual labeling and the use of metric measurements.

___ 52. Unit-pricing involves placing the price per ounce (or some other standard measure) on or near a product.

___ 53. A warranty explains what a seller promises about its product.

___ 54. In Canada, producers must guarantee their product even if they do not give a written warranty..

Answers to True-False Questions

1. T, p. 243	19. F, p. 252	37. T, p. 257
2. T, p. 244	20. F, p. 252	38. T, p. 259
3. F, p. 244	21. F, p. 252	39. F, p. 260
4. T, p. 245	22. T, p. 252	40. T, p. 259
5. F, p. 246	23. F, p. 252	41. F, p. 259
6. F, p. 247	24. T, p. 252	42. T, p. 262
7. T, p. 248	25. T, p. 253	43. T, p. 263
8. T, p. 249	26. T, p. 253	44. T, p. 263
9. T, p. 249	27. F, p. 254	45. T, p. 263
10. F, p. 250	28. T, p. 254-255	46. F, p. 265
11. T, p. 250	29. T, p. 254-255	47. F, p. 265
12. F, p. 250	30. F, p. 254-255	48. F, p. 266
13. T, p. 250	31. T, p. 254-255	49. F, p. 266
14. T, p. 250	32. T, p. 254-255	50. T, p. 266
15. F, p. 250	33. T, p. 255	51. T, p. 267
16. F, p. 250	34. F, p. 256	52. T, p. 267
17. F, p. 250	35. T, p. 256	53. T, p. 267
18. F, p. 251	36. F, p. 256	54. T, p. 268

Multiple-Choice Questions (Circle the correct response)

1. According to the text, the term "product" means:
    a. any tangible item that satisfies needs.
    b. goods but not services.
    c. the need-satisfying offering of a firm.
    d. any item that is mass produced by a firm.
    e. all of the above.

2. Regarding quality:
    a. the best credit card may not be the one with the highest credit limit.
    b. the best clothing may not be a pair of slacks, but a pair of jeans.
    c. the best computer may not be the most powerful one.
    d. All of the above are true.
    e. None of the above is true.

3. Marketing mix planning for services
    a. is easier than for physical goods because services do not need to be stored.
    b. is more likely to be influenced by economies of scale.
    c. must consider where the service is produced.
    d. All of the above are true.
    e. None of the above is true.

4. The set of all products a firm sells is called its:
    a. product line.
    b. individual products.
    c. product assortment.
    d. tangible products.

5. The text's consumer product classes are based upon:
    a. methods of distribution.
    b. NAICS codes.
    c. the nature of the products.
    d. the way people think about and shop for products.
    e. the way firms view their products.

6. Which of the following is *not* included as a product class in the classification system for consumer products given in the text?
    a. Convenience products
    b. Staple products
    c. Specialty products
    d. Shopping products
    e. Durable products

7. As Carla Tomas was doing her weekly supermarket shopping, she walked down the pet food aisle to pick up her usual six cans of brand "X." cat food. However, she came upon a special display of a new, highly advertised brand and decided to try it instead. In this case, the cat food she bought is:
    a. an impulse product.
    b. a specialty product.
    c. an unsought product.

d.   a homogeneous shopping product.

e.   a staple product.

8.   You are stranded in your automobile during a snowstorm. You decide to walk to the closest service station for tire chains. In this case you would consider the tire chains as:

a.   emergency products.

b.   staple products.

c.   impulse products.

d.   shopping products.

e.   specialty products.

9.   Mr. Beza feels that most people are too emotional and status-minded concerning their automobile purchases. "An automobile's only function is transportation," he says, "and those high-priced 'chrome-wagons' can't do anything that most lower priced cars won't do." Beza only considers Fords, Chevrolets, and Plymouths when he looks around for a new car and he feels all these cars are alike. For him automobiles are:

a.   a specialty product.

b.   a homogeneous shopping product.

c.   a convenience staple product.

d.   a heterogeneous shopping product.

e.   a staple product.

10.   Specialty products would be best described as having:

a.   brand insistence and inelastic demand.

b.   brand preference and inelastic demand.

c.   brand insistence and elastic demand.

d.   brand preference and elastic demand.

e.   a relatively high price and durability.

11.   Which of the following statements about consumer products is *true*?

a.   Convenience products are those that customers want to buy at the lowest possible price.

b.   Shopping products are those products for which customers usually want to use routinized buying behaviour.

c.   Specialty products are those that customers usually are least willing to search for.

d.   Unsought products are not shopped for at all.

e.   None of the above statements are true.

12.   Motels are a good example of:

a.   convenience products.

b.   shopping products.

c.   specialty products.

d.   unsought products.

e.   Could be any of the above.

13.   Which of the following is *not* a general characteristic of most business products?

a.   Buyers tend to buy from only one supplier.

b.   Their demand is derived from the demand for final consumer products.

c.   Industry demand may be inelastic while each company's demand may be elastic.

d.   Buying is basically concerned with economic factors.

e.   All of the above are characteristics for most business products.

14.   Tax regulations affect business buying decisions because:
      a.   expense items are depreciated.
      b.   capital items are written off over several years.
      c.   installations are expensed in one year.
      d.   capital items are expensed in one year.

15.   The business product classes discussed in the text are based on:
      a.   how sellers think about products.
      b.   how buyers see products.
      c.   how the products are to be used.
      d.   all of the above.
      e.   both b and c.

16.   Which of the following is *not* one of the business product classes discussed in the text?
      a.   Professional services
      b.   Farm products
      c.   Component parts
      d.   Accessory equipment
      e.   Fabrications

17.   Which of the following business products to be purchased by a firm is *most* likely to involve top management in the buying decision?
      a.   Raw materials
      b.   Accessory equipment
      c.   Operating supplies
      d.   Installations
      e.   Component parts

18.   Which of the following would *not* be classified as accessory equipment?
      a.   Of rice typewriters
      b.   Filing cases
      c.   Portable drills
      d.   All of the above might be accessory equipment.
      e.   None of the above is likely to be accessory equipment.

19.   Raw materials are usually broken down into two broad categories, which are:
      a.   domestic animals and crops.
      b.   farm products and natural products.
      c.   forest products and mineral products.
      d.   maintenance materials and operating materials.
      e.   farm products and chemicals.

20.   Which of the following would *not* be considered as a component part by an auto manufacturer?
      a.   Automobile batteries
      b.   Steel sheets
      c.   Automobile jacks
      d.   Tires

e. All of the above can be considered component parts, except when they are sold in the replacement market.

21. A marketing manager for a firm that produces component parts should keep in mind that:
    a. most component buyers prefer to rely on one reliable source of supply.
    b. the replacement market for component parts generally requires the same marketing mix as the one used to serve the original equipment market.
    c. any product originally sold as a component part becomes a consumer product when sold in the replacement market.
    d. the original equipment market and the replacement market for component parts should be viewed as separate target markets.
    e. All of the above are true statements.

22. Supplies may be divided into three main categories. Lubricating oils and greases for machines on the production line would be classified as:
    a. maintenance items.
    b. production items.
    c. operating supplies.
    d. repair supplies.
    e. accessories.

23. A "brand name" is:
    a. any means of product identification.
    b. a word used to identify a seller's products.
    c. the same thing as "branding."
    d. the same thing as a "trademark".
    e. All of the above.

24. Which of the following conditions would *not* be favourable to branding?
    a. Dependable and widespread availability is possible
    b. Economies of scale in production
    c. Fluctuations in product quality due to inevitable variations in raw materials
    d. Product easy to identify by brand or trademark
    e. Large market with a variety of needs and preferences

25. What degree of brand familiarity has a manufacturer achieved when the firm's particular brand is chosen out of habit or past experience, even though various "name" brands are available?
    a. Brand rejection
    b. Brand preference
    c. Brand recognition
    d. Brand insistence
    e. Nonrecognition of brand

26. Which of the following statements about the Trademarks Act is *true?*
    a. It spells out what kinds of brand names can be protected.
    b. Registration under the Trademarks Act only applies to licensed brands.
    c. The Trademarks Act makes registration of a brand name mandatory.
    d. Registering under the Trademarks Act does not help protect a trademark to be used in foreign markets.

e.   Legally prevents another company from using a trademark in Canada that might be "confused with the registered trademark..

27.   A firm that has decided to brand all its products under one label is following a policy of:
a.   dealer branding.
b.   generic branding.
c.   family branding.
d.   manufacturer branding.
e.   None of the above.

28.   Which of the following statements about manufacturer or dealer brands is *true?*
a.   Dealer brands are distributed only by chain-store retailers.
b.   Dealer brands may be distributed as widely or more widely than many manufacturer brands.
c.   Dealer brands are the same as "licensed brands."
d.   Manufacturer brands are sometimes called private brands.
e.   All of the above are true.

29.   A wholesaler might develop a dealer brand because it:
a.   permits the wholesaler to raise prices.
b.   usually leads to faster turnover of products.
c.   usually leads to less inventory carrying costs.
d.   usually cuts his promotion costs.
e.   protects against channel changes by manufacturers.

30.   Which of the following statements regarding the "battle of the brands" is *true?*
a.   It is pretty well over as the dealers now control the marketplace.
b.   Middlemen have no real advantages in the battle of the brands.
c.   If the present trend continues, manufacturers will control all middlemen.
d.   Manufacturer brands may be losing ground to dealer brands.
e.   The battle of the brands has increased the differences in price between manufacturer brands and dealer brands.

31.   Which of the following statements about the strategic importance of packaging is *false?*
a.   A package may have more promotional impact than a firm's advertising efforts.
b.   A new package can become the major factor in a new marketing strategy by significantly improving the product.
c.   Packaging is concerned with promoting, protecting, and enhancing.
d.   Better packaging always raises total distribution costs.
e.   A package should satisfy not only the needs of consumers but also those of business and organizational customers.

32.   The Textile Care Labeling Program:
a.   suggests voluntary informative labeling of textiles with respect to their weight, and volume.
b.   made unit pricing mandatory.
c.   encouraged each firm to use a different size package, so consumers would have more choice.
d.   prohibits the use of universal product codes as a substitute for marking prices on retail products.

     e.   requires that all garments and other textiles be labeled with their washing and dry cleaning instructions.

33.   The Competition Act:
     a.   requires that all firms provide written warranties for all products.
     b.   requires that a warranty must be clearly written, if one is offered.
     c.   requires that all warranties be strong warranties.
     d.   legislates that all warranties be for at least one year.
     e.   protects consumers against misleading warranties.

Answers to Multiple-Choice Questions

1. c, p. 243	12. e, p. 250	23. b, p. 256
2. d, p. 244	13. a, p. 249	24. c, p. 260
3. c, p. 245	14. b, p. 252	25. b, p. 259
4. c, p. 247	15. e, p. 252	26. e, p. 259
5. d, p. 249	16. e, p. 252-255	27. c, p. 262
6. e, p. 249	17. d, p. 252-255	28. b, p. 263
7. e, p. 250	18. d, p. 253	29. e, p. 263
8. a, p. 250	19. b, p. 253	30. d, p. 263
9. b, p. 250	20. b, p. 254	31. d, p. 263
10. a, p. 250	21. d, p. 254	32. e, p. 267
11. d, p. 250	22. c, p. 254	33. e, p. 268

Additional Questions to Test Your Understanding (Fill in the Blanks)

1. Briefly explain why the consumer product classes and the business product classes are important to marketing managers.

   _____

   _____

   _____

   _____

   _____

2. Based on your own experience, provide two examples of how package can create or help create a "new" product.

   a. _____

   _____

   _____

   b. _____

   _____

   _____

3. Provide an example of how warranty policies or service guarantees can generate goodwill (happier more satisfied customers) and repeat customers.

   _____

   _____

   _____

   _____

   _____

4. Match each of the following terms with the correct definition listed below:

   Heterogeneous   shopping products   brand rejection   derived demand
   individual brand   expense item   warranty

   a. _____ - A product whose total cost is treated as a business expense in the year it is purchased.

   b. _____ - A separate brand name is used for each product when it is important for each of the products to have a separate identity

c. _____ - Explains what a seller promises about their product.

d. _____ - Potential customers will not buy a brand unless its image is changed.

e. _____ - Products that the customer sees as different – and wants to inspect for quality and suitability.

f. _____ - The demand for business products derives from the demand for the final consumer products.

Answers to Additional Questions

1. Consumer product classes are based on how consumers think about and shop for products. Business product classes are based on how buyers think about products and how the products will be used. (p. 249)

2. a. Microwable, expandable bags for popcorn created a new kind of "popcorn. b. Single use disposable cameras are another way of packaging film, but they also create a new product.

3. See discussion of Pizza Hut, General Motors and the Hampton Inn chain on page 268-269

4.
    a. expense item , p. 252
    b. individual brand, p. 262
    c. warranty, p. 267
    d. brand rejection, p. 257
    e. heterogeneous shopping products, p. 250
    f. derived demand, p. 252

Name: _____   Course & Section: _____

Exercise 9-1

Classifying consumer products

Introduction

Consumer product classes are based on *the way people think about and buy products.* However, different groups of potential customers may have different needs and buying behaviour for the same product. Thus, the same product could be placed in two or more product classes--depending on the needs and behaviour of target customers. Therefore, product planners should focus on specific groups of customers (i.e., market segments) whose needs and buying behaviour are relatively homogeneous.

This exercise will give you some practice in using consumer product classes. As you do the exercise, you will see that the product classes have very little meaning unless they are related to specific target markets.

Assignment

The buying behaviour of several customers or potential customers is described below for the Kodak Disc camera. (A disc camera uses a disc shaped film). Assume in each situation that the customer being described is representative of a particular group of customers--all possessing the same needs and exhibiting similar buying behaviour. Then: (a) indicate in which consumer product class the product should be placed based on the characteristics of each group of customers and (b) state *why* you placed the product in this class. Use the following classes, which are described on pages 249-251 in the text.

Staple convenience product   Heterogeneous shopping product
Impulse convenience product   Specialty product
Emergency convenience product   New unsought product
Homogeneous shopping product   Regularly unsought product

The first situation has been answered for you as an example.

1. Tamara Zanavich, a college student, wished to purchase a camera as a birthday gift for her boyfriend. Although Tamara could only afford to spend about $70, she wanted a camera of reasonably good quality--but also one that would be easy to operate. Knowing very little about cameras, Tamara asked a salesperson at the Campus Camera Shop for his advice. He recommended that she buy a Kodak Disc camera because of its low price and many convenient features.

   Product Class: *Heterogeneous shopping product.*

   Reason: *Customer spends time and effort to compare quality and features, has little concern for brand, and is not too concerned about price as long as it is within her budget.*

9-16

2.   Dennis Dahl walked into a Super Kmart Centre and told the clerk at the camera counter that he wanted to buy a pocket camera with a built-in flash. The clerk said the store carried several such cameras, including the Kodak Disc. "I'll take the one with the lowest price," Dennis told the clerk.

Product Class:

_____

Reason:

3.   Priya Hothi was at her cousin's house and saw some photographs that her cousin had taken with a Kodak Disc camera. She was so impressed by the quality of the pictures that she decided to purchase the same camera. The next day she went to a nearby camera store and found that the store did not have the camera in stock--although it did have other "pocket cameras" in stock in the same price range. The salesperson in the store assured her that the others were just as good. However, Priya ignored this advice and tried two other stores that were also out of stock. Getting frustrated, Priya was ready to drive downtown to a large camera store when she came upon a display of Kodak Disc cameras in a nearby department store. She quickly bought one--even though she felt the price would probably be lower at the camera store.

Product Class:

_____

Reason:

4.   While deep-sea fishing off the Florida Keys, Scott Griffin caught a large swordfish. He decided that his friends back home would never believe his "fish story" if he did not have pictures. However, he did not have a camera. As soon as the boat got back to the dock, Scott went to a nearby tourist shop. He was pleased to see a display of Kodak Disc cameras, but was sorry to see a much higher price than the same camera sold for in his hometown. He bought one anyway, because he wanted to take some pictures right away before the fish was taken away to the fish market.

Product Class:

_____

Reason:

5.   Paul Chu teaches high school science courses. He spends most of his leisure time doing amateur photography. In fact, he enjoys photography so much that for several years he has volunteered to teach the advanced photography workshop offered by the city recreation department. He has won several awards for his photographs of mountain landscapes. Paul has even earned extra cash by selling some of his photos to companies that print postcards. Several of his friends have encouraged him to turn professional, but he prefers using his talents mainly as a hobby.

Product Class:

_____

Reason:

6.   While Caroline Beauchamp was shopping in her local supermarket, she came upon a special display of Kodak Disc cameras. At first, she doubted the product quality because they were priced quite low compared to her friend's Minolta camera. However, remembering all the Kodak advertisements she had seen on television and in magazines, she decided to buy one to take photographs of her grandchildren who were visiting for the week.

Product Class:

_____

Reason:

Question for Discussion

What implications do your answers to the above exercises have for Kodak when planning its marketing strategies? Be specific?

Exercise 9-2

Classifying business products

Introduction

Compared to consumer product buyers, business product buyers do relatively little shopping. The accepted practice is for the seller to come to the buyer. This means that business product classes based on shopping behaviour are *not* useful. The business product classes are determined by *how buyers see products* and *how the products will be used.*

The business product classes may be easier to use than consumer product classes, because business and organizational buyers tend to have similar views of the same products. Another reason is that the way a purchase is treated for tax purposes affects its classification. The treatment is determined by the Revenue Canada rather than the buyer--so little variation is possible.

However, it is possible that a product may be placed in different classes by two buyers because of how they view the purchase. A "small" truck might be classified as an "accessory" by a large manufacturer, while a small manufacturer would view the same truck as an important "installation." Thus, how the customer sees the product is the determining factor--and it will affect marketing mix planning!

Assignment

This exercise focuses on the essential differences between business product classes. After carefully reading the following cases, indicate which type of business product each case is *primarily* concerned with. Use the following classes:

Installations	Component materials
Accessories	Supplies
Raw materials	Professional services
Component parts	

Then explain your answers, taking into consideration the various characteristics of each type of product as explained in the text on pages 252-255. The first case is answered for you as an example.

1. Tracy Knight manages airplane maintenance for a major airline. As chief mechanic she knows which parts often need replacing and orders seals, O-rings, and gasket kits in large quantities so she will always have them on hand.

   a) Product Class: *Supplies (repair items)*

   b) Reason: *Although the engine parts are component parts when a plane is manufactured, Knight keeps these replacement parts on hand so they are supplies--just like oil and grease. They are not raw materials because they are not further processed for sale to consumers.*

2. Marketing Advantage is a marketing research company that helps clients improve their management and marketing decision making--through data collection and evaluation. The firm employs specialists in consumer, industrial, transportation, medical, and government research. It offers clients national field surveys, consumer mail panels, test marketing facilities, shopping centre interviews, group interviewing facilities, and a telephone interviewing centre--in addition to sophisticated computer and data analysis programs.

   a) Product Class:

   _____

   b) Reason:

3. Wes Lambert is the marketing manager for All-Secure, Inc., a company that makes expensive rigid camera cases and equipment like tripods for independent film production companies. He is currently planning to introduce a lightweight, flexible tripod for use with professional video cameras.

   a) Product Class:

   _____

   b) Reason:

4. Sei Nomi's company makes rechargeable power supplies for use with portable computers. The power supplies are designed to make it fast and easy for manufacturers of notebook size computers to install them as the computer is moving down an assembly line.

    a) Product Class:

    _____

    b) Reason:

5. The office staff for *Kemler's Old Car Buying Guide* are debating whether to add a computerized voice-mail system. One advocate of the idea argues that "all the other car magazines are using voice-mail to take classified ads. The customer can leave the ad--along with a credit card number--whenever it is convenient. Clearly, it's the wave of the future." Tom Kemler, who inherited the business from his grandfather has a different opinion: "These systems cost too much. And they won't bring in any more ads--they'll just encourage people to call in ads at the last minute right at our deadline."

    a) Product Class:

    _____

    b) Reason:

6. Faye Wilder runs a company that makes electronic connectors. Manufacturers use them in computers and a wide range of electronic equipment to join groups of wires to internal components. Some manufacturers contract for purchase directly with Wilder, but because these connectors must all conform to worldwide standards, they are also sold "off the shelf" by many wholesale distributors.

    a) Product Class:

    _____

    b) Reason:

7. Prestige Fruits Company buys peaches and other fruits from hundreds of small growers in Ontario. The fruits are accumulated, sorted, candied and then sold to candy companies, bakeries, and other food processing firms.

    a) Product Class:

    _____

    b) Reason:

Question for Discussion

Which types of products would most likely be associated with the following kinds of buying: (a) new-task buying, (b) straight rebuy, (c) modified rebuy? Why? Illustrate with examples from Exercise 9-2.

Exercise 9-3

Achieving brand familiarity

Introduction

In hopes of developing a strong "customer franchise," Canadian firms spend billions of dollars annually to promote brands for their products. Nevertheless, many brands are, for practical purposes, valueless because of their *nonrecognition* among potential customers. In addition, while obtaining *brand recognition* may be a significant achievement--given the many nondescript brands on the market--this level of brand familiarity does not guarantee sales for the firm. To win a favourable position in monopolistic competition, a firm may need to develop *brand preference* or even *brand insistence* for its products.

Why are some firms more successful than others in their branding efforts? The reasons are not always clear. Unfortunately, brand loyalty, like many aspects of buying behaviour, remains a rather mysterious phenomenon. In general, a firm probably must produce a good product and continually promote it, but this alone may not ensure a high level of brand familiarity--particularly if the firm does not direct its efforts toward some specific target market.

This exercise gets at some important problems in branding--such as conditions favourable to branding--and the difficulty of achieving brand familiarity for certain types of products. As you do the exercise, you may begin to wonder if brands are really relevant for some product classes. You may also wish to speculate about how much effort is spent promoting brands to consumers who have no use for the product in question--or for whom brand names are meaningless.

Assignment

1.   List from *memory* (DO NOT DO ANY "RESEARCH") up to five brand names for each of the following product types. List the first brands that come to mind. If you cannot think of *any* brands for a particular product type, write "none" in the Brand 1 column.

Product	Brand 1	Brand 2	Brand 3	Brand 4	Brand 5
Bottled Water					
Frozen Yogurt					
Automobiles					
Soft Drinks					
Jeans					
Cellular phones					

2.	What level of brand familiarity do you think exists among the majority of consumers for each of the following products?

Product Types		Level of Brand Familiarity
a)	Bottled Water:	_____
b)	Frozen Yogurt:	_____
c)	Automobiles:	_____
d)	Soft drinks:	_____
e)	Jeans:	_____
f)	Cellular phones:	_____

3.	From the product types listed in Questions 1 and 2, indicate for which one branding would be *most appropriate* and explain what conditions make branding so favourable for that product type.

Product type: _____

Conditions:

4.	From the product types listed in Questions 1 and 2, indicate for which one branding would be *least appropriate* and explain what conditions make branding so unfavourable for that product type.

Product type: _____

Conditions:

Question for Discussion

Why would a firm want to "license" the use of another firm's brand name?

Exercise 9-4

Comparing branded product offerings

Introduction

Most manufacturers of consumer products use *manufacturer brands* (often called "national brands") to try to develop a loyal group of customers for their products. At the same time, more and more wholesalers and retailers are offering consumers *dealer brands* (sometimes called "private brands") to try to develop channel and store loyalty. As a result, millions of dollars are spent each year for promotion in a "battle of the brands."

The "battle of the brands" takes many forms--and attitudes toward brands vary a lot both among consumers and marketers. Some retailers tend to stock mainly manufacturer brands. Meanwhile, some manufacturers--particularly in the shoe industry--have opened up their own retail outlets to promote their own brands.

To add to the "battle of the brands," some food retailers also carry *generic products*--unbranded products in plain packages (or unpackaged!)--to appeal to price-conscious consumers. This gives consumers even more products to choose from--but may make it more difficult and confusing to determine the "best buy."
This exercise is designed to give you additional insight into the "battle of the brands." You are asked to make price comparisons between manufacturer brands and dealer brands--and then decide which is the "better buy."

Assignment

1.   Visit a large chain supermarket and record the prices of the items listed on the next page. For each item, select one manufacturer brand and one dealer brand. Record the name of the manufacturer brand and then its price. If no dealer brand is available, write the price of the generic product in the dealer column. If the store carries neither a dealer brand nor a generic product, write the price of the manufacturer brand in that column also. Completely fill in all columns so that you can compare the totals.

2.   Which do you think is the "better buy"--manufacturer brands or dealer brands? Why? What factors did you take into consideration in deciding that is the better buy?

PRICE COMPARISON CHART			
Store Visited:		Date:	
Item/Size	Name of Manufacturer Brand	Price of Manufacturer brand	Price of Dealer Brand
Spaghetti Sauce/26 oz.			
Ketchup/24 oz.			
Mayonnaise/32 oz.			
Chick. Noodle Soup/10.75 oz.			
Ground Coffee/34.5 oz.			
Coffee Creamer/22 oz.			
Peanut Butter/18 oz.			
Toasted Oats Cereal/15 oz.			
Sliced Peaches, can/15 oz.			
Sweet Corn, can/15.25 oz.			
Stuffing Mix/6 oz.			
Bacon, Sliced/16 oz.			
Popcorn, Microwave/10.5 oz.			
Fudge Brownie Mix/20 oz.			
Sugar/5 lb.			
Vegetable Oil/48 oz.			
Orange Juice/64 oz.			
Milk/1 gal.			
Cola/2 litre			
Dog Food/37.5 lb.			
Paper Towels/Big Roll			
Aluminum Foil/75 sq. ft.			
Plastic Sandwich Bags/100 ct.			
Bathroom Tissue/4-pack			
Trash Bags, kitchen/20 count			
Shampoo+Conditioner/13.5 oz.			
Liquid Bleach/96 oz.			
Liquid Antiacid/8 oz.			

Question for Discussion

Why would a manufacturer be willing to produce dealer brands for a supermarket if it already is producing and advertising a similar product with its own brand name?

Exercise 9-5

Branding decision

This exercise is based on computer-aided problem number 9--Branding Decision. A complete description of the problem appears on page 271 of Wong/Shapiro, 11th edition.

1. After some thought, Wholesteen's marketing manager has concluded that there might be a side effect of the FoodWorld proposal which she had not considered earlier. Specifically, she had not planned to reduce her promotion spending if she accepted the FoodWorld proposal. Yet, FoodWorld would be doing some of its own promotion for the FoodWorld brand. As a result, Wholesteen could reallocate some of its promotion money to attract new customers in areas where it had not been doing promotion. She is interested in evaluating this idea more closely, and would like to know how much sales (in cases) of the Wholesteen brand would have to increase (beyond the 90,000 cases she was expecting from the proposed arrangement) to make the same profit the firm makes at present. (Hint: use the What If analysis to vary the total number of cases of the Wholesteen brand in the right hand column and display the total profit for the current situation and the proposed situation. Repeat the process with new minimum and maximum quantity values until you find a quantity that produces about the same profit.)

    Total Profit earned under current arrangement   _____

    Number of cases to make about the same Profit   _____

    Less, number of cases expected under current proposal   90,000

    Equals, increase in number of cases needed   _____

    Explanation:

    _____

    _____

    _____

2. Even if Wholesteen were able to attract some new customers, the marketing manager knows that it might take awhile. In the meantime, she is worried about profits. One idea she has is to make a counterproposal of her own. She is thinking about accepting the proposal if FoodWorld is willing to pay a higher price for the cases produced under the FoodWorld brand. She would like to set a price for those cases so that her firm's total profits would stay about the same as now. What price per case for the FoodWorld brand would result in about the same profits as at present? (Hint: use the "What If" analysis to vary the price per case for the FoodWorld brand and display the total profit for the current situation and the proposed situation. Repeat the process with new minimum and maximum price values until you find a price that produces about the same profit.)

Target price for FoodWorld brand per case _____

List some factors that will affect whether FoodWorld might agree or disagree with this price:

_____

_____

_____

_____

_____

Chapter 10

Product Management and New-Product development

Chapter Summary

- **Understand how product life cycles affect strategic planning.**
  There are four main stages to a product's life cycle. Managers face a different set of conditions and must make different decisions at each stage. *Market introduction* is a period of low sales volume when the product is first introduced. Promotion is necessary to increase awareness of the benefits and uses of this new product offering. Next is the period called *market growth*, which is a time of fast sales growth and rising industry profits. As competitors enter the market with similar products, profits begin to level out and than start to decrease. Many firms fail at this stage because they fail to properly consider the changes in the competitive environment. During the *market maturity* stage, industry sales level off and competition increases. Profit continues to decline as promotional activities are increased and prices are cut. The final stage is *sales decline*, where new products replace the old ones. Price competition increases, though firms with strong brands may be profitable to the very end.

- **Know what is involved in designing new products and what "new products" really are.**
  A new product is one that is new in any way for the company concerned. A fresh idea can be turned into a new product, or a change to an existing product can also make the product new. Because of strong competition it is necessary for a firm to continually develop new products, otherwise its existing products will earn less and less. In the end, the company will go out of business.

- **Understand the new-product development process.**
  Many firms follow an organized new-product development process in an attempt to avoid expensive product failures. One such process involves five steps: (1) idea generation, (2) screening, (3) idea evaluation, (4) development of product and marketing mix, and (5) commercialization.

- **See why product liability must be considered in screening new products.**
  Producers may be held responsible for injuries related to their products, no matter how the items are used or how well they are designed. Sellers are legally liable to pay damages to individuals who are injured by defective or unsafe products. These damages could exceed the company's insurance coverage, or even the assets of the firm. Marketing managers must be sure that their products are safe for use by the public.

- **Understand the need for product and brand managers.**
  Product managers, or brand managers who are in charge of a single product or brand make sure that that attention on these products/brands is not forgotten in the everyday rush of business. They can also manage the new-product development process. However, in some

cases a product champion is often given the responsibility for managing the activities associated with a product's development.

Important Terms

product life cycle, p. 275
market growth, p. 276
market introduction, p. 276
market maturity, p. 277
sales decline, p. 277
fashion, p. 287

fad, p. 288
new product, p. 289
concept testing, p. 294
product liability, p. 293
product (brand) managers, p. 299

True-False Questions

_____ 1.   The product life cycle is divided into four major stages: market introduction, market growth, market maturity, and market saturation.

_____ 2.   A firm's marketing mix usually must change--and different target markets may be appealed to--as a product moves through the different stages of its life cycle.

_____ 3.   Industry sales and profits tend to rise and fall together as a product moves through its life cycle.

_____ 4.   The market introduction stage is usually extremely profitable due to the lack of competitors.

_____ 5.   Industry profits tend to reach their peak and start to decline during the market growth stage--even though industry sales may be growing rapidly.

_____ 6.   Industry profits decline throughout the market maturity stage because aggressive competition leads to price cutting and increased expenditures on persuasive promotion.

_____ 7.   During the sales decline stage, new products replace the old--and all firms remaining in the industry find themselves operating at a loss.

_____ 8.   In general, product life cycles appear to be getting longer due to a decline in product innovation.

_____ 9.   A fashion is the currently accepted or popular style.

_____ 10.   A fad is an idea that is fashionable only to certain groups who are enthusiastic about it--but these groups are so fickle that a fad is even more short-lived than a regular fashion.

_____ 11.   Once a firm introduces a product to a market, it has no other choice but to watch its product move through the remaining stages of the product life cycle.

____ 12. Strategy planning can sometimes extend product life cycles, delaying the move from market maturity to sales decline.

____ 13. The same product may be in different life cycle stages in different markets.

____ 14. While a lot of strategy planning is necessary to introduce a new product, no strategy is required to get rid of a dying product.

____ 15. According to the text, a new product is one that is new in any way for the company concerned.

____ 16. Twelve months is the longest time that any product may be called "new" according to the Industry Canada.

____ 17. Since new products are vital to the survival of most firms, the objective of the new-product development process should be to approve as many new-product ideas as possible.

____ 18. Product planners should consider long-term welfare in addition to immediate satisfaction--and therefore should offer "pleasing products" instead of "desirable products."

____ 19. The Hazardous Products Act gives Industry Canada the right to either ban or regulate the sale of potentially dangerous products.

____ 20. Product liability means the legal obligation of sellers to pay damages to individuals who are injured by defective or unsafe products.

____ 21. Concept testing is done before any tangible product has been developed--and involves marketing research to determine potential customers' attitudes towards the new-product idea.

____ 22. The development step (in new-product development) involves the testing of physical products as well as test marketing--something that must be done for all products before commercialization.

____ 23. The specific organization arrangement for new-product development may not be too important--as long as there is top-level support.

____ 24. Product managers sometimes have profit responsibilities and much power, but often they are "product champions" who are mainly involved in planning and getting promotion done.

Answers to True-False Questions

1. F, p. 275	9. T, p. 287	17. F, p. 289
2. T, p. 275	10. T, p. 288	18. F, p. 293
3. F, p. 276	11. F, p. 288	19. T, p. 293

4. F, p. 276
5. T, p. 276
6. T, p. 277
7. F, p. 277
8. F, p. 287

12. T, p. 286
13. T, p. 285
14. F, p. 284-285
15. T, p. 289
16. T, p. 289

20. T, p. 293
21. T, p. 294
22. F, p. 294
23. T, p. 297
24. T, p. 297-298

Multiple-Choice Questions (Circle the correct response)

1. The product life cycle has four stages. Which of the following is *not* one of these?
    a. Market introduction
    b. Market growth
    c. Market maturity
    d. Economic competition
    e. Sales decline

2. During the *market introduction* stage of the product life cycle:
    a. considerable money is spent on promotion while place development is left until later stages.
    b. products usually show large profits if marketers have successfully carved out new markets.
    c. most potential customers are quite anxious to try out the new-product concept.
    d. funds are being invested in marketing with the expectation of *future* profits.
    e. product and promotion are more important than place and price.

3. Which of the following statements regarding the *market growth* stage of the product life cycle is *false*?
    a. Innovators still earn profits--but this stage is less profitable for them than the previous stage.
    b. This is the time of peak profitability for the industry.
    c. Many competitors enter the market resulting in much product variety.
    d. The sales of the total industry are rising fairly rapidly as more and more customers buy.
    e. Monopolistic competition is common during this stage.

4. Regarding product life cycles, good marketing managers know that:
    a. all competitors lose money during the sales decline stage.
    b. they are getting longer.
    c. industry sales reach their maximum during the market growth stage.
    d. firms earn their biggest profits during the market introduction stage.
    e. industry profits reach their maximum during the market growth stage.

5. A particular industry is experiencing no real sales growth and declining profits in the face of oligopolistic competition. Demand has become quite elastic--as consumers see competing products as almost homogeneous. Several firms have dropped out of the industry, and there has been only one recent new entry. Firms in the industry are attempting to avoid price-cutting by budgeting huge amounts for persuasive advertising. In which stage of the product life cycle are firms in this industry competing?
    a. Market maturity
    b. Sales decline
    c. Market growth
    d. Market introduction
    e. Product renewal

6. Marketing managers should recognize that:
    a. product life cycles appear to be getting longer.
    b. every segment within a market has the same product life cycle.

c.	the product life cycle describes the sales and profits of individual products, not industry sales and profits.
d.	firms that enter mature markets have to compete with established firms for declining industry profits.
e.	None of the above is a true statement.

7.	In planning for different stages of the product life cycle, strategy planners must be aware that:
a.	losses can be expected during the market introduction stage.
b.	the life cycles of mature product-markets can be extended through strategic product adjustments.
c.	offering the product to a new market segment may start a whole new life cycle.
d.	products can be withdrawn from the market before the sales decline stage--but even here a phase-out strategy is usually required.
e.	All of the above are true statements.

8.	Which of the following statements about "new products" is *false?*
a.	In order for it to be considered new, there should be a functionally significant change in the product--according to Industry Canada.
b.	A product should be considered "new" by a particular firm if it is new in any way for that company.
c.	Industry Canada considers six months as the maximum time that a product should be called "new."
d.	it must be entirely new or changed in a "functionally significant or substantial respect.", according to Industry Canada.
e.	A product should be considered "new" by a firm if it is aimed at new markets.

9.	Regarding the new-product development process,
a.	screening criteria should be mainly quantitative--because qualitative criteria require too much judgment.
b.	concept testing tries to see how the new product works in the hands of potential customers.
c.	it tries to "kill" new ideas that are not likely to be profitable.
d.	market tests should be conducted for all new product ideas before commercialization.
e.	All of the above are true.

10.	Which of the following types of products provides low immediate satisfaction but high long-run consumer welfare?
a.	Salutary products
b.	Pleasing products
c.	Desirable products
d.	Deficient products
e.	Generic products

11.	The Industry Canada under the Hazardous Products Act can:
a.	order costly repairs of "unsafe products."
b.	back up its orders with fines.
c.	order returns of "unsafe products."
d.	back up its orders with jail sentences.
e.	ban the sale of unsafe products.

12. Product or brand managers are commonly used when a firm:
   a. has several different kinds of products or brands.
   b. wants to eliminate the job of the advertising manager.
   c. has one or a few products--all of which are important to its success.
   d. wants to eliminate the job of sales manager.
   e. wants one person to have authority over all the functional areas that affect the profitability of a particular product.

Answers to Multiple-Choice Questions

1. d, p. 275
2. d, p. 276
3. a, p. 276-277
4. e, p. 277-288

5. a, p. 277
6. d, p. 285-288
7. e, p. 285-288
8. d, p. 289

9. c, p. 292
10. a, p. 291-92
11. e, p. 293
12. a, p. 299

Additional Questions to Test Your Understanding (Fill in the Blanks)

1. Match the following terms with their correct definition listed below.

Market maturity   Concept testing   Fashion
Product liability   Product Managers   Market introduction

a. _____ - The current accepted or popular style.

b. _____ - Managers of specific products

c. _____ - the legal obligation of sellers to pay damages to individuals who are hurt by defective or unsafe products.

d. _____ - when sales are usually low during the period when a new idea is introduced to the market.

e. _____ - getting reactions from customers as to how well a new product idea fits their needs.

f. _____ - industry sales are leveling off

2. List the five steps of the new-product development process.

a. _____

b. _____

c. _____

d. _____

e. _____

3. Briefly explain why pioneers might encourage competitors to enter a market.

_____

_____

_____

_____

Answers to Additional Questions

1.
   a. Fashion, p. 287
   b. Product managers, p. 299
   c. Product liability, p. 293
   d. Market introduction, p. 276
   e. Concept testing, p. 294

      f.   Market maturity, p. 277

2.
      a. Idea generation
      b. Screening
      c. Idea evaluation
      d. Development
      e. Commercialization

All can be found in Exhibit 10-4 on page 291.

3.   Sometimes building customer interest in a new product idea is simply too big for one company. More than one company investing in promotion to build demand may stimulate the growth of the entire product market.

Exercise 10-1

Identifying a product's stage in the product life cycle

Introduction

This exercise is designed to improve your understanding of the product life cycle--a valuable model for marketing strategy planning. For example, the product life cycle can help decide if and when it will be to a company's advantage to add, change, or drop a given product. Further, where a product is along its life cycle suggests a workable blend of the "four Ps."

Assignment

Read the following five cases carefully and for each one:

a)   Decide which stage of the product life cycle best describes the situation in the case--considering the relevant product-market.

b)   Briefly explain your answer, including such factors as profitability, number of competitors, place, promotion, and pricing.

1.   Yanni Karish, legendary founder of Enlightened Computer Company, has announced that his computer company will no longer manufacture computer hardware. Instead, the company will focus its effort on developing high performance, *graphically-oriented software* for use in navigating the Internet and searching for information on the World Wide Web. Some experts applaud Karish's decision to focus on software for the World Wide Web, which takes advantage of the explosive growth of interest in the Internet and the revolution it is prompting in computing. However, Netware, Novell, Microsoft, IBM, and other firms that helped create the market for network software already have a formidable head start.

a)   Stage of product life cycle:

_____

b)   Explanation:

_____

_____

_____

2. Opti Lenses Corporation has announced that it will no longer produce *hard contact lenses.* A spokesman for the company said that the firm's share of the market for hard contact lenses had grown in each of the last 5 years, but that the overall market was shrinking as more consumers were switching to other alternatives--including disposable contacts, gas permeable lenses, and even surgical procedures such as radial keratomy. Opti Lenses' management has indicated that its decision was motivated by the need to pursue more profitable opportunities. The firm's sales manager also said that the decision was hastened by the fact that several other firms serving this market had begun to focus on "ill-conceived price promotions" that were eroding what profit might be possible from serving those consumers who still prefer the old-style hard lenses.

    a)   Stage of product life cycle:

    _____

    b)   Explanation:

    _____

    _____

    _____

3. Technics Stereo Systems is just entering the fast-growing, but increasingly competitive market for "home theatre" sound systems. Like other available systems, the Technics line creates excellent "surround sound" that is like what you hear in a movie theatre. The Technics marketing manager is confident that he can capture a profitable share of the market because his firm's system has an integrated control unit that automatically coordinates the settings for various components--say, the TV, the stereo system, a cable box, and a VCR--even if they are from different manufacturers. All the user has to do is press the "on" button on the remote control and set the volume. Well-known competitors like Pioneer and Sony still do not have anything to match the ease-of-use of the Technics model. In addition, to attract support from traditional retailers of home electronics products, Technics is offering a very low wholesale price. Even at the very low suggested retail price, this will make the Technics receiver very profitable for the retailers. Technics' marketing manager says that this very aggressive pricing will pay off. He predicts that in the next decade home theatre systems will replace standard stereo receiver systems--and that already prices of the surround sound systems are dropping rapidly. He says that this will stimulate even faster growth in the home theatre market.

    a)   Stage of product life cycle:

    _____

    b)   Explanation:

    _____

    _____

    _____

4.   Personal Edge, Inc., one of the nation's largest producers of personal care products, has just announced plans to sell a new shampoo called Herbal Plus. The company is spending heavily on magazine and TV ads that will promote Herbal Plus as "The shampoo that everyone can use daily. No other shampoo is as gentle on your hair or provides as clean and natural a scent." Free samples of Herbal Plus will be attached to packages of other Personal Edge products, and magazine ads will include cents-off coupons. Despite intense competition, Personal Edge expects its new product to capture a 5 percent share of the slowly growing shampoo market.

   a)   Stage of product life cycle:

   _____

   b)   Explanation:

   _____

   _____

   _____

5.   One of the largest food manufacturers is testing a new product for the large soft-drink market--a patented paper cup coated with a secret formula. All the consumer has to do is add water and it becomes a carbonated beverage! It is no longer necessary to carry home six-packs or eight-packs. There are no empty bottles or cans to return, and less storage space is needed. The product can also be distributed through normal wholesale channels rather than requiring the special distribution networks now used by the bottling industry. Therefore, the product offers economy as well as convenience.

   a)   Stage of product life cycle:

   _____

   b)   Explanation:

   _____

   _____

   _____

Question for Discussion

What alternatives should a firm consider when it finds some or all of its products in the market maturity stage of the product life cycle?

Exercise 10-2

New-product development process

Introduction

The product life cycle shows us that markets and competition are dynamic. Over time old products are replaced with new ones. And as markets mature, firms usually face increasing price competition and erosion of their profit margins. To succeed in spite of these pressures, firms must constantly look for new market opportunities--and that often means identifying and developing new product ideas--and effective strategies to go with them.

While the new-product development process is crucial to the survival and success of most firms, it is also a challenge. Even the best-run companies sometimes "miss" opportunities that--after the fact--seem obvious. And too often companies go ahead and introduce new products that turn out to be costly failures. Marketing managers can increase the odds of success in this area by really understanding the steps of the new-product development process--and what it takes to generate and screen new-product ideas.

This exercise is intended to help develop your skills in this area.

Assignment

The short descriptions that follow provide information about different companies. In each case, there is at least one major problem with the way the company is currently approaching the new-product development process. Read and evaluate each statement carefully, and then explain:

a)   your diagnosis of the problem, and

b)   your recommendation for what the company should do as a substitute for what is described in the case situation.

1. Caliber Cycles, Inc. has been successful producing and marketing high performance motorcycles. In searching for new product opportunities, the company became interested in small size, three wheel all-terrain vehicles (ATVs) designed for children in the 10- to 15-year age group. The head design engineer for the company thought that the company's expertise in designing motorcycles would apply directly to this popular new product. In addition, many of the dealers who carry the firm's motorcycles are interested in the idea. However, one of them noted that there have been many accidents involving three-wheel ATVs--and suggested that the company check into product liability insurance. When this was discussed back at the firm, the engineer said that he did not see a big problem. "After all," he said, "our ATVs will be as safe as others that are available. And in addition the accidents that occur are invariably the fault of the user. We can't be held responsible for user-errors if the product is properly designed and manufactured."

   a) the problem:

   b) your recommendation:

2. Aiwa, Inc. produces and sells special types of wire used in a variety of telecommunication applications. The firm's initial growth came from sales of a new wire that was used by cellular telephone service companies when setting up transmission stations. However, growth in that market has slowed. Moreover, at present, most of the other products offered by the firm are similar to those available from a variety of other suppliers. Jennifer Lopez, the marketing manager for the company, recently scheduled a meeting with the company president to discuss problems of falling profits. Jennifer expressed concern that the company did not have a specific person responsible for identifying new products. The president pointed out that few other firms in their industry had such a position--and generally argued that new-product thinking was the responsibility of everyone in the firm. After further discussion, the president agreed to let Lopez send out a memo to all company employees encouraging them to be alert to new product ideas--and to submit any ideas to the research and development department for analysis of their technical feasibility.

   a) the problem:

   b) your recommendation:

3.   Pinnacle Drug Company has developed a promising new nonprescription tablet to relieve the symptoms of allergy sufferers. The idea has successfully passed the screening and idea evaluation stages of the company's new-product development process. The company has also completed concept tests and produced some tablets. Now, the head of the new-product development group has sent the following memo to the marketing department. "Our laboratory tests have satisfied the Food and Drug Administration criteria and we are ready to move ahead with a final test market prior to commercialization. I want you to start thinking about this now. If the product does well in the test market, we will need to develop the rest of the marketing mix. We will want to come up with an attention-getting package design--one that will really stand out on a drugstore shelf. We will also need to decide on the brand name we would use in a national distribution. For now, we will just price the product in test market at the same price as our cold tablets. So final pricing decisions will also need to be made. And, of course, we will need to decide what type of promotion to use--and what message we want to get across to potential customers. I wanted to alert you to these exciting developments so that you could be getting your ideas together. We want to be ready to move quickly into commercialization if the test market is successful."

a)   the problem:

b)   your recommendation:

4.   Qualtex Medical Supplies Corporation produces a variety of sterile storage containers used in hospital operating rooms. Recently, large companies like Johnson & Johnson have been aggressive in this market, and they seem to have had better success in identifying new-product opportunities. The sales manager at the company recently sent a memo to the firm's salespeople outlining problems related to the firm's weak financial position. He ended the memo with a plea: "To increase our profits in coming years, we must move ahead aggressively with new-product ideas. The president of the company fully backs this thrust. He has established a new-product screening committee with members from different departments of the firm. You are in contact with the customer--and we need for you to submit your ideas. We promise to carry forward with marketing research on every good idea that comes in. Our objective is to really get behind your ideas--and turn them into products."

a)   the problem:

b)   your recommendation:

Question for Discussion

The text emphasizes that many of the new products that are developed and introduced prove to be expensive failures. Who pays the cost of these failures? Is it just the owners of the companies that introduced them?

Exercise 10-3

Grown stage competition

This exercise is based on computer-aided problem number 10--Growth Stage Competition. A complete description of the problem appears on page 302 of Wong/Shapiro, 11th edition.

1.   As competition increases over time, AgriChem is likely to get a reduced share of the market. However, at the same time, the overall market will be growing. What market share, unit sales, and profit is AgriChem's marketing managers expecting in the current year and each of the next five years-- assuming that the overall market grows at a rate of 200,000 units a year? What will AgriChem's long run profit be (that is, the sum of the profit for the current year and profits for each of the next five years)?

Year	Share (percent)	Unit Sales	Profit
0	_____	_____	_____
1	_____	_____	_____
2	_____	_____	_____
3	_____	_____	_____
4	_____	_____	_____
5	_____	_____	_____

Long Run (Total) Profit _____

2.   AgriChem's marketing manager knows that competitors will force prices down over time, and he expects to lose market share as competitors enter the market. However, he also thinks that lower prices will stimulate demand and contribute to growth in the market. In fact, he is thinking about cutting his price to $12.50 now--to try to spur more growth in market demand while he still has a larger share. He thinks that if he cuts his price to $12.50 this year that the annual growth in sales might increase to 280,000 units a year for the current year and each of the next five years. However, a price cut now would probably also drive prices down even faster during the next five years. He wants to evaluate the effect of this potential price change on AgriChem's expected long-run profits. Complete the table on the next page to evaluate this situation. (Hint: set the current price on the spreadsheet to $12.50, and set expected unit growth each year to 280,000. Then use the What If analysis to vary years in the future from a minimum of 0 to a maximum of 5 and display AgriChem's price for each year, its unit sales, and its profit.)

Year	Price	Unit Sales	Profit
0	$12.50	_____	_____
1	_____	_____	_____
2	_____	_____	_____
3	_____	_____	_____
4	_____	_____	_____
5	_____	_____	_____

Long Run (Total) Profit _____

3. How do profits for the current year and the first year in the future compare for the two different pricing/growth situations?

_____

_____

_____

_____

4. How do long-run profits (say, for the current year and next five years) compare for the two different pricing/growth situations?

_____

_____

_____

_____

5. Drawing on your analysis, discuss why it is important for a marketing manager to try to anticipate how the market will change over the product life cycle.

_____

_____

_____

_____

Chapter 11

Place: Channel Systems and Physical Distribution

Chapter Summary

- **Understand what product classes suggest about place objectives.**
  Different consumer and business product classes need different marketing mix considerations, and in particular the amount of market exposure in a given geographic area. Product classes can be an effective means to determine place objectives. These decisions must consider that different market segments may classify the same product in different ways. However, since people in the same target market will have similar attitudes, knowing how to classify the product can help choose the right balance of place objectives.

- **Understand why some firms use direct channel systems while others rely on intermediaries and indirect systems.**
  A firm may choose direct distribution to maintain control of the entire marketing job. They may be able to serve the target customers at a lower price or work more effectively than intermediaries. Some firms prefer the direct contact with customers they achieve through handling their own distribution channels. Indirect channels may be best if it is not possible to sell to target customers in other ways. Geographic restrictions may also force a manufacturer to sell through wholesalers. Intermediaries already have expensive infrastructure in place, and may thus be cheaper than establishing direct channels.

- **Understand how and why marketing specialists develop to make channel systems more effective.**
  Through specialization and/or economies of scale, marketing intermediaries and facilitators are often able to perform the marketing functions better – and at a lower cost – than producers or consumers can. Discrepancies in quantity and assortment develop a need for different types of specialists. Specialists can be more efficient because they are closer to the customer and can easily relay information back to the supplier.

- **Understand how to develop cooperative relationships and avoid conflict in channel systems.**
  A channel captain is useful for directing the activities of the entire channel and tries to avoid, or solve, channel conflicts. The best way to avoid conflict is to get everyone in the channel focused on a common product-market and on the common objective of satisfying the end customer.

- **Know how channel members in vertical marketing systems shift and share functions to meet customer needs.**
  Vertical channel systems are focused on a specific target market. They may be corporate owned, administered, or contractual in nature. Each offers a different level of co-operation among channel members and a different basis of control. The combination of common

product-market focus and formal systems and agreements helps to minimize channel conflict.

- **Understand the difference between intensive, selective, and exclusive distribution.**
  Intensive distribution involves selling the product through all responsible and suitable wholesalers or retailers who will stock the product. Selective distribution involves selling the product through only those intermediaries who will give the product special attention. Exclusive distribution limits the sale of the product to a single intermediary within a particular geographic area.

- **Understand the physical distribution concept and how it affects decisions about customer service levels, costs, and the use of new technology.**
  The physical distribution concept reflects a belief that all transporting, storing, and product-handling activities of a business and a whole channel system should be coordinated as one system that seeks to minimize the cost of distribution for a given customer service level. Firms must harmonize their efforts to determine what levels of service to provide to best meet the needs of the customers at the end of the channel, and how to do so at the lowest cost.

  Information management and the ability to coordinate activities across several firms and levels in the distribution channel is key to PD. The use of computer technology and the applications it enables, such as EDI and supply chain management, are constantly changing the face of PD.

Important Terms

channels of distribution, p. 307
place, p. 307
accumulating, p. 309
discrepancy of assortment, p. 309
regrouping activities, p. 309
discrepancy of quantity, p. 309
assorting, p. 310
bulk-breaking, p. 310
sorting, p. 310
universal functions of marketing, p. 310
facilitators, p. 312
intermediary, p. 312
coverage, p. 313
distribution cost, p. 313
promotional intensity, p. 313
direct marketing, p. 316
traditional channel systems, p. 318
channel captain, p. 320

corporate channel systems, p. 324
vertical integration, p. 324
vertical marketing systems, p. 324
administered channel systems, p. 326
contractual channel systems, p. 326
ideal market exposure, p. 326
exclusive distribution, p. 327
intensive distribution, p. 327
selective distribution, p. 327
dual distribution, p. 330
refusal to supply, p. 330
logistics/physical distribution (PD), p. 332
reverse channels, p. 332
customer service level, p. 333
supply chains, p. 335
total-cost approach, p. 335
electronic data interchange (EDI), p. 336

True-False Questions

____ 1. The Place part of the marketing mix is concerned with building channels of distribution and providing the time, place, and possession utilities needed to satisfy target customers.

____ 2. A channel of distribution is any series of firms or individuals who participate in the flow of goods and services from producer to final user or consumer.

____ 3. Product classes help solve Place problems and in particular how much market exposure will be needed in each geographic area.

____ 4. A marketing manager's decisions on Place have long-range effects and are usually harder to change than Product, Price, and Promotion decisions.

____ 5. Although seldom used, direct-to-user channels are usually better than channels that use middlemen.

____ 6. The Internet makes it easier for firms to have direct access to customers.

____ 7. Most consumer products are sold through middlemen.

____ 8. There is no difference between *direct distribution* and *direct marketing.*

____ 9. A direct instead of indirect channel is probably a better choice for a producer with limited financial resources.

____ 10. Discrepancies of quantity exist because producers specialize in making one or a few items—while customers want many items and probably prefer not to shop at different stores for each item.

____ 11. Because few customers can consume a big part of any producer's output, the large quantities that mass production makes possible generally cause a discrepancy of assortment.

____ 12. Collecting larger quantities of similar products, the accumulating process, creates a discrepancy of quantity but permits economies of scale.

____ 13. Bulk-breaking involves dividing larger quantities into smaller quantities as products get closer to the final market.

____ 14. The sorting process is usually handled by middlemen--when they put together a variety of products to give a target market what it wants.

____ 15. The assorting process means sorting products into the grades and qualities desired by different target markets.

____ 16. Marketing specialists should develop to adjust discrepancies of quantity and assortment only if these discrepancies must be adjusted.

____ 17. A channel system can work well only if its members have accepted a common product-market commitment and are all strongly market-oriented.

____ 18. In a traditional channe1 system the various channel members make little or no effort to cooperate with each other.

____ 19. Clearly, a producer should always act as "channel captain"--because he is in the best position to help direct the channel as an integrated system of action.

____ 20. Vertical marketing systems are channel systems in which the whole channe1 focuses on the same target market at the end of the channel.

____ 21. Corporate channel systems involve corporate ownership all along the channel.

____ 22. In regard to the development of the channel system, vertical integration means acquiring firms, which operate at different levels of channel activity.

____ 23. Any administered channel system--by definition--is also a contractual channel system.

____ 24. Because of the importance of Place in a firm's marketing mix, marketing managers should always seek maximum market exposure for their products.

____ 25. Ideal market exposure makes a product widely enough available to satisfy the target customers' needs--but not exceed them.

____ 26. An intensive distribution policy refers to the marketing manager's desire to sell through all responsible and suitable wholesalers and retailers.

____ 27. Since it is not necessary to obtain 100 percent coverage of a market to justify or support national advertising, some firms now using intensive distribution might be wise to switch to selective distribution and use only the better middlemen to distribute and promote their products.

____ 28. Exclusive distribution is likely to be used by a producer--to help control prices and the service offered in a channel.

____ 29. Exclusive distribution is illegal in Canada.

____ 30. Dual distribution occurs when a manufacturer uses several competing channels to reach the same target market--perhaps using several middlemen in addition to selling directly itself.

____ 31. Reverse channels are used to retrieve products that customers no longer want.

____ 32. According to the physical distribution concept, a firm might lower its total cost of physical distribution by selecting a higher cost transportation alternative.

____ 33. The total cost approach to PD involves evaluating each possible PD system— and identifying all of the costs of each alternative.

___ 34. Electronic data interchange sets a standard for communication between different firms' computer systems.

___ 35. A higher physical distribution service level may mean both higher costs and higher profits.

___ 36. Logistics—that is the transporting, storing, and handling of goods within individual firms and along channel systems—accounts for half the cost of marketing.

___ 37. Customer service level is a measure of how rapidly and dependably a firm can deliver what customers want.

___ 38. Marketing managers should be careful to avoid offering customers a level of physical distribution service that might increase storing or transporting costs.

___ 39. According to the physical distribution concept, a firm might lower its total cost of physical distribution by selecting a higher cost transportation alternative.

___ 40. Improved order processing can sometimes have the same effect on customer service levels as faster, more expensive transportation.

Answers to True-False Questions

1. T, p. 307	15. F, p. 310	29. F, p. 329
2. T, p. 307	16. T, p. 310	30. T, p. 330
3. T, p. 314	17. F, p. 318	31. T, p. 332
4. T, p. 314	18. T, p. 318	32. T p. 332
5. F, p. 315	19. F, p. 320	33. T, p. 333
6. T, p. 315	20. T, p. 324	34. T, p. 336
7. T, p. 316	21. T, p. 324	35. T, p. 333
8. F, p. 316	22. T, p. 324	36. T, p. 332
9. F, p. 317	23. F, p. 326	37. T, p. 336
10. F, p. 309	24. F, p. 326	38. F, p. 336
11. F, p. 309	25. T, p. 326	39. T, p. 332-334
12. T, p. 309	26. T, p. 327	40. T, p. 332-334
13. T, p. 310	27. T, p. 327	
14. F, p. 310	28. T, p. 327	

Multiple-Choice Questions (Circle the correct response)

1. A channel of distribution:
    a.   is any series of firms or individuals who participate in the flow of goods and services from producer to final user or consumer.
    b.   must include a middleman.
    c.   must have at least three-members--a manufacturer, a wholesaler, and a retailer.
    d.   All of the above are true statements.
    e.   None of the above is a true statement.

2. The "Place" variable deals with the creation of:
    a.   time and place utilities only.
    b.   time, place, possession, and form utilities.
    c.   time utility only.
    d.   time, place, and possession utilities.
    e.   place and possession utilities only.

3. Marketing specialists develop to adjust "discrepancies" in the marketplace. Which of the following best explains the concept of "discrepancies"?
    a.   There are many more consumers than there are producers.
    b.   The assortment and quantity of products wanted by a customer may be different than the assortment and quantity of products normally produced by a manufacturer.
    c.   Supply and demand is no longer determined by market forces because "big business" is more powerful than the individual consumer.
    d.   Price is not always a reliable measure of a product's quality.
    e.   Although most manufacturers claim to be marketing-oriented, most firms would rather produce what they want to sell rather than what customers want to buy.

4. Discrepancies of quantity occur because:
    a.   some consumers have more money than others.
    b.   individual producers tend to specialize while individual consumers want a broad assortment of products.
    c.   consumers demand more product variety than producers can make.
    d.   to obtain economies of scale, individual producers often make larger quantities of products than individual consumers normally want to buy.
    e.   there are many more consumers than producers.

5. If you were a retailer attempting to supply a wide variety of products for the convenience of your customers, which of the following "regrouping activities" would you be *most* involved in?
    a.   Sorting
    b.   Accumulating
    c.   Bulk-breaking
    d.   Assorting
    e.   Breaking bulk

6. When a channel has a "product-market commitment":
    a.   all members focus on the same target market at the end of the channel.
    b.   its members attempt to share the various marketing functions in appropriate ways.

c.   there is no need for a channel captain to develop.

d.   all of the above.

e.   a and b above--but not c.

7.   In "traditional channel systems"

     a.   the producer is usually responsible for assorting.

     b.   only one middleman is used at each level of the channel.

     c.   it is easy to coordinate the necessary marketing functions.

     d.   members at each level of the channel often have a very different view of who the competitors are.

     e.   the producer sets the objectives for all channel members.

8.   Ideally, a "channel captain":

     a.   has sufficient market power to force his policies on other channel members.

     b.   is a manufacturer.

     c.   is a strong retailer or wholesaler.

     d.   is assigned this role by majority vote among channel system members.

     e.   earns his position by effective leadership.

9.   If Wal-Mart were to purchase the Zenith Radio Corporation, this would be an example of:

     a.   vertical integration.

     b.   internal expansion.

     c.   horizontal integration.

     d.   an administered channel system.

10.   Which of the following statements about channel systems is *true?*

     a.   Some administered channel systems have achieved the advantages of vertically integrated systems while retaining more flexibility.

     b.   All vertical marketing systems are also contractual channel systems.

     c.   The independence of firms in traditional channel systems has led to channel efficiencies because of greater freedom of decision making.

     d.   Indirect channel systems seem to be generally more effective than direct channels.

     e.   Corporate channel systems are competitively superior to administered channel systems.

11.   The best level of market exposure for a product

     a.   always costs more, but the higher costs lead to higher sales and profits.

     b.   is the level, which will result in the highest level of attention by middlemen.

     c.   is the one, which minimizes distribution costs.

     d.   is intensive distribution.

     e.   depends on how much effort potential customers are willing to put into shopping for a product.

12.   A manufacturer that tries to sell a product through any *responsible* and *suitable* wholesaler or retailer who will stock and/or sell the product is seeking what degree of market exposure?

     a.   Exclusive distribution

     b.   Intensive distribution

     c.   Selective distribution

13. Which of the following statements about "ideal" market exposure is *true?*
    a.   A manufacturer should aim for maximum market exposure.
    b.   As a firm moves from intensive to exclusive distribution, it loses more and more control over price and service.
    c.   It may be necessary to avoid intensive distribution to avoid dealing with middlemen who buy too little compared to the cost of working with them.
    d.   Intensive distribution refers to the desire to sell through any and every retail outlet.
    e.   All of the above are true statements.

14. Marketing managers should know that:
    a.   Canada prohibits exclusive distribution.
    b.   vertical arrangements between manufacturers and middlemen, which limit sales by customer or territory, may be legal according to Canadian law.
    c.   horizontal arrangements among competing manufacturers or middlemen, which limit sales by customer or territory, are always considered illegal.
    d.   all of the above are true.

15. Although some middlemen may resent this approach, a manufacturer may have to use "dual distribution" because:
    a.   present channel members are doing a poor job.
    b.   the firm desires to reach different target markets.
    c.   big retail chains want to deal directly.
    d.   antitrust regulations prohibit relying on just one channel system.
    e.   both a and c above.

16. The physical distribution customer service level is important because:
    a.   it is a measure of how rapidly and dependably a firm delivers what its customers want.
    b.   it may result in lost sales if it is too low.
    c.   it may result in lower profits if it is too high.
    d.   All of the above.

17. According to the "physical distribution concept":
    a.   transporting, storing, and product-handling are independent activities.
    b.   all transporting, storing, and product-handling activities of a business and a whole channel system should be coordinated as part of one system.
    c.   inventories should be based on production requirements.
    d.   the production department should be responsible for warehousing and shipping.
    e.   the lowest-cost distribution system is the best alternative.

18. Which of the following statements reflects a marketing-oriented approach to physical distribution?
    a.   "We should create a position of physical distribution manager and give him authority to integrate all physical distribution activities to minimize the total cost of distribution."
    b.   "We should aim to keep our customers fully satisfied 100 percent of the time as this will increase our sales and give us a competitive advantage."
    c.   "We should replace our warehouses with distribution centres to speed the flow. of products and eliminate all storage."

d. "We should choose the physical distribution alternative that will minimize the total cost of achieving the level of customer service our target market requires."

e. All are equally "marketing-oriented."

19. The "total cost approach" to physical distribution management:
   a. emphasizes faster delivery service and thus favours the use of airfreight over railroads.
   b. often ignores inventory carrying costs.
   c. might favour a high-cost transportation mode if storage costs are reduced enough to lower total distribution costs.
   d. seeks to reduce the cost of transportation to its minimum.
   e. All of the above are true.

20. A marketing-oriented physical distribution manager would *insist* that:
   a. the storage function be eliminated to reduce inventory costs.
   b. efficiency in physical distribution can be best achieved by minimizing costs.
   c. emphasis must be on maximizing the customer service level.
   d. both customer service level and total distribution costs be considered.
   e. none of the above.

21. Electronic data interchange:
   a. puts information in a standardized format.
   b. makes inventory reports more accessible.
   c. is common in domestic and international communication.
   d. replaces many paper forms with electronic versions
   e. all of the above

Answers to Multiple-Choice Questions

1. a, p. 307
2. d, p. 307
3. b, p. 309
4. d, p. 309
5. d, p. 310
6. e, p. 318
7. d, p. 318

8. e, p. 337
9. a, p. 324
10. a, p. 326
11. e, p. 326
12. b, p. 327
13. c, p. 326
14. d, p. 329

15. e, p. 330
16. d, p. 333
17. b, p. 332
18. d, p. 332-334
19. c, p. 335
20. d, p. 332-334
21. e, p. 336

Additional Questions to Test Your Understanding (Fill in the Blanks)

1. Match each of the following terms with the correct definition listed below.

Facilitators   Corporate Channel Systems   Bulk-breaking
Channel Captain   Distribution Cost   Sorting
Total-cost approach   Supply Chains   Coverage

       a. _____ - Firms that provide one or more of the marketing functions other than buying or selling.

       b. _____ - Involves dividing larger quantities into smaller quantities as products get closer to the final market.

       c. _____ - Often develop by vertical integration and have corporate ownership all along the channel.

       d. _____ - Directs the activities of a whole channel and tries to avoid or solve channel conflicts.

       e. _____ - Separating products into grades and qualities desired by different target markets.

       f. _____ - The percentage of the target market that is reached by the channels of distribution.

       g. _____ - The amount that is paid to members of the distribution in order to achieve the desired levels of coverage and promotional intensity.

       h. _____ - The complete set of firms and facilities and logistics activities that are involved in procuring materials, transforming them into intermediate or finished products, and distributing them to customers.

       i. _____ - Evaluating each PD system and evaluating all of the costs of each alternative.

2. List three reasons why it is important to manage channel relationships in a traditional channel system.

a. _____

_____

_____

b. _____

_____

_____

c. _____

_____

_____

3. Give two reasons for using a direct distribution system.

a. _____

_____

_____

b. _____

_____

_____

4. Give two reasons for using an indirect distribution system.

a. _____

_____

_____

b. _____

_____

_____

5. Briefly describe the cost-service tradeoff and give an example from the text of a cost-service trade.

a. _____

_____

b. _____

_____

Answers to Additional Questions

1.
   a. facilitators, p. 312
   b. bulk-breaking, p. 310
   c. corporate channel systems, p. 324
   d. channel captain, p. 320
   e. sorting, p. 310
   f. coverage, p. 313
   g. distribution cost, p. 313
   h. supply chain, p. 335
   i. total cost approach, p. 335

2.
   a. Channel members in traditional channel systems often make little or no effort to cooperate with each other. (p. 318)

b. Vertical conflicts occur between firms at different levels of the channel of distribution, e.g. between a producer and a retailer regarding the amount of shelf space used by the retailer for the producer's product. (p. 318)

c. Horizontal conflicts occur between firms at the same level in the channel of distribution, e.g., a furniture retailer with a complete line of furniture on display discovers that a nearby competitor is discounting special orders of the same line of furniture. (p. 320)

3.

a. Service firms will use direct distribution if the service has to be produced in the presence of the customer. (p. 316)

b. A company wants complete control over the marketing job. (p. 316)

4.

a. When customers have an established buying pattern. (p. 317)

b. Financial reasons , direct distribution requires a large investment and a company may not have enough resources. (p. 317)

5.

a. Most physical distribution decisions involve compromises (or tradeoffs) between costs, the level of customer service and the total sales. (p. 334)

b. Xerox will deliver 90% of all emergency repair parts in 24 hours. Customers would prefer to have all parts delivered within 24 hours, but the cost would be too high to Xerox. (p. 335)

Exercise 11-1

Evaluating the costs of adjusting discrepancies of quantity and assortment in channel systems

Introduction

If market segmentation were carried to its extreme, every customer would have a set of "tailor-made" goods and services. From an economic standpoint, this normally would not be practical, of course. And fortunately, it is not necessary--since it is often possible to find reasonably sized groups of consumers having relatively homogeneous needs. This often leads to "economies of scale"--that lower costs to customers.

By their very nature, however, mass production and mass consumption cause discrepancies of quantity and assortment. So, activities for adjusting these discrepancies are needed. The *regrouping activities* are: accumulating, bulk-breaking, sorting, and assorting. These activities can be carried out by the manufacturer or the consumer. Like many activities, however, they are generally performed best by specialists. This is why marketing middlemen develop--and often become important members of channels of distribution.

Assignment

The following case shows the role of marketing middlemen (particularly wholesalers) in creating and adjusting discrepancies of quantity and assortment. Questions appear at various points through the case--to test your understanding of the material. Read the case carefully and answer the questions *as they appear.* It is important that you understand the concepts involved, even though the case has been simplified to aid analysis. So think about the implications for a highly developed economy such as the United States.

RAINBOW REPUBLIC

The Rainbow Republic is a small developing country that recently experienced an industrial revolution. The country's 100 basic commodities are produced by 100 specialized firms, each of which makes only one product. All of the products are in turn sold through a network of 2,000 equal-sized retailers who are scattered all around the country.

The Cosmic Company produces sunstars (a consumer staple) for the Rainbow Republic. Due to large fluctuations in demand, the sunstars cannot be manufactured in large quantities--and therefore cost $12.50 each to produce. Each week Cosmic's salespeople have to call on all of the retailers to solicit their orders for sunstars. This results in a relatively high selling cost of $2.00 per each unit sold. Since orders are generally quite small, order processing costs amount to about 50 cents per unit. Finally, the necessity of shipping many small orders to retailers results in transportation costs of $1.00 per unit. The price Cosmic charges for each unit is determined by adding on 50 percent of the *total* unit cost of producing, selling, and delivering the sunstars. Each retailer, then, takes a 40 percent markup on the cost they are charged by Cosmic.

1. How much do consumers in the Rainbow Republic pay for sunstars? Show your work (and label your numbers). The retail price of sunstars is _____

2. What discrepancies of quantity and assortment exist in the Rainbow Republic? Be specific.

Consumers in the Rainbow Republic complained about the high prices they were being asked to pay for sunstars and other commodities. They blamed retailers for the high prices--demanding that the government take some action to reduce the retailers' high markups. However, retailers in turn blamed the high prices on the operating practices of manufacturers. Manufacturers acknowledged inefficiencies in their operations, but contended that such problems were unavoidable given the country's present distribution system.

After thinking over the situation quite carefully, the country's economic advisers concluded that the best solution would be to change the nation's distribution system. They recommended that 10 wholesale establishments be added to facilitate the distribution of manufactured commodities. The welfare minister protested, however, that the addition of more middlemen would only serve to *raise* prices instead of lowering them. Here, the economists countered with the following list to show the advantages of employing wholesalers in the Rainbow Republic:

a) The presence of wholesalers would tend to stabilize demand for manufacturers, allowing them to take advantage of mass production techniques. It was estimated that manufacturing costs could be cut in half by producing products in larger quantities.

b) Since manufacturers would only have to deal with 10 wholesalers who buy in large quantities instead of 2,000 retailers, their unit selling costs would decrease by 60 percent. Furthermore, since each wholesaler would only be required to sell to 200 retailers, the wholesale selling costs would amount to only about 25 cents per unit for most commodities.

c) Order processing costs would decrease 50 percent for manufacturers, because wholesalers would order in large quantities. However, it will still cost wholesalers about 25 cents per unit to process each order from the retailers.

d) By shipping bulk quantities to the wholesalers, the manufacturers could take advantage of carload freight rates, thereby cutting their shipping costs to about 50 cents per unit. Also, since their orders would travel shorter distances, the wholesalers could ship products at a rate of 30 cents per unit.

e) Because they deal in large quantities of merchandise, the wholesalers would operate with only a 20 percent markup on total unit cost. Moreover, retailers could cut their markups down to 25 percent, since they would each be dealing with only one wholesaler rather than with 100 manufacturers--and therefore would have lower costs.

3. Assuming that the economist's estimates are accurate, calculate the new retail price for sunstars if Cosmic were to distribute them through wholesalers. Show your work (and label your numbers).

The new retail price for sunstars would be _____.

4. Should the Rainbow Republic adopt the plan to use wholesalers in its distribution system? ___

Yes or No? Why?

5. Explain how the addition of wholesalers would serve to adjust discrepancies of quantity and assortment in the Rainbow Republic. Be specific.

Question for Discussion

Which marketing functions were added or eliminated with the addition of wholesalers to the Rainbow Republic's macro-marketing system?

Exercise 11-2

Determining market exposure policies

Introduction

Once a producer decides to use middlemen (wholesalers and retailers) to help distribute its products, it must decide what degree of market exposure will be best: *exclusive distribution, selective distribution,* or *intensive distribution.* Contrary to popular opinion, maximum exposure is not always desirable. The ideal market exposure should meet--but not exceed--the needs of target customers. As one moves from exclusive distribution to intensive distribution, the total marketing cost may increase--and the quality of service provided by middlemen may actually decline.

When deciding about the desired market exposure, a marketing manager should consider the functions which middlemen will be asked to perform and the product class for his product. The product classes summarize some of what is known about the product--including what the target customers think of it, their willingness to shop for it, and the amount of personal attention and service they want. The product class often determines the "ideal" market exposure.

Of course, there sometimes is a difference between a product's *ideal* market exposure and the exposure, which it can achieve. Middlemen are not always willing to carry a new product, especially when several similar products are already on the market. Similarly, middlemen who are interested in carrying a product may not have the opportunity, unless the producer wants them as a channel partner.

Assignment

This exercise will give you some practice in determining the "ideal" degree of market exposure for a company. Six cases are presented below--with the first serving as an example. Read each case carefully and then indicate (a) the product class, which is involved, and (b) the degree of market exposure (intensive, selective, or exclusive) which you think would be "ideal." Then in part (c), explain *why* you think the indicated degree of market exposure would be ideal. State any assumptions that you have made. *Note:* "Ideal" here means the degree of market exposure which will satisfy the target customers' needs (but not exceed them) *and* will be achievable by the producer. For example, a new producer of "homogeneous" cookies might desire intensive distribution, but agree to sell to only a few food chains because it knows it will not be able to obtain intensive distribution with its undifferentiated cookies. So its "ideal" is selective distribution, and it will adjust the rest of its marketing mix accordingly.

Note: Exhibits 11-3 and 11-4 on pages 311 and 312 of the text may be helpful in completing this exercise.

1.	Aragosa Dinettes, Inc. manufactures a wide line of kitchen tables and chairs for sale throughout Canada. The products are distributed through retail outlets. Retailers are supposed to stock a large assortment of tables and chairs, along with a large inventory of replacement parts. The tables and chairs are usually shipped to the retailers unassembled. According to a recent cost study, 30 percent of Rockwell's retailers account for about 80 percent of the company's sales.

a)	Product class: *Heterogeneous shopping products*

b)	"Ideal" market exposure: *Selective distribution*

c)	Why?	*The recent cost study shows that a small percentage of retailers are producing most of the business. These middlemen might do an even better job if given more assistance and less direct competition from retailers carrying the same products. Since customers are willing to shop around, reducing the number of outlets would be possible--and might benefit consumers through larger retail inventories and increased customer service.*

2.	James River Paper (JRP) recently introduced Absorb, a new double-thick paper towel aimed at families with children. Primarily an industrial products manufacturer, JRP had produced paper towels for a few large grocery chains to sell as their own dealer brand. But Absorb was its first attempt at marketing a consumer product under its own brand. So far, results are not encouraging. Only a few wholesalers have taken on the line. Most are very reluctant to handle Absorb, claiming that retail shelves are already overcrowded with paper towels.

a)	Product class:

_____

b)	"Ideal" market exposure:

_____

c)	Why?

_____

_____

_____

_____

_____

3.	Ciao Footwear designs and manufactures a high-quality line of fashionable shoes that are popular among young professional women. The line is quite expensive--and it is sold through specialty shops that handle only this type of fashion shoe (including competing brands). Ciao will only work with retailers who agree to stock a large variety of sizes and colours of Ciao shoes. They also must agree to promote the Ciao line very aggressively. In return, Ciao agrees not to distribute its line to other retailers within the specialty shop's immediate trading area. Since continuing promotion seems to be necessary in this highly competitive market, advertisements for Ciao shoes appear regularly in fashion magazines targeted at professional women and on select cable TV broadcasts, including broadcasts of women's tennis tournaments.

a)	Product class:

_____

b)	"Ideal" market exposure:

_____

c)	Why?

_____

_____

_____

_____

_____

4.	File 'n Store, Inc. makes and sells a low-priced line of file cabinets for use in offices.. One style of cabinets is designed to store standard size business papers, and another style is designed for computer output. The files are sold directly to universities and other institutions--and indirectly through wholesalers to office equipment dealers. File 'n Store's files sell to final customers (not the middlemen) at prices ranging from about $90 to $300. Most dealers handle several competing brands of file cabinets, including some "high-quality" brands that sell for as much as $1,000.

a)	Product class:

_____

b)	"Ideal" market exposure:

_____

c)	Why?

_____

_____

_____

_____

5.   International Tractor, Inc. (ITI) manufactures a full line of farm machinery--including tractors, graders, and materials-handling equipment. ITI farm products are distributed through over 500 independent dealers scattered throughout Canada. Typically, there is only one ITI dealer near any rural community, although there may be several other dealers who sell competing equipment. Many of ITI's dealerships are quite small, and the company lacks adequate dealers in several key market areas. To further complicate matters, price wars between dealerships are becoming common as industry sales continue to decline. In fact, some ITI dealers often find themselves competing directly with other ITI dealers--since many farmers travel 100 kilometres or more to purchase new equipment.

a)   Product class:
_____

b)   "Ideal" market exposure:
_____

c)   Why?
_____

_____

_____

_____

_____

6.   Keepsake Designs, Ltd. manufactures decorative items for the home. It recently added beaded bamboo curtains to its product line. Designed for use in open doorways or as room dividers, the curtains are available in several colours and can be mounted easily on curtain rods. They are priced at $20 per set and measure six feet long by three feet wide. Like most of the company's products, the curtains are sold in gift shops, hobby shops, and specialty shops such as "Basket Ville" franchise outlets. Initial sales for the curtains have been quite promising. The product seems to have good "eye appeal," according to one shop owner. Apparently, the early customers had not planned to buy anything like bamboo curtains, but once they saw them displayed in the store, they could not resist buying them.

_____

Question for Discussion

How do you think each firm should try to achieve the "ideal" degree of market exposure you discussed above? Are there any legal constraints they should consider?

Name: _____   Course & Section: _____

Exercise 11-3

Evaluating physical distribution alternatives

Introduction

Within the framework of marketing strategy planning, logistics managers seek to provide the level of customer service that satisfies the needs of the firm's target market. Given some specified level of customer service, it is also the logistics manager's job to provide that service at the lowest cost possible. This total cost approach is based on the idea of "tradeoffs" among parts of the distribution system.

For example, a logistics manager may be making a tradeoff when he or she decides to lower transportation costs, because such a move usually results in larger inventory costs. Following the total cost approach, you would not try to minimize with transportation *or* inventory costs. Instead, you would design and operate the physical distribution system in a way that would *minimize the total cost of offering the desired customer service level.* The following exercise will illustrate this idea in greater detail.

Assignment

Read the following case and answer the questions that follow.

PARAGON COMPANY

The Paragon Company is studying its physical distribution system to see if the system needs to be remodeled. Currently, Paragon's industrial component product is manufactured at the firm's plant in Toronto and then shipped by train to several branch warehouses across Canada. When an order is received at the Toronto plant, the order is relayed to the branch warehouse closest to the customer. The products are then shipped directly to the customer by truck. Paragon tries to maintain a 70 percent customer service level--that is, it tries to deliver 70 percent of its orders to the customer within three days after the orders are received.

Recently, several company managers have expressed dissatisfaction with the present distribution system. Paragon's sales manager feels that the 70 percent service level is inadequate--and should be increased to at least 90 percent by adding more warehouses. The production manager wants to cut the service level to 20 percent, to even out his production schedule--although the traffic manager claims this will increase transportation costs too much. Finally, the finance manager has suggested that the firm try to minimize its total distribution costs by providing whatever level of customer service it can while operating at the lowest possible total cost.

To help resolve this conflicting advice from his top managers, Paragon's president asked his assistant to analyze the relationship between alternative customer service levels and physical distribution costs. The results of this analysis are shown in Figure 12-1.

FIGURE 12-1
Distribution Costs at Different Customer Service Levels

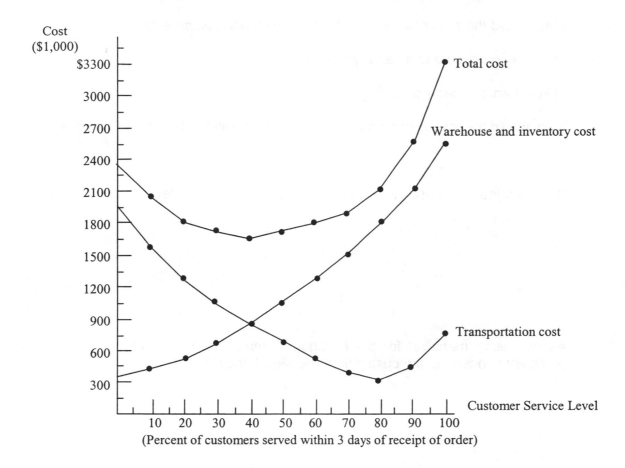

1. At what customer service level would the total cost of distribution be *minimized* as the finance manager suggests? What would the minimum total cost be?

   Customer service level _____%   Total cost $ _____

2. According to Figure 12-1, what is Paragon's total cost of physical distribution at its present 70 percent customer service level?
   $_____

3. What would the total cost be if a 90 percent service level were adopted, as the sales manager desires?
   $ _____

4.   What would the total cost be if a 20 percent service level were adopted, as the production manager has suggested?

$ _____

5.   What would the *total cost* be if Paragon attempted to *minimize* its:

a)   warehouse and inventory costs $ _____

b)   transportation costs $ _____

6.   What would the total cost be if Paragon were to *maximize* its customer service level?

$ _____

7.   Based on the information in Figure 12-1, what is the optimal level of customer service?

8.   As marketing manager for the Paragon Company, what advice would you give the president concerning the customer service level decision?

Question for Discussion

What determines the level of service that customers expect?

Exercise 11-4

Integrating physical distribution

Introduction

Successful marketers must pay attention to the distribution customer service they provide their customers. They also must worry about the cost of the service they provide--because ultimately the price of a product should cover the cost. Deciding on the right balance between the distribution customer service level and the costs of transporting and storing is sometimes difficult--and identifying how best to achieve that balance can be even more of a challenge. The job of integrating all of the logistics activities is even more complicated when it requires coordination among different firms in a channel. But the job must be done and done well. One firm can't just reduce its own PD costs if that raises costs somewhere else in the channel--or reduces the service level. For example some business customers may demand just-in-time delivery or expect the convenience and speed of electronic data interchange (EDI)--because that is what is required to make the whole channel more competitive.

Many marketing managers know about the physical distribution concept, but it's easy to fall into the trap of just accepting 'a firm's PD system as "the way it's always been"--never even bothering to think about how to improve it. This exercise gives you practice in analyzing different PD situations--and in applying the concepts discussed in Chapter 11 to improve a marketing strategy.

Assignment

Read each of the following situations carefully. Identify the major PD problem(s) and then make specific suggestions about how you might improve the strategy. State any assumptions that you think are important to your recommendation. In your answer, be sure to show that you understand the various concepts--including the different storing and transporting alternatives--discussed in the text. The first problem is answered for you as an example of the approach to take. But keep in mind that there may be more than one "correct" answer in each situation. The solution will depend, in part, on your creativity!

1. Triangle Orthodontics is a partnership of oral surgeons who correct teeth alignments for patients who live in a medium-size town. Recently, Triangle Orthodontics contracted to provide care to members of Blue Cross dental plans, and they agreed that Blue Cross could do a survey to evaluate patient satisfaction. The doctors were surprised to find that many patients gave them a low rating--primarily because of the inconvenience involved in' being fitted for braces. Orthodontist clinics in a large city keep a complete assortment of braces on hand, but that is not feasible for a small clinic with limited space. So Triangle Orthodontics orders braces from a wholesaler by phone the day a patient's cast is removed, and then the patient schedules another appointment to come back the next day--after the wholesaler delivers the brace-to have it fitted.

Problem: *Fitting of the braces may not be the most important part of what the doctors do, but the unavailability of braces when patients (customers) expect them results in a breakdown in satisfaction with the service. The anxiety of a day without the brace probably doesn't help.*

Recommendation: *Although it may not be possible to stock all of the different types and sizes of braces, the clinic might try to stock one each of the most frequently used braces. Even a "less-than-complete" inventory might avoid many of the problems. Further, and perhaps more important, the timing of the demand for a particular size and type of brace does not arise as a surprise. Most patients have had a cast on for a number of weeks before they come in for the appointment to have it removed. It should be a simple matter for the clinic to order needed braces several days before each patient's cast-removal appointment. Earlier ordering could solve the problem--and increase satisfaction.*

2.   BrickOven Bakeries makes a variety of sugar-free cookies that are sold by several large supermarket chains in lower mainland British Columbia. Data from the stores' checkout computers is automatically linked to the BrickOven Bakeries in Vancouver so that each day's production run, and the shipments to each store, can exactly match the assortment needed to refill each store's display. This reduces inventory costs and also results in fresh cookies. While studying sales figures, the BrickOven Bakeries marketing manager noticed that during the previous two months there had been no sales of Almond cookies at one store. On investigation, the manager discovered that a case of Almond cookies were crushed in transit. The shattered cookies--clearly visible through their plastic bags-- had been placed on the rack by a stock clerk. Because no customers were buying the damaged cookies, none passed through the checkout scanners, and no replacements were ordered.

a)   Problem:

b)   Recommendation:

3. EuroMotor Works (EMW) is a manufacturer of family automobiles and has enjoyed real success in serving a small, but profitable, segment of the Canadian market. EMW's vehicles are renown for safety and durability. But this success brings problems. EMW must provide dealers with repair parts for five different models, many of which have changed significantly over the years. Yet, the success of EMW's strategy depends on strong service from dealers--to keep customers happy, word-of-mouth favourable, and repeat sales strong. The company operates 4 Canadian parts warehouses and ships to dealers by common carrier truck. As the number of older models still in service has increased, dealers have begun to complain about the long re-stock time *and* the large number of parts they must keep in stock to handle the discontinued models. Some customers face a long wait for parts before the dealer can fix a car.

a) Problem:

b) Recommendation:

4. SunShadow Designs is the second largest producer of high quality coated fabrics used for outdoor awnings for fine homes, restaurants, and hotels, and in other applications--including boat covers. SunShadow Designs sells fabric directly to the thousands of awning fabricators who serve customers in their local markets. Once a consumer selects a fabric from a sample and tells a fabricator what to make, the fabricator calls the regional SunShadow Designs sales rep and places an order. Each week's orders are then processed through the home office and the bulky fabric is shipped by truck to the fabricator from either the company's BC or Quebec warehouse. This approach reduces transportation costs and makes it easier to manage the inventory in the warehouse. Although many fabricators are loyal to SunShadow Designs fabric, a new competitor from Europe has been taking a share of the market, apparently in large part because it is able to fill orders within a week rather than the three weeks it takes, on average, for SunShadow Designs. The SunShadow Designs marketing manager does not expect the new competitor to be able to survive, however, because its delivered prices are about 10 percent higher.

a) Problem:

b) Recommendation:

5.   Stylco Furniture makes a wide variety of stylish upholstered sofas and chairs. Over time, an increasing share of the company's business has come from special orders which consumers place through furniture stores, most of which handle a number of competing lines. As special orders increased, Stylco slowly increased the choices among upholstery fabrics--and the firm now offers more than 250 colours and patterns. Some customers seem to be delighted with this unique array of choices. Even so, sales have slowly tapered off--and at a recent dealer meeting, several retailers complained that not many customers were willing to wait eight to twelve weeks for Stylco to produce and deliver a custom order. Stylco's sales manager urged the retailers to carry more chairs and sofa in stock, so that they could sell more Stylco furniture "off the display floor."

a)   Problem:

b)   Recommendation:

Question for Discussion

Given the difficulties of coordinating physical distribution activities in a channel, wouldn't it be easier and cheaper for most manufacturers to make all the important PD decisions--and then deal only with middlemen who will accept those decisions.

Exercise 11-5

Intensive vs. selective distribution

This exercise is based on computer-aided problem number 11--Intensive versus Selective Distribution. A complete description of the problem appears on pages 338-339 of Wong/Shapiro, 11th edition.

1. Hydropump's marketing manager thinks that the type of channel relationship possible with selective distribution would make it possible to get a large share (40 percent) of the pumps sold by its hot-tub dealers. But he realizes that the actual percent might vary. He thinks that the percent could be as low as 35 percent, or go as high as 45 percent. He wants to evaluate the effect that this might have on expected profits. Do a What If analysis, based on the selective distribution alternative, varying Hydropump's percent of dealer unit sales between 35 percent and 45 percent and displaying Hydropump's unit sales and profit, and then complete the missing numbers in the table below.

Percent of Dealer Unit Sales	Expected Unit Sales	Expected Profit
35	_____	_____
37	_____	_____
_____	9,880	193,200
43	_____	_____
44	_____	_____
45	_____	_____

2. How important is it that Hydropump win at least a 40 percent share of the dealers' unit sales? Explain your reasons.

_____

_____

_____

_____

_____

3. Hydropump's marketing manager thinks that the hot-tub dealers will pay more attention to the company's product if they get a higher than normal level of attention and help from Hydropump sales reps. However, a sales rep would only be able to spend the extra time with each dealer if he is responsible for fewer accounts. If each rep is assigned only 47 dealers, instead of 70, how many more sales reps would be needed, and how much would personal selling costs increase?

   number of sales reps needed at 47 dealers per rep _____

   personal selling cost for this number of sales reps _____

   less, personal selling cost for 4 sales reps $72,000

   equals, increase in personal selling cost   _____

4. With this change in the sales force, Hydropump's manager is confident that the firm will get at least 40 percent--and perhaps as high as 50 percent--of the pumps sold by the dealers. Evaluate Hydropump's likely profit in this situation--and then compare it with your previous analysis (above). Would you recommend that Hydropump add the extra sales reps? Discuss your reasons.

   _____

   _____

   _____

   _____

   _____

   _____

   _____

   _____

Chapter 12

Retailers, Wholesalers, and Their Strategy Planning

Chapter Summary

- **Understand how retailers plan their marketing strategies.**
  Many retailers are stuck in the production-oriented approach, which leads to the failure of three-fourths of all new retailing ventures within their first year. Retailers must understand the demographics of the market they wish to compete in and come to a thorough understanding of the marketing environment – from laws and regulations to competitor analysis. Awareness of these factors will allow retailers to make important decisions on target market selection and on how best to meet the emotional and social needs of their customers.

  Retail marketing mixes have seven Ps that are critical to their success. The traditional four Ps of *product, price, place* and *promotion* are joined by *personnel* (type and quality of assistance available), *personalized services* (return policies, ability to customize, hours, other extras), and *physical facilities* (store layout, washrooms, interior elements). The retailer must be flexible to adapt the retail marketing mix in the face of rapid competitive changes.

- **Know about the many kinds of retailers that work with producers and wholesalers as members of the channel systems.**
  Retailers are seen as the last link to consumers in the indirect channel of distribution. The number and type of *retailers* to carry the product is a crucial decision. The type of *retailers* affects the channel management and control of the firm's ability to manage its marketing plans. The distinctions between various types of retailers are diminishing as an increasing number of retailers are moving towards scrambled merchandising.

- **Understand the differences among conventional and non-conventional retailers – including Internet merchants and others who accept the mass-merchandising concept.**
  Most conventional retailers are single line or limited line stores, e.g. a retailer selling clothes (or apparel) is a single line, while a retailer selling only just shoes or just formal wear is limiting the single line of clothes. They can satisfy their customer better, because they can adjust to suit specific customers. They try to build long-term relationships and want to be the place to shop for a certain type of product.

  Non-conventional retailers use a number of different models and reject the conventional retailer's idea that demand in a given geographic area is fixed. The *mass-merchandising concept*, which is that retailers should offer, lower prices to get faster turnover and greater sales volumes.

- **Understand scrambled merchandising and the "wheel of retailing."**
  Many retailers are moving towards scrambled merchandising – carrying any product line they think they can sell profitably. These types of retailers believe that one-stop shopping and store location are both valued by the customer.

The wheel of retailing assumes that new types of retailers enter the market as low status, low margin, low price operators and then evolve into more conventional retailers offering more services with higher operating costs and higher prices.

- **See why size or belonging to a chain can be important to a retailer.**
  Many large producers gravitate toward chains or large stores for the distribution of their goods due to the high efficiency of selling to volume buyers. These firms are able to make large-volume sales and reach a large number of customers while making relatively few sales calls. The chain or large store benefits because they are able to capitalize on the maximum order discount due to their large order size.

- **Know what progressive wholesalers are doing to modernize their operations and marketing strategies.**
  Progressive wholesalers are showing a greater interest in their customers' needs by developing new strategies that better suit their customers' businesses. Many wholesalers offer a host of new services while others have worked to create closer relations to the customers. Modern wholesalers offer some services at minimum cost, and then charge additional fees for any special services required. Other changes include the use of computers to manage inventory, allowing a wholesaler to spend their time with their most profitable customers.

- **Know the various kinds of merchant wholesalers and agent intermediaries and the strategies that they use.**
  Wholesaling functions really are variations on the basic marketing functions. Different types of wholesalers can be distinguished on the basis of the set of functions they perform and include merchant wholesalers, who own the products they sell; service wholesalers, who provide all wholesaling functions; and limited-function wholesalers, who provide only some wholesaling services.

- **Understand why retailing and wholesaling have developed in different ways in different countries.**
  Many new retailing approaches that have developed in different countries have rapidly spread all over the world. There are some exceptions. Retailing in less developed countries are more likely to be characterized by small shops selling very small amounts to a few customers. In other countries retailing is regulated to protect smaller retailers. However retailing change is taking place throughout the world under the influence of the global expansion of mega-retailers.

- **See why the Internet is affecting both retailing and wholesaling.**
  New technologies, and in particular the Internet, are changing the way retailers interface with both buyers and suppliers. Buyers are getting greater service, more convenience, and access to better information. Suppliers are gaining more accurate and timely information to assist in planning activities.

Important Terms

True-False Questions

____ 1.   Retailing covers all of the activities involved in the sale of products to final consumers.

____ 2.   Thousands of new retailing ventures fail during the first year in Canada.

____ 3.   A consumer's choice of a retail store appears to be based almost entirely on emotional needs--economic needs have almost no influence.

____ 4.   Canadian total retail sales are close to 250 billion dollars annually.

____ 5.   A limited-line store will typically carry a broader assortment than a single-line store.

____ 6.   Limited-line stores may carry several lines of merchandise--but with a very limited assortment of products within each line.

____ 7.   A specialty shop is a type of limited-line store that usually is small, has a distinct personality, and aims at a carefully defined market segment by offering knowledgeable salespeople, better service, and a unique product assortment.

____ 8.   Department stores are becoming less important and their share of retail business has declined continuously since the 1970s.

____ 9.   Conventional retailers believe in a fixed demand for a territory and have a "buy-low and sell-high" philosophy.

____ 10. The mass-merchandising concept says that retailers should offer low prices to get faster turnover and greater sales volumes--by appealing to larger markets.

____ 11. A well-managed supermarket can generally count on a net profit level of only about 1 percent of sales.

____ 12. Catalogue showroom retailers have become quite successful in Canada using their strategy of stocking little inventory and delivering by mail.

____ 13. Supercentres are very large stores that may carry food and drug items.

____ 14. The average mass-merchandiser has a store that is about the same size as an average supermarket.

____ 15. Supercentres are simply large mass-merchandisers that carry many more shopping products.

____ 16. Single-line mass-merchandisers attract large numbers of customers with their large assortment and low prices in a single product category.

____ 17. Convenience food stores limit their assortment to those "pickup" or "fill-in" items that are needed between major shopping trips to a supermarket, and thus earn smaller profits as a percent of sales.

___ 18. Automatic vending has low operating costs because labour costs are very low.

___ 19. Although it's an expensive method of selling--door-to-door retailers may be especially useful for the sale of unsought products.

___ 20. Telephone and mail-order retailing grew for a while, then declined, but the Internet is helping to turn things around again.

___ 21. Cable TV channels devoted to home shopping are holding their own and may never decide to open websites on the Internet.

___ 22. The Internet is JUST another aspect of how low-margin mass-merchandisers appeal to large target markets with discount prices.

___ 23. Retail sales on the Internet are expected to grow rapidly.

___ 24. The Internet makes it harder to do comparison shopping of products and prices.

___ 25. All major retailing developments can be explained by the "Wheel of Retailing" theory—that describes a recurring retail cycle from low cost and low prices to higher cost and higher prices.

___ 26. "Scrambled merchandising" is a way of describing the activities of modern retailers who are willing to carry "unconventional" assortments of products—anything they can sell profitably.

___ 27. Loblaws accounts for more than 30% of grocery products sold in Canada.

___ 28. One of the incentives to corporate chain development is the availability of economies of scale.

___ 29. Voluntary chains are formed by independent retailers in their efforts to compete with corporate chains—while cooperative chains operate similarly except that they are sponsored by wholesalers.

___ 30. The very high failure rate among franchise operations explains why franchises are becoming less popular.

___ 31. Franchise holders now account for about half of all retail sales.

___ 32. Around the world, mass-merchandising is more popular in less-developed nations because they need the lower prices more.

___ 33. Information technology is making it easier for producers and consumers to connect without the use of wholesalers.

___ 34. Many manufacturers and retailers have realized that wholesaling functions are not always necessary, so wholesalers have been eliminated at an increasing rate since the 1970s.

_____ 35. Most modern wholesalers have become more streamlined in their operations, more computerized in controlling their inventories, and more selective in their distribution policies.

_____ 36. Recent trends in wholesaling indicate that wholesaling will survive, even though some wholesalers may disappear.

_____ 37. All wholesalers perform the following functions for their customers: anticipate needs, regroup products, carry stocks, deliver products, grant credit, provide information and advisory service, provide part of buying function, and own and transfer title to products.

_____ 38. The typical merchant wholesaler's operating expenses amount to about 25 percent of sales.

_____ 39. The fact that many manufacturers have set up their own sales branches suggests that the use of wholesalers usually make distribution costs unnecessarily high.

_____ 40. A producer who uses a direct channel system normally is also considered a wholesaler--because he must take over the wholesaling functions that an independent wholesaler might provide.

_____ 41. Merchant wholesalers don't necessarily provide all of the wholesaling functions, but they do take title to the products they sell.

_____ 42. Service wholesalers provide all of the wholesaling functions--while limited-function wholesalers provide only certain functions.

_____ 43. A general merchandise service wholesaler may represent many different kinds of manufacturers and supply many different kinds of retailers.

_____ 44. Even though cash-and-carry wholesalers are limited-function wholesalers, they operate like service wholesalers, except that the customer must pay cash.

_____ 45. Drop-shippers own the products they sell--but do not actually handle, stock, or deliver them.

_____ 46. Truck wholesalers' operating costs are relatively high because they provide a lot of service relative to how much they sell.

_____ 47. Rack jobbers are limited-function wholesalers, with relatively high operating costs, who help retailers offer a more attractive assortment of products--especially nonfood items.

_____ 48. Catalogue wholesalers should probably be classified as retailers--since they sell out of catalogs.

___ 49. A manufacturer who has the capability of operating its own distribution facilities but lacks customer contacts should consider the use of agent middlemen to facilitate the buying and selling functions.

___ 50. Agent middlemen are less common in international trade than in Canadian markets because merchant wholesalers can both sell products and handle the financing.

___ 51. The key role of manufacturers' agents is to provide well-established customer contacts for new products--while assuming all the risks of taking title to the products they handle.

___ 52. A broker's "product" is information about what buyers need--and what supplies are available.

___ 53. A small manufacturer with limited financial resources whose only skills are in production should probably consider contracting with a selling agent to act, in effect, as the firm's marketing manager.

___ 54. The primary advantage of auction companies is that they facilitate buying by description.

Answers to True-False Questions

1. T, p. 343	19. T, p. 355	37. F, p. 370
2. T, p. 343	20. T, p. 355	38. F, p. 371
3. F, p. 343-344	21. F, p. 355	39. F, p. 370
4. T, p. 343	22. F, p. 356	40. F, p. 371
5. F, p. 348	23. T, p. 356	41. T, p. 371
6. F, p. 348	24. F, p. 358	42. T, p. 371
7. T, p. 350	25. F, p. 361	43. T, p. 371
8. T, p. 350	26. T, p. 359	44. T, p. 372
9. T, p. 348	27. T, p. 347	45. T, p. 372
10. T, p. 351	28. T, p. 347	46. T, p. 372
11. T, p. 351	29. F, p. 348	47. T, p. 372
12. F, p. 352	30. F, p. 347	48. F, p. 372
13. F, p. 353	31. T, p. 348	49. T, p. 373
14. F, p. 352	32. F, p. 351	50. F, p. 373
15. F, p. 353	33. T, p. 367-368	51. F, p. 373-374
16. T, p. 352	34. F, p. 367-368	52. T, p. 374
17. F, p. 354	35. T, p. 368	53. T, p. 375
18. F, p. 354	36. T, p. 369	54. F, p. 375

Multiple-Choice Questions (Circle the correct response)

1. Which of the following best describes what "retailing" involves?
    a. The sale of consumer products to wholesalers, retailers, or final consumers.
    b. The performance of all merchandising activities except promotion and pricing.
    c. The sale of both business and consumer products.
    d. The sale of products to final consumers.
    e. All of the above describe what retailing involves.

2. Which of the following are *not* "conventional retailers" according to the text?
    a. General stores
    b. Single-line stores
    c. Supermarkets
    d. Limited-line retailers
    e. All of the above

3. Which of the following would be considered a *limited-line* retailer?
    a. Supermarket
    b. Gas station
    c. Mass-merchandiser
    d. Drugstore
    e. Bakery shop

4. Specialty shops:
    a. generally try to become well known for the distinctiveness of their line and the special services offered.
    b. generally carry complete lines--like department stores.
    c. carry specialty products almost exclusively.
    d. generally use a mass-marketing approach.
    e. All of the above are true.

5. Department stores:
    a. are often frowned upon by the retailing community because they provide too many customer services.
    b. normally are large stores, which emphasize depth and distinctiveness rather than variety in the lines they carry.
    c. are very popular with some consumers--and thus may be the only way to reach these market segments.
    d. are still growing rapidly in number, average sales per store, and share of retail sales.
    e. All of the above are true statements.

6. The idea underlying the mass-merchandising concept is that:
    a. a big profit on each item sold won't earn much if sales volume is low.
    b. inventory is a big cost, so everything you stock should be out on a shelf where it can be seen by the mass market.
    c. a store should "buy low and sell high" if it's going to make a profit.
    d. it is better to sell more at the same price--since total revenue will increase.
    e. All of the above are true.

7. Which of the following statements about supermarkets is *true*?

a. Supermarkets should be classified as "conventional retailers."
b. Net profits after taxes in supermarkets usually run about 1 percent of sales--or less.
c. Annual sales for supermarkets average about $50 million.
d. They typically carry 15,000 product items.
e. All of the above are true statements.

8. Catalogue showroom retailers:
a. are essentially mail-order sellers.
b. must charge above-average prices to cover the costs of printing and distributing catalogs to consumers.
c. stress convenience as their most distinguishing feature.
d. minimize handling costs by keeping their inventories in backroom warehouses until customer orders are placed.
e. All of the above are true statements.

9. Large departmentalized retail stores that are larger than supermarkets and follow the discount house's philosophy of emphasizing lower margins to achieve faster turnover are called:
a. department stores.
b. mass-merchandisers.
c. category killers.
d. specialty shops.
e. box stores.

10. The "supercentre concept":
a. is just another name for the mass-merchandising concept.
b. essentially refers to large department stores, which have adopted supermarket-style operating procedures and methods.
c. is concerned with providing all of the customer's routine needs at a low price.
d. probably will not be accepted by mass-merchandisers.
e. All of the above are true.

11. The modern convenience (food) stores are successful because they offer:
a. wide assortments.
b. low prices.
c. expanded customer service.
d. the right assortment of "fill-in" items.
e. All of the above.

12. Which of the following statements about telephone and direct-mail retailing is *true?*
a. It is hard to target customers using direct-mail retailing.
b. Mail-order retailers tend to have lower operating costs than conventional retailers.
c. All mail-order retailers offer both convenience products and shopping products.
d. Although mail-order retailers have increased in number in the United States, their profit margins are less than those of most other types of retailers.
e. Mail-order retailers place their primary emphasis on low-price merchandise.

13. Electronic shopping via the Internet:
a. is expected to grow even faster with the availability of interactive cable services.

b. is better strong on cable TV where whole channels are devoted to it.
c. allows shoppers to order almost any kind of product from their home by phone.
d. None of the above are true statements.

14. Which of the following statements is *false?*
a. All types of retailers are now establishing a presence on the Internet.
b. Shopping on the Internet is easier when you know exactly what you're looking for.
c. The economic impact of the Internet has already been phenomenal.
d. Shopping on the Internet makes it easy to compare products and prices.
e. None of the above is false.

15. The "Wheel of Retailing" theory suggests that:
a. retail stores do not have life cycles.
b. retailing profits tend to be cyclical.
c. only the largest retailers have a chance to survive in a fast-moving economy.
d. new types of retailers enter as low-price operators and eventually begin to offer more services and charge higher prices.
e. only discounters can survive in the long run.

16. Which of the following concepts is best illustrated by a retail bakery that sells wristwatches?
a. The "superstore"
b. Scrambled merchandising
c. Time-sharing
d. The "wheel of retailing" theory
e. Mass-merchandising

17. Canadian market data indicate that:
a. thousands and thousands of new retail ventures go out of business in the first year.
b. there are more manufacturers and wholesalers than there are retailers in Canada
c. the large number of small retailers make working with them inexpensive.
d. the really large retailers account for a rather small percentage of total retail sales.
e. all of the above are true.

18. A group of retailers banding together to establish their own wholesaling organization would be known as a:
a. cooperative chain.
b. voluntary chain.
c. consumer cooperative.
d. corporate chain.
e. franchise.

19. Franchisors:
a. are similar to voluntary chain operators.
b. often provide franchise holders with training.
c. usually receive fees and commissions from the franchise holder.
d. reduce their risk of starting a new retailing business.
e. All of the above are true statements.

20. The development of new, more efficient retailers around the world is dependent upon:
    a. the political and legal environment.
    b. the technological environment.
    c. the social and cultural environment.
    d. the economic environment.
    e. all of the above.

21. Which of the following is *least likely* to occur in retailing in the future?
    a. Conventional retailers will continue to feel a profit squeeze.
    b. Scrambled merchandising will decline.
    c. There will be more vertical arrangements between producers and retailers.
    d. There will be an increase in in-home shopping.
    e. Stores will continue to make shopping more convenient.

22. Which of the following is *not* a typical wholesaling function?
    a. provide market information to a producer.
    b. grant credit to customers.
    c. supply capital to pay the cost of carrying inventory.
    d. all of the above are typical wholesaling functions.
    e. none of the above is a typical wholesaling function.

23. Which of the following statements is *least relevant* in explaining how wholesaling is changing with the times?
    a. The need for wholesaling services has increased.
    b. Wholesalers have modernized their warehouses and physical handling facilities.
    c. Wholesalers have become more selective in their choice of customers--as many small retailers were clearly unprofitable.
    d. Many wholesalers no longer require each customer to pay for all of the services they provide *some* customers.
    e. Wholesalers have streamlined their operations to cut costs and improve profits.

24. Which of the following types of wholesalers has the *highest* operating expenses as a percent of sales?
    a. Manufacturers' agents
    b. Manufacturers' sales branches
    c. Brokers
    d. Drop-shippers
    e. Merchant wholesalers

25. Manufacturers' sales branches:
    a. have very low sales per branch.
    b. are mainly used in weak market areas, where there is not enough business for other types of wholesalers.
    c. operating costs would be even lower than they are now if manufacturers didn't "charge" them with extra expenses.
    d. handle about a third of all wholesale sales.
    e. serve the same basic needs as do brokers.

26. The two basic types of merchant wholesalers are:
    a. single-line and specialty.
    b. service and limited-function.

c. service and general merchandise.
d. single-line and limited-function.
e. agents and brokers.

27. Regarding merchant wholesalers, which of the following statements is TRUE?
    a. They own (take title to) the products they sell.
    b. Merchant wholesalers are the most numerous wholesalers and handle over half of all wholesale sales.
    c. General merchandise wholesalers of consumer products handle a broad variety of nonperishable items, including both convenience and shopping products.
    d. A specialty wholesaler generally would offer a narrower range of products than a single-line wholesaler.
    e. All of the above are true.

28. Which of the following types of wholesalers do *not* carry stocks for their customers?
    a. Cash-and-carry wholesalers.
    b. Rack jobbers.
    c. Truck wholesalers.
    d. Drop-shippers.
    e. Catalog wholesalers.

29. Which of the following statements about rack jobbers is *true?*
    a. Rack jobbers specialize in hard-to-handle assortments of products.
    b. Rack jobbers provide retailers with specialized information about consumer preferences.
    c. Rack jobbers are practically full-service wholesalers.
    d. Rack jobbers apply their knowledge of local retail preferences in many stores.
    e. All of the above are true statements.

30. A type of middleman that does *not* take title to the products is known as:
    a. an agent intermediary.
    b. a limited-function wholesaler.
    c. a rack jobber.
    d. a merchant wholesaler.
    e. a drop-shipper.

31. Which of the following statements *is false?*
    a. Agent generally do not take title to products they sell.
    b. Manufacturers' agents usually do not represent competing manufacturers.
    c. Brokers are often used because of the seasonal nature of production or demand.
    d. Manufacturers' agents generally have more authority over prices and terms of sale than do selling agents.
    e. Agent middlemen are very common is international trade.

32. Turgo, Inc. has just developed a new convenience product for which it wants intensive distribution nationally. It expects a low initial demand and wants to keep selling costs as low as possible while keeping control of marketing. This is Turgo's first product and working capital is small. Which of the following channels would be best?
    a. Turgo's own sales force direct to retailers.
    b. Manufacturers' agents to merchant wholesalers to retailers.
    c. Brokers to consumers.

    d.   Turgo's own sales force direct to merchant wholesalers to retailers.

    e.   Selling agents to merchant wholesalers to retailers.

33.   The principal function of a broker is to:

    a.   transport acquired products.

    b.   facilitate inspection of products.

    c.   establish a central market.

    d.   bring buyers and sellers together.

    e.   distribute grocery products.

34.   The Jory Co. handles the entire output of several small clothing manufacturers on a national basis. The firm has almost complete control of pricing, selling, and advertising. In addition, Jory often provides working capital to the producers, who have very limited financial resources. In return, Jory is paid a substantial commission on all sales. The Jory Co. is a:

    a.   selling agent.

    b.   full-service wholesaler.

    c.   manufacturers' agent.

    d.   broker.

    e.   none of the above.

Answers to Multiple-Choice Questions

1. d, p. 343	13. a, p. 356	25. d, p. 370
2. c, p. 348	14. c, p. 367-69	26. b, p. 371
3. e, p. 348	15. d, p. 361	27. e, p. 371
4. a, p. 350	16. b, p. 359	28. d, p. 371-372
5. c, p. 350	17. a, p. 343	29. e, p. 372
6. a, p. 351	18. a, p. 347	30. a, p. 373
7. b, p. 351	19. e, p. 348	31. d, p. 373-374
8. d, p. 352	20. e, p. 365	32. b, p. 343
9. b, p. 352	21. b, p. 375-376	33. d, p. 374
10. c, p. 353	22. d, p. 370	34. a, p. 373
11. d, p. 354	23. a, p. 367-369	
12. b, p. 355	24. e, p. 371-373	

Additional Questions to Test Your Understanding (Fill in the blanks)

1. Briefly describe "scrambled merchandising" and provide one example from your own experience?

   _____

   _____

   _____

   _____

   _____

2. What are the seven Ps of a retailer's marketing mix?

   a. _____

   b. _____

   c. _____

   d. _____

   e. _____

   f. _____

   g. _____

3. Briefly explain why mega-retailers such as Bennetton and Wal-Mart going global.

   _____

   _____

   _____

   _____

   _____

4. Briefly describe four methods used to modernize wholesalers by streamlining their operations, cutting unnecessary costs and improving their profits.

   a. _____

   _____

   _____

   b. _____

   _____

   _____

c. _____

_____

_____

d. _____

_____

_____

Answers to Additional Questions

1. Scrambled merchandising is the practice of many retail outlets to carry any product line they think they can sell profitably. An example this type of retailer would be Hy & Zells, whose primary business is selling drug related products, but is also selling grocery packaged goods and perishables. (p. 359)

2.
   a. product
   b. price
   c. promotion
   d. place
   e. personnel
   f. physical facilities
   g. personalized service

   (p. 345)

3. The mega-retailers are going global because their home markets are saturated with competition. At home they are sharing stagnant consumer markets with an increasing number of firms attempting to copy their success. (p. 365)

4. See discussion on pages 367-369

Exercise 12-1

Identifying and analyzing retail stores

Introduction

Retailing involves the sale of products to final consumers. There are almost two hundred thousand retailers in Canada. However, as discussed in the text, there are many different types of retailers and they vary both in size and method of operation. Marketing managers of consumer products at all channel levels must understand retailing--for if the retailing effort is not effective, the products may not be sold and *all* members of the channel will suffer. Likewise, consumers must be concerned with retailing--because their standard of living is partly dependent on how well retailing is done.

The purpose of this exercise is to focus your attention on the retailers who serve *your* community. What types of stores are there? How do they operate? Who are their target customers? Why might there be different types of retailers selling *basically* the same kinds of products?

Assignment

Listed below are several types of retail stores that were discussed in the text. For each type:

a)   Give the name and address of a store in your community that illustrates this type.

b)   Briefly describe the store in terms of its *width* and *depth* of assortment. Is it a single-line or limited-line store or a "scrambled merchandiser"? Does the store stress high turnover or low turnover products?

c)   Briefly describe the store in terms of its price/service blend (is the store price-oriented or service-oriented) and estimate whether the store's gross margin is in the *low range* (below 20 percent), *medium range* (20-35 percent), or *high range* (over 35 percent).

Note: If your community does not have a particular store type, write "none" under part (a) and then answer parts (b) and (c) in terms of how you *think* that type of store would operate.

1. *Limited-Line "Conventional " Retailer*

   a) Store name and address:

   _____

   b) Assortment:

   _____

   c) Price/Service blend:

   _____

   d) Gross margin range:

   _____

2. *Department Store*

   a) Store name and address:

   _____

   b) Assortment:

   _____

   c) Price/Service blend:

   _____

   d) Gross margin range:

   _____

3. *Supermarket*

   a) Store name and address:

   _____

   b) Assortment:

   _____

   c) Price/Service blend:

   _____

   d) Gross margin range:

   _____

4. *Catalog Showroom*

   a) Store name and address:

   _____

   b) Assortment:

   _____

c)   Price/Service blend:

_____

d)   Gross margin range:

_____

5.   *Mass-Merchandiser*

      a)   Store name and address:

_____

      b)   Assortment:

_____

      c)   Price/Service blend:

_____

      d)   Gross margin range:

_____

6.   *Single-Line Mass-Merchandiser*

      a)   Store name and address:

_____

      b)   Assortment:

_____

      c)   Price/Service blend:

_____

      d)   Gross margin range:

_____

7.   *Convenience (Food) Store*

      a)   Store name and address:

_____

      b)   Assortment:

_____

      c)   Price/Service blend:

_____

      d)   Gross margin range:

_____

8. *Internet Merchant (does not need to be based in your community, but can be)*

   a) Store name and address:

   _____

   b) Assortment:

   _____

   c) Price/Service blend:

   _____

   d) Gross margin range:

   _____

Question for Discussion

Why are there so many different types of retailers in the United States? What implications does this have for marketing strategy planning?

Exercise 12-2

Choosing the right kind of wholesaler

Introduction

Wholesalers are less dominant than they once were, but they are still a very important part in our economy. Wholesalers have become more specialized, so a marketing manager who must select a wholesaler must be concerned not only with finding a "good one," but also finding the right *type* of wholesaler.

There are two important types of wholesalers--*merchant wholesalers* and *agent middlemen.* The most important difference between the two types is that merchant wholesalers take title to (own) the products they handle, while agent middlemen do not. There are several types of merchant wholesalers and agent middlemen-and each performs different tasks. A marketing manager should select the type best suited to his marketing strategy. The various types of wholesalers are:

A.   *Merchant Wholesalers*

   1.   *Service Wholesalers*--including general merchandise, single-line and specialty whole-salers.
   2.   *Limited-Function Wholesalers*--including cash and carry, drop-shippers, truck whole-salers, catalog wholesalers, and rack jobbers.

B.   *Agent Intermediaries*--including auction companies, brokers, manufacturers' agents, and selling agents.

Assignment

This exercise will give you some practice in choosing the right type of wholesaler. Each of the following cases describes a situation in which a buyer or seller *might* want to use one or more types of merchant wholesalers or agent middlemen. Read each case carefully and then indicate which type(s) of wholesaler(s) would be most appropriate for each situation. Then explain your answer.

The first case is answered for you as an example.

1. CanMex Food Company was started in Winnipeg in 1970 by a Mexican immigrant. Over the years, the company's spicy corn chips have become a snack food favourite in the greater Winnipeg metropolitan market. In fact, CanMex's chips have become so popular that the company is now planning to open new plants in Vancouver and Montreal and to expand its market coverage across the whole of Canada. However, the marketing manager for the company doubts that CanMex can afford to set up the same plant-to-retailer delivery service in the new market areas as it now operates in the Winnipeg area.

    a) Type of Wholesaler: *Merchant wholesaler--truck wholesaler*

    b) Explanation: *The perishability of these products and the wide variety of outlets suggests the need for wholesalers who specialize in carrying stock and delivering on a frequent basis. There might be some specialty wholesalers willing to do this job--but truck wholesalers have specialized in this area for some years and might better understand the needs of the appropriate target markets. There still might be a problem in "selling" them on taking on this company's line.*

2. Willa Honea has been managing a picture frame shop that she owned with her husband. That seemed like an interesting thing to do when she graduated from college, but now she wants to start her own business. She thinks that the growing interest in health food opens up some interesting opportunities. With money borrowed from her father, she made a down payment on a bakery, which formerly belonged to a local cookie manufacturer. As her first product, she decided to produce a unique honey and bran muffin. She "discovered" the recipe for this tasty product while travelling in Switzerland, and she is certain that it can be a profitable item if she can distribute it through health food stores and nutrition centres. A number of the health food stores in her area have already expressed interest in carrying the muffins. However, Willa knows that she needs to obtain wider distribution--i.e. outside her present area--to be successful. One of the problems with expanding distribution, however, is that the muffins use no preservatives--so they are perishable.

    a) Type of Wholesaler:

    _____

    b) Explanation:

    _____

    _____

    _____

3. PowerSecure Corporation--a large manufacturer of backup ("uninterruptible") power supplies and battery packs for computer systems--has decided to produce and sell a new line of automobile batteries. The company deliberately avoided the highly competitive consumer replacement market in the past--but now feels that it has a product that is much longer lasting than any battery currently on the market. PowerSecure plans to distribute its new batteries through gasoline service stations, automotive stores, hardware stores, and mass-merchandisers. At the present time, the company has very limited financial resources--due to the cost of expanding its manufacturing facilities to produce the new line of batteries.

    a) Type of Wholesaler:

    _____

    b) Explanation:

    _____

    _____

    _____

4. TripleA Windows produces a line of insulated windows that are used for residential and commercial construction and remodeling. It supplies lumberyards, large glass contractors, and home-builders throughout a three-state area. TripleA uses its own trucks for deliveries within a hundred miles--and ships carload quantities by railroad. Currently, five sales reps call directly on its present customers. The company is faced with large swings in demand, however, and has had difficulty finding new customers.

    a) Type of Wholesaler:

    _____

    b) Explanation:

    _____

    _____

    _____

5. Vaneet Harish recently developed a patented recycling process for diseased trees. Officials from nearby cities--lacking any ecologically acceptable alternatives for disposing of trees that have been cut down--have agreed to deliver their trees free of charge to Harish's plant. There, the trees are processed and converted into products such as wood chips for landscaping, bark mulch, railroad ties, and patio blocks. However, Harish has little marketing experience and know-how. Usually buyers come to him by word of mouth--and then he is not sure how to price his products. The firm is in trouble financially and may have to declare bankruptcy unless Harish can locate a steady and sizable market for his products. However, he has no funds to hire a sales rep or to promote his products.

a)   Type of Wholesaler:

_____

b)   Explanation:

_____

_____

_____

6.   Industrial Coatings Co. (ICC) offers a full line of custom paint pigments, rust preventive coatings, and polishing compounds to a variety of industrial customers. Recently, a manufacturer of fibreglass hot-tubs asked ICC to develop a special polishing compound that could remove small scratches and blemishes from its new tubs. The polish worked so well that ICC decided that it might do well in the consumer market--not only for hot-tubs but also for standard fibreglass tubs and shower enclosures. A test market in Hamilton, Ontario--that relied on distribution through select hardware stores, hot-tub outlets, and even some mass-merchandisers--proved quite successful. Now, ICC has decided to sell the polish in other large cities--including Halifax, Montreal, Ottawa, Toronto, Winnipeg, Calgary, and Vancouver. ICC has the financial resources to manufacture the product and handle physical distribution to these areas. However, the company does not have any established contacts with the relevant retailers in these markets. Further, ICC is reluctant to hire new sales reps to promote its only consumer product.

a)   Type of Wholesaler:

_____

b)   Explanation:

_____

_____

_____

7.   Jessica Falk is marketing manager for Nature's Best, Inc., a firm that processes and markets premium grade frozen and canned vegetables. In recent years, Thelma has been expanding distribution of the Nature's Best brand. She does not expect more sales growth this year, but large increases are expected over the next few years. The company had planned to expand production capacity as it was needed, but that plan changed when several small vegetable processing plants came on the market. Nature's Best got the processing plants at a very low price because they had not been able to find enough business at profitable prices and were near bankruptcy. Falk is glad to know that the company now has the capacity to serve expanding market opportunities, but in the meantime she is looking for some way to quickly "get rid of" fairly large quantities of processed peas, corn, and other vegetables that were acquired with the processing plants.

a) Type of Wholesaler:

_____

b) Explanation:

_____

_____

_____

8. Mary Eng is the owner and president of ConnectIt, Inc. Her father started the firm after immigrating to Canada in 1970, and it became a respected supplier of brass electrical connectors. Most of the firm's business in the early years came from a relatively small number of electric power companies who placed large orders as they expanded their service in fast-growing areas of Southern Ontario. After her graduation from an electrical engineering program in 1996, Mary encouraged her father to shift the firm's focus to making specialized connectors used by firms that assemble electronic parts. In the past, the firm relied primarily on a network of manufacturers' agents who called on customer firms all over Canada. Now that Mary has taken over the reins of the firm, she wants to do a better job of reaching overseas markets. There are many thousands of small and large companies in countries all over the world that might use her very specialized connectors. Many of these firms don't have local suppliers but instead order the wide variety of supplies and parts they need from wholesalers in various countries. These wholesalers attract the firms' business with web sites and print materials that describe in detail the thousand and thousands of products that they carry.

a) Type of Wholesaler:

_____

b) Explanation:

_____

_____

_____

Question for Discussion

Why are there so many different types of wholesalers?

Exercise 12-3

Analyzing channels of distribution

Introduction

A channel of distribution consists of different people performing different functions. They are linked together by a common interest in marketing products that someone needs and wants. At one end of the channel are producers and at the other end are customers, and often there are "middlemen" in between.

Most products are *not* distributed directly from the manufacturer to the consumer or final user. The Internet is opening up new possibilities in the area, but middlemen will play an important role in many channels long into the future. In fact, the variety of middlemen has actually increased over the years. Middlemen exist because they perform some necessary functions--often more efficiently and economically than could either manufacturers or consumers.

This exercise focuses on several important types of middlemen. The objective is to determine what specific functions and activities each middleman performs--and to understand the role each plays in the distribution channel. Further, the exercise illustrates that while one type of middleman can sometimes be substituted for another--in other situations different types of middlemen perform complementary functions. Thus, while one channel may be longer than some others, it may also be faster, more economical, or more effective.

Assignment

The activities of several types of middlemen are described below in five cases. For each middleman described:

A.   Identify the *general type* of middleman (a full-service merchant wholesaler, a limited-function merchant wholesaler, or an agent middleman) *and* the *specific type* of middleman (rack jobber, broker, etc.).

B.   Diagram the channel or *channels* of distribution that are described in the case, using the following letters.

(M)	for Manufacturers	A	for Agent Middlemen
R	for Retailers	W	for Full-Service Wholesalers
(C)	for Consumers or Final Users	L	for Limited-Function Middlemen

The first case has been completed as an example.

1. Sammy Sayer sells carload quantities of chemicals to industrial users--for several chemical manufacturers. Sayer takes title to the products he sells. However, he does not take physical possession of them, although he often arranges for transporting the products. One part of his business that is costly is the frequent need to provide credit to small customers.

    a) General Type: *Sayer is a limited-function merchant wholesaler.*

        Specific Type: *drop-shipper*

    b) Diagram of the Channel:

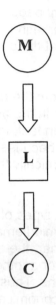

2. Heritage Textiles, Inc., is the manufacturer of HeritageWear brand acrylic fabrics. HeritageWear is the leading brand of fabric used in manufacturing waterproof awnings for stores, hotels, and homes. There are about 1,000 "fabricators" around the country who use HeritageWear to produce custom awnings for their clients. The fabricators order HeritageWear from distributors. The distributors maintain inventories (usually at a number of different branch locations) so that they can provide fast delivery of HeritageWear. The distributors also offer the fabricators credit, and they carry a complete assortment of grommets, zippers, snaps, metal poles, and other items the fabricators need to make awnings. Heritage Textiles has six salespeople who call on the distributors.

    a) General Type:

    _____

        Specific Type:

    _____

    b) Diagram of the Channel:

3. Recently, Heritage Textiles has developed new fabric designs for use in making cushions for outdoor furniture. However, Heritage's traditional distributors have not done a very good job of seeking out orders from the hundreds of small manufacturers who produce outdoor furniture. As a result, Heritage has turned to people like Sally McDonald for additional help in reaching this market. McDonald, who also represents producers of a number of other noncompeting lines, aggressively promotes HeritageWear to manufacturers of outdoor furniture in her region. McDonald earns a commission of 6 percent on all of the sales she generates. When McDonald calls in an order, Heritage ships the fabric directly to the furniture manufacturer.

a) General Type:

_____

Specific Type:

_____

b) Diagram of the Channel:

4. Eagle Distributors is a hardware wholesaler who sponsors a voluntary chain of independent hardware retailers. In addition to the usual wholesaling functions, Eagle provides special services for its affiliated stores: its own "dealer brand" products at very competitive prices, free-standing advertising inserts for distribution in the retailer's local newspaper, other merchandising assistance, employee training programs, store location and design assistance, and accounting aid. Merchandise economies are achieved through group buying, and a modern distribution centre is used to lower operating costs.

Some retailers who handle only small assortments of hardware items are too small to benefit from membership in the chain. Eagle operates a subsidiary to provide a smaller assortment of household items (such as extension cords, spray paint, screw drivers) for these "unaffiliated" customers. Retailers must provide their own transportation. The products are priced attractively--considering the small order quantities--but no credit is offered.

a) General Type:

_____

Specific Type:

_____

b) Diagram of the Channel:

5. Potluck Pottery, a small company in Dorval, Quebec, produces handcrafted pottery plates, cups, bowls, and vases. The owners of Potluck Popery want to focus on designing and producing pottery, not on the administrative and financial responsibilities of the business. As a result, they have worked out an arrangement with Kilnware, Inc., a wholesaler that basically operates as a "marketing manager" for Potluck Popery. Kilnware finds retail gift shops to carry the pottery--and handles pricing, selling, advertising, and all paperwork on orders, including billing and collections. Kilnware earns a large commission on all sales, but Potluck's owners like the arrangement because all they need to do is arrange transportation to get the pottery to the retailers.

    a)   General Type:

_____

            Specific Type:

_____

    b)   Diagram of the Channel:

6. ElectroNet is an Internet-based firm that works with manufacturers of a wide variety of electronic parts and components and helps them quickly liquidate excess or obsolete inventory. ElectroNet does not actually buy the inventory; rather, it sells the inventory (usually as a complete "lot") on a commission basis by putting a detailed description of what is for sale on its web site and then selling it to the highest bidder. For example, Specialty Control manufactures circuit boards used to control electric motors. Current models of Specialty Control circuit boards are usually sold to distributors who supply manufacturers of various types of electronic equipment. However, when Specialty Control introduces a new model, it turns to ElectroNet to sell off its remaining inventory of the discontinued model. Many of the firms that bid on the products listed on ElectroNet's web site are in developing nations where there is demand for the products, even if they are not on the cutting edge of technology.

    a)   General Type:

_____

            Specific Type:

_____

    b)   Diagram of the Channel:

Question for Discussion

Are salespeople middlemen? Where are salespeople shown in channel diagrams?

Exercise 12-4

Selecting channel intermediaries

This exercise is based on computer-aided problem number 13--Selecting Channel Intermediaries. A complete description of the problem appears on pages 378-379 of Wong/Shapiro, 11th edition.

After further discussion, the owner of Giftware Distributing--the merchant wholesaler--says that he might take on some, or even all, of the responsibility for advertising the Art Glass items to gift stores--if Art Glass will sell to him at a lower price--to help cover the advertising expense. Art Glass is considering this idea--and trying to decide what type of arrangement makes the most sense.

1. Art Glass' marketing manager has decided that it will help him analyze the decision if he first figures out how much Giftware will earn under the current arrangement--assuming that Giftware sells 4,500 units. Although he did not include this calculation in the spreadsheet, he can calculate the total dollar markup because he knows how much Giftware would pay for each item and Giftware's selling price. What is the total dollar markup (contribution to profit) for Giftware?

    Giftware's selling price per item: $ _____

    less, Art Glass' price to Giftware: $ _____

    equals, Giftware's markup per unit: $ _____

    multiplied times the total units sold: 4,500

    equals total $ markup (contribution to
    profit) earned by Giftware: $ _____

2. Since Art Glass is considering spending $8,000 on advertising to support Giftware's marketing effort, and since Giftware is expected to sell about 4,500 units, what is the expected advertising cost per unit?

    Advertising expenditure per unit: $ _____

3. Use the spreadsheet to calculate the profit contribution to Art Glass if it sells to Giftware at $10.25 a unit, and Giftware does the advertising needed to sell 4,500 units (that is, so that Art Glass has no advertising expense). Would this be a better arrangement for Art Glass than what it was originally considering? Briefly, explain why or why not?

   Art Glass' Total Contribution to Profit with this plan: $ _____

   Explanation:

   _____

   _____

   _____

   _____

4. Art Glass' marketing manager thinks that Giftware would be more likely to agree to an arrangement in which Art Glass pays for some of the "up front" advertising expense. He is thinking about offering to pay half of the proposed $8,000 advertising expense. If this plan is used (and Giftware sells 4,500 units), what price should Art Glass charge to enable it to make the same profit contribution as it would if it paid for all of the advertising and sold to the wholesaler at the $12.00 price? (Hint: change the advertising expense on the spreadsheet, and use the What If analysis to vary Art Glass' selling price).

   Art Glass' selling price to make about the same contribution if it pays for only half of the advertising expense:

   Art Glass' price to Giftware $ _____

   Total profit contribution to Art Glass $ _____

5. At Art Glass' price in question 4, how much would Giftware have left as a "contribution to profit" if it sold 4,500 units and paid $4,000 for advertising expense? (Please show your calculations below. Please label the numbers you use.)

   Giftware's "contribution to profit" $ _____

6. Art Glass' marketing manager wants to know how this advertising cost-sharing arrangement would compare to the original proposal (that is, with Art Glass paying all of the advertising expense but getting a higher price from Giftware) if Giftware were able to sell 5,000 units, rather than the expected 4,500.

Art Glass' contribution to profit:

from 5,000 units sold at $12.00 with $8,000 ad expense: $ _____

from 5,000 units sold at $_____ with $4,000 in ad expense: $ _____

7. Would Giftware be motivated to work harder at selling Art Glass' products under the proposed ad cost-sharing arrangement than it would if it bought at the higher price but with Art Glass paying all the advertising expense)? Briefly, explain why or why not?

_____

_____

_____

_____

_____

_____

_____

Chapter 13

Promotion— Introduction to Integrated Marketing Communications

Chapter Summary

- **Know the advantages and disadvantages of the promotion methods a marketing manager can use in strategy planning.**
  Personal selling involves face-to-face interaction between salespeople and customers, allowing for instantaneous feedback and adaptation on the part of the salesperson. The downside of personal selling is its high cost. *Mass selling* involves targeting a large number of potential customers through advertising and promotion. *Advertising* is any paid form of non-personal presentation of ideas, goods, or services by an identified sponsor, while *publicity* is any unpaid form of presentation. *Sales promotion* refers to promotion activities (other than those listed above) that stimulate interest, trial, or purchase. Sales promotion can be implemented quickly and deliver faster results than other promotion methods.

- **Understand the integrated marketing communications concept and why most firms use a blend of different promotion methods.**
  Each promotion method has its own strengths and weaknesses. Combining promotion methods gives the marketer a comprehensive set of tools. Choosing the right balance between the various promotion tools will result in integrated marketing communications. Care should be taken that all the different forms of promotion convey a complete and consistent message to the target customer.

- **Understand the importance of promotion objectives.**
  Good marketing managers are interested in (1) reinforcing present attitudes or relationships that might lead to favourable behaviour, or (2) actually changing the attitudes and behaviour of the firm's target market. In establishing your promotion objectives it is useful to determine who you want to inform, persuade, or remind, and why. These objectives are unique to each company, and may even vary by promotion method.

- **Know how new customer-initiated interactive communication is different.**
  New interactive technologies are making it easier for customers to search for information on their own. Customer-initiated communication begins with a customer driven search process. The customer then decides how much information they wish to receive, and when satisfied may take action, which may be immediate. As new customer approaches occur, marketers are now able to personalize the messages available for their customers. One of the fastest growing areas for customer-initiated communication is the Internet.

- **Understand how direct response promotion is helping marketers develop more targeted promotion blends.**

Direct response promotion is designed to prompt immediate feedback from potential customers. It is a form of direct communication between the seller and an individual customer other than personal selling. Databases of consumer profiles are used to generate mailing lists, phone numbers, and broadcast information, allowing the firm to direct its promotion toward its target customers.

- **Know how typical promotion plans are blended to get an extra push from intermediaries and help from customers in pulling products through the channel.**
  Pushing a product through a channel means using normal promotion efforts to sell the entire marketing mix to possible channel members. Producers usually take on most of the responsibility for the pushing effort, although most wholesalers and some other intermediaries take on some of the promotional activities. The overall message being communicated is likely to be most effective when all of the individual messages are carefully integrated. On the other hand, when producers focus their promotional activities on creating consumer demand, consumers will ask intermediaries for the product, thereby creating a pull. Most often push and pull strategies are used in some combination.

- **Understand how promotion blends typically vary over the adoption curve and product life cycle.**
  The adoption curve shows when different groups accept ideas. There is a need to change promotional strategies as time passes and new stages of the adoption process begin. This curve helps to explain why a product goes through the product life cycle stages. In the *market introduction,* stage the objective is to inform and build primary demand. As more competitors enter the market in the *market growth* stage, the promotional emphasis shifts to building selective demand and to persuading customers to buy the company's own brand. In the *market maturity* stage, strategies that are more aggressive and personal selling are needed to compete against the new market entrants. Total dollars allocated to promotion are likely to rise. As the product enters the *sales decline* stage, total dollars spent on promotion tend to decrease as firms cut costs in an attempt to remain profitable. Firms may sometimes inject new funds into promotion at this stage to slow down the cycle.

- **Understand how to determine how much to spend on promotion efforts.**
  There is rarely enough money to do all the promotion that you want to do. Small firms may find that they are unable to use mass media and must instead focus their promotion efforts on methods with a higher cost per person "reached". Different ways of setting the promotion budget include (1) percentage of sales, (2) matching competitors, (3) dollars per sales unit, (4) percentage of uncommitted revenue, and (5) based on the task to be done.

Important Terms

integrated marketing communications (IMC), p. 383

personal selling, p. 383

promotion, p. 383

advertising, p. 384

mass selling, p. 384

publicity, p. 385

sales promotion, p. 385

advertising managers, p. 386

decoding, p. 391

encoding, p. 391

message channel, p. 392

direct marketing, p. 395

pushing, p. 399

pulling, p. 401

adoption curve, p. 403

innovators, p. 403

True-False Questions

_____ 1. Promotion is communicating information between seller and potential buyer or others in the channel--to influence attitudes and behaviour.

_____ 2. Advertising is any form of nonpersonal presentation of ideas, goods, or services.

_____ 3. Sales promotion refers to activities such as personal selling, advertising and publicity.

_____ 4. All sales promotion is aimed at final consumers or users.

_____ 5. In total, personal selling is more expensive than advertising.

_____ 6. Planning of promotion blends can be best accomplished by placing specialists in charge of each promotion method; for example, the firm might appoint a sales manager, an advertising manager, and a sales promotion manager to weigh the pros and cons of the various approaches and come up with an effective blend.

_____ 7. To avoid conflicts, it is usually best for sales promotion to be handled by a firm's advertising manager and sales manager--not by a sales promotion specialist.

_____ 8. An effective blending of all of the firm's promotion efforts should produce integrated advertising communications.

_____ 9. All of a firm's different communications to a target market should be consistent.

_____ 10. The overall objective of promotion is to affect behaviour.

_____ 11. The three basic objectives of promotion are to inform, persuade, and/or remind.

_____ 12. The AIDA model consists of four promotion jobs: attention, information, desire, and action.

_____ 13. Much of what we call promotion is really wasted effort because it does not really communicate.

14. A major advantage of personal selling is that the source can get immediate feedback to help direct subsequent communication efforts.

15. The term "noise" refers only to distorting influences within the message channel, which reduce the effectiveness of the communication process.

16. If the right message channel is selected, problems related to encoding and decoding in the communication process will be avoided.

17. The communication process is complicated by the fact that receivers are usually influenced not only by the message but also by the source and the message channel.

18. Direct marketing is direct communication between a seller and an individual customer using a promotion method other than face-to-face personal selling.

19. Unfortunately, direct-response promotion is limited to mail.

20. A firm that wants to send a specific message to a clearly identified target market probably should seriously consider using integrated direct marketing.

21. Firms who use direct-response promotion need to be very sensitive to ethical and environmental concerns.

22. Interactive information technologies are changing the traditional communication process to a customer-initiated process.

23. In customer-initiated interactive communication, action is more immediate than in the traditional communication process.

24. There is no one right promotion blend for all situations.

25. Salespeople should usually be expected to do all the promotion to middlemen.

26. One reason personal selling is important in promotion to middlemen is that marketing mixes often have to be adjusted from one geographic territory to another.

27. Promotion to employees is especially important in service-oriented industries where the quality of the employees' efforts is a big part of the product.

28. "Pulling a product through the channel" means using normal promotion effort to help sell the whole marketing mix to possible channel members.

29. The large number of potential customers practically forces producers of consumer products and retailers to emphasize advertising and sales promotion.

30. Since business customers are much less numerous than final consumers, it is more practical to emphasize mass selling in the promotion blends aimed at

these markers.

____ 31. The adoption curve focuses on the process by which an individual accepts new ideas.

____ 32. Publicity in technical journals is likely to be a more effective method of promotion than personal selling for reaching extremely innovative business firms.

____ 33. The late majority is influenced more by other late adopters—rather than by advertising.

____ 34. Situations that may affect the promotion blend are the stage in the product life cycle and the nature of competition.

____ 35. During the market introduction stage of product life cycles, promotion must pioneer acceptance of the product idea--not just the company's own brand—to stimulate primary demand.

____ 36. In the market growth stage of the product life cycle, promotion emphasis must begin to shift from stimulating selective demand to stimulating primary demand for the company's own brand.

____ 37. In the market maturity stage, the promotion blend of consumer products firms rely almost exclusively on advertising to consumers.

____ 38. Firms in monopolistic competition may favour mass selling because they have differentiated their marketing mixes somewhat--and have something to talk about.

____ 39. Budgeting for marketing expenditures as a percentage of either past or forecasted sales leads to larger marketing expenditures when business is good and sales are rising--and to reduced spending when business is poor.

____ 40. The most sensible approach to budgeting marketing expenditures is the "task method."

Answers to True-False Questions

1. T, p. 383	15. F, p. 390	29. T, p. 403
2. F, p. 384	16. F, p. 391	30. F, p. 402
3. F, p. 385	17. T, p. 391	31. F, p. 403
4. F, p. 385	18. T, p. 395	32. T, p. 385
5. T, p. 383	19. F, p. 395	33. T, p. 405
6. F, p. 386	20. T, p. 395	34. T, p. 405-406
7. F, p. 386	21. T, p. 396	35. T, p. 405
8. F, p. 383	22. T, p. 395	36. F, p. 405
9. T, p. 383	23. T, p. 395	37. F, p. 405
10. T, p. 383	24. T, p. 399	38. T, p. 406

11. T, p. 389
12. F, p. 390
13. T, p. 390
14. T, p. 383

25. F. p. 400
26. T, p. 400
27. T, p. 401
28. F, p. 401

39. T, p. 407
40. T, p. 407

Multiple-Choice Questions (Circle the correct response)

1.   Promotion does *not* include:
        a.   personal selling.
        b.   advertising.
        c.   publicity.
        d.   sales promotion.
        e.   Promotion includes all of the above.

2.   Personal selling is more appropriate than mass selling when:
        a.   the target market is large and scattered.
        b.   there are many potential customers and a desire to keep promotion costs low.
        c.   flexibility is not important.
        d.   immediate feedback is desirable.
        e.   All of the above are true.

3.   Sales promotion activities:
        a.   try to stimulate interest, trial or purchase.
        b.   always, involve direct face-to-face communication between sellers and potential customers.
        c.   usually, take a long time to implement.
        d.   are usually a good substitute for personal selling and advertising.
        e.   All of the above.

4.   Sales promotion can be aimed at:
        a.   final consumers or users.
        b.   middlemen.
        c.   the company's own sales force.
        d.   all of the above.
        e.   only a and b above.

5.   Deciding on the appropriate promotion blend is a job for the firm's:
        a.   advertising agency.
        b.   marketing manager.
        c.   advertising manager.
        d.   sales manager.
        e.   sales promotion manager.

6.   Promotion is intended to make a firm's demand curve:
        a.   become more elastic--while shifting it to the right.
        b.   become more inelastic--while shifting it to the left.
        c.   become more elastic--while shifting it to the left.
        d.   become more inelastic--while shifting it to the right.

7.   Which basic promotion objective should be emphasized by a firm whose products very similar to those offered by many competitors?
        a.   Communicating
        b.   Persuading
        c.   Reminding
        d.   Informing
        e.   Reinforcing

8. The AIDA model's four promotion jobs are getting:
   a. awareness, interest, demand, action.
   b. attention, interest, desire, action.
   c. action, interest, desire, acceptance.
   d. awareness, interest, decision, acceptance.

9. Which of the following is *not* one of the basic elements in the communication process?
   a. Feedback
   b. Receiver
   c. Encoding
   d. Dissonance
   e. Message channel

10. Communication is *most difficult* to achieve when:
    a. the source and the receiver are not in face-to-face contact with each other.
    b. immediate feedback is not provided.
    c. any trace of "noise" remains in the message channel.
    d. the source and the receiver do not have a common frame of reference.
    e. the encoder does not do the decoding.

11. Direct response promotion may include:
    a. Telephone
    b. Print
    c. E-mail
    d. Internet
    e. All of the above

12. To communicate a very specific message to a very select, well-identified group of consumers, one probably should use:
    a. magazines aimed at special-interest groups.
    b. newspapers.
    c. television.
    d. integrated direct-response promotion marketing.
    e. radio.

13. The Calmar Corporation is introducing a new product next month. To prepare for the introduction, the marketing manager is having his sales force call on distributors to explain the unique features of the new product, how the distributors can best promote it, and what sales volume and profit margins they can reasonably expect. In addition, Calmar is budgeting 2 percent of its estimated sales for magazine advertising. This is an example of:
    a. selective distribution.
    b. a "pulling" policy.
    c. exclusive distribution.
    d. a "pushing" policy.
    e. intensive distribution.

14. Which of the following statements about the *target of promotion* and promotion blends is *true?*
    a. There is no one right promotion blend for all situations.

b. Promotion to middlemen emphasizes personal selling.
c. Promotion to employees involves pushing.
d. Promotion to final consumers is usually a combination of pushing and pulling.
e. All of the above are true.

15. Regarding planning a promotion blend, a good marketing manager knows that:
a. the job of reaching all the people in a "buying centre" is made easier by their low turnover.
b. there is not much chance of economies of scale in promotion.
c. it is seldom practical for salespeople to carry the whole promotion load.
d. salespeople can be very economical since they devote almost all of their time to actual selling activities.
e. None of the above is true.

16. Jaime Garriss is strongly influenced by her peer group--and she often adopts a new product only after they have pressured her to try it. She makes little use of mass media and salespeople as sources of information. In terms of the adoption curve, she would be in what category?
a. Laggard
b. Late majority
c. Early adopter
d. Innovator
e. Early majority

17. During the market introduction stage of the product life cycle, the basic objective of promotion is to:
a. spend more money on promotion than competitors.
b. remind customers about the firm and its products.
c. inform the potential customers of the product.
d. stimulate selective demand.
e. persuade the early majority to buy the product.

18. Which of the following is the most sensible approach to budgeting for marketing expenditures?
a. Budget expenditures as a percentage of either past or forecasted sales.
b. Set aside all uncommitted sales revenue--perhaps including budgeted profits.
c. Base the budget on the amount required to reach predetermined objectives.
d. Match expenditures with competitors.
e. Set the budget at a certain number of cents or dollars per sales unit--using the past year or estimated year ahead as a base for comparison.

Answers to Multiple-Choice Questions

1. e, p. 383
2. d, p. 383
3. a, p. 385
4. d, p. 385
5. b, p. 386
6. d, p. 388

7. b, p. 389
8. b, p. 389-390
9. d, p. 390
10. d, p. 391
11. e, p. 395
12. d, p. 396

13. d, p. 399
14. e, p. 399
15. c, p. 400
16. b, p. 404
17. c, p. 405
18. c, p. 407

Additional Questions to Test Your Understanding (Fill in the blanks)

1. List and briefly describe the two forms of mass selling?

   a. _____ -

   _____

   _____

   _____

   b. _____ -

   _____

   _____

   _____

2. Match each of the following specialist with the correct job description listed below:

Sales Manager   Advertising Manager   Sales Promotion Manager

   a. _____ - Manage their company's mass selling efforts on television, and in newspapers, magazines, and other media. Their job is to choose the right media and develop the ads.

   b. _____ - Manage their company's sales promotion efforts. In some companies have independent status and report directly to the marketing manager.

   c. _____ - Concerned with managing personal selling. Often id responsible for building good distribution channels and implementing Place policies.

3. Which promotion blends should be used with the following product-life cycle stages?

   a. Market Introduction – Use

   _____

   _____

   _____

   b. Market Growth – Use

   _____

   _____

   _____

   c. Market Maturity – Use

   _____

      d.   Sales Decline – Use

_____

Answers to Additional Questions

1. a. Advertising – Any paid form of nonpersonal presentation of ideas, goods, or services by an identified sponsor. (p. 384)
     b. Publicity – Any unpaid form of nonpersonal presentation of ideas, goods, or services (p.385)

2.
     a. Advertising Managers, (p. 386)
     b. Sales Promotion Managers, (p.387)
     c. Sales Managers, (p. 386)

3.
     a. Use personal selling and sales promotion. (p. 405)
     b. Use mass selling (advertising and publicity) and personal selling. (p. 405)
     c. Use mass selling and sales promotion for consumer products. Business products may require aggressive personal selling and perhaps more advertising.(p. 405)
     d. Use more targeted promotion to reach customers who still want the product and increase promotion to try to slow the sales decline stage at least temporarily. (p. 406)

Exercise 13-1

The traditional communication process in promotion

Introduction

Promotion must communicate effectively--or it is wasted effort. Yet, it is often difficult to achieve effective communication. The communication process can break down in many different ways.

Understanding the whole communication process can improve promotion. As discussed in more detail in the text (see pages 390-391 and Exhibit 13-5), the major elements of the traditional communication process include:

- a source,
- encoding,
- a message channel,
- decoding,
- a receiver,
- feedback, and
- noise.

Each of these different elements can influence the effectiveness of a firm's promotion effort--so marketing managers need to consider each element when planning or modifying their promotion. The whole promotion effort may fail because of a failure in just one element.

This exercise is designed to enhance your understanding of the traditional communication process in promotion planning. The focus here is on specific elements of the process.

Assignment

Listed below are several descriptions of different promotion situations. In each case, there is a problem with the promotion effort. For some reason, communication has not been effective. You may see different elements of the promotion process that may be related to the problem. However, the focus of each situation is on a specific element of the process. Therefore, for each situation, write down *one* element (from the list above) that you think is the major problem. Then, briefly explain why you think that element is a problem, and how the communication process might need to be changed to correct the problem. (Note: your recommendation may include changing one or more elements of the traditional communication process other than the one that you noted as the major problem.)

1. A company that produces expensive leather briefcases for business executives wants to expand its sales in overseas markets. In Canada, the company's ads--placed in business magazines—show a group of well-dressed men and women executives preparing for a meeting. Each executive has a briefcase, and the headline for the ad says "If you want respect, it's as important to look professional as it is to act professional. " The company adapted this same copy thrust to a Japanese ad that featured Japanese models. However, the effort was a failure. In Japan, there are still very few women in high executive positions, and for many target customers the ad did not help to create a "prestige" image for the company's products.

    a)   Problem element of the communication process:

    _____

    b)   Explanation:

2. A company has been doing advertising for its line of weight-loss diet supplements. The supplements are targeted to overweight, middle-aged men and women. The company's ads appear on TV exercise programs that are viewed by the same target market. In the ad, a trim professional model explains the product and how safely and effectively it works. However, the ads do not seem to be effective. Apparently, the overweight viewers do not believe that a trim model really knows about the difficulties of losing weight.

    a)   Problem element of the communication process:

    _____

    b)   Explanation:

4. A student newspaper on a college campus wants to increase revenues by attracting more faculty subscriptions. Very few faculty currently subscribe. A study by students in a marketing research course found that many faculty do not subscribe because they think that the price of a subscription is much higher than is actually the case. The subscription manager has placed large ads in the paper that clearly show how little it actually costs to subscribe, but so far faculty response has been very disappointing.

    a) Problem element of the communication process:

    _____

    b) Explanation:

5. Home-Based Life Insurance Company has equipped its sales agents with notebook computers so they can quickly do a detailed, personalized analysis of a prospect's needs and present the results with on-screen graphs--while working with the prospect. The company thought that the computers would be especially helpful for presentations about its combined insurance and retirement-savings products--which are targeted at retired professionals who are interested in leaving a "nest-egg" for their grandchildren. However, since the agents started using the on-screen presentations, their ratio of "closes" (signed contracts) to sales calls has dropped for the retiree market segment. One of the retirees commented to the salespeople that "we old people don't want all this razzle-dazzle, we just want to hear what you have to say about the plan." However, most of the agents continue to use the notebook computers anyway--because of its powerful presentation graphics.

    a) Problem element of the communication process:

    _____

    b) Explanation:

Question for Discussion

Does a marketer who has set up a web site on the Internet to enable interactive communications initiated by customers need to worry about the elements of the traditional communication process? Explain your thinking.

Exercise 13-2

Using the adoption curve to develop promotion blends

Introduction

We have continually stressed that each of the "four Ps" should be matched with the needs and characteristics of target markets. However, marketing mix planning can get more complicated in the promotion area. Even though a target market may have fairly homogeneous needs--*groups of people within this market may differ considerably in their sources of information and how quickly they adopt new products.* Therefore, marketing managers may need to use several promotion blends--over time--to communicate effectively with this target market.

Promotion blend planning should use the adoption curve--which shows when different groups accept ideas. Five adopter groups are commonly used: innovators, early adopters, the early majority, the late majority, and laggards.

As outlined in the text (see pages 403-405), a unique pattern of communication exists within and between each of these adopter groups. Therefore, each may require its own promotion blend.

Assignment

This exercise is designed to show how an understanding of the adoption curve can be helpful when planning promotion blends. Read the following case and then *develop a promotion blend for each adopter group* within the firm's target market. Outline in detail what kind of mass selling, personal selling, and sales promotion you would use, if any, to reach each adopter group. Be specific. For example, if you decide to advertise in magazines, give examples of the magazines you would use. Above all, be creative-it's expected of you!

After you outline your promotion blend for each adopter group, explain *why* you chose that particular blend in the space marked "Comments." Here, you should consider some of the important characteristics of each adopter group--as discussed in the text.

Note that you are only being asked to focus *on promotion to final consumers.* The firm would also have to do some promotion work in the channels-just to obtain distribution--and adoption curve thinking should be applied to middleman adoption too. However, all of this promotion activity should be ignored here--because we want to focus on the way that final consumers would accept the product and its impact on promotion planning.

Mediamax, Ltd.--one of the world's largest manufacturers of electronic equipment--has just announced the introduction of a revolutionary new "personal information system" called the Ultimedia. Aimed primarily at the "serious consumer" market, the Ultimedia features a fascinating combination of features and capabilities. It can play and record sound, perform calculations, and display text, numbers, pictures and other images on a small (4" diametre) high resolution display screen. It also has built-in software for jotting down notes, maintaining an appointment calendar, and performing calculations. One electronics magazine described the Ultimedia as "like a personal CD player/recorder, a programmable calculator, a personal organizer, and a dictating machine all rolled into one exquisite, hand-held design." The sound quality of the Ultimedia is exceptional. In fact, in the past this quality of sound could only be achieved with prerecorded compact discs. However, rather than relying on CDs to store music the Ultimedia uses a new optical disk technology. An optical disk looks like a standard 3.5" computer floppy disk, but it can store as much information as a CD. Further, information (music, software, data) is stored on these optical disks in a digital format. Digital recording has been standard on computers for years, but the development of the optical storage disk has made it possible to incorporate a *"digital enhancement"* system that reduces static and distortion when recording or playing music. This means that the user can record collections of tapes or CDs--and get a higher quality sound than was possible with the original. Further, the Ultimedia has *automatic indexing*--so the Ultimedia electronically "marks" the beginning of any material stored on the disk--whether it is music or dictation. This allows the user to easily and quickly skip over a selection and "search" for a particular song or message. While such features can be found on some CD players and multimedia computers, the Ultimedia is the first system to offer high quality digital recording on a high capacity removable media that can handle music as well as standard "computer-type" files. Further, one optical disk can store many more songs than a standard CD.

The Ultimedia also offers several other important benefits. With its built-in rechargeable lithium battery, small case, light weight (about the same as a Sony DiscMan), and stereo headset, the unit is truly portable and can be used anywhere--at home, school or office, on trips, while taking a walk, or at the beach. In addition, it features an innovative system of "user friendly" instructions (the user selects either on-screen or audio instructions) and controls so that is so simple even a child can automatically "program" any of the Ultimedia's functions. For example, it will play back a selection of songs in any order, any number of times, while the user is at the same time updating calendar entries or doing calculations.

The Ultimedia also has a unique "digital dubbing" feature and built in microphone. This allows the user to simultaneously listen to and record (or "edit") a selection on the optical disk. For example, users can listen to and then modify previously recorded reminders (such as a daily "to do" list). This may be used for dictation, or the user can even play an instrumental selection and add in his or her own voice track. In combination, all of these features make the Ultimedia one of the world's most sophisticated consumer audio recorders.

The Ultimedia has a manufacturer's suggested list price of $595--but it is expected to retail for about $295. This price is not out of line when one considers the unique capabilities of the Ultimedia--but the price is much higher than consumers are used to paying for a CD player, a dictating machine, a personal organizer, or a programmable calculator. Further, some of the possible uses of the unit will never have occurred to potential customers. For example, the dictation and "edit" feature of the Ultimedia makes it easy for the user to create and update an "audio" appointment calendar, address book, phone list, or even diary. Therefore, promotion may be critical for the new unit--which will be distributed through electronics retailers, some computer and stereo dealers, and selected electronics equipment mass-merchandisers.

Mediamax, Ltd. managers are not sure what promotion blend to use to introduce this new recorder. One manager has noted that some customers will adopt the Ultimedia faster than others--and therefore the promotion blend may have to vary over time. Therefore, they are asking you to advise them.

**Suggested Promotion Blends for Communicating with Potential
Consumers in Each Adopter Group**

1.   Innovators

    a)   Market characteristics:

    _____

    _____

    _____

    _____

    b)   Promotion blend:

    _____

    _____

    _____

    _____

    c)   Comments:

    _____

    _____

    _____

    _____

2. Early adopters

a) Market characteristics:

_____

_____

_____

_____

b) Promotion blend:

_____

_____

_____

_____

c) Comments:

_____

_____

_____

_____

3. Early majority

a) Market characteristics:

_____

_____

_____

_____

b) Promotion blend:

_____

_____

_____

_____

c)   Comments:

_____

_____

_____

_____

4.   Late majority

   a)   Market characteristics:

_____

_____

_____

_____

   b)   Promotion blend:

_____

_____

_____

_____

   c)   Comments:

_____

_____

_____

_____

5.   Laggards

   a)   Market characteristics:

_____

_____

_____

_____

b)   Promotion blend:

_____

_____

_____

_____

c)   Comments:

_____

_____

_____

_____

Question for Discussion

Which of the adopter categories is probably the most important from the viewpoint of the marketing strategy planner? That is, which is most crucial in launching a successful new product? Why?

Exercise 13-3

Selecting a
Communications Channel

This exercise is based on computer-aided problem number 13--Selecting a Communications Channel. A complete description of the problem appears on page 410 of Wong/Shapiro, 11th edition.

Helen Troy had almost decided to go with advertising on FM radio--given the numbers on the original spreadsheet. This would result in a "cost per buyer" of about $8.65. At that point, the sales rep for the magazine space called and suggested that Troy consider some new information.

1.   First, the rep said it was hard to verify the actual number of readers--but that some of his 200,000 magazines are actually read by two or three people. He stressed that, when this "pass-along circulation" is included, the actual number of readers is greater than 200,000--probably between 230,000 and 250,000. Troy decided to evaluate this new information with her spreadsheet. Do you think it should influence her decision? Briefly, explain why.

_____

_____

_____

_____

2.   The magazine's sales rep also told Troy about a new "quantity discount." The magazine has reduced the rate for a one-page ad to $1,500 when an advertiser agrees to place five or more ads in one year. How does the lower ad rate affect the two kinds of costs? (Note: do this analysis and subsequent analyses assuming 240,000 readers--for the reasons described in the question above.)

          $ _____ cost per aware prospect $ _____ cost per buyer

3.   As in question 2, companies that do more advertising often get lower advertising rates. Briefly, discuss how this might affect their ability to compete with other firms.

_____

_____

4. The magazine's sales rep has also told Troy that the magazine has just started to include a "reader service" card in each issue--so readers can follow up on advertising of interest by simply returning the postage-paid card. Troy will receive all of the names--and her salespeople can follow up with personal phone calls. Troy is optimistic that this could help identify good prospects and increase the percentage of "awares" converted to buyers from a low of the expected 1.5 percent to as high as 2.5 percent. Given the increased number of readers due to pass-along circulation, the rate discount for placing five or more ads, and the reader interest card, evaluate the "new" situation-- regarding use of the magazine. How does it compare with the original spreadsheet proposal for the radio campaign? Briefly, summarize your conclusions based on your analysis. (Hint: one approach is to do a What If analysis--varying the percent of awares who will buy and comparing these results with the results for the radio ad.)

Chapter 14

Personal selling

Chapter Summary

- **Understand the importance and nature of personal selling.**
  Personal face-to-face selling allows the salesperson to adjust to the situation and the customer – taking culture and behaviour into consideration – making it more effective than advertisements and displays. Both the salesperson and the customer can ask questions and receive instant feedback. Personal selling can be very expensive in terms of a per "sales contact cost". It is often the company's largest single operating expense.

- **Know the three basic sales tasks and what the various kinds of salespeople can be expected to do.**
  (1) *Order getters* establish relationships with new customers. They must have an in-depth knowledge of the product, their firm, and their customer's business to help customers solve their problems. (2) *Order takers* sell to regular, established customers. Sales are often routine, with follow-ups to ensure customer satisfaction. Order takers work on improving the relationship with the customer and are involved with training and informing customers on their products. (3) *Supporters* help the order getters, but do not usually take orders. They are focused on enhancing customer relationships and generating orders in the long term.

- **Know how sales technology affects the way sales are performed.**
  First, technology is actually performing sales tasks, and second is to use information technology to support the salesforce. The use of e-commerce applications to share inventory levels, orders, etc. is an example of technology performing sales tasks. In terms of sales support, software tools like spreadsheet analysis, electronic presentations, time management, sales forecasting, customer contact and shelf-space management are now available to the salesperson.

- **Know what the sales manager must do – including selecting, training, and organizing salespeople – to carry out the personal selling job.**
  Salespeople are often divided by task, account type, or sales territory. The sales manager must establish the best possible number of sales reps by determining how much one salesperson can do in a specific time and how much total work needs to be done in that same period. Sales candidates are often carefully screened, including background checks and psychological tests. Once hired, salespeople need to be taught about the company, products, presentations, relationships with customer, and professional selling skills.

- **Understand how the right compensation can help motivate and control salespeople.**
  Salespeople should be paid in such a manner that they want to do – for personal reasons – what is best for the company. That involves setting (1) the level of compensation, and (2) the method of payment. The three most common payment plans are (1) straight salary, (2) straight commission, (3) a combination of the two. The sales manager should pick a compensation plan that offers a balance between security and incentive to sell. A straight salary, in combination with close supervision, allows for greater managerial control, but offers fewer incentives for people to sell.

- **Understand when and where to use the three types of sales presentations.**

  Prepared sales presentations are memorized presentations that are *not* adapted for each customer, and are prepared statements that include a close. Prepared sales presentations are used when a short presentation is practical, or when a sales pitch is being offered by an unskilled salesperson. Because they treat all customers equally, they will work with some and not with others. *Consultative selling* requires the salesperson to develop a good understanding of the customer before trying to close the sale. The salesperson may speak about some general benefits of the product or service, as a way to generate interest. Customer goals are then determined. The salesperson then shows how the product meets the identified needs of the customer and attempts to close the sale. This approach is often used when there are subtle differences in the target customers. The selling formula approach starts with a prepared presentation outline, and then leads the customer through some logical steps and attempts to close the sale. The salesperson should communicate key points early and then shift the focus to the customer as time progresses. The selling formula approach is used for similar customers and by relatively untrained salespeople.

Important Terms

order getters, p. 417
order-getting, p. 417
order takers, p. 420
order-taking, p. 420
missionary salespeople, p. 422
supporting salespeople, p. 422
technical specialists, p. 422
team selling, p. 423
major accounts sales force, p. 424
sales territory, p. 424

telemarketing, p. 424
job description, p. 431
sales quota, p. 435
prospecting, p. 436
close, p. 438
consultative selling approach, p. 438
prepared sales presentation, p. 438
sales presentation, p. 438
selling formula approach, p. 439

True-False Questions

_____ 1. It should be the responsibility of the sales manager--not the marketing manager--to make final decisions about how many and what kinds of salespeople are needed.

_____ 2. Personal selling has declined in importance to the point that there are now more Americans employed in advertising than in personal selling.

_____ 3. Professional salespeople do not just try to sell the customer—they try to help him buy.

_____ 4. Some salespeople are expected to act as marketing managers for their own geographic territories and develop their own marketing mixes and strategies.

_____ 5. Three basic sales tasks are found in most sales organizations—although in some situations one salesperson might have to do all three tasks.

_____ 6. Good order getters are essential in sales of business installations and accessory equipment.

_____ 7. Sales representatives for progressive merchant wholesalers often serve as advisors to their customers--not just as order takers.

_____ 8. Unsought consumer products often require order getters--to convince customers of the product's value.

_____ 9. A wholesaler's order takers handle so many items that they usually will not--and probably should not--give special attention to any particular items.

_____ 10. A consumer product manufacturer using an indirect channel system has little need to use missionary salespeople.

_____ 11. A business product manufacturer may benefit considerably by using technical specialists, even though a direct channel of distribution and order getters are used.

_____ 12. A major accounts sales force sells directly to very large accounts.

_____ 13. Telemarketing has none of the benefits of a personal visit.

_____ 14. The big advantage of telemarketing is that it saves time, but a disadvantage is that its costs are high.

_____ 15. A sales territory is a geographic area that is the responsibility of one salesperson or several working together.

_____ 16. The first step in deciding how many salespeople are needed is to estimate how much work can be done by one person in some time period.

_____ 17. Companies are using new information technology tools to change how sales tasks and responsibilities are planned and handled.

_____ 18. Information technology does not change the basic nature of sales tasks, but it does change the way and how well those tasks are done.

_____ 19. The only costs associated with new information technology tools in the area of personal selling are price-related.

_____ 20. A good job description should not be too specific--since the nature of the sales job is always changing.

_____ 21. A written job description can be helpful in setting the level of compensation for salespeople, because it shows whether any special skills or responsibilities are required that will command higher pay levels.

_____ 22. All new salespeople should receive the same kind of sales training.

_____ 23. A combination compensation plan will usually provide the greatest incentive for a salesperson to increase sales.

_____ 24. The most popular compensation method is the straight commission plan.

_____ 25. A sales manager's control over a salesperson tends to vary directly with what proportion of his compensation is in the form of salary.

_____ 26. Many firms set different sales objectives--or sales quotas--to adjust the compensation plan to differences in potential in each territory.

_____ 27. Basically, prospecting involves following all the leads in the target market--and deciding how much time to spend on which prospects.

_____ 28. Some kind of priority system is needed to guide sales prospecting--because most salespeople will have too many prospects.

_____ 29. The prepared (canned) sales presentation probably would be appropriate for the majority of retail clerks employed by convenience stores.

_____ 30. A salesperson's request for an order is called a close.

_____ 31. The consultative selling approach requires less skill on the part of the salesperson than the prepared approach.

_____ 32. An effective office equipment salesperson might use a selling formula sales presentation.

_____ 33. The AIDA sequence is helpful for planning a consultative selling sales presentation--but not for a selling formula sales presentation.

1. F, p. 414	12. T, p. 424	23. F, p. 433
2. F, p. 415	13. F, p. 424	24. F, p. 433
3. T, p. 416	14. F, p. 424	25. T, p. 434
4. T, p. 417	15. T, p. 425	26. T, p. 435
5. T, p. 417	16. T, p. 425	27. T, p. 436
6. T, p. 417	17. T, p. 425	28. T, p. 437
7. T, p. 419	18. T, p. 430	29. T, p. 438
8. T, p. 420	19. F, p. 430	30. T, p. 438
9. T, p. 419	20. F, p. 431	31. F, p. 438
10. F, p. 420	21. T, p. 431	32. T, p. 439
11. T, p. 420	22. F, p. 432	33. F, p. 440

Multiple-Choice Questions (Circle the correct response)

1. Which of the following statements about personal selling is *true?*
    a.   As a representative of his company, a salesperson's job is to sell the customer rather than to help him buy.
    b.   Today's salesperson is really only responsible for "moving products."
    c.   The modern salesperson's sole job is to communicate his company's story to customers.
    d.   Some sales representatives are expected to be marketing managers in their own geographic territories.
    e.   A beginning salesperson could not expect to be responsible for a sales volume as large as that achieved by many retail stores.

2. A salesperson might have to perform three basic sales tasks. Choose the *correct* description of these tasks from the following:
    a.   *Supporting:* the routine completion of sales made regularly to the target customers.
    b.   *Order getting:* confidently seeking possible buyers with a well-organized sales presentation designed to sell a good, service, or idea.
    c.   *Order taking:* purpose is to develop goodwill, stimulate demand, explain technical aspects of product, train the middleman's salespeople, and perform other specialized services aimed at obtaining sales in the long run.
    d.   All of the above are correct.
    e.   None of the above are correct.

3. Order-getting salespeople would be required for which one of the following jobs?
    a.   Helping a buyer plan and install a computer system.
    b.   Helping drug retailers find new ways to display and promote their products.
    c.   Seeking orders from food retailers for a new brand of cake mix which has been added to the company's line.
    d.   "Helping" an indecisive supermarket customer select the kind of meat she should buy for dinner.
    e.   All of the jobs call for order takers.

4. Chemco, Inc., a three-year-old producer of chemicals, has just hired a manufacturers' agent. The agent
   a. is probably replacing a company order getter who built up the territory.
   b. should assume that Chemco will not ever hire its own sales force for the territory.
   c. may lose the business when the territory gets to the point where it can be handled by an order taker.
   d. All of the above are equally likely.
   e. None of the above is a good answer.

5. A large appliance manufacturer has adequate wholesale and retail distribution--but is concerned that the middlemen do not push its products aggressively enough--because they also carry competitive lines. The manufacturer should hire some:
   a. missionary salespeople.
   b. order getters.
   c. order takers.
   d. technical specialists.
   e. manufacturers' agents.

6. Which of the following statements *is false?*
   a. Team selling involves different specialists--to handle different parts of the selling job.
   b. A major accounts sales force is used to sell to small retailers who are not covered by wholesalers in the channel.
   c. Carefully selected sales territories can reduce the cost of sales calls.
   d. The first step in deciding how many salespeople are needed is to estimate how much work can be done by one person in some time period.
   e. Telemarketing provides salespeople with many of the benefits of a personal visit--including the ability to modify the message as feedback is received.

7. Information technology is having a profound impact on personal selling through the use of software for:
   a. spreadsheet analysis.
   b. electronic presentations.
   c. time management.
   d. sales forecasting.
   e. all of the above.

8. With regard to the level of compensation for salespeople, a marketing manager should recognize that:
   a. order takers generally are paid more than order getters.
   b. the appropriate level of compensation should be suggested by the job description.
   c. a good order getter will generally be worth less to a firm than a good technical specialist.
   d. the firm should attempt to pay all its salespeople at least the going market wage for order getters.
   e. salespeople should be the highest-paid employees in the firm.

9. The sales manager of the Bubba Beanbag Corp. wishes to compensate his sales force in a way, which will provide some security, incentive, flexibility, and control. The company should offer its sales force:

a. straight salaries.
b. straight commissions.
c. a combination plan.
d. a value plan.
e. a bonus plan.

10. Regardless of the sales volume, the least expensive type of sales force compensation system is always:
a. straight salary.
b. straight commission.
c. a combination plan.
d. None of the above.

11. Wilma Rogers works as a telephone salesperson for the Catalogue Division of Sears. Her primary job is to call customers with Sears charge accounts to inform them about sales items and ask if they would like to order the sales items. Which of the following kinds of sales presentations would be best for Wilma to use?
a. Prepared sales presentation.
b. Selling formula approach.
c. Consultative selling approach.
d. Missionary approach.
e. Target market presentation.

12. Danny White sells life insurance for a Canada Maritime Assurance. He locates customers by selecting names out of a telephone directory and calling to arrange an appointment. He begins each presentation by explaining the basic features and merits of his product--eventually bringing the customer into the conversation to clarify the customer's insurance needs. Then he tells how his insurance policy would satisfy the customer's needs and attempts to close the sale. Danny's sales presentation is based on the:
a. consultative selling approach.
b. selling formula approach.
c. canned presentation approach.
d. target market approach.
e. missionary approach.

Answers to Multiple-Choice Questions

1. d, p. 415-416
2. b, p. 417-418
3. c, p. 417
4. c, p. 418

5. a, p. 422
6. b, p. 423
7. e, p. 425
8. b, p. 435-436

9. c, p. 433
10. d, p. 438-40
11. a, p. 433-434
12. b, p. 419-420

Additional Questions to Test Your Understanding (Fill in the blanks)

1. What are the four basic features to remember when deciding upon a compensation plan for a company's salesforce?

   a. _____

   b. _____

   c. _____

   d. _____

2. List the four major areas that should be covered in a company's sales training program:

   a. _____

   b. _____

   c. _____

   d. _____

3. Briefly, describe the activities of supporting salespeople.

   _____

   _____

   _____

   _____

4. Match the terms with the correct definition.

Order taker   Prospecting   Sales quota   Team selling
Telemarketing   Job description   Missionary salespeople

   a. _____ - Supporting salespeople who work for producers, calling on their intermediaries and their customers.

   b. _____ - Sell to regular or established customers, complete most sales transactions, and maintain relationships with customers.

   c. _____ - The specific sales or profit objective a salesperson is expected to achieve.

   d. _____ - Calling on customers and prospects over the telephone.

   e. _____ - Following all the leads in a target market to identify potential customers.

   f. _____ - A written statement of what a salesperson is expected to do.

   g. _____ - When different sales reps work together on a specific account.

Answers to Additional Questions

1.
    a. control
    b. incentive
    c. flexibility
    d. simplicity
    (pp. 434-435)

2.
    a. company policies
    b. product information
    c. building relationships with customers
    d. professional selling skills
    (p. 432)

3. They help order-oriented salespeople, but do not try to get orders themselves. Their activities are aimed at enhancing the relationship with the customer and getting sales in the long run. In the short run, they are ambassadors of goodwill who may provide specialized services . (p. 422)

4.
    a. Missionary Salespeople, p. 422
    b. Order Taker, p. 420
    c. Sales Quota, p. 435
    d. Telemarketing, p. 424
    e. Prospecting, p. 436
    f. Job Description, p. 431
    g. Team Selling, p. 423

Exercise 14-1

Analyzing the nature of the personal selling task

Introduction

Personal selling may involve three basic tasks: (1) *order getting,* (2) *order taking,* and (3) *supporting.* Each task may be done by different individuals--or the same person may do all three. While we use these terms to describe salespeople by referring to their *primary* task, it is important to keep in mind that many salespeople do all of the three tasks to some extent.

Consider, for example, a sales rep for a manufacturer of an established consumer good that is distributed through wholesalers. Since the product is established in the marketplace, the sales rep's primary task would probably be order taking--obtaining routine orders from regular wholesale customers. The same rep may also be expected to do other secondary tasks, however. For example, he or she may be expected to get orders from new wholesale customers--and so would also do order getting at times. Further, the rep might also spend part of the time helping the wholesaler's sales force--by informing retailers about the company's product, building special store displays, and so forth. In this case, the sales rep would be doing a supporting task.

This exercise focuses on the basic differences among the three selling tasks. In some cases, these differences may be rather clear. In other cases, the differences may be quite difficult to see. To determine what kind of sales rep is needed to handle a particular personal selling job, we will try to distinguish between the *primary* and *secondary* selling tasks. *Note: the words "primary* n *and "secondary" are used in this way in this exercise only--they do not appear in the text.*

Assignment

Six cases are presented below to show how the selling tasks may vary. In some of the cases, the sales rep will perform both primary and secondary selling tasks, while in others only the primary selling task will be discussed. Read each case and then indicate (a) the *primary* selling task *usually required to effectively carry out the specified job* and (b) any secondary selling task(s) that *may also be described in the case.* Then explain your answer in the space marked "Comments. " The first case is answered for you as an example.

1. Danielle Browning, in her third semester at University, works part-time at the Campus Drug Store. During the week, Danielle works afternoons waiting on customers at the lunch counter. On weekends, she usually operates the cash register at the candy and cigarette counter--in addition to handling bills for public utilities. According to her boss, Danielle is a very good worker.

    a) Primary selling task: *Order-taking*

    b) Secondary selling task: *Possibly order-getting*

c)   Comments: *No order getting is specifically mentioned, but she may do some occasionally. For example: "Would you like to try some of our fresh strawberry pie today? It's delicious!"*

2.   The Great Outdoors Equipment Company is a large merchant wholesaler that distributes chain saws, lawnmowers, and other outdoor power equipment. Great Outdoors sells to retailers and also sells direct to large end-users--such as golf courses and cemeteries. Recently Great Outdoors decided to target local government (city and county) buyers--who purchase equipment to maintain parks, roadside areas, and public schools and hospitals. In the past, these buyers often just purchased equipment from local retailers. Glen Martin, a sales rep for Great Outdoors, was assigned responsibility for identifying who influenced these purchase decisions, and for persuading them either to buy from Great Outdoors or at least allow Great Outdoors to bid on their next order. In addition, Martin has been successful in getting Great Outdoors on their city's and province's list of approved vendors. That means that various municipal and provincial agencies can select equipment from the Great Outdoors catalog and submit a purchase order without a lot of additional red tape. Martin follows up with the warehouse manager to make certain that these orders are shipped promptly.

a)   Primary selling task:

_____

b)   Secondary selling task:

_____

c)   Comments:

3.   Vida Medus, a marketing major in college, went to work for Frito-Lay as soon as she graduated. While she hopes to become a brand manager some day, Vida is a district sales representative--calling on supermarkets, grocery stores, and convenience stores. Her job is to build special displays, inform store managers of new products, provide merchandising assistance, review customer complaints, and occasionally to suggest special orders for the stores she visits. Vida is paid a straight salary--plus a bonus when sales in her district are good. (Note: Frito-Lay uses merchant wholesalers to distribute its products.)

a)   Primary selling task:

_____

b)   Secondary selling task:

_____

c)   Comments:

4. For twenty years, Marcus Stadler has been a manufacturers' agent. Based in Montreal, Quebec, he represents a variety of noncompeting manufacturers of parts and components used in the production of recreational vehicles ("vans") and boats. For example, he calls on the many small producers of boats in the Georgian Bay area and sells them the special water-resistant fabrics and chrome-plated hardware that they need for boat interiors. His customers also include the "conversion shops" that customize vans and RVs, as well as large boatyards that repair and renovate older boats. He also calls on a number of very large boating supply wholesalers. Marcus has worked at getting to know his customers really well. Because of the variety and complexity of the lines he represents, he spends much of his time checking his customers' parts inventories. This gives him continual customer contact--and provides a useful service. He also finds some time to seek new customers--and is always looking for new producers to represent. Recently, however, the producer of one of Marcus' most profitable lines switched to another agent. Apparently, the producer was concerned that Marcus had not been aggressive enough in promoting its products; the company was especially concerned that a competing European producer represented by another agent was getting an increasing share of the market. Marcus was bitter about losing the account. "I built their Georgian Bay business from scratch--and now they're dropping me cold," he complained. "I handle too many products to devote all of my time to just one manufacturer's offerings."

    a) Primary selling task:

    _____

    b) Secondary selling task:

    _____

    c) Comments:

5. Lori Park is a "sales engineer" with Creative Packaging Corporation--which specializes in foam and air "bubble" packaging materials. Producers use these packaging materials to protect their products inside shipping cartons during shipping. Creative Packaging has a line of standard products but also will produce custom packaging materials if that is what a customer needs. The company does advertising in trade magazines, and each ad includes a response card. When a prospect calls to inquire about Creative Packaging products, Matthews is sent out to analyze the customer's packaging needs. She determines how much protection is needed and which packaging product would be best. After finishing her work, Matthews reports back to her sales manager --who assigns another sales rep to handle the rest of the contacts with the customer.

    a) Primary selling task:

    _____

    b) Secondary selling task:

    _____

    c) Comments:

6.   Melanie Chang is paying most of her own college expenses by selling Avon personal care products door-to-door. At first, Melanie did not like her job, but lately has been enjoying it more--and doing very well. As Melanie puts it, "Once you learn the knack of getting your foot in the door, sales come easily and the commissions add up fast. After all, people like our products and the convenience of in-home buying."

a)   Primary selling task:

_____

b)   Secondary selling task:

_____

c)   Comments:

Question for Discussion

Three different kinds of sales presentations are discussed in the text: the *prepared, consultative,* and *selling formula* presentations. Which of these three kinds of sales presentations would be most appropriate for each of the sales reps described in Exercise 14-1? Why?

Exercise 14-2

Selecting the appropriate kind of salesperson

Introduction

Many people believe that a good salesperson must always be an aggressive, extroverted type of individual with highly developed persuasive skills. Such is not the case, however. Studies have shown, for example, that middle-class shoppers often prefer salespeople who tend to be passive and impersonal. Thus--like all other ingredients of a firm's marketing mix--the kind of salesperson needed depends on the needs and attitudes of the firm's target market.

In addition, the firm must keep its basic promotion objectives in mind. The selling task is not always one of persuasion--but may involve informing or reminding target customers about the company's products and/or the company itself. Therefore, it is often desirable to use order takers--or supporting salespeople-rather than order getters.

Selecting the right kind of salesperson is an important strategy decision. Using the wrong kind of salesperson to handle a specific selling situation may do a firm more harm than good.

Assignment

This exercise will give you practice in selecting the appropriate kinds of salespersons. Several situations involving a need for personal selling are described below. For each situation, indicate which of the following kinds of salespeople would be *most* appropriate--and then explain why in the space provided.

        A.   Order getter

        B.   Order taker

        C.   Missionary salespeople

        D.   Technical specialist

The first situation is answered for you as an example.

1.   A video rental store needs a person to operate its checkout counter.

   a)   Type of salesperson: *Order taker*

   b)   Reason: *The chief task is to complete transactions, which the customers have begun by coming to the store and making a selection.*

2.   A producer of hand soaps--that sells to retail food stores and drugstores through their normal wholesale suppliers--wants to get retailer promotional support and shelf space for a new line of liquid soaps.

   a)   Type of salesperson:

   b)   Reason:

3.   A group of CGI systems managers who have taken early retirement want to hire a salesperson to promote their new business which is performing "MIS Audits"--evaluating the expense and effectiveness of firms' current management information systems and offering suggestions for improvement. Some firms do this type of evaluation themselves, but many companies do not have the technical or management expertise to know about all of the alternative ways the MIS might be improved.

   a)   Type of salesperson:

   b)   Reason:

4.   A group of lawyers wants to sell prepaid legal services to unions and other employee groups; although the idea has been popular in other areas of the country, they are the first law firm to offer this service in their city.

   a)   Type of salesperson:

   b)   Reason:

5. A company that manufactures radio equipment for commercial aircraft wants to add a new salesperson to be responsible for global positioning satellite systems (a type of radio receiver which can compute a plane's position based on satellite signals) with its existing customers, a small number of very large commercial aircraft manufacturers.

a) Type of salesperson:

b) Reason:

6. A maker of industrial dishwashing machines (used by institutions and very large restaurants) wants to take advantage of lower freight tariffs to expand the market for its existing product line.

a) Type of salesperson:

b) Reason:

7. A manufacturer of specialized light bulbs needs someone to call on automobile companies to determine their needs for new models and to work with the company's engineers and pricing staff to develop new proposals.

a) Type of salesperson:

b) Reason:

8. A real estate developer is about to open the model homes for a new subdivision and wants to hire a salesperson that is experienced in new home sales.

a) Type of salesperson:

b) Reason:

9.	A new firm that hopes to offer a series of "wellness" programs--including exercise classes, stress-reduction seminars, and diet plans--for employees of large companies needs a salesperson to call on the personnel managers of prospect firms, explain the service, and negotiate contracts.

	a)	Type of salesperson:

	b)	Reason:

10.	A distributor of "stock" steel (steel bars, pipes and so on, used by fabricators to make things out of steel) needs an "inside" counter salesperson. The duties are primarily telephone work, processing orders from existing customers, and helping "walk-in" customers.

	a)	Type of salesperson:

	b)	Reason:

11.	A producer of a line of skin care products--including sun-block lotions, hand creams, and facial cleansers--needs some people to provide free samples and information about new products to dermatologists.

	a)	Type of salesperson:

	b)	Reason:

Question for Discussion

What kind of sales compensation plan--straight salary, straight commission, or a combination plan--would be appropriate in the above situations? Why? What factors must be considered in choosing a sales compensation plan?

Exercise 14-3

Sales compensation

This exercise is based on the computer-aided problem - Sales Compensation. A complete description of the problem appears on page 442 of Wong/Shapiro, 11th edition.

1. Franco Welles knows that his estimates of "expected sales" are just that--estimates. He wants to know what the effect will be on the two compensation plans if unit sales are less or more than expected--but otherwise as he initially planned them. Use the Spreadsheet to fill in the blanks in the following tables, and indicate by marking " < " (less than) or " > " (greater than) which plan gives the highest compensation to the rep and the highest contribution to Nanek in each of the situations.

Sales Volume as Planned			
	Commission	< or >	Combination
Units of A	4000		3600
Units of B	1000		1250
Compensation (TC)			
Contribution			

Actual Volume Less than Planned			
	Commission	< or >	Combination
Units of A	3600		3240
Units of B	500		625
Compensation (TC)			
Contribution			

Actual Volume Greater than Planned			
	Commission	< or >	Combination
Units of A	4400		3960
Units of B	1500		1875
Compensation (TC)			
Contribution			

2. From the analysis of the three tables above, how do the two compensation plans perform from the perspective of Nanek?

_____

_____

_____

_____

3. Franco Welles and the new rep agree to start on the combination plan as originally formulated, but the rep points out that Product A is a mature line and unit sales would surely increase if the rep has authority to cut prices. Welles estimates that each $5 price cut might increase sales by 10 percent--that is, 360 more units than his original estimate. To test this idea, Welles constructs the following table to see the effect on total revenue, total compensation and profit contribution.

Price	Unit Sales	Total Revenue	Total Compensation	Profit Contribution
110	3600			
105	3960			
100	4320			
95	4680			
90	5040			

4. Examine the figures you have entered into the table and discuss the implications of what happens to Total Revenue, Total Compensation, and Profit Contribution as the price is lowered.

_____

_____

_____

_____

Chapter 15

Advertising and sales promotion

Chapter Summary

- **Understand why a marketing manager sets specific objectives to guide the advertising effort.**
  The marketing manager needs to set advertising objectives that grow out of the firm's overall marketing strategy. These objectives are used to help guide the implementation and purpose of the advertising, as well as to guide decisions as to which medium is best suited for conveying the message to the target audience. The objectives will also dictate whether product or institutional advertising should be pursued.

- **Understand when the various kinds of advertising are needed.**
  Product advertising attempts to sell a product, often aimed at final users or channel members. There are three key types of product advertising: pioneering, competitive and reminder. *Pioneering advertising* is used to develop primary demand for a product category rather than for a specific brand. This is typically done in the early stages of the product life cycle. *Competitive advertising* tries to develop selective demand for a specific brand, occurring as the product life cycle progresses. *Reminder advertising* tries to keep the product's name before the public. This is useful in the market maturity or sales decline stages of the product life cycle. *Institutional advertising* promotes an organization's image, reputation, or ideas instead of a specific product. The basic objective is to develop good will or to improve relations with various groups.

- **Understand how to choose the best medium.**
  To choose the best medium, the marketing manager must consider (1) the promotion objectives, (2) who the target market is, (3) the funds available for advertising, and (4) the nature of the media, including reach, frequency, impact and cost. The medium should be matched to the advertising objectives already set out by the company.

- **Understand the main ways that advertising in the Internet differs from advertising in other media.**
  The Internet is an additional medium for advertising and sales promotion programs. It has new capabilities to interact with and engage the consumer in a two-way flow of information and communication.

- **Understand how to plan the best message – that is, the copy thrust.**
  The AIDA concept short for "*getting* attention, *holding* interest, *arousing* desire, and *getting* action", is a useful framework for planning copy direction and look. Attention is important because without getting attention it will not matter how many people see the ad. The method of getting attention should not detract from the ad, but instead lead to interest. To hold the interest of the viewer/reader/listener, the tone of the ad must fit with the experiences and attitudes of the target consumers, as well as providing evidence that convinces the customer

of the validity of the advertisement's claims. Doing so will arouse desire, convincing customers that the product can meet their needs. Finally, the ad should call for action, encouraging interested customers to make a purchase.

- **Understand what advertising agencies do and how they are paid.**
  Advertising agencies are specialists in planning and handling mass-selling details for advertisers. They work independently of the advertiser, and thus are able to offer an outside view. Most agencies are paid a commission of approximately 15% on media and production costs. Some are paid on a fee for service basis, while very few are paid on a fee-for-result basis.

- **Understand how to advertise legally.**
  Government often takes a role in determining what kinds of advertising are allowable, fair, and appropriate. Provisions in Canada's *Competition Act* are designed to prevent misleading advertising. In addition, *Consumer and Corporate Affairs Canada (a part of Industry Canada)* has introduced new legislation and used stricter enforcement as a result of efforts by Canadian consumer activists. Differences in rules mean that a marketing manager may face very specific limits in different countries. Local experts may need to be consulted to ensure compliance with local laws.

- **Understand the importance and nature of sales promotion.**
  Sales promotion can often be implemented quickly, and generates quicker results than advertising. The focus is usually on generating short-term results by overcoming consumer price resistance with the use of coupons. Spending on promotion is increasing and accounts for more spending than does advertising. There is a particularly heavy use of sales promotion in mature markets, which causes price sensitive customers to switch back and forth between brands. It is argued that sales promotion just contributes to lower profits, and is often done only to counter competitors' promotions. Sales promotion can be difficult to manage, and it is easy to make large, costly mistakes.

- **Know the advantages and limitations of different types of sales promotion.**
  There are many forms of sales promotions. *Free trials* encourage customers to switch brands, and if the customer likes the new brand, lead to a permanent growth in sales. *Price-off coupons* lead to short-term increases in sales. The downside is that after the discount period, sales will probably return to the original level or even decline if customers have used the coupons to stock up. *Trade promotion* stresses price-related matters, often entailing merchandise allowances, promotion allowances, and sales contests. *Sales promotions* for employees encourage getting new customers, selling a new product, or selling a company's entire line. Contests, bonuses on sales, or holding sales meetings at fancy resorts are often used as incentives.

Important Terms

True-False Questions

_____ 1. Advertising expenditures grew continuously from world War II until the mid-1980s, but since then, the trend has been down.

_____ 2. Canadian firms spent more than $11 billion dollars on advertising alone in 2001.

_____ 3. The top 25 advertisers in Canada account for more than 50% of all advertising expenditures..

_____ 4. Advertising objectives should be very specific--even more specific than personal selling objectives.

_____ 5. A firm whose objective is to help buyers make their purchasing decision should use institutional advertising.

_____ 6. Pioneering advertising should be used in the market introduction stage of the product life cycle to develop selective demand for a specific brand.

_____ 7. The objective of competitive advertising is to develop selective demand (demand for a specific brand).

_____ 8. Direct competitive advertising involves making product comparisons with competitive brands, while indirect competitive advertising focuses solely on the advertiser's products.

_____ 9. Canada like the U.S. bans comparative advertising that involves specific brand comparisons using actual product names.

_____ 10. Reminder advertising is likely to be most useful when the firm has achieved brand preference or brand insistence for its products.

_____ 11. Advertising allowances are price reductions to firms further along in the channel to encourage them to advertise or otherwise promote the firm's products locally.

_____ 12. The main reason cooperative advertising is used is that large manufacturers usually can get lower media rates than local retailers.

_____ 13. Regardless of a firm's objectives, television advertising is generally more effective than newspaper or magazine advertising.

_____ 14. A major advantage of using "cost per thousand" data to aid in media selection is that this approach is very helpful for target marketing.

_____ 15. Some advertising media are "must buys"--meaning that the FTC requires firms to use such media.

_____ 16. Content on a website is similar to traditional advertising.

_____ 17. There are very good measures of how many people are exposed to Internet ads.

_____ 18. When a website sets fees based on actual sales, it is using the same method as traditional media does to set fees.

_____ 19. Copy thrust means what is to be communicated by an ad's words and illustrations.

_____ 20. The first job in message planning is to determine how to get attention.

_____ 21. Global ads have not been very successful because they emphasize mass marketing instead of target marketing.

_____ 22. Advertising agencies are specialists in planning and handling mass selling details for advertisers.

_____ 23. With the growth of mega-agencies, it will only be a matter of time before small agencies disappear.

_____ 24. Normally, media have two prices: one for national advertisers and a lower rate for local

_____ 25. The 15 percent commission system of ad agency compensation is most favoured by large national advertisers of consumer products.

_____ 26. Advertising effectiveness can be measured quite simply and accurately just by analyzing increases or decreases in sales.

_____ 27. The Canadian Radio and Television Commission control the content of all radio and television ads.

_____ 28. The media itself and Canadian industry associations also regulate advertising content.

_____ 29. Spending on sales promotion is growing, but never at the expense of advertising and personal selling.

_____ 30. One basic reason for increased use of sales promotion by consumer products firms is that they are competing in mature markets.

_____ 31. The effect of most sales promotions is long-lasting.

_____ 32. Sales promotion aimed at final consumers usually is trying to increase demand and speed up the time of purchase.

_____ 33. Sales promotion aimed at middlemen--sometimes called trade promotion--stresses price-related matters.

1. F, p. 447	12. F, p. 457	23. F, p. 471
2. T, p. 447	13. F, p. 458	24. T, p. 472
3. F, p. 448	14. F, p. 462	25. F, p. 472
4. T, p. 453	15. F, p. 464	26. F, p. 473
5. F, p. 454	16. F, p. 464	27. T, p. 478
6. F, p. 454	17. F, p. 467	28. T, p. 478
7. T, p. 454	18. F, p. 467	29. F, p. 448-450
8. F, p. 455	19. T, p. 468	30. T, p. 450
9. F, p. 456	20. T, p. 468	31. F, p. 481
10. T, p. 456	21. T, p. 470	32. T, p. 480
11. T, p. 457	22. T, p. 471	33. T, p. 481

Multiple-Choice Questions (Circle the correct response)

1. Advertising spending as a percent of sales dollars is largest for:
    a.   malt beverages.
    b.   perfumes and cosmetics.
    c.   games and toys.
    d.   investment advice.
    e.   dairy products.

2. The largest share of total advertising expenditures in the United States goes for:
    a.   newspaper advertising.
    b.   television (including cable) advertising.
    c.   magazine advertising.
    d.   direct-mail advertising.
    e.   radio advertising.

3. Regarding "good" advertising objectives:
    a.   Given no clearly specified objectives, advertising agencies may plan campaigns that will be of little benefit to advertisers.
    b.   Advertising objectives often are not stated specifically enough to guide implementation.
    c.   Advertising objectives should be more specific than personal selling objectives.
    d.   The objectives should suggest which kinds of advertising are needed.
    e.   All of the above are true.

4. Which of the following statements about advertising objectives is *false?*
    a.   They should be as specific as possible.
    b.   They should be more specific than personal selling objectives.
    c.   They usually are quite clear from the nature and appearance of an advertisement.
    d.   They should flow from the overall marketing strategy.
    e.   They should set the framework for an advertising campaign.

5. "Better things for better living through chemistry" is an example of:
    a.   pioneering advertising.
    b.   reminder advertising.
    c.   competitive advertising.
    d.   institutional advertising.
    e.   cooperative advertising.

6. The message "Drink milk every day" is an example of which type of advertising?
    a.   Pioneering
    b.   Competitive
    c.   Indirect action
    d.   Reminder
    e.   Direct action

7. Thad Gibson developed an innovative machine to make a more effective and less expensive bottle cap. He found a backer, produced a model, photographed it, and placed an advertisement in a food canners' magazine explaining how caps could be made as needed--right in the canner's plant. Much of the ad copy tried to sell the

convenience and inventory cost-saving features of in-plant production as needed, rather than purchasing large quantities. Gibson's advertising was trying to develop:
a.   selective demand.
b.   primary demand.
c.   derived demand.
d.   elastic demand.

8.   Regarding comparative advertising, which of the following statements is NOT true?
a.   Comparative advertising may actually help the competitor.
b.   Canada bans the use of comparative advertising.
c.   Comparative advertising is intended to stimulate selective demand.
d.   Comparative advertising means making comparisons in which competitors' products are actually named.
e.   Guidelines about the evidence needed to support superiority claims are clear and specific.

9.   Comparative ads:
a.   have been banned by Industry Canada.
b.   attempt to develop primary demand.
c.   have been banned on television because of their tendency to deceive consumers.
d.   have consistently pleased consumers.
e.   that actually name the competitor's brand are illegal.

10. "Cooperative" advertising refers to the practice of:
a.   producers and middlemen sharing in the cost of advertising which is done by the producer.
b.   producers doing some advertising and expecting their middlemen to cooperate by providing the rest of the promotion blend.
c.   the producer paying for all of the advertising which is done by its middlemen.
d.   middlemen doing advertising which is partially paid for by the producer.
e.   middlemen picking up the promotion theme of the producer and carrying it through.

11. The choice of the "best" advertising medium depends upon:
a.   the promotion objectives.
b.   the budget available.
c.   the target markets.
d.   the characteristics of each medium.
e.   All of the above.

12. A media buyer knows that:
a.   the local newspaper will probably be a must buy for targeting consumers.
b.   a 30-second commercial on television may be too expensive.
c.   a Yellow Pages listing will probably be a must buy for serving local markets.
d.   website advertising will probably be a must buy for firms targeting business buyers in overseas markets.
e.   All of the above.

13. Regarding Internet advertising, which of the following statements is true?

a. It is likely that a few portal websites will become for the Internet what the networks once were for television.
b. As with traditional media, getting lots of exposure for Internet ads doesn't help if viewers are not in the firm's target market.
c. Context advertising monitors the content a net surfer is viewing and then serves up related ads.
d. Pointcasting displays an Internet ad only to those individuals who meet certain qualifications.
e. All of the above.

14. Which of the following statements about advertising agencies is *false?*
a. advertising agencies are specialists with an outside view that work for advertisers.
b. most advertising agencies are small--with 10 or fewer employees.
c. the largest advertising agencies account for most of the billings.
d. All of the above *are false.*
e. None of the above *are false.*

15. Which of the following statements about advertising agencies and compensation methods is *true?*
a. The 15 percent commission system is no longer required--and some advertisers have obtained discounts or fee increases.
b. The traditional compensation arrangements between advertisers and agencies might make it difficult for an agency to be completely objective about low cost media.
c. Some advertisers--especially business products manufacturers--were quite satisfied with the traditional compensation arrangements whereby the agency did the advertiser's advertising work in return for the normal discount allowed by the media.
d. The agencies earn commissions from media only when time or space is purchased at the national rate (as opposed to local rates).
e. All of the above are true statements.

16. Which of the following statements about measuring advertising effectiveness is *false?*
a. The most reliable approach is to check the size and composition of media audiences.
b. Some progressive advertisers are now demanding laboratory or market tests to evaluate the effectiveness of advertisements.
c. No single technique or approach has proven most effective.
d. When specific advertising objectives are set, then marketing research may be able to provide feedback on the effectiveness of the advertising.
e. Ideally, management should pretest advertising before it is run rather than relying solely on the judgment of creative people or advertising "experts."

17. Sales promotion:
a. usually lasts for only a limited time period.
b. spending is growing rapidly.
c. involves a wide variety of activities which often require the use of specialists.
d. can make the personal selling job easier.
e. All of the above are true statements.

18. Sales promotion:
    a. to consumers usually is trying to increase demand or speed up the time of purchase.
    b. aimed at middlemen is sometimes called trade promotion.
    c. might include free samples of a product.
    d. aimed at employees is common in service firms.
    e. all of the above.

Answers to Multiple-Choice Questions

1. b, p. 448
2. b, p. 448
3. e, p. 453
4. c, p. 453
5. d, p. 457
6. a, p. 456
7. b, p. 454

8. e, p. 455
9. a, p. 456
10. d, p. 457
11. e, p. 458
12. e, p. 462-464
13. e, p. 464
14. e, p. 471

15. e, p. 472
16. a, p. 473-476
17. e, p. 479
18. e, p. 480

Additional Questions to Test Your Understanding (Fill in the blanks)

1. List the five basic strategy decisions that marketing managers and advertising managers should make regarding advertising, after advertising objectives have been chosen.

   a. _____

   b. _____

   c. _____

   d. _____

   e. _____

2. What are the three categories of product advertising? Describe each category and indicate when it is used in relation to the product life cycle stages.

   a. _____ -

   _____

   _____

   _____

   b. _____ -

   _____

   _____

   _____

   c. _____ -

   _____

   _____

   _____

3. Match the following terms with the correct definitions listed below.

Advertising allowances   Copy thrust   Product Advertising
Comparative advertising   Competitive advertising

   a. _____ - What an advertisement's words and illustrations should communicate.

   b. _____ - An extreme form of direct competitive advertising that involves making specific brand comparisons using actual product names.

   c. _____ - Price reductions to firms farther along in the channel to encourage them to advertise or promote the firm's products locally.

d. _____ - Advertising that tries to sell the product.

e. _____ - Advertising that tries to develop selective demand for a specific brand.

4. Should a copy thrust be used globally?

_____

_____

_____

_____

_____

_____

Answers to Additional Questions

1.
   a. Who the target is.
   b. What kind of advertising to use.
   c. How to reach customers (via which types of media).
   d. What to say to them (copy thrust).
   e. Who will do the work – the firm's own advertising department or outside agencies.
   (p. 452)

2.
   a. Pioneering advertising – It tries to develop primary demand for a product category rather than demand for a specific brand. It is usually used in the early stages of the product life cycle (market introduction and market growth), and it informs potential customers about the new product and helps turn them into adopters. (p. 454)

   b. Competitive advertising – it tries to develop selective demand for a specific brand. It is usually used in the market growth and market maturity product life cycle stages. It may be direct (aims for immediate buying action) or indirect (points out product advantages to affect future buying decisions). (p. 454)

   c. Reminder advertising – it tries to keep the product's name before the public. It may be used when the product has achieved brand preference or insistence, perhaps in the market maturity or sales decline stages of the product life cycle. It is used primarily to reinforce previous promotion. (p. 456)

3.
   a. Copy Thrust, p. 468
   b. Comparative Advertising, p. 455
   c. Advertising Allowances, p. 457
   d. Product Advertising, p. 454

e. Competitive Advertising, p. 454

4. Using a copy thrust globally has worked for a few firms, such as Coca Cola and Gillette. However, most firms who use this approach experience terrible results. They lose sales because they do not develop advertising messages – and entire marketing mixes – aimed at specific target markets. (p. 470)

Exercise 15-1

Identifying different kinds of advertising

Introduction

Perhaps because of the high cost of advertising, some companies try to use multi-purpose ads to reach several promotion objectives at the same time. Studies have shown, however, that such ads often fail to produce *any* of the desired effects. On the contrary, several special-purpose ads are much more likely to stimulate positive responses than a single multi-purpose ad. Thus, a marketing manager usually should use different kinds of advertising to accomplish different promotion objectives.

This exercise is designed to show the different kinds of advertising that can be used--and to show the various objectives an advertisement might have. While doing the assignment, you should see that promotion objectives may be only indirectly concerned with increasing sales--and that a firm may have other reasons for advertising. Try to guess what these "other reasons" are--and how they might relate to a company's overall marketing mix.

Assignment

Using recent magazines and newspapers (or, if you wish, the Internet), find advertisements to *final consumers* which illustrate the following kinds of advertising (as defined in the text):

        A.   Institutional
        B.   Pioneering
        C.   Direct competitive
        D.   Indirect competitive
        E.   Comparative
        F.   Reminder

Clip out the ads (or print out any Internet ads)--and for each ad attach a separate sheet of paper indicating:

a)   what kind of advertising the ad illustrates.
b)   at what target market, if any, the ad appears to be aimed.
c)   the general and specific objectives of each ad--e.g., to inform consumers (general) about three new product improvements (specific).
d)   the name of the magazine or newspaper in which the ad appeared (or, in the case of ads on the Internet, the a brief description of the website where it appeared).

Question for Discussion

When one overall objective of a company's marketing activities must be to sell its products, why would advertisements have objectives such as those you indicated for your examples?

Exercise 15-2

Determining advertising objectives and the appropriate kind of advertising

Introduction

About 1910 George Washington Hill--president of the American Tobacco Company--is said to have made this now-famous quote: "I am convinced that 50 percent of our advertising is sheer waste, but I can never find out which half." Today, there are many business executives who share Mr. Hill's feelings. Billions of dollars are spent each year creating clever--and sometimes annoying--ads which often appear to be poorly designed and largely ineffective.

Actually, it is extremely difficult to measure the effectiveness of advertising--because companies often lack clearly defined advertising objectives. In hopes of remaining competitive, advertisers often budget some fixed percent of their sales dollars to advertising without any specific objectives in mind--other than to just "promote the product."

Like all business expenditures, however, there is no reason for making advertising expenditures unless the company has some specific purpose in mind. Since the advertising objectives selected will largely determine the kind of advertising that is needed, companies should set specific advertising objectives that are tied to their overall marketing strategies.

Assignment

This exercise will give you some practice determining the kind of advertising that may be needed to obtain some specific advertising objectives. Described below are several situations in which some kind of advertising may be necessary or desirable. For each situation: (a) indicate what *general* (i.e., inform, persuade, and/or remind) and *specific* objectives the advertising probably would be meant to achieve; and (b) indicate which of the following kinds of advertising would be *most* appropriate to accomplish that objective.

> A. Pioneering advertising
> B. Direct competitive advertising
> C. Indirect competitive advertising
> D. Reminder advertising
> E. Institutional advertising

The first situation is answered for you as an example.

1. A print ad shows an insurance adjuster with a clipboard in hand watched by a family with grateful expressions on their face. The only "copy" is a single line: "You're in good hands with Allstate."

    a) Advertising objectives: *Remind. This ad assumes that consumers already know that Allstate is in the domestic casualty insurance market and builds on other advertisements that have given greater details about product benefits.*

    b) Kind of advertising: *Reminder.*

2. Print advertisements for a producer of designer clothing simply feature the designer's "brand name" and a picture of scantily clad models frolicking in romantic situations.

    a) Advertising objectives:

    _____

    _____

    _____

    b) Kind of advertising:

    _____

3. Enterprise uses testimonials from satisfied customers to differentiate itself from competing car rental services. In particular, it promotes its service of delivering a car to you--at home, at the office, or on vacation. Its slogan says, "Pick Enterprise. We'll pick you up."

    a) Advertising objectives:

    _____

    _____

    _____

    b) Kind of advertising:

    _____

4. In an attempt to reposition its high performance multimedia, laptop computers towards the higher end of the market, Toshiba's print ads include a table comparing product benefits of its multimedia laptops with features and service of IBM and Apple laptop computers.

   a) Advertising objectives:

   _____

   _____

   _____

   b) Kind of advertising:

   _____

5. Charter Clinics radio advertisement describes the symptoms and serious consequences of misaligned teeth, and explains that most health insurance policies cover treatment for this condition. At the end, the ad gives a toll-free number for Charter as the announcer encourages the friends and families of depressed people to "seek help today, even if not from Charter."

   a) Advertising objectives:

   _____

   _____

   _____

   b) Kind of advertising:

   _____

6. For several decades Texaco has sponsored broadcasts of the Metropolitan Opera House on classical music stations. Since many of the stations are public radio stations, there are no formal "pitches" for individual products, but the host uses the line: "You can trust your car to the man with the Texaco star."

   a) Advertising objectives:

   _____

   _____

   _____

b) Kind of advertising:

_____

7. Buick takes out single-page advertisements in national business magazines to tout the amenities of owning its Riviera. Its ads mention, "You can get a supercharged engine, a CD player with six speakers, and an ashtray big enough for two cigars. It's not for carpooling, but then, neither are you. You're due. Definitely due."

a) Advertising objectives:

_____

_____

_____

b) Kind of advertising:

_____

8. The metropolitan transportation district receives a grant from the provincial and federal Ministry of Environments to advertise bus services to promote clean air by switching commuters from single-occupancy cars. Billboards and TV time are too expensive, so the bus company uses the money to purchase placard ads inside its own buses. The copy says: "Save gas--take the bus!"

a) Advertising objectives:

_____

_____

_____

b) Kind of advertising:

_____

9. British Airways in Hong Kong uses print advertisements that feature one of four Chinese flight attendants and builds on the airline's image as "global and caring in the eyes of Chinese consumers." The emphasis is on its people, not its product or fares.

a) Advertising objectives:

_____

_____

_____

b) Kind of advertising:

_____

10. A print advertisement for Rolls Royce automobiles features an attractive couple driving a Rolls convertible in front of New York's Plaza hotel. The driver of a Mercedes sedan looks on and there is also a Lincoln in the background. The ad copy is a single line: "Simply the best motor car in the world."

a) Advertising objectives:

_____

_____

_____

b) Kind of advertising:

_____

Question for Discussion

Would there be difficulties in evaluating the effectiveness of ads for the situations mentioned in Exercise 15-2? Why?

Exercise 15-3

Sales promotion

This exercise is based on computer-aided problem - Sales Promotion. A complete description of the problem appears on page 484-485 of Wong/Shapiro, 11th edition.

1.   The PTA likes the idea of the T-shirt promotion, but is concerned about the "front-end" costs. Thus, it has decided to order only 400 T-shirts at $2.40 each, the minimum order from the supplier. In addition, the PTA has decided to evaluate a variation of the president's idea--offering a choice of a regular ticket at $5.00 or a ticket with a T-shirt at $6.50. If the PTA used this approach and sold 400 tickets with T-shirts and 200 tickets without T-shirts, how much money--net--would the PTA earn? How would this compare with what the PTA would earn if it sold the same total number of tickets at $5.00 each--with the first 400 purchasers getting a free T-shirt.

      $ _____ money earned by PTA using 2 prices (with and without T-shirt)

      $ _____ money earned by PTA selling all tickets at $5.00 and giving away 400 T-shirts

2.   Another possibility is that the game would attract the "normal" number of ticket buyers at $5.00 a ticket, but that not all of the higher priced tickets with a T-shirt would be sold. If 300 tickets were sold at $5.00 and only 300 people bought the higher priced tickets with the T-shirt, how much money would the PTA earn?

      $ _____ money earned by the PTA.

3.   Spreadsheet analysis helped the PTA evaluate various possibilities, but it is still uncertain how to proceed. The group thinks there will be a lot of interest in the T-shirts--but they worry that they will cause dissatisfaction and lose potential ticket sales if they order the minimum and then run out of T-shirts. One member of the group has proposed an idea that might solve the problem.

      He recommends a "sweepstakes" approach. Specifically, he suggests that they sell all the tickets at a regular price of $5.50--but that every person who has a ticket with a winning number will be given a T-shirt at the game. 400 winning numbers will be drawn from a bowl during the game. He thinks this will stimulate the most interest--and allow the PTA to place the minimum T-shirt order.

      If the PTA uses this approach, how many extra tickets will it have to sell to pay for the T-shirt promotion?

      _____ extra tickets to pay for the T-shirt promotion

If 700 tickets are sold, how much money will be earned for the PTA?

$ _____ money earned if 700 tickets are sold.

4. If the PTA earns $3,000 from the game, they will be able to buy new uniforms for the school band. If they use the sweepstakes approach, about how many tickets would they have to sell to be able to buy the new uniforms? (Hint: use the What If analysis to vary the number of tickets sold, and display the amount of money earned.)

_____ number of tickets to sell to be able to buy new uniforms

5. Based on your analysis of this problem, briefly comment on the following quote: "Companies spend too much money on sales promotion. It just adds to the cost of marketing."

_____

_____

_____

_____

_____

_____

Chapter 16

Pricing Objectives and Policies

Chapter Summary

- **Understand how pricing objectives should guide strategy planning for pricing decisions.**
  As with each of the four Ps, pricing objectives must flow from, and fit with all marketing and company level objectives. There are three key types of pricing objectives: profit-oriented, sales-oriented, and status quo-oriented (stay the same). Profit oriented objectives are used when a firm wants to earn a certain profit level (e.g. 15% of sales revenue, increase profit be 5% over last year, or 8% return on Investment (**ROI**)). Sales-oriented objectives are used when the company wants to achieve some level of unit sales (e.g. 10,000 DVD players per month), dollar sales (e.g. $1,025,000 annual sales), or market share (increase Canadian market share to 12%) Status quo-oriented objectives are typical when a market is stagnant (no growth). This can mean trying to keep prices stable, instead of declining, matching competitors' prices, or avoiding competition entirely.

- **Understand choices the marketing manager must make about price flexibility.**
  The marketing manager must set introductory prices when entering a market. To do so they must consider where in the life cycle their product is and how fast it is moving. They must also decide how to price their product compared to competitors.
  Among the choices a company has is a *one-price policy*, meaning that all customers who purchase products under the same conditions and in the same quantities are offered the same price. Or, it can adopt a *flexible price policy* and charge different prices to different customers even if they buy under the same conditions and the same quantities.

- **Know what a marketing manager should consider when setting the price level for a product in the early stages of the product life cycle.**
  A firm may choose to use a *skimming price policy* to sell to the top of the market before targeting more price sensitive consumers. In contrast, the firm can use a *penetration price policy*, by selling to the entire market at a single low price. *Introductory price dealing* is the practice of using temporary discounts to attract new customers.

- **Understand the many possible variations of a price structure, including discounts, allowances, and who pays transportation costs.**
  Pricing policies are often developed in such a way as to result in value pricing, setting a fair price that results in superior value for the larger market. *Discounts* are reductions from the list price given by the seller to buyers. These discounts are usually based on the buyer giving up some seller provided marketing service or doing it themselves. *Discounts* can be based on quantity, seasonal, trade, and cash discounts, or different payment options may be given. *Allowances* are given to the final consumer, customer or channel member for doing something or accepting less of something. This may include advertising, stocking allowances, push money, or trade-in-allowances.

Transportation costs are sometimes included in the list price, or free delivery may be offered as an additional incentive to close a deal. Types of transportation policies include free on board (FOB), zone pricing, uniform delivered pricing and freight absorption costing.

- **Understand the value-pricing concept and its role in obtaining a competitive advantage and offering target customers superior value.**
  Value pricing means setting a price for a specific marketing mix that really gives the target market superior value. It does not mean cheap, rather the focus is on customer needs and wants and how well the entire marketing mix meets those needs. Remember that in the end the value price relationship is related to the firm's target market perception.

- **Understand the legality of price level and price flexibility policies.**
  The *Competition Act* provides a framework for business conduct in Canada. One of the areas this act covers is pricing practices. Pricing practices that are regulated are: (1) *Price fixing*, which involves competitors getting together to raise lower or stabilize prices is illegal in Canada; (2) *Price discrimination*, which means giving different prices or promotional allowances to different customers is if it is based on quantity, but is illegal if not; (3) *Predatory pricing*, which is pricing a product so low as to keep other competitors out of the market is illegal; (4) *Resale price maintenance* is illegal, but manufacturers can use a suggested list price (SRP), as long as retailers know that they can charge a lower price without being discriminated against.

Important Terms

profit maximization objective, p. 492

target return objective, p. 492

sales-oriented objective, p. 493

administered prices, p. 494

status quo objectives, p. 494

flexible-price policy, p. 495

one-price policy, p. 495

skimming price policy, p. 498

introductory price dealing, p. 500

penetration pricing policy, p. 500

basic list prices, p. 501

discounts, p. 501

quantity discounts, p. 501

cumulative quantity discounts, p. 502

noncumulative quantity discounts, p. 502

seasonal discounts, p. 502

cash discounts, p. 503

net, p. 503

sale price, p. 503

trade (functional) discount, p. 503

2/10, net 30, p. 503

advertising allowances, p. 504

allowances, p. 504

everyday low pricing, p. 504

push money (or prize money) allowances, p. 504

stocking allowances, p. 504

trade-in allowance, p. 504

F.O.B., p. 505

freight absorption pricing, p. 505

rebates, p. 505

uniform delivered pricing, p. 505

zone pricing, p. 505

value pricing, p. 506

price fixing, p. 508

True-False Questions

____ 1. Any business transaction in our modern economy can be thought of as an exchange of money, the money being the Price for something of greater value.

____ 2. The "something" that Price buys is different for consumers or users than it is for channel members.

____ 3. A target return objective is often used in a large company to evaluate several different divisions or products.

____ 4. Profit maximization objectives are undesirable from a social viewpoint, because profit maximization necessarily leads to high prices.

____ 5. Instead of setting profit-oriented objectives, a marketing manager should follow sales-oriented objectives because--in the long run--sales growth leads to big profits.

____ 6. Market share objectives provide a measurable objective--but an increase in market share does not always lead to higher profits.

____ 7. Status quo pricing objectives do not ever make sense if the firm intends to develop an overall marketing strategy that is aggressive.

____ 8. Instead of letting daily market forces determine their prices, most firms set their own administered prices.

____ 9. A one-price policy means offering the same price to all customers who purchase products under essentially the same conditions and in the same quantities.

____ 10. Flexible pricing is seldom used anymore in Canada because it does not help selling.

____ 11. A skimming pricing policy is especially desirable when economies of scale reduce costs greatly as volume expands--or when the firm expects strong competition very soon after introducing its new product.

____ 12. A penetration pricing policy might be indicated where there is no "elite" market--that is, where the whole demand curve is fairly elastic--even in the early stages of the product's life cycle.

____ 13. Introductory price dealing is the same thing as using a penetration pricing policy.

____ 14. In mature markets, competitor prices will have an impact on the firm's pricing strategy.

____ 15. Basic list prices are the prices final consumers (or business customers) are normally asked to pay for products.

16. Discounts from the list price may be granted by the seller to a buyer who either gives up some marketing function or provides the function for himself.

17. Noncumulative quantity discounts apply only to individual orders.

18. Cumulative quantity discounts tend to encourage larger single orders than do noncumulative quantity discounts.

19. The following is an example of a seasonal discount: A local supermarket gives 4 litres of milk free with every order of $10.00 or more, provided the purchases are made on either Monday, Tuesday, or Wednesday--that normally are slow days in the food business.

20. Cash discounts are used to encourage buyers to pay their bills quickly--meaning they are granted to buyers who pay their bills by the due date.

21. The following terms of sale appear on an invoice: 2/10, net 30. A buyer who fails to take advantage of this cash discount offer is--in effect—borrowing at an annual rate of 36 percent a year.

22. A mass-merchandiser that allows government employees to purchase products at 10 percent below the store's normal selling prices is using a trade or functional discount.

23. Common occurrences of sale prices and deals are a signal that the basic marketing strategy is constantly changing.

24. Everyday low pricing starts with a low list price that does not change instead of starting with a high list price that changes frequently.

25. Allowances are typically given only to consumers, not to middlemen customers.

26. Stocking allowances have been around for a long time and are just another way for middlemen to make extra profit.

27. Push Money is given to retailers by manufacturers or wholesalers to pass on to their salespeople in return for aggressively selling particular items.

28. Trade-in allowances are price reductions given for used products when similar new products are bought.

29. A retailer is usually willing to redeem a producer's coupons since they increase his sales to consumers and because he is paid by the producer for handling the coupons.

30. Rebates give the producer a way to be sure that final consumers, instead of middlemen, get an intended price reduction.

31. F.O.B. pricing simplifies a seller's pricing--but may narrow his target market

because customers located farther from the seller must pay more for transporting costs and may buy from nearby suppliers.

32. With zone pricing, an average freight charge is made to all buyers within certain geographic areas.

33. Uniform delivered pricing--that is used when the seller wishes to sell his products in all geographic areas at one price--is most often used when transportation costs are relatively high.

34. Freight absorption pricing means absorbing freight cost so that a firm's delivered price will meet the nearest competitor's.

35. Value pricing means setting a fair price level for a marketing mix that really gives the target market superior customer value.

36. Wal-Mart motto "The low price on the brands you trust" means that they use EDLP and not value pricing..

37. Sellers who may appear to emphasize below-the-market prices in their marketing mixes may really be using different marketing strategies--not different price levels.

38. A firm can usually increase profits by pricing higher than the market, if it claims to be using value pricing..

39. One of the purposes of the Competition Act is to ensure that small and medium sized firms have an equitable opportunity to compete in the Canadian economy.

40. I f "price discrimination' is based on the location of the buyer it is legal.

41. Only the company can be charged in a case of price fixing.

42. Price fixing is illegal if it raises or stabilizes prices--but not if it results in lower prices.

43. Although price fixing is illegal under the Competition Act, there are no penalties for managers who ignore these laws.

44. Predatory pricing, if it is done to drive out foreign competition is legal in Canada.

45. Suggested Retail prices are legal in Canada so long as the retailer does not charge less than the suggested price.

46. A producer could legally refuse to give a wholesale discount to a large retail grocery chain that buys direct--although the chain might handle a larger volume than small wholesalers.

47. Under the *Competition Act*, it is legal for a firm to provide push money,

advertising allowances, or other promotion aids to its customers, as long as such allowances are made available to all customers in equal dollar amounts.

Answers to True-False Questions

1. F, p. 490	17. T, p. 502	33. F, p. 505
2. T, p. 490-491	18. F, p. 502	34. T, p. 505
3. T, p. 492	19. T, p. 502	35. T, p. 505
4. F, p. 493	20. F, p. 503	36. F, p. 506
5. F, p. 493	21. T, p. 503	37. T, p. 507
6. T, p. 494	22. F, p. 503	38. F, p. 506
7. F, p. 494	23. F, p. 503	39. T, p. 508
8. T, p. 494	24. T, p. 504	40. F, p. 508
9. T, p. 495	25. F, p. 504	41. F, p. 508
10. F, p. 495	26. F, p. 504	42. F, p. 508
11. F, p. 498	27. T, p. 504	43. F, p. 508
12. T, p. 500	28. T, p. 504	44. F, p. 509
13. F, p. 500	29. T, p. 504-505	45. F, p. 509
14. T, p. 501	30. T, p. 505	46. F, p. 509
15. T, p. 501	31. T, p. 505	47. T, p. 508
16. T, p. 501	32. T, p. 505	

Multiple-Choice Questions (Circle the correct response)

1. Which of the following would be *least likely* to be included in the "something" part of the "price equation" as seen by channel members?
   a. Promotion aimed at customers
   b. Rebates
   c. Price-level guarantees
   d. Sufficient margin to allow chance for profit
   e. Convenient packaging for handling

2. If a marketing manager for a large company wants to compare the performance of different divisions of his firm, which of the following pricing objectives would he be most likely to pursue?
   a. Status quo
   b. Market share
   c. Target return
   d. Profit maximization
   e. Sales growth

3. Profit maximization pricing objectives:
   a. usually are achieved when the producer's sales volume is high.
   b. may be in the interest of both producers and consumers
   c. result in high prices.
   d. are never used in combination with penetration pricing
   e. None of the above is a good answer.

4. With respect to pricing objectives, a marketing manager should be aware that:
   a. profit maximization objectives generally result in high prices.
   b. status quo pricing objectives can be part of an extremely aggressive marketing strategy.
   c. target return objectives usually guarantee a substantial profit.
   d. sales-oriented objectives generally result in high profits.
   e. All of the above are true statements.

5. Prices are called "administered" when:
   a. they are determined through negotiations between buyers and sellers.
   b. they fall below the "suggested list price."
   c. a marketing manager has to change his strategy every time a customer asks about the price.
   d. government intervenes to ensure that prices fluctuate freely in response to market forces.
   e. firms set their own prices for some period of time--rather than letting daily market forces determine their prices.

6. In contrast to flexible pricing, a one-price policy:
   a. means that the same price is offered to all customers who purchase products under the same conditions.
   b. involves setting the price at the "right" level from the start--and holding it there.
   c. generally results in rigid prices, which change very infrequently.
   d. means that delivered prices will be the same to all customers.
   e. All of the above.

7. Which of the following factors would be *least favourable* to a skimming price policy?
   a.   The firm has no competitors.
   b.   The quantity demanded is very sensitive to price.
   c.   The product is in the market introduction stage of its life cycle.
   d.   The firm follows a multiple target market approach.
   e.   The firm has a unique, patented product.

8. The Gill Corp. is introducing a new "me-too" brand of shampoo in market maturity. To speed its entry into the market--without encouraging price competition with other shampoo producers--Gill should consider using:
   a.   a penetration pricing policy.
   b.   a flexible-price policy.
   c.   a skimming price policy.
   d.   introductory price dealing.
   e.   an above-the-market price-level policy.

9. The Stark Corporation purchases large quantities of iron castings from a well-known producer. Stark receives a discount, which increases as the total amount ordered during the year increases. What type of discount is involved here?
   a.   Seasonal discount
   b.   Cumulative quantity discount
   c.   Brokerage allowance
   d.   Noncumulative quantity discount
   e.   Cash discount

10. The terms "3/20, net 60" mean that:
   a.   in effect, the buyer will pay a 27 percent interest rate if he takes 60 days to pay the invoice.
   b.   the buyer must make a 3 percent down payment--with the balance due in 20 to 60 days.
   c.   a 3 percent discount off the face value of the invoice is permitted if the bill is paid within 60 days--otherwise, the full face value is due within 20 days.
   d.   the invoice is dated March 20 and must be paid within 60 days.
   e.   None of the above is a true statement.

11. The Bowman Co., a producer of sports equipment, gives its retailers a 2 percent price reduction on all products with the expectation that the dealers will advertise the products locally. Apparently, Bowman believes that local promotion will be more effective and economical than national promotion. This is an example of:
   a.   "push money."
   b.   a brokerage allowance.
   c.   a cash discount.
   d.   a trade (functional) discount.
   e.   an advertising allowance.

12. Some producers give "*this*" to retailers to pass on to the retailers' salesclerks in return for aggressively selling particular items or lines.
   a.   brokerage commissions
   b.   advertising allowances
   c.   trade discounts

d.   "push money" allowances
e.   cash discounts

13.   A producer in Quebec sold some furniture to a firm in Halifax. If the *seller* wanted title to the products to pass immediately--but still wanted to pay the freight bill--the invoice would read:
a.   F.O.B. delivered.
b.   F.O.B. seller's factory--freight prepaid.
c.   F.O.B. Baltimore.
d.   F.O.B. seller's factory.
e.   F.O.B. buyer's warehouse.

14.   If a buyer purchases a shipment of products from a seller in another city and the invoice reads "F.O.B. shipping point,"
a.   the seller pays the freight bill and keeps title to the products until they are delivered.
b.   the seller pays the freight bill but title to the products passes to the buyer at the point of loading.
c.   the buyer pays the freight but the seller keeps title to the products until delivery.
d.   the buyer pays the freight and gets title to the products at the point of loading.
e.   Both a and c.

15.   Which of the following statements about geographic pricing policies is *true*?
a.   Zone pricing penalizes buyers closest to the factory.
b.   Uniform delivered pricing is more practical when transportation costs are relatively low.
c.   Freight absorption pricing may increase the size of market territories.
d.   F.O.B. pricing tends to reduce the size of market territories.
e.   All of the above are true statements.

16.   One of the main purposes of the" *Competition Act*" is to:
a.   prevent manufacturers from taking high markups.
b.   eliminate price competition on manufacturers' brands.
c.   give small and medium sized companies an equal chance to compete in the Canadian market place.
d.   permit different types of retail outlets to charge different retail prices.
e.   guarantee retailers some profit.

17.   Price fixing:
a.   is always illegal.
b.   is prohibited by the Food and Drug Act.
c.   is illegal if it raises or stabilizes prices--but not if it lowers prices.
d.   is technically illegal--but there is very little that the federal or provincial governments can do about it.
e.   All of the above are true statements.

18.   According to the _____ Act, it is unlawful to practice price discrimination between different purchasers if quantities are similar.
a.   Consumer and Corporate Affairs
b.   Fair-Trade
c.   Competition

d.   Hazardous Materials
e.   Ant-Combine

19.   A manufacturer might try to defend himself against charges of predatory pricing by claiming that:
     a.   the price discrimination occurred as a defensive measure.
     b.   the price differentials only injured the competition temporarily.
     c.   the price differentials were justified based on cost differences in production and/or distribution.
     d.   the buyers were from different areas.
     e.   Any of the above could make predatory pricing legal.

20.   The manufacturers suggested retail price is great for consumers, unfortunately retailers who use it can only:
     a.   use a flexible pricing policy.
     b.   Sell to all its customers at uniform prices.
     c.   Grant a lower price to a buyer because of a large-quantity purchase.
     d.   Get a special advertising allowance and pass none of the savings on to consumers.
     e.   Charge a lower price, if they want to.

Answers to Multiple-Choice Questions

1. b, p. 491	8. d, p. 500	15. e, p. 505
2. c, p. 492	9. b, p. 502	16. c, p. 508
3. b, p. 493	10. a, p. 503	17. a, p. 508
4. b, p. 492-494	11. e, p. 504	18. c, p. 508
5. e, p. 494	12. d, p. 504	19. c, p. 509
6. a, p. 495	13. b, p. 505	20. e, p. 509
7. b, p. 498	14. d, p. 505	

Additional Questions to Test Your Understanding (Fill in the blanks)

1. What are the four price related strategy decision areas that a marketing manager, guided by the company's pricing objective, should consider and decide upon in setting a company's pricing policies?

   a. _____

   b. _____

   c. _____

   d. _____

2. List the advantages and disadvantages of a one-price policy:

   a. Advantages:

   _____

   _____

   _____

   b. Disadvantages:

   _____

   _____

   _____

3. List the advantages and disadvantages of a flexible-price policy:

   a. Advantages:

   _____

   _____

   _____

   b. Disadvantages:

   _____

   _____

   _____

4. What are four standard types of allowances and why are they used?

   a. _____ -

   _____

   _____

b. _____ -

_____

_____

c. _____ -

_____

_____

d. _____ -

_____

_____

Answers to Additional Questions

1.
   a. How flexible prices will be.
   b. A what level prices will be set over the product life cycle.
   c. To whom and when discounts and allowances will be given.
   d. How transportation costs will be handled.

See Exhibit 16-1 and page 489

2.
   a. Advantage: Administrative convenience and maintenance of goodwill among customers. (p. 495)
   b. Disadvantage: A rigid one-price policy can be undercut by competitors. (p. 495)

3.
   a. Advantage: The salesperson can make price adjustments, having considered the prices charged by competitors, the relationship with the customer, and the customer's bargaining ability. (pp. 495-498)
   b. Disadvantage: Can cause unhappy customers and real conflict in the channel. The time needed for bargaining and increase the time spent on a single customer, which can increase sales costs. (p. 495-498)

4.
   a. Advertising Allowance – These are price reductions given to channel members to encourage them to advertise or otherwise promote the supplier's products locally. (p. 504)
   b. Stocking Allowance – These are cash allowances or free merchandise given to retailers by manufacturers or wholesalers to get shelf space. They are used mainly to encourage supermarket chains to handle new product. (p. 504)
   c. Push Money (or prize money) allowances – These are cash allowances given to retailers by manufacturers or wholesalers to pass on to the retailers' salesclerks for aggressively selling certain items/products. (p. 504)
   d. Trade-in Allowance – This allowance is a price reduction given for used products when similar new products are bought. Trade-ins give the marketing manager and easy way to lower the effective price without reducing the basic list price. (p. 504)

Exercise 16-1

Using discounts and allowances to improve the marketing mix

Introduction

Most price structures have a basic list price from which various discounts and allowances are subtracted. *Discounts* (not to be confused with discount selling) are reductions from list price that are given by a seller to a buyer who either gives up some marketing function or provides the function himself. Several types of discounts are commonly used, including:

a)   Cumulative quantity discounts
b)   Noncumulative quantity discounts
c)   Seasonal discounts
d)   Cash discounts
e)   Trade (functional) discounts

Allowances are similar to discounts. They are given to final consumers, customers or channel members for doing "something" or accepting less of "something." Different types of allowances include:

a)   Advertising allowances
b)   Push money or prize money allowances
c)   Trade-in allowances
d)   Stocking allowances

While many firms give discounts and allowances as a matter of custom, they should be viewed as highly useful tools for marketing strategy planning. As outlined in the text, each type is designed for a specific purpose. Thus, some firms offer buyers a choice of several discounts and allowances.

The purpose of this exercise is to illustrate how discounts and allowances can be used in marketing strategy planning. The emphasis will be on recognizing opportunities to improve a firm's marketing mix. In Exercise 16-2, we will discuss various legal restrictions that may affect a firm's policies regarding discounts and allowances.

Assignment

Presented below are five cases describing situations in which a firm *might* want to add or change some discount or allowance--as part of its marketing mix. Read each case carefully and then answer the questions, which follow.

1.   Oak Trace Apartments offers two-bedroom apartments with the same basic "roommate" floor plan that is popular with other student-oriented apartments in the area. In August and early September, there is no difficulty in attracting tenants at the "going rate" of $650 per month rent. Although there is a penalty for breaking the lease, each year a number of unexpected vacancies occur at the end of the first semester when some students graduate or drop out of school, move to a dorm, or find someone new with whom to live. Of course, the same thing happens at other apartments, so in late December and early January there are always more empty apartments than new renters. As a result, competition for tenants is usually intense. In this "buyer's market," student renters look for the best deal--and apartment managers dread the idea of having an empty apartment that brings in no rent for the spring semester.

      a)   What type of discount or allowance would you recommend in this situation? Why?

2.   Elite Speakers, Ltd. manufactures expensive stereo speakers that are sold through manufacturers' agents to selected retailers who specialize in high-quality stereo component systems. Most of Elite's stereo speakers are sold on credit. In fact, Elite usually is not paid until its retailers manage to sell the speakers themselves. While this service is convenient and necessary for most of its customers, it places a heavy financial burden on Elite. Recently, for example, the company was forced to postpone production of a promising new product due to a lack of cash.

      a)   Should Elite consider using discounts or allowances to solve its financial problem? Why? If so, what type would be best? Why?

3. Accu-Treat, Inc. manufactures a large assortment of fertilizers, weed killers, plant nutrients, and insecticides. Accu-Treat's products are sold across southern Ontario through merchant wholesalers (distributors) who supply not only farmers but also plant nurseries, landscaping services, hardware stores, and lumberyards. Accu-Treat's production manager recently complained to the firm's marketing manager that "the sales force needs to do a better job of smoothing out sales. In the fall and winter--when there is little planting activity--we have extra capacity. Then, in the spring all of the orders come in at once--and we have to pay overtime to get everything produced. It is not just a matter of putting items in our warehouse. We need to get the orders. We have bills to pay."

    a) Could Accu-Treat's problem be due in part to a lack of appropriate discounts or allowances? Why? Is so, what type might be best for the company to adopt? Explain.

4. PowerPro Electrical Supply Company sells a wide assortment of products to electricians, electrical contractors, and general building contractors in the area around Calgary, Alberta. PowerPro's line includes almost everything its customers might need--ranging from wire, electrical tape, circuit breaker boxes, conduit, switches, outlet boxes, lighting fixtures, and a wide variety of electrician's tools and equipment. In addition, like most other electrical wholesalers in the area, PowerPro offers free delivery to the construction site. Despite PowerPro's efforts to promote itself as "the most economical source for all your needs," most of its customers split their business among a number of different electrical supply wholesalers. When PowerPro's owner complained about this, one of his counter clerks offered an explanation: "The person having the work done usually doesn't care what electrical supply house gets the business--so the different electricians just call whoever comes to mind first."

    a) Could discounts or allowances be useful to PowerPro Electrical Supply? Why? If so, what type would be best? Explain.

5. Maple Leaf Furniture Co. produces a line of high quality reproductions of Early Canadiana style beds, dressers, tables and chairs. Maple Leaf 's furniture is distributed nationally through a network of carefully selected furniture retailers. When Maple Leaf first introduced its line, sales grew rapidly--in part because of its ongoing advertising in national home furnishings magazines. Now, however, sales are flat--and in some areas falling. Other producers have come out with similar lines, and most retailers now carry several competing brands. The company is concerned about what it considers "a lack of adequate promotion support at the retail level."

a) Could Maple Leaf Furniture Company use discounts or allowances to obtain additional promotion support at the retail level? Why? If so, what type would you recommend? Why?

b) What would be the advantages and limitations of your recommendation relative to other approaches?

6. Claire's Shop has just purchased $10,000 worth of fashionable accessories for teens from Capture, Inc. The invoice for the accessories included the terms "3/10, net 60."

a) What do the terms 3/10, net 60 mean?

b) Suppose Claire's Shop pays the invoice 10 days after receipt. What amount should it pay Capture, Inc.?

c)   If Claire's Shop does not pay the invoice until 60 days after receipt, it will in effect be borrowing money at a high interest rate. Calculate what the effective interest rate would be in this case. (Assume a 360 day year.)

d)   What conditions would make it sensible for Capture, Inc. to offer these terms?

Question for Discussion

Do discounts and allowances really offer marketing managers a great deal of flexibility in varying their marketing mixes? Explain.

Name: _____   Course & Section: _____

Exercise 16-2

How legislation affects pricing policies

Introduction

Pricing legislation is a very complex area. Even legal experts cannot always provide their clients with clear-cut advice in pricing matters. This is due in part to the vague way in which many laws have been written by legislators--and in part to the fact that no two situations are ever exactly alike. It is up to the courts and government administrative bodies, to interpret pricing legislation. And their interpretation of laws has tended to vary a lot, depending on the political environment.

Nevertheless, a marketing manager should try to understand the legal environment--and know how to work within it. Legislation and legal cases often tend to focus on pricing matters, because prices are highly visible elements of the marketing mix. Business managers have a lot of freedom to charge whatever prices they choose--subject to the forces of competition. But they must be aware of and work with the restrictions that do exist. Ignorance of the law is no excuse. The penalties for violating pricing laws are tough--even jail!

This exercise is designed to increase your understanding of the pricing provisions of the Competition Act. The intent is not to make you a legal expert--but rather to be sure you understand the kinds of pricing activities, which *might* be illegal. A review of pages 508-509 of the text would be helpful.

Assignment

The following five cases describe pricing activities, which *might* be judged illegal in certain circumstances. Study each case carefully and then answer the questions that follow. Be sure to identify the law (or laws) that are *most relevant* to each situation *as it is described.*

1. Jumping Jeans Ltd., a retail sportswear chain, has four locations in Toronto and plans to open its first store in a Montreal suburb next month. The new sales manager has proposed a two-for-the-price–of-one jeans sales for the first week of Montreal operations. She estimates at least 2000 customers will come to the Montreal store for this special opening week offer. However, she plans to stock only 1000 jeans for this sale. She plans to advertise the special offer in major Montreal newspapers, but there will be no mention of limited quantities. There are also no plans to give rain checks (coupons that would allow customers to buy at the same price when more stock arrives). The president of Jumping Jacks is worried that the special may be illegal and asks the company's lawyer to comment on the promotion.

   Do you think the president's concerns are valid in this case? Give reasons for your position?

2. PharmCo, Inc.--a large manufacturer of pharmaceuticals--sells its consumer products exclusively through drug wholesalers--who sell to retail druggists. Wholesalers are allowed a "chain discount" of 35 percent and 10 percent off the manufacturer's suggested retail list prices. The wholesalers are then expected to pass the 35 percent discount on to retailers. Recently a large retail drug chain approached PharmCo about buying direct. PharmCo agreed to sell direct to the chain--and offered a discount of 35 percent. However, the chain wanted the additional 10 percent usually given to wholesalers. The chain would buy in greater quantities than most of the wholesalers. PharmCo felt this would be unfair to those retail druggists who must buy through wholesalers--and refused the chain's request on the grounds that such a discount would be illegal.

   Do you agree with PharmCo? Why or why not?

3.   The Better Business Bureau (BBB) recently received a telephone call from an angry consumer who wished to complain about Best Deal Electronics--an electronics discount chain with nine stores in the surrounding area. The consumer had gone to Best Deal to buy some items listed in an "inventory clearance sale" advertisement. The first item was a "top-name" colour TV marked down from $450 to $200. Upon arrival at the store, he found only one of the featured TVs in stock--a floor model in very poor condition. The salesclerk apologized--and suggested that the customer buy one of the store's other models at "regular everyday low prices" ranging from $199 on up. The consumer then asked to see a video camera that--according to the ad--was "originally priced at $1,295" and "now reduced to only $795." The salesclerk pointed to a dusty camera in a case near the back of the store. On closer inspection, the customer realized that the camera was a three-year-old model that did not have any of the features found on new cameras--even one that regularly sold for less than $795. An official from BBB sympathized with the consumer and said that his agency had received many similar complaints about Best Deal. He went on to say, however, that there was very little anyone could do--other than to avoid shopping at such stores.

Comment on the Better Business Bureau's analysis of the above situation. Are Best Deal's pricing practices deceptive and/or illegal? Can anything be done in such situations?

4.   Libby Corporation produces a wide line of canned foods--including "Early," one of the leading brands of canned corn. The wholesale selling price for a case (48 cans) of Early corn is $9.60--which includes a 5 percent trade discount for the wholesaler. Libby also gives a 10 percent quantity discount to wholesalers who buy in carload quantities. Wholesalers normally pass the quantity discount along to their customers in the form of lower prices. The identical corn is also sold to a few large food chains for use as dealer brands. The cans are sold under different labels at $8.00 per case (minus the 10 percent quantity discount if earned). Libby allocates 3 percent of its net sales of Early corn toward national advertising.

Suppose the Government under the Competition Act were to take a close look at Libby's pricing methods to see whether the manufacturer was violating federal pricing legislation. What aspects of Libby's pricing policies do you think might be questioned based on what is presented above? Why?

5.   Gabriella Glover, a rising manager at Kanata Canada Corporation (KCC), has just been given responsibility for pricing products sold in KKC's Corn Products division. Because the division's products are based on corn, the firm's costs vary a lot depending on the cost of corn, which is set in the agricultural commodity market. In light of that, Glover has always wondered how the firm has been able to maintain consistently high prices and attractive profits. However, she is told that another executive, Pepe Moralez, will help her to better understand the firm's pricing approaches. Moralez says that as far as he is concerned the firm's customers are the enemy--they're the ones pushing for low prices. He also argues that competitors in the same industry are friends--because it's in their interest as well as KKC's interest to keep prices high. Moralez suggests that he and Gabriella play golf with the pricing manager for a competing firm and make it clear that they have very similar interests in the worldwide market.

What would government lawyers think about Moralez's comments? If the meeting with the competitor takes place, what law would be most relevant?

6. As marketing manager for SeaBreeze Carpets Ltd., you have been asked to approve the following ad for use in next weeks newspaper:

SeaBreeze Carpets Ltd. Special Carpet Sale
Top-Quality Broadloom $10.95 per metre
Usually $15.95 per metre or more
Hurry! Limited Quantity

You immediately telephone the sales manager for further details about the proposed sale stock. He advises you that over 75 metres are available for sale. In addition he has a substantial stock of similar carpet that is regularly priced at $11.95 per yard. As well the sales manager tells you that the carpet to be advertised was priced at $16.95 per metre when it was first introduced four years ago. The $15.95 price applied as recently as last year when this carpet was discontinued due to manufacturing problems.

Do you see any ethical or moral reasons for not approving this advertisement? If you approve it will SeaBreeze be vulnerable to prosecution for false or deceptive advertising? Why or Why not?

Question for Discussion

According to one point of view, the Competition Act benefits consumers by prohibiting pricing practices, which may tend to injure competition. Another point of view, however, holds that the act only serves to protect inefficient competitors and thus may actually be harmful to consumers. Which view do you agree with? Why? How can we determine which view is "right?"

Exercise 16-3

Cash discounts

This exercise is based on computer-aided problem - Cash Discounts. A complete description of the problem appears on page 511 of Wong/Shapiro, 11th edition.

1. Tulkin has several variables to consider as he tries to decide what cash discount terms to offer. One thing he has noticed about his current situation (with 90 percent of his customers taking the cash discount) is that his ratio of cash discounts to total invoice amounts is .027--or about 3 percent. It occurred to him that another alternative might be to leave his terms the way they are for the short term, but increase his prices by about 3 percent. If he does this--so that, the average invoice is about $927 instead of $900--and everything else stays the same, what will happen to his total <u>net</u> sales (after the cash discounts are taken)?

    For 120 customers:

    Net sales without price increase $ _____

    Net sales with 3.0 percent price increase $ _____

2. Tulkin realizes that if he increases his list price some price-sensitive retailers will switch to other wholesalers. If he increases the price, how many customers can he "afford" to lose before his net sales are back to the level he had before the price increase?

    Number of customers to earn about the same net sales _____

3.   In thinking about price-sensitive customers, Tulkin feels he may be able to promote his favourable invoice terms to attract customers away from other wholesalers who have already changed to less favourable terms. He recognizes that drawing attention to his invoice terms will probably mean that more customers will take the cash discount. He also knows he might still have to change his terms of sale later--but thinks he could hang on to some of the new customers once they become aware of his good service and quality products. If he keeps his invoice terms the same--and 95 percent of the customers take the cash discount--how many new customers will Tulkin have to attract to increase his net sales by about $5,000? What will his expected gross sales and total monthly cash discount amount be in this case?

Net sales with 120 customers,
   90 percent taking discount $ _____

plus target increase in net sales $ _____5000_____

equals, new target for net sales $ _____

Number of customers required to achieve
   target net sales, assuming
   95 percent take the discount   _____

expected gross sales with that many customers $ _____

expected cash discount with that many customers $ _____

4. Tulkin feels this plan may work--so he wants to see how things might look later if and when he reduces his terms closer to what competitors are charging--2/10, net 30. He figures he would not lose customers at that point--since others would already be offering similar terms. He is not certain how many customers will take the cash discount with the new terms--but he estimates that it will be between 40 percent and 60 percent. He is uncertain how his net sales might vary over that percentage range. To help answer this question, prepare a table that shows how his net sales, the total dollar value of cash discounts, and the ratio of cash discounts to invoice face value would change as the percentage of customers that take the discount varies between 40 percent and 60 percent.

Percent Taking Discounts	Total Cash Discounts	Net Dollar Sales	Ratio Discount to Face Value
40			
42			
44			
46			
48			
50			
52			
54			
56			
58			
60			

Chapter 17

Price Setting in the Business World

Chapter Summary

- **Understand how most wholesalers and retailers set their prices – using markups.**
  The markup is the percentage of the selling price that has been added to the cost in order to achieve the selling price. Many intermediaries use a standard markup percentage that they apply to all their products. This makes setting price easier. Managers often set the standard markup close to the gross margin.

  High markups do not always mean big profits because they may result in prices that are too high. Low prices may increase inventory turns, which may in turn increase profits.

- **Understand why turnover is so important in pricing.**
  A low turnover rate increases inventory carrying costs and ties up working capital. For calculations, see the discussion on "Marketing Arithmetic" in the Student Centre of the text's Web site at www.mcgrawhill.ca\college\WongShapiro11.

- **Understand the advantages and disadvantages of average cost pricing.**
  Average-cost pricing means adding a reasonable markup to the average cost of the product. Average-cost pricing is simple, but may on occasion lead to significant losses. This pricing method does consider cost variations at varying levels of output.

- **Know how to use break-even analysis to evaluate possible prices.**
  The breakeven analysis evaluates whether a firm can cover its costs at a given price level. Often, charts depicting the total costs (total fixed costs plus total variable costs) and total revenues are used to help determine the break-even point (**BEP**) The BEP (in units) can be calculated by dividing the total fixed costs by the fixed-cost contribution per unit. It is important to note that each price has its own BEP. Break-even analysis is useful for analyzing costs, but it does not consider the effect of price on the quantity that consumers want.

- **Understand the advantages of marginal analysis and how to use it for price setting.**
  Marginal analysis focuses on the changes in total revenue and total cost that occur with the sale of "one more unit". This shows the firm how profit changes at different prices, and can help to find the most profitable price. It can also help calculate the amount of profit the firm gives up if it pursues non-profit oriented pricing objectives.

  Marginal analysis shows that when a firm is looking for the best price to charge it should lower the price – to increase the quantity it will sell – as long as the last unit it sells will produce an extra profit.

- **Understand the various factors that influence customer price sensitivity.**
  There are a six factors that influence customer price sensitivity: (1) *availability of substitutes* – when customers have substitute ways of satisfying a need, they are likely to be more

price-sensitive; (2) *Ease of price comparison* – the impact of substitutes is greatest when it is easy for customers to compare prices; (3) *Cost sharing* – People tend to be less price sensitive when somebody else is paying or they are sharing the bill; (4) *Amount spent* – The greater the total expenditure, the more price sensitive the customer; (5) *Significance of end benefit* – The greater the greater the importance or significance of the end benefit, the less price sensitive the customer is; (6) Sunk investments – Customers are sometimes less price sensitive if they already have a "sunk investment" (invested money in training, systems, service equipment, etc.) that is related to the purchase.

- **Know the many ways that price setters use demand estimates in their pricing.**
  Prices can be set below the *reference price* to achieve a perceived superior value in the minds of the target customer. *Leader prices* are used to attract customers into the store in the hope that they will purchase other more profitable items. *Bait pricing* involves attracting the customers into the store with a product at a low price, then trying to get them to spend more money on a higher priced product. This, if successful will expand the demand for higher-quality products.

  Psychological factors also affect demand. Some consumers do not respond to changes in price within a certain range, whereas they do when the price is above or below that range. In addition, *odd-even pricing* is also used to make prices appear cheaper in the minds of target customers. *Prestige pricing* involves setting high prices to suggest high quality or high status products.

Important Terms

markup, p. 516
markup chain, p. 517
stockturn rate, p. 518
average-cost pricing, p. 519
average cost, p. 520
average fixed cost, p. 520
average variable cost, p. 520
total cost, p. 520
total fixed cost, p. 520
total variable cost, p. 520
experience curve pricing, p. 523
target return pricing, p. 523
break-even analysis, p. 524
break-even point (BEP), p. 524
long-run target return pricing, p. 524
fixed-cost (FC) contribution per unit, p. 525
marginal analysis, p. 526
marginal cost, p. 527

marginal revenue, p. 527
marginal profit, p. 528
rule for maximizing profit, p. 528
reference price, p. 532
value in use pricing, p. 532
leader pricing, p. 533
bait pricing, p. 534
odd-even pricing, p. 534
price lining, p. 534
psychological pricing, p. 534
demand-backward pricing, p. 535
full-line pricing, p. 536
prestige pricing, p. 536
complementary product pricing, p. 537
product-bundle pricing, p. 537
bid pricing, p. 538
negotiated price, p. 539

True-False Questions

_____ 1. Markup (dollars) means the dollar amount added to cost of products to get the selling price--or markup (percent) means a percentage of the selling price that is added to the cost to get the selling price.

_____ 2. According to the definition of markup given in the text, a product that a retailer buys for $2.00 would be priced at $3.20 if the retailer applied a markup of 60 percent.

_____ 3. Considering the large number of items the average retailer or wholesaler carries--and the small sales volume of any one item--a markup approach to pricing makes sense.

_____ 4. A producer--whose product sells for $24--distributes its product through wholesalers and retailers who traditionally use a "markup chain" of 20 percent and 40 percent, respectively. Therefore, the retail-selling price of this product is $50.

_____ 5. A wholesaler or retailer concerned with increasing profits should consider using a smaller markup as a way of achieving a substantial increase in turnover.

_____ 6. "Stockturn rate" means the number of times a firm's beginning inventory is sold in a year.

_____ 7. Producers commonly use a cost-oriented pricing approach--adding a standard markup to obtain their selling price.

_____ 8. Because average-cost pricing consists of adding a "reasonable" markup to the average cost of a product, it assures the producer of earning a profit at any level of output.

_____ 9. Total fixed cost is the sum of those costs that are fixed in total--no matter how much is produced.

_____ 10. Total variable cost would include items such as wages paid to workers, sales commissions, and salaries paid to top executives.

_____ 11. The rate of growth of total cost as output increases is not affected by total fixed cost.

_____ 12. Average cost is obtained by dividing total cost by the related total quantity.

_____ 13. Average fixed cost increases as the total quantity produced increases.

_____ 14. Average variable cost is obtained by dividing total variable cost by the number of units produced.

_____ 15. Because of economies of scale, all average and total costs tend to decline as the quantity produced increases.

16. Average-cost pricing works best when demand conditions are changing rapidly and substantially.

17. Experience curve pricing is like average-cost pricing—except that, prices are based on an estimate of future average costs.

18. Unlike the average-cost curve approach, target return pricing assures that the target return is achieved--even if the quantity that is actually sold is less than the quantity used in setting the price.

19. Those who use long-run target return pricing assume that short-run losses and above-normal profits will average out in the long run--thus allowing the firm to achieve its long-run target return objectives.

20. Break-even analysis suggests that once a firm reaches its break-even point, profit will keep increasing with every additional unit sold.

21. Although break-even analysis considers the relationship of total revenue and total cost, it may not solve the firm's pricing problem because the assumed price may not be tied to realistic demand estimates.

22. The traditional goal of economic analysis--to maximize profits--is a reasonable one because if you know how to make the biggest profit, you can always adjust your price to pursue other objectives--while knowing how much profit you are giving up.

23. Marginal analysis helps the marketing manager make the best pricing decision by focusing on the last unit which would be sold--to determine how total revenue and total cost would be affected.

24. Since marginal revenue is the change in total revenue which results from the sale of one additional unit of a product--and since this extra unit will be sold while charging a positive price for all items--marginal revenue can never be negative.

25. Marginal cost--that is the change in total cost that results from producing one more unit--might also be defined as the change in total variable cost that results from producing one more unit.

26. To maximize profit--the firm should produce that output where the difference between marginal revenue and marginal cost is the greatest.

27. Marginal analysis indicates that--to maximize profits--a firm should be willing to increase the quantity it will sell until the marginal profit of the last unit is at--or near--zero.

28. If marginal costs can be covered in the short run—even though all fixed costs cannot--the firm should remain in operation.

29. Marginal analysis can only be done when a manager is sure that both the cost and demand information is complete and correct.

_____ 30. A marginal analysis cannot be done for most firms because they do not know the shape of their demand curve..

_____ 31. Value in use pricing is setting prices that will capture some of what customers will save by substituting the firm's product for the one currently being used.

_____ 32. Reference prices do not vary from one customer to another for the same basic type of purchase (for example, paperback books).

_____ 33. Leader pricing is most common in oligopoly situations—where most firms will raise or lower their price only after the industry leader raises or lowers its price.

_____ 34. Items featured in "bait pricing" are real bargains priced low to get customers into the store to buy these and other items.

_____ 35. Psychological pricing assumes that some price changes will not affect the quantity sold.

_____ 36. Retailers who use "odd-even pricing" seem to assume that they face a rather jagged demand curve--that slightly higher prices will substantially reduce the quantity demanded.

_____ 37. Although price lining may result in higher sales, faster turnover, and simplified buying--it also increases the retailer's total inventory requirements and often leads to greater markdowns.

_____ 38. Henry Ford's decision to build a car for the "masses"—setting "a price so low as to force everybody to the highest point of efficiency"--is an example of demand-backward pricing.

_____ 39. Prestige pricing is possible when target customers think that high prices mean high quality or high status--and the demand curve for this market slopes down for a while and then bends back to the left again.

_____ 40. A producer that offers a complete line (or assortment) of products should not be overly concerned about full-line pricing if it is aiming at different target markets for each of its products.

_____ 41. Complementary product pricing is setting prices on several products as a group.

_____ 42. Firms that use product-bundle pricing usually set the overall price so that it's cheaper for the customer to buy the bundle than to buy each item separately.

_____ 43. The major job in bid pricing is assembling all of the costs--including the variable and fixed costs--that should apply to each job.

_____ 44. Bargaining may involve the whole marketing mix, not just the price level in arriving at a negotiated price.

1. T, p. 516	16. F, p. 522	31. T, p. 532
2. F, p. 516	17. T, p. 523	32. F, p. 532
3. T, p. 516	18. F, p. 523	33. F, p. 533
4. T, p. 517	19. T, p. 524	34. F, p. 534
5. T, p. 517	20. T, p. 524	35. T, p. 534
6. F, p. 518	21. T, p. 524	36. T, p. 534
7. T, p. 519	22. T, p. 525	37. F, p. 534
8. F, p. 519	23. T, p. 526	38. T, p. 536
9. T, p. 520	24. F, p. 527	39. T, p. 536
10. F, p. 520	25. T, p. 527	40. T, p. 536
11. T, p. 520	26. F, p. 527	41. T, p. 537
12. T, p. 520	27. T, p. 528	42. T, p. 537
13. F, p. 520	28. T, p. 528	43. T, p. 538
14. T, p. 520	29. F, p. 529	44. T, p. 539
15. F, p. 523	30. F, p. 529	

Multiple-Choice Questions (Circle the correct response)

1. A certain product retails for $100. How much does this product cost the retailer if his markup is 33 1/3 percent?
    a. $25.00
    b. $33.00
    c. $50.00
    d. $75.00
    e. $66.67

2. The markup approach to price setting used by most middlemen:
    a. makes little sense--given the large number of items carried and the small sales volume of any one item.
    b. is very inflexible because the same markup percent must be applied to all products.
    c. often uses the trade (functional) discount allowed by the manufacturer.
    d. is quite complicated--because each product has a different delivered cost.
    e. All of the above.

3. A certain item is sold at retail for $50. The retailer's markup is 25 percent *on cost.* The wholesaler's markup is 25 percent *on selling price.* What is the manufacturer's selling price?
    a. $30.00
    b. $32.00
    c. $28. 10
    d. $35.11
    e. $25.00

4. With respect to markups and turnover, a marketing manager should be aware that:
    a. a low stockturn rate increases inventory carrying costs.

b. depending on the industry, a stockturn rate of 1 or 2 may be quite profitable.
c. high markups do not always mean big profits.
d. speeding turnover often increases profits because the firm's operating costs are a function of time and the volume of goods sold.
e. All of the above are true statements.

5. Which of the following statements about average-cost pricing is *true*?
   a. The chief merit of this approach is that it is based on well-researched pricing formulas.
   b. It consists of adding a "reasonable" markup to the average cost of a product.
   c. This method takes into consideration cost variations at different levels of output.
   d. It assumes that the average cost for the next period will be different from that of the last period.
   e. All of the above are true statements.

6. Average-cost pricing:
   a. consists of adding a "reasonable" markup to the average cost of a product.
   b. uses demand-oriented pricing formulas.
   c. does not allow for cost variations at different levels of output.
   d. focuses on the differences between fixed and variable costs.
   e. Both a and c are true.

7. Total cost usually:
   a. is zero at zero quantity.
   b. grows at a rate determined by increases in total variable cost.
   c. is the sum of total fixed and total marginal costs.
   d. grows at a rate determined by increases in total fixed cost.
   e. None of the above is a true statement.

8. The *major* weakness of average-cost pricing is that:
   a. it always leads to losses instead of profits.
   b. costs decline and rise at different levels of output.
   c. demand is ignored.
   d. average fixed cost increases as the quantity increases.
   e. All of the above.

9. Average cost pricing will result in *larger* than expected profit:
   a. most of the time.
   b. if the average fixed cost estimate is based on a quantity that is smaller than the actual quantity sold.
   c. if the average total cost is higher than expected.
   d. only if the manager makes arithmetic errors in computing average variable cost.
   e. None of the above is correct.

10. When a firm seeks to obtain some specific percentage return on its investment (or a specific total dollar return), it is using:
    a. break-even pricing.
    b. experience curve pricing.
    c. "what the traffic will bear" pricing.
    d. target return pricing.
    e. average-cost pricing.

11. A manufacturer who uses "target return" pricing sold 1,000 units of his product last year. He wants to earn a profit of at least $20,000 in the coming year. If his fixed costs are $40,000 and his variable costs equal $20 per unit, what price would he charge (assuming that he could still sell 1,000 units)?
   a. $60
   b. $40
   c. $80
   d. $120
   e. Cannot be determined with information given.

12. Break-even analysis assumes that:
   a. variable cost is constant per unit but varies in total.
   b. average fixed costs increases as quantity increases.
   c. the demand curve slopes downward and to the right.
   d. average variable cost first decreases and then increases as quantity increases.
   e. All of the above.

13. Assume that a producer's fixed costs amount to $240,000, its variable costs are $30 per unit, and it intends to sell its portable washer to wholesalers for $50. Given this information, the break-even point is:
   a. 8,000 units.
   b. 12,000 units.
   c. 14,000 units.
   d. 20,000 units.
   e. almost 50,000 units.

14. Given the following data, compute the BEP *in dollars:*
       Selling price = $1.25
       Variable cost = $ .75
       Fixed cost = $45,000
   a. $36,000
   b. $60,000
   c. $90,000
   d. $112,500
   e. None of the above.

15. Break-even analysis can be used for:
   a. relating prices to potential demand.
   b. comparing various assumed pricing alternatives.
   c. finding the most profitable price.
   d. estimating future sales.
   e. All of the above.

16. Trying to find the *most profitable* price and quantity to produce:
   a. requires average-cost pricing.
   b. requires an estimate of the firm's demand curve.
   c. is easy once the average fixed cost is known.
   d. is only sensible if demand estimates are exact.
   e. All of the above are true.

17. Because a firms "marginal revenue" is always greater than its marginal costs:
    a.   Firms should increase their production.
    b.   MR is always shown above the corresponding down-sloping demand curve on a graph.
    c.   is only the change in total costs that results from the sale of one more unit of a product.
    d.   Does not tell the firm anything about the profit made from that one additional sale.
    e.   None of the above are true.

18. The change in total cost that results from producing one more unit is called:
    a.   average variable cost.
    b.   marginal cost.
    c.   average fixed cost.
    d.   total variable cost.
    e.   average total cost.

19. To maximize profit, a firm should:
    a.   produce that output where marginal revenue is at a maximum.
    b.   produce that output where marginal cost is just less than or equal to marginal revenue.
    c.   produce that output where marginal cost is greater than marginal revenue.
    d.   try to maximize the difference between marginal revenue and marginal cost.
    e.   produce that output where marginal profit is at a maximum.

20. A marketing manager should be aware that the most profitable level of output:
    a.   is where total revenue equals total cost.
    b.   is where the difference between marginal revenue and marginal cost is the greatest.
    c.   is where the vertical difference between total revenue and total cost is the greatest.
    d.   is where marginal revenue is at a maximum.
    e.   Both b and c are correct.

21. In applying traditional economic analysis, a firm has discovered two break-ever points--rather than a single break-even point. This means that:
    a.   the firm's demand curve cannot be down-sloping.
    b.   there is a profitable operating range, which surrounds the point of maximum profit.
    c.   seeking the maximum profit point is likely to prove fruitless.
    d.   the firm has not experienced any economies or diseconomies of scale.
    e.   None of the above--there can never be more than one break-even point.

22. Profit-maximizing firms cannot use marginal analysis because:
    a.   marginal revenue curves are horizontal and elasticity of demand is equal to one.
    b.   Can never exactly plot a firms demand curve.
    c.   Costs will change over time, so there is always some inaccuracy.
    d.   unless they accept that the figures are estimations.

23. A "price leader" should recognize that:
    a.   "conscious parallel action" has been ruled illegal.

b.　　other firms in the industry are sure to raise their prices if they raise it first.

c.　　price cutting may occur if the "followers" are not able to make a reasonable profit at the market price.

d.　　marginal analysis is not applicable because of the kinked demand curve.

e.　　it may backfire if consumers only buy the price leader items.

24.　An equipment producer is introducing a new type of paint sprayer to sell to automobile body-repair shops. The sprayer saves labour time in painting the car, makes it possible to get as good a job with less expensive paint, and requires less work polishing after the car is painted. This company should use:

a.　　leader pricing.

b.　　bait pricing.

c.　　complementary product pricing.

d.　　odd-even pricing.

e.　　value in use pricing.

25.　The manager of Green's Dress Shop has concluded that her customers find certain prices very appealing. Between these prices are whole ranges where prices are apparently seen as roughly equal--and price cuts in these ranges generally do not increase the quantity sold (i.e., the demand curve tends to drop vertically within these price ranges). Therefore, the manager has decided to price her dresses as close as possible to the top of each price range. This is known as:

a.　　prestige pricing.

b.　　bait pricing.

c.　　leader pricing.

d.　　psychological pricing.

e.　　odd-even pricing.

26.　The practice of setting different price levels for different quality classes of merchandise--with no prices between the classes--is called:

a.　　full-line pricing.

b.　　prestige pricing.

c.　　price lining.

d.　　odd-even pricing.

e.　　psychological pricing.

27.　"Demand-backward" pricing:

a.　　is like leader pricing.

b.　　has been called "market-minus" pricing.

c.　　requires no demand estimates.

d.　　is usually performed by retailers.

e.　　All of the above are true statements.

28.　Setting relatively high prices on products with perceived high status is known as:

a.　　price lining.

b.　　odd-even pricing.

c.　　leader pricing.

d.　　prestige pricing.

e.　　bait pricing.

29.　Which of the following statements about "full-line pricing" is *true?*

a. A marketing manager usually attempts to price products in the line so that the prices will seem logically related and make sense to potential customers.
b. Most customers seem to feel that prices in a product line should be somewhat related to cost.
c. The marketing manager must try to recover all his costs on the whole product line.
d. Not all companies that produce a variety of products must use full-line pricing.
e. All of the above are true statements.

30. With regard to bid pricing, a marketing manager should be aware that:
a. the customer is always required to accept the lowest bid.
b. since it costs very little to submit a bid, most firms try to bid for as many jobs as possible.
c. the same overhead charges and profit rates usually apply to all bids.
d. a big problem is assembling all the costs--including the variable and fixed costs that apply to a particular job.
e. All of the above are true statements.

Answers to Multiple-Choice Questions

1. e, p. 516	11. c, p. 523	21. b, p. 528
2. c, p. 516	12. a, p. 524	22. d, p. 529
3. a, p. 516-17	13. b, p. 524	23. d, p. 534
4. e, p. 517-18	14. d, p. 524	24. e, p. 532
5. b, p. 519	15. b, p. 525	25. d, p. 534
6. e, p. 519	16. b, p. 526	26. c, p. 534
7. b, p. 520	17. d, p. 527	27. b, p. 536
8. c, p. 519	18. b, p. 527	28. d, p. 536
9. b, p. 519	19. b, p. 527	29. e, p. 536
10. d, p. 523	20. c, p. 528	30. d, p. 538

Additional Questions to Test Your Understanding (Fill in the blanks)

1. Match each of the following terms with the correct definition below:

Markup Chain   Stockturn Rate   BEP
Leader Pricing   Reference Price   Complementary Product Pricing
Prestige Pricing   Marginal Cost   Price Lining

a. _____ - The price consumers expect to pay for many of the products they purchase.

b. _____ - The number of times the average inventory is sold in a year.

c. _____ - Setting some very low prices to get customers into retail stores.

d. _____ - Setting prices on several products as a group.

e. _____ - The quantity where the firm's total cost will just equal its total revenue.

f. _____ - The sequence of markups firms use at different levels in a channel that determines the price structure in the whole channel.

g. _____ - Setting a few price levels for a product line and then marking all items at these prices.

h. _____ - The change in total cost that results from producing one more unit.

i. _____ - Setting a high price to suggest high quality or service.

2. What is the purpose for doing a break-even analysis?

_____

_____

_____

_____

3. What is the major disadvantage of a break-even analysis?

_____

_____

_____

_____

4. List six factors that have an influence on price sensitivity.

a. _____

b. _____

c. _____

d. _____

e. _____

f. _____

Answers to Additional Questions

1.
   a. Reference Price, p. 532
   b. Stockturn Rate, p. 518
   c. Leader Pricing, p. 533
   d. Complementary Product pricing, p. 537
   e. BEP, p. 524
   f. Markup Chain, p. 517
   g. Price Lining, p. 534
   h. Marginal Cost
   i. Prestige Pricing, p. 540

2. A break-even analysis evaluates whether a firm will be able to break-even, i.e. cover all of its costs, with a particular price. (p. 524)

3. A break-even analysis is a cost-oriented approach that does not consider the effect of price on the quantity that consumers will want. (p. 525)

4.
   a. Availability of substitutes (p. 531)
   b. Ease of price comparisons (p. 531)
   c. Cost sharing (p. 531)
   d. Amount spent (p. 531)
   e. Significance of the end benefit (p. 532)
   f. Sunk investments (p. 532)

Exercise 17-1

Elements of cost-oriented price setting

Introduction

This exercise is designed to familiarize you with the arithmetic of cost-oriented pricing. Because most firms use cost-oriented methods to set prices, it is important that you understand these methods. Retailers and wholesalers, for example, use traditional markups that they feel will yield a reasonable rate of profit. You should be aware of how markups are figured. And you should know how stock turnover is calculated. Further, you should understand how the various types of costs differ, how they relate to each other, and how they affect profits as the sales volume varies.

Note: before starting this exercise, it is highly recommended that you review "Marketing Arithmetic" in the Student Centre of the text's Web site at www.mcgrawhill.ca\college\wongshapiro11.

Assignment

Answer the following set of problems. Show your work in the space provided.

1.   The usual retail price of an item is $100.00. The manufacturer's cost to produce the item is $40.00. Retailers take a 50 percent markup and wholesalers take a 10 percent markup. (Note: markup is calculated on selling price, unless otherwise indicated.)

   a)   What is the retailer's markup in dollars? _____

      b)   What is the wholesale price? _____

      c)   What is the manufacturer's price? _____

      d)   What is the manufacturer's markup percentage? _____

      e)   What is the manufacturer's markup percentage *on cost*? _____

2.   The Burberry Manufacturing Company is trying to set its price on an item that will sell at retail for $80.00.

      a)   For retailers to earn a markup of 25 percent, what should the wholesale price be?

            _____

b)   For the wholesalers in 2a to earn a markup of 10 percent, what should the manufacturer's price be?

_____

3.   Complete the following table by filling in the blanks. *Hint:* start with the first column and work to the right, column by column.

			Quantity produced		
Item	0	1	2	3	4
Total Cost	____	____	____	____	$400
Total fixed cost	$120	____	____	____	____
Total variable cost	____	____	$140	____	____
Average cost	N/A*	____	____	$110	____
Average fixed cost	N/A*	____	____	____	____
Average variable cost	N/A*	$70	____	____	____

* Note: N/A means not applicable (because at zero output there is not an average cost per unit).

4.   a)   Using the data from Question 3, plot the total cost, total fixed cost, and total variable cost curves on the following graph.

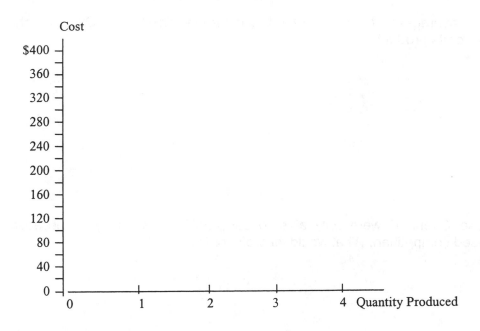

      b)   Using the data from Question 3, plot the average cost, average fixed cost, and average variable cost curves on the following graph.

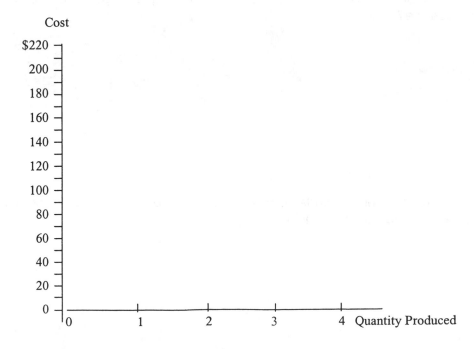

5.   Overland Corp. has fixed costs of $2,000,000 and average variable costs of $100 per unit at all levels of output. It wishes to earn a profit of $300,000 this year--which is an increase of 10 percent over last year when Overland sold 5,000 units of its product.

   a)   Use the average-cost pricing method to determine what price Overland should charge for its product.

   b)   Suppose Overland were only able to sell 4,000 units this year because of increased competition. What would its profit (or loss) be?

   c)   Suppose Overland's sales increased to 7,000 units this year. What would its profit (or loss) be?

   d)   Based on your answers to parts a, b, and c, what do you conclude about the effectiveness of average-cost pricing?

6.   Suppose in Question 5 that Overland had decided to use "target return" pricing instead of average-cost pricing. Suppose further that it wished to earn a 20 percent return on its investment of $500,000.

   a)   What price should Overland charge for its product?

   b)   What would Overland's return on investment be if it were only able to sell 4,000 units?

   c)   What would Overland's return on investment be if its sales increased to 7,000 units?

Question for Discussion

Why do so many firms use cost-oriented pricing methods when such methods have so many obvious shortcomings?

Exercise 17-2

Using break-even analysis to evaluate alternative prices

Introduction

Break-even analysis can be a very useful tool for evaluating alternative prices--especially when the prices being considered are realistic from a demand point of view. Break-even analysis shows how many units would have to be sold--or how much dollar volume would have to be achieved--to just cover the firm's costs at alternative prices. A realistic appraisal of the likelihood of achieving the break-even point associated with each alternative price might show that some prices are clearly unacceptable--that is, there would be no way that the firm could even reach the break-even point, let alone make a profit.

The mechanics of break-even analysis are relatively simple--once you understand the concepts and assumptions. This exercise reviews these ideas and then has you apply them to a common decision making situation.

Assignment

Read each of the following problems carefully--and fill in the blanks as you come to them. Where calculations are required, make them in the space provided--and show your calculations to aid review.

1.   Study the break-even chart in Figure 17-2a on the next page and answer the following questions:

    a)   According to Figure 17-2a, at what quantity, total revenue, and price will the firm break even?

        Quantity _____ Total Revenue _____ Price _____

    b)   The firm's total fixed cost in this situation is: _____

    c)   The firm's average variable cost (AVC)is: _____

    d)   Using the information in Figure 17-2a, plot the firm's *demand curve (D), average fixed cost curve* (AFC), and *average variable cost curve* (AVC) in Figure 17-2b on the next page. Label each curve and both axes.

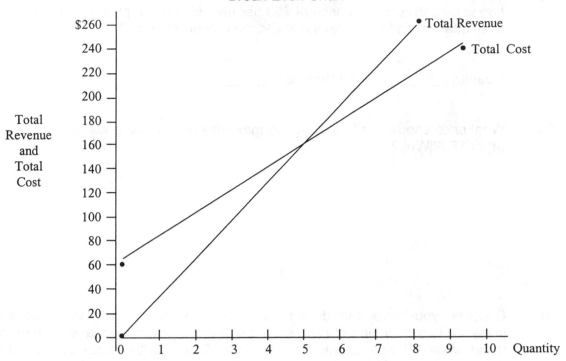

FIGURE 17-2a
Break-Even Chart

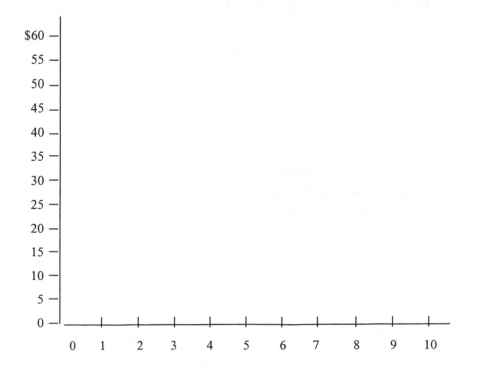

FIGURE 17-2b

e)   Using Figure 17-2a, draw the total revenue curve that would be relevant if the firm were considering a price of $50 per unit. Given this price of $50 per unit, at what quantity and total revenue would the firm break even?

Quantity _____   Total Revenue _____

f)   What price should the firm charge to maximize profits--the price you calculated in (a) or $50? Why?

2.   a)   Suppose you were considering going into the car-washing business and investing in a new kind of car-washing unit that is more mechanized than the usual ones--but also has higher fixed costs. Calculate the break-even point in dollars and units if the usual price of $4.00 per car were charged. The variable cost per car is estimated at $2.00. The total fixed cost per year (including depreciation, interest, taxes, fixed labour costs, and other fixed costs) is estimated at $320,000.

BEP in $ _____   BEP in units _____

b)   There is some possibility that there will be increased price cutting in your proposed market in the near future. Calculate the BEPs for the situation in (a) if the retail price drops to $3.50 per car.

BEP in $ _____   BEP in units _____

c)   There is also a possibility that the new washing unit will deliver a better job for which some people will be willing to pay more. Calculate the new BEPs if it were possible to raise the retail price to $4.50.

BEP in $ _____ BEP in units _____

d)   Should you go into the car-washing business in *any* of the above situations? Explain.

Question for Discussion

Looking at Figures 17-2a and 17-2b, what does break-even analysis assume about the nature of demand and about the competitive environment? Is break-even analysis relevant for monopolistic competition?

Exercise 17-3

Setting the most profitable price and quantity to produce

Introduction

Demand must be considered when setting prices. Ignoring demand curves does not make them go away. Usually, a market will buy more at lower prices--so total revenue my increase if prices are lowered. But this probably will not continue as the price gets closer to zero. Further, total cost--and perhaps average costs--will increase as greater quantities are sold.

So, if a firm is at all interested in making a profit (or avoiding losses), it should consider demand and cost curves *together*. This exercise shows how this can be done--and emphasizes that not all prices will be profitable.

Assignment

Figure 17-3 shows the Bullseye Manufacturing Company's estimated total revenue and total cost curves for the coming year. Study this figure carefully and answer the questions, which follow.

FIGURE 17-3

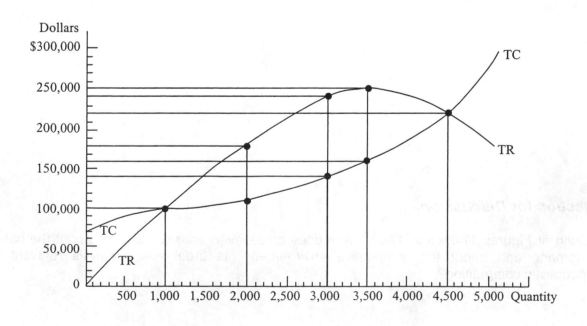

1. Complete the following chart by referring to Figure 17-3--the graph of Bullseye's total costs and revenues.

Quantity	Total Cost	Average Cost	Total Revenue	Price*	Total Profit (Loss)
1,000	___	___	___	___	___
2,000	___	___	___	___	___
3,500	___	___	___	___	___
4,500	___	___	___	___	___

* Remember: Total Revenue = Price x Quantity

   Total Profit = Total Revenue – Total Cost

Using the information from Question 1, and Figure 18-3, answer Questions 2-11.

2. The maximum amount of profit Bullseye can earn is: $ _____

3. Bullseye has total fixed costs of: $ _____

4. Given that Total Revenue = Price X Quantity, what should Bullseye's price be if it wants to get the most total revenue it can and plans to sell:

   a.   1,000 units: _____

   b.   2,000 units: _____

   c.   3,500 units: _____

   d.   4,500 units: _____

5. What would Bullseye's average cost per unit be at:

   a.   1,000 units: _____

   b.   2,000 units: _____

   c.   3,500 units: _____

   d.   4,500 units: _____

6.	To maximize its *total revenue*, Bullseye should sell (check the correct response):

___a.	1,000 units.

___b.	2,000 units.

___c.	3,500 units.

___d.	4,000 units.

___e.	more than 4,500 units.

7.	Figure 17-3 indicates that Bullseye's demand curve is (check the correct response):

___a.	horizontal.

___b.	vertical.

___c.	downward-sloping from left to right.

___d.	upward-sloping from left to right.

8.	Bullseye's demand curve is (check the correct response):

___a.	elastic.

___b.	inelastic.

___c.	unitary elastic.

___d.	elastic up to 3,500 units and inelastic beyond 3,500 units.

___e.	inelastic up to 3,500 units and elastic beyond 3,500 units.

9.	Bullseye's *average* cost curve is (check the correct response):

___a.	horizontal.

___b.	U-shaped.

___c.	vertical.

___d.	upward-sloping from left to right.

10. Bullseye will *lose money* if it sells (check the correct response):

___a. less than 1,000 units.

___b. less than 4,500 units.

___c. more than 3,500 units.

___d. more than 4,500 units.

___e. both a and d are correct.

11. Bullseye will *break even* if it sells (check the correct response):

___a. 1,000 units.

___b. 2,000 units.

___c. 3,500 units.

___d. 4,500 units.

___e. both a and d are correct.

12. To *maximize profit,* Bullseye should sell (check the correct response):

___a. 1,000 units.

___b. 2,000 units.

___c. 3,500 units.

___d. 4,500 units.

___e. more than 4,500 units.

Question for Discussion

Should a firm in monopolistic competition try to sell as many units as it can produce? Why or why not? State your assumptions.

Exercise 17-4

Using marginal analysis to set the most profitable price and quantity to produce

Introduction

Too many firms seem to ignore demand--depending almost blindly on cost-oriented pricing. A firm might operate quite profitably using cost-oriented pricing--but could it earn larger profits by charging a different price? The firm has no way of answering this question unless it also considers demand. When both costs and demand are known (or estimated), marginal analysis can be used to determine the most profitable price and the most profitable quantity to produce. Of course, in the short run the firm's objective may *not* be to maximize profit. In this case, marginal analysis can be used to show how much profit is "lost" when the firm pursues some other objective--such as maximizing sales.

This exercise gives you practice in working with the concepts of marginal analysis by applying them to the graph (Figure 17-4) on the next page. This graph shows curves for demand (D), average cost (AC), marginal revenue (MR), and marginal cost (MC) at different price and quantity combinations. (Review the discussion of marginal analysis on pages 527-31 of the text). Note that the graph in this exercise is different from the graph (Exhibit 17-10, page 530) used to illustrate marginal analysis in the text. Thus, this exercise gives you an opportunity to look at marginal analysis issues from a different point of view. However, you will see that you can answer the questions in this exercise by applying the concepts discussed in the text.

Assignment

Use Figure 17-4 on the next page to answer the following questions:

1.   At what price would 184 units be sold? _____

2.   How many units would be sold if the firm priced its product at $24? _____

3.   At what output (quantity) _____ and price _____ would the average cost per unit be *minimized?*

4.   At what output _____ and price _____ would the firm break even?

5.	At what output _____ and price _____ would the firm maximize its *total revenue?*

6.	At what output _____ and price _____ would the firm maximize its *total profit?*

7.	What will the average profit per unit be when the firm maximizes its total profit? _____

8.	What is the maximum amount of profit this firm can earn? _____

FIGURE 17-4

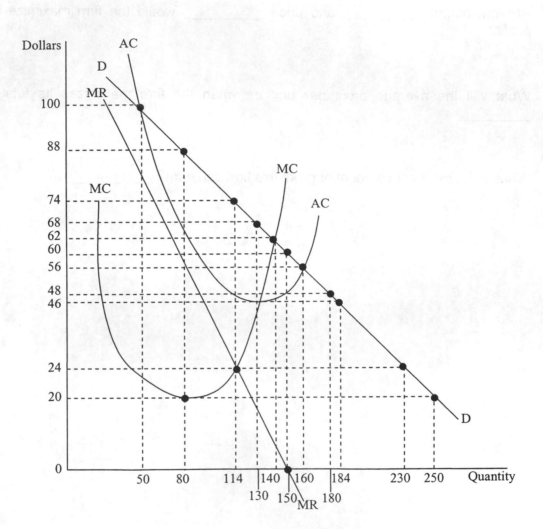

Question for Discussion

Why do so few firms use demand-oriented pricing? Is it an impossible task?

Exercise 17-5

Break-even/profit analysis

This exercise is based on computer-aided problem --Break-Even/Profit Analysis. A complete description of the problem appears on pages 541 of Wong/Shapiro, 11th edition.

1.   The marketing manager is interested in how the break-even point--in both units and sale dollars-- changes as fixed costs vary. Do a What If analysis (using the break-even column on the left side of the spreadsheet) to vary fixed costs between $27,000 and $33,000 (that is, plus or minus 10 percent from the initial $30,000 level). See how the break-even point changes and fill in the missing numbers in the table below. Then, briefly explain the pattern you observe.

Fixed Cost Level	Break-Even (Units)	Break-Even ($ Sales)
$ 27,000		$
$	72,000	$
$ 30,000		$
$		$ 95,400
$ 33,000		$

Explanation:

_____

_____

_____

_____

_____

2. The marketing manager is also interested in how variable cost changes affect break-even. If fixed cost remains at $30,000 and price and other variables stay the same, what happens to the break-even points (units and dollar sales) as the variable cost varies between $.72 and $.88--that is, plus or minus 10 percent from the initial value of $.80 a unit? As you did above, fill in the missing values in the table on the next page, and briefly explain the pattern you observe.

Average Variable Cost	Break-Even (Units)	Break-Even ($ Sales)
$ .72		$
$	68,182	$
$ .80		$
$		$ 105,882.00
$ .88		$

Explanation:

_____

_____

_____

_____

_____

3. The marketing manager is also considering what happens if fixed costs and variable costs change at the same time. For the two combinations of fixed cost and variable cost shown below, what are the break-even points in units and dollars?

Fixed Cost	Variable Cost	Break-Even (Units)	Break-Even ($ Sales)
$ 27,000	$ 0.84		$
$ 33,000	$ 0.76		$

In the first situation above, fixed cost decreased and variable cost increased from the original (spreadsheet) situation. In the second, fixed cost increased and variable cost decreased. Once the break-even point is achieved, which of these combinations would earn profits the fastest as additional units are sold? Briefly explain why.

_____

_____

_____

_____

Chapter 18

Developing innovative marketing plans

Chapter Summary

- **Know the content of and differences among strategies, marketing plans, and a marketing program.**

  A marketing strategy consists of a target market and a marketing mix, which is comprised of the four Ps. This is the overall big picture of what the firm will do in some target market. A marketing plan includes time-related details, as well as expected costs and revenues for the given strategy. The marketing program is a combination of the various marketing plans in use at the firm.

- **Understand, in detail, all of the elements of the marketing strategy planning process and the strategy decisions for the four Ps.**

  Exhibit 18-1 on page 546, shows the "narrowing down" marketing planning process. The marketing planning process: (1) Begins with an identification of customers needs and other segmentation factors. (2) Considers the company's objectives and goals, (3) analyses current and future competitors. (4) Uses a S.W.O.T. analysis to identify and list their firm's weaknesses and strengths, so that that manager can focus on the opportunities that match with the company's strengths. (5) Segments and defines the target market. (6) Differentiates and positions the firms offering. (7) Finally, develops a marketing mix using the 4 Ps.

  The 4 Ps should be creatively blended – in order to develop the best mix for the target market. In addition, each element of the marketing mix decision must work well with all the others.

- **Understand why the product classes and typical mixes should be considered when developing a marketing plan.**

  Marketers often do not know all they would like to about their target customers. To cope with this dilemma, identifying the proper product class is helpful because it suggests how a typical product should be promoted and distributed using past successes and failures as a guideline. Similarly, using a typical mix can act as a starting point, though one should be cautioned that a typical marketing mix for a given product class may not be right for all situations. It is often when a marketing mix is differentiated that the firm can offer customers some unique value.

- **Understand ways the marketing strategy and marketing plan is likely to change at different stages of the product life cycle.**

  Exhibit 18-3 demonstrates some strategies for each of the 4 Ps and to respond to competition over the product life cycle. Remember that markets change continuously, which means that strategies must allow for adjustment to different conditions.

- **Understand the basic forecasting approaches and why they are used to evaluate the profitability of potential strategies.**

  Forecasting future sales, costs, and profitability is important when planning an effective strategy. There are many ways of forecasting market potential and sales, all of which can be grouped into two basic forecasting methods: (1) *extending past behaviour*, and (2) *predicting future behaviour*.

  Extending past behaviour into the future requires understanding why variations in sales exist. This can be difficult and time consuming. Once the reasons for sales variations are known it is usually possible to develop a specific forecast of future behaviour. One weakness of this method is that it assumes past and present conditions will be the same in the future. Extending past behaviour relies on quantitative data.

  In contrast, predicting future behaviour does not rely entirely on quantitative data, Instead it may use one or more of the following: a "jury of executive opinion", estimates from sales people, surveys, and market tests. These methods are used to predict what will happen in the future, rather than assuming the past will repeat itself.

- **Know what is involved in preparing a marketing plan, including estimates of costs and revenue and specification of other time-related details.**

  Depending on the situation, estimating the costs for a particular marketing may be easy or difficult. Two ways costs for similar activities can be obtained are from the marketing department or from competitors' annual reports. Although both these methods are valid, the best approach is to use the task method (the estimated cost and budget for each activity is based on the job to be done). Then the marketing manger can use a "spreadsheet analysis" to compare profitability under different "what if" scenarios", such as various price points or costs.

  A marketing plan should also include time-related details (a schedule), since implementation plans can take 6 months to several years. A time frame should be integrated with expected sales and profits, so the actual results can be compared with the plan. This allows the marketing manager to control the implementation against specific performance goals at specific times.

  Finally a marketing plan should outline the reasons why each decision was made, providing important background information that is relevant to marketing mix and target market decisions.

- **Understand the different ways a firm can plan to become involved in international marketing.**

  There are six ways in which a firm can become involved in international markets: (1) *Exporting*, is selling some of what the firm produces to foreign markets. Exporting requires some knowledge of the foreign market, but specialists are often able to help when the producer is unfamiliar with foreign business practices and markets. (2) *Licensing* is selling the right to use some process, trademark, patent, or other right for a fee or royalty. (3) *Contract manufacturing* means turning over production to another party while retaining the marketing process. (4) *Management contracting* means that the seller provides only management skills while others own the production and distribution facilities. (5) *Joint venturing* is a domestic firm partnering with a foreign firm, requiring a large commitment from both parties, who must agree on a joint plan. (6) *Wholly owned subsidiaries* are separate firms owned by the parent company, giving the firm complete control over the marketing plan and operations.

  A firm's overall marketing program should be developed so it is adaptable to different countries. It is often not possible to develop a detailed country specific plan without a "local feel", so local managers should be given a great deal of freedom in their planning. However, the firm should keep tight control over the implementation.

Important Terms

True-False Questions

_____ 1. A marketing strategy is a "big picture" of what a firm will do in some target market--while a marketing plan includes the time-related details for that strategy--and a marketing program is a combination of the firm's marketing plans.

_____ 2. There are usually more different strategy possibilities than a firm can pursue.

_____ 3. A S.W.O.T. analysis is one way to zero in on a marketing strategy that is well-suited to the firm.

_____ 4. Even if you don't know as much as you would like about potential customers' needs and attitudes, knowing how they would classify your product--in terms of the product classes--can give you a starting point in developing a marketing mix.

_____ 5. When marketers fully understand the needs and attitudes of their target markets, they may be able to develop marketing mixes that are obviously superior to "competitive" mixes.

_____ 6. Typically, marketing variables should change during a product's life cycle.

_____ 7. Target-market potential is an estimate of how much a whole market segment might buy.

_____ 8. National economic forecasts available in business and government publications are often of limited value in forecasting the potential of a specific market segment.

_____ 9. A major limitation of trend extension is that it assumes that conditions in the past will continue unchanged into the future.

_____ 10. The factor method of sales forecasting tries to find a relation between a company's sales and some other factor that is readily available.

_____ 11. A factor is a variable that shows the relation of some other variable to the item being forecasted.

_____ 12. "Canadian Markets" an annual publication of the Financial Post is the most widely used source to determine market size and importance.

_____ 13. A leading series is a time series that, for some reason, changes in the opposite direction but ahead of the series to be forecasted.

_____ 14. Indices are statistical combinations of several time series.

_____ 15. "Trend-projecting" forecasting techniques should probably be supplemented by a "jury of executive opinion" or some other type of judgmental approach.

_____ 16. Instead of relying heavily on salespeople to estimate customers' intentions, it may be desirable for a firm to use marketing research techniques such as surveys, panels, and market tests.

_____ 17. The best approach for estimating the costs of various parts of a marketing strategy is the task method.

_____ 18. A spreadsheet analysis is a useful tool for demonstrating how sales and profits change over a range of prices.

_____ 19. The marketing plan serves as a blueprint for what the firm will do, including the time-related details.

_____ 20. Planning the time-related details of a marketing plan can be greatly aided by use of PERT--that stands for Product Evaluation and Rating Techniques.

_____ 21. A marketing plan should contain the marketing mix decisions, but not the reasons for those decisions because that would make the plan too long.

_____ 22. Finding the best marketing program requires some juggling among the various plans-- comparing profitability versus resources needed and available.

_____ 23. When a manufacturer moves into exporting, it usually is primarily concerned with selling some of what the firm is currently producing to foreign markets.

_____ 24. Licensing is a relatively easy--but risky--way to enter foreign markets.

_____ 25. Management contracting--in international marketing--means turning over production to others, while retaining the marketing process.

_____ 26. A domestic firm wishing to enter international marketing can use a joint venture--, which simply involves entering into a partnership with a foreign firm.

_____ 27. If a foreign market looked really promising, multinational corporations might set up a wholly-owned subsidiary--which is a separate firm owned by a parent company.

_____ 28. A multinational company is one that earns over 30 percent of its total sales or profits by exporting domestic production to foreign markets.

Answers to True-False Questions

1. T, p. 545	11. T, p. 554	21. F, p. 564
2. T, p. 546	12. T, p. 555	22. T, p. 564
3. T, p. 546	13. F, p. 556	23. T, p. 566
4. T, p. 548	14. T, p. 556	24. F, p. 566
5. T, p. 548	15. T, p. 557	25. F, p. 629
6. T, p. 551	16. T, p. 557	26. T, p. 567
7. T, p. 552	17. T, p. 558	27. T, p. 567
8. T, p. 553	18. T, p. 558	28. F, p. 568
9. T, p. 553	19. T, p. 562	
10. T, p. 554	20. F, p. 562	

Multiple-Choice Questions (Circle the correct response)

1. The main difference between a "strategy" and a "marketing plan" is:
    a.   that a plan does not consider the firm's target market.
    b.   that a plan includes several strategies.
    c.   that time-related details are included in a plan.
    d.   that resource commitments are made clearer in a strategy.
    e.   There is no difference.

2. Developing a "marketing plan":
    a.   means selecting a target market and developing a marketing mix.
    b.   involves nothing more than assembling the four Ps better than your competitors.
    c.   is easy--and profits are virtually guaranteed--provided that a firm fully understands the needs and attitudes of its target market.
    d.   All of the above are true statements.
    e.   None of the above is a true statement.

3. A manufacturer of a consumer product is trying to establish brand recognition and preference in monopolistic competition. The firm places considerable emphasis on channel development and is becoming somewhat less selective in its choice of middlemen. Promotion is both informative and persuasive--as the firm is seeking to increase both primary and selective demand. Prices in the industry are competitive--but there has been little price-cutting to date. What stage of the product life cycle is this firm's situation characteristic of?
    a.   Market introduction
    b.   Market growth
    c.   Market maturity
    d.   Sales decline

4. As defined in the text, target-market potential is:
    a.   what a market segment might buy (from all suppliers).
    b.   how much a firm can hope to sell to a market segment.
    c.   how much the firm sold to a market segment in the last year.
    d.   the size of national income for the coming year.

5. A good marketing manager knows that:
    a.   market potential is an estimate of how much a firm can hope to sell to a particular market segment.
    b.   sales forecasts should be developed BEFORE marketing strategies are planned.
    c.   a firm's sales forecast probably will be less than the estimated market potential.
    d.   sales forecasts are estimates of what a whole market segment might buy.
    e.   All of the above are true.

6. You have been asked to develop a sales forecast for one of your company's major products. What would be the most logical *starting point?*
    a.   Determine why the company's sales fluctuate the way they do.
    b.   Consider the prospects for the economy as a whole.
    c.   Determine your industry's prospects for the near future.
    d.   Analyze regional sales for this product for last year.
    e.   Perform marketing research into consumer buying habits.

7. The trend-extension method often can be useful for forecasting annual sales, but it depends upon the assumption that:
   a. the forecast is for a new product.
   b. sales during the coming period will be about the same as the previous period.
   c. there will be big changes in market conditions.
   d. the general growth (or decline), which has been seen in the past, will continue in the future.
   e. the firm will continue to improve its marketing mixes.

8. *Financial Post's* "Canadian Markets" is based on:
   a. the population in a market.
   b. the retail sales in a market.
   c. the income in a market.
   d. All of the above.
   e. Only a and c above.

9. Given the complexity of buyer behavior, sales forecasts for established products are likely to prove more accurate if based on:
   a. market tests.
   b. trend extension.
   c. a single factor.
   d. several factors.

10. Sales forecasters often try to find business indicators that change before sales and thus will help predict future sales. These indicators are called:
    a. correlation coefficients.
    b. time series.
    c. leading series.
    d. trend extenders.
    e. input-output measures.

11. Palladin Specialist, Inc., has developed a new product about which it is quite excited. Which of the following sales forecasting methods would be *least appropriate*?
    a. Market tests
    b. Sales force estimates
    c. Trend extension
    d. Jury of executive opinion
    e. A survey of customers

12. Which of the following sales forecasting techniques would be most useful for the marketing manager of a business products manufacturer facing intense competition?
    a. Sales force estimates
    b. Jury of executive opinion
    c. Use of a national economic forecast
    d. Trend extension of past sales
    e. Multiple-factor method

13. A company, which wants to objectively estimate the reaction of customers to possible changes in, its marketing mix should use:
    a. trend extension.
    b. jury of executive opinion.

c. sales force estimates.
d. surveys, panels, and market tests.
e. None of the above.

14. Flow-charting techniques such as CPM and PERT:
a. require that all marketing activities must be done in sequence.
b. do not indicate how long a project will actually take to complete.
c. identify the tasks, which must be performed to achieve predetermined objectives.
d. require complex mathematical tools and analysis.

15. A marketing program can be best described as consisting of several:
a. marketing plans.
b. advertising campaigns.
c. marketing mixes.
d. operational decisions.
e. target markets.

16. When a business firm in one country sells a firm in another country the right to use some process, trademark, or patent for a fee or royalty--this practice is called:
a. exporting.
b. contract manufacturing.
c. joint ventures.
d. licensing.
e. management contracting.

17. To minimize its own risks, the Boomtown Petroleum Corp. of Calgary, Alberta, operates a South American oil refinery, which is wholly owned by residents of that country. Boomtown is engaged in an activity known as:
a. management contracting.
b. a joint venture.
c. exporting.
d. licensing.
e. contract manufacturing.

18. A multinational corporation:
a. is any Canadian based corporation with direct investments in several foreign countries.
b. is one, which sells the right to use some process, trademark, patent, or other right for a fee or royalty to foreign firms.
c. is a worldwide enterprise, which makes major decisions on a global basis.
d. is any firm, which earns over 30 percent of its sales and profits in foreign markets.
e. All of the above are true statements.

Answers to Multiple-Choice Questions

1. c, p. 545
2. e, p. 545-546
3. b, p. 552
4. a, p. 552
5. c, p. 552
6. b, p. 552-553

7. d, p. 553
8. e, p. 555
9. d, p. 557
10. c, p. 556
11. c, p. 557
12. a, p. 555

13. d, p. 557
14. c, p. 562
15. a, p. 564
16. d, p. 566
17. a, p. 566
18. c, p. 568

Additional Questions to Test Your Understanding (Fill in the blanks)

1. What is a S.W.O.T. analysis?

_____

_____

_____

_____

_____

_____

_____

2. What are the three levels of forecasts?

   a. _____

   b. _____

   c. _____

3. What are the two basic approaches to forecasting?

   a. _____

   b. _____

4. What is a "jury of executive opinion" and why a marketing manager should not rely exclusively on this forecasting method?

_____

_____

_____

_____

_____

_____

_____

Answers to Additional Questions

1. A "*S.W.O.T. analysis*" is a useful aid for zeroing in on a feasible strategy. It identifies and lists the firm's strengths, weaknesses, opportunities and threats. A good S.W.O.T. analysis helps the manager focus on a strategy that takes advantage of the firm's opportunities and strengths while avoiding its weaknesses and threats to its success. (p. 546)

2.
    a. National Income forecast
    b. Industry Sales forecast
    c. Specific company and product forecasts
        (p.553)

3.
    a. Extending past behaviour
    b. Predicting past behaviour
    (p. 553)

4. A "jury of executive opinion" combines the opinions the opinions of experienced executives, perhaps from marketing, production, finance, purchasing, and top management. Each executive estimates market potential and sales for the coming years. Then they try to work out a consensus. A marketing manager should not rely on this forecasting method because the results may not be very good. There may be too much extending of the past, and some of the executives may have little contact with outside market influences. (p. 557)

Exercise 18-1

Using the "Survey of Buying Power" to estimate market and sales potential

Introduction

All marketers are faced with the ongoing problem of forecasting market and sales potentials. Forecasting is as much an art as a science--and many different forecasting methods can be used. Regardless of which method is used, the forecast should be based on data that is as accurate, reliable, and up-to-date as possible.

Many forecasters rely very heavily on data published in *the Financial Post annual survey of Canadian Markets and CMA data from Statistics Canada*" (see pages 555-556 of the text). Forecasters also rely on market data published in *Sales and Marketing Management's* annual "*Survey of Buying Power*". The "Survey" provides data on three important market characteristics--population, retail sales, and "Effective Buying Income." Population is reported by age group. Retail sales are shown for five store categories. "Effective Buying Income" (similar to disposable income) is broken down into median household and three income groups. Further, the data is broken down geographically according to Census Metropolitan Area, counties, and cities.

While there is a long period between updates of Canadian census data, the "Survey of Buying Power" and "Canadian Markets" data is published each year. Moreover, "Survey" and "Canadian Markets" estimates have been shown to do a good job of updating the census data on which they are based. A disadvantage, however, is that "Survey" and "Canadian Markets" data, like all published data, may not be available in the exact form a particular firm desires. Most firms find it necessary to modify the data or supplement it with other data--before making their forecasts.

Probably the most widely used part of the "Survey" is the "Buying Power Index" (BPI), a weighted index of three variables--population, retail sales, and Effective Buying Income--that measures a market's *ability* to buy as a percentage of the total Canadian potential. The BPI is calculated by giving a weight of 2 to its percent of the Canadian population, a weight of 3 to its percent of Canadian retail sales, and a weight of 5 to the market's percent of Canada. Effective Buying Income. The sum of those three weighted percents (population, retail sales, and effective buying income) is then divided by 10 to arrive at the BPI--as shown in the formula below:

BPI = 2(% Canadian Population) + 3(% Canadian Retail Sales) + 5(% Canadian Effective Buying Income)

10

For example, suppose Anytown, Canada, had about 1 percent of the Canadian population, about 4 percent of Canadian retail sales, and about 5 percent of the total Canadian. Effective Buying Income. Then the BPI for Anytown is found by substituting these percentages into the formula above:

$$\frac{2(1)+3(4)+5(5)}{10} = 3.9$$

Thus Anytown's market potential--relative to all of Canada--would be 3.9 percent. So if Canadians were expected to buy $10,000,000 worth of "gadgets" during the coming year, the population of Anytown might be expected to buy 3.9 percent X $10,000,000, or $390,000 worth of gadgets.

There is nothing sacred about the weights used to calculate the BPI. Many firms tailor the index to their own needs by applying a different set of weights or adding additional variables to the index based on their past experience. A manufacturer of snowmobiles, for example, might add a weather variable, such as average inches of snowfall, to the BPI. A potential pitfall in applying the BPI is that because it is broadly based, the BPI is said to be most useful for "mass products sold at popular prices." Thus, for more expensive products, or for products that are used regionally, the BPI may need to be modified by taking additional buying factors into account. For example, a simple BPI calculation won't help to predict the number of snow shovels we could expect to sell in Victoria, BC and Halifax, NS. However, including an additional variable--such as average number of inches of snowfall each winter--might help to make reliable estimates.

Assignment

The purpose of this exercise is to familiarize you with the Survey of Buying Power and the Buying Power Index--and to show how they are used in forecasting market and sales potential. Before examining a sample table from the *Survey,* we will begin with a review of the calculations used to produce the standard BPI. Answer each of the following questions and show your work in the space provided.

1.   Suppose that Strawberry Fields accounts for 3 percent of the Canadian population, 3 percent of Canadian retail sales, and 4 percent of the nation's Effective Buying Income. Calculate Strawberry Fields' "Buying Power Index."

2.   Look at the sample table from the *Survey of Buying Power* reproduced on the next page. The table summarizes population information, retail sales by store group, information about effective buying income, and shows the BPI. Next, study the headings carefully to learn the format for listing by Metropolitan area (in bold print), counties that make up that Metropolitan area (indented and listed under each Metropolitan area) and finally cities in that county. Now, reading from Figure 18-1, provide the following information:

For the Metropolis Metropolitan area:

        the total population: _____

        the total Effective Buying Income: _____

the Buying Power Index: _____

For Regions County in the Metropolis Metro area:

the total population: _____

For Metropolis (the city):

the Buying Power Index: _____

Figure 18-1
Sample of Pages from Sales & Marketing Management's Survey of Buying Power: Metro and County Totals

Province: Ontario

METRO AREA COUNTY · City	Population Total Pop-ulation (000s)	% of Population by Age Group 18-24	25-34	35-49	50+	House-holds (000s)	Retail Sales by Store Group ($000) Total Retail Sales	Food	Eating & Drinking Places	Gen-eral Mdse.	Furn-iture/ Furn-ishings/ Appli-ances	Auto-motive	Effective Buying Income Total EBI ($000)	Median Hsld. EBI	% of Households by EBI Group $20,000-$34,999	$35,000-$49,999	$50,000 & over	Buy-ing Power Index
METROPOLIS	260.2	12.2	17.3	27.9	19.2	103.6	2,999,501	525,192	432,303	304,860	182,133	660,874	5,024,497	39,919	21.3	18.0	38.1	.1163
REGIONS	260.2	12.2	17.3	27.9	19.2	103.6	2,999,501	525,192	432,303	304,860	182,133	660,874	5,024,497	39,919	21.3	18.0	38.1	.1163
· Metropolis South	81.2	23.7	18.4	24.6	17.8	35.5	1,602,708	268,101	246,771	142,011	129,516	304,425	1,618,013	33,409	21.8	14.7	33.3	.0452
· Metropolis North	57.4	7.6	16.4	25.4	22.4	22.2	771,282	132,991	85,375	61,538	31,383	227,700	916,833	36,965	24.5	21.0	31.9	.0247

3.   Based on the Buying Power Index, if total Canadian annual sales for a consumer product are predicted to be 6,000,000 units next year, how many would you estimate will be sold in the Metropolis *Metro Area* (show your work):

_____ units

4.   Based on the Buying Power Index, how many of the units above in question 3 would you expect to be sold in the city of Metropolis (show your work)?

_____ units

5.   If your firm has about a 25 percent share of the market for the product in questions 3 and 4 above, how many units would your firm expect to sell in the city of Metropolis?

_____ units

6.   Suppose that a producer of a new luxury car was trying to determine the sales potential in the Metropolis metro area--to determine whether or not to establish a dealership there. Would the BPI be useful for this purpose? Why or why not?

Question for Discussion

Would the "Survey of Buying Power" data be more useful to "mass marketers" or "target marketers"? Why?

Exercise 18-2

Adjusting marketing strategies over the product life cycle

Introduction

A marketing manager must take a dynamic approach to marketing strategy planning. Markets are continually changing--and today's successful strategy may be tomorrow's failure. Competitive advantages are often achieved and maintained by firms who are best able to anticipate and respond positively to changes in their marketing environment. Some changes may be completely unpredictable, of course--but other changes may be somewhat predictable and should be planned for in advance. Otherwise, by the time the planner realizes that some important changes have taken place, it may be too late to adjust an existing strategy or, if necessary, to plan a new strategy.

Among the changes that are more predictable--and, which should be considered, when developing marketing plans--are the typical changes in marketing mix variables that are often made over the course of a product life cycle. Exhibit 18-3 on page 552 of the text shows some of these typical changes.

Assignment

This exercise stresses how marketing strategies may need to be adjusted over the product life cycle. Read the following case and follow the instructions.

CREATEQUIP FREEZE-DRY APPLIANCES FOR FOOD

Createquip, Inc. manufactures a broad line of electric equipment for industrial buyers. Its sales and profits have stopped growing in recent years--and the firm's top executives are anxious to diversify into the consumer products market. However, they do not want to enter a new market with just another "me too" product. Instead, they hope to discover a real "breakthrough opportunity"--an unsatisfied market with large profit potential.

For several years, Createquip's marketing research and product planning departments have been working together in search of an innovative new product for the firm's entry into the consumer market. Now, the top executives believe that they have finally found such a product. The new product is a "freeze-dry appliance" for food. The unit makes it easy for consumers to make instant versions of just about any food--just as freeze-dried coffee makes great instant coffee. The unit can process almost any type of food (ranging from eggs and hamburger to oatmeal, rice, and fruits), which is available at any supermarket. It has the capacity to cook up to two-pound batches of a food product and convert it to freeze-dried

Figure 18-2
Planned Changes in Marketing Strategy for Createquip
Over the Course of Its Product Life Cycle

Item	Market Introduction Stage
Target Market Dimensions	
Nature of Competition	
Product	
Place	
Promotion	
Price	

Market Growth Stage	Market Maturity Stage

"pellets." Whenever the consumer is ready, the freeze-dried pellets can be put in a microwave oven with water and heated to produce fresh-tasting soups, sauces, gravy, drinks--and hundreds of other items which are otherwise time consuming to cook in small quantities. With the unit, a gourmet cook would be able to make fancy sauces on an impulse, an office worker could create a favourite type of homemade soup to take to work without the mess, and busy singles could keep pellets ready for when there's no time to go to the store or cook something from scratch. At first the new product idea seemed strange--perhaps even hard to believe--but in tests with consumers it has generated a very favourable response. Moreover, the freeze-dry unit is inexpensive and easy-to-operate, and it is expected to retail for about $100.

Createquip's marketing manager believes the new product will appeal to convenience-oriented families-- and also health-conscious people who want to make their own "instant" foods but with ingredients that are more nutritious and without the preservatives typically found in packages at the store. The marketing manager feels the product has almost unlimited potential--citing the rapid growth of prepared and instant foods and the wide use of microwave ovens. Further, the firm's research and development staff is sure that it will take any potential competitors at least two years to introduce a similar product.

The electric freeze-dry unit is really a revolutionary new concept--and will probably require a major promotion effort to gain consumer acceptance. Moreover, Createquip has no established channels of distribution in the consumer products market--and middlemen may be reluctant to handle an unproven product which lacks a well-known brand name. In addition, the firm is not sure what pricing policies to adopt, because it has no previous experience in the consumer products market.

To further complicate the strategy planning efforts, Createquip's marketing manager recognizes that the marketing strategy will need to be modified over time--as the new product passes through the various stages of its life cycle. So that the firm will be in a position to adjust quickly to changing market conditions, the president has asked the marketing manager for an overview of future marketing strategies for the freeze-dry unit--as well as the beginning strategy.

1.   Assume the role of marketing manager for Createquip, Inc. and fill in Figure 18-2 to show how your marketing strategy for the electric freeze-dry unit would vary over the stages of its product life cycle. (See Exhibit 18-3 on page 552 of the text for some general ideas about what you might include in your answers.) Be specific.

Question for Discussion

What kind of product will the "freeze-dry" unit be--that is, what product class--and what type of marketing mix would be typical for such a product? Are there any other factors that should be taken into account in planning the marketing mix for this product?

Chapter 19

Implementing and Controlling Marketing Plans: Evolution and Revolution

Chapter Summary

- **Understand how information technology is speeding up feedback for better implementation and control.**

  Marketing managers are able to capitalize on the advances in information technology to obtain almost instantaneous feedback on their marketing plans, gathering data on sales, expenses, and profits. Many companies are using satellite transmission and fibre-optic cable links to communicate with their salesforce via e-mail, laptops, PDA's and cell phones making data quickly and easily accessible from any remote location. A firm that is able to receive fast feedback on decisions can often use that feedback to develop a competitive advantage by spotting potential problems early or fine-tuning a smooth running implementation.

- **Know why effective implementation is critical to customer satisfaction and profits.**

  The challenge of implementing a marketing plan may include hundreds or even thousands of operational decisions, which may be handled by a few people or, in the case of large corporations, by hundreds of people. Careful coordination and communication is required for these decisions to be well executed. If the original marketing plan is a good one and the implementation done well, customers will be satisfied. In contrast, a good plan that is implemented poorly will result in unhappy customers. When many firms with similar product offerings follow the same strategy, customers are often won or lost depending on the quality of the implementation.

  Implementation activities can be either external or internal. In either case, they all must be consistent with the objectives of the overall strategy and with other decisions of the plan. The three general objectives that apply to all implementation efforts are – to get the job done (1) better, (2) faster, (3) at a lower cost.

- **Know how total quality management can improve implementation – including implementation of service quality.**

  Total quality management (**TQM**) can be used to improve any implementation effort. With TQM, everyone in the firm is concerned about quality to better service customer needs. Good-quality products satisfy customers, while the cost of poor quality is the loss of customers and good will.

  Firms that adopt TQM are always looking for ways to improve implementation through *continuous improvement*. This is done through a process of identifying what has gone right and what has gone wrong. As problems are identified, solutions are found to improve quality one step at a time. Similarly, service industries must manage quality through employee training and empowerment to maintain customer satisfaction.

- **Understand how sales analysis can aid in marketing strategy planning.**
  The detailed breakdown of a company's sales records can be very informative. Routine sales analyses prepared each week, month, or year may show trends, allowing managers to check their hypotheses and assumptions. With the growth of computer technology, such forecasts can be done easily and relatively inexpensively. Computer programs that draw graphs and figures are often used to make it easy to see patterns, helping the manager cope with large amounts of data.

- **Understand the differences in sales analysis, performance analysis using performance indexes.**
  Where sales analysis provides detailed breakdowns of a company's sales records, performance analysis looks for exceptions or variations from the planned performance. In a simple sales analysis, the figures are merely listed or graphed, not compared against standards. In performance analysis, managers make comparisons.

  A performance index is used to check on performance effectiveness by comparing what did happen with what should have happened. The performance index is a quantitative measure used to show the relationship between two values. This helps the marketing manager see if the firm's marketing plans are working correctly.

- **Understand the differences between the full-cost approach and the contribution margin approach.**
  Allocating costs can be tricky since some costs are likely to be fixed for the short term while other costs are likely to be common to several products or customers. Using the *full-cost approach*, all costs are allocated to products, customers, or other categories, including all fixed costs and common costs. This method allows the marketing manager to determine the profitability of various products, customers and so on.

  The *contribution-margin* approach does not allocate all costs in all situations.

  Another approach is when comparing various alternatives, it may be more helpful to consider only those costs that are directly related to a specific alternative(s). This method assumes that fixed costs do not change in the short run, and thus focuses on variable costs rather than total costs.

- **Understand how planning and control can be combined to improve the marketing management process.**
  Developing a plan and tracking actual performance is an important step in ensuring a firm is meeting its target performance level. As time passes, actual sales can be compared with the projected outcome. If performance is less than expected, corrective action in the form of improved implementation or new, more realistic strategies can be put into practice. As a rule, the shorter the planning and control period, the easier it is to correct problems before they become emergencies.

- **Understand what a marketing audit is and when and where it should be used.**
  A marketing audit is a systematic and unbiased review and appraisal of the basic objectives and policies of the marketing function. The audit looks at the company's current plans and objectives to see if they are still the best plans the firm can offer in the face of continually changing customer attitudes and competition. A marketing audit looks at the overall business and evaluates the whole marketing program. To get an unbiased expert and objective opinion, it is often best to hire an outside organization to perform the audit.

Important Terms

control, p. 575
total quality management (TQM), p. 580
continuous improvement, p. 582
Pareto chart, p. 582
fishbone diagram, p. 583
benchmarking, p. 586
sales analysis, p. 588

performance analysis, p. 591
performance index, p. 593
iceberg principle, p. 596
full-cost approach, p. 597
contribution-margin approach, p. 598
marketing audit, p. 601

True-False Questions

____ 1. Control is the feedback process that helps the marketing manager learn how ongoing plans and implementation are working and how to plan for the future.

____ 2. New information technologies help speed decision-making within the company and the implementation process outside the company.

____ 3. Total quality management works because everyone in the firm is concerned about quality to better serve customers' needs.

____ 4. The commitment to constantly make things better one step at a time is called continuous improvement.

____ 5. In a Pareto chart, problem causes are ordered from least frequent to most frequent.

____ 6. The fishbone diagram is a visual aid that helps managers figure out why things go wrong.

____ 7. A company may benchmark each of its sales reps against its other sales reps or against a competitor's sales reps.

____ 8. Because of the 80/20 rule--traditional accounting reports are usually of great help to marketing managers in controlling their plans and programs.

____ 9. Routine sales analyses are best done by manually reviewing data stored in sales invoice files.

____ 10. The best way to analyze sales data is to break it down by geographic region and customer type.

____ 11. Sales analysis provides a detailed breakdown of company sales records, but with no attempt to compare them against standards. Performance analysis seeks exceptions or variations from planned performance.

____ 12. A performance index is a number--such as a baseball batting average--that shows the relation of one value to another.

____ 13. A well-designed performance analysis will not only solve marketing problems--but may also be used to forecast sales.

____ 14. For most firms, the biggest obstacle to using sales and performance analysis--and marketing cost analysis-- is not the amount of data processing that is required--but rather the need for marketing managers to insist that the necessary data be collected.

____ 15. The "iceberg principle" suggests that while averaging and summarizing data can be helpful to managers--they should be sure that these summaries do not hide more than they reveal.

____ 16. The full-cost approach requires that difficult-to-allocate costs be split on some basis.

____ 17. Although the contribution-margin approach focuses management attention on variable cost--rather than total cost--it is likely to lead to the same marketing decisions as the full-cost approach.

____ 18. While full-cost analysis is especially useful for evaluating alternatives, the contribution-margin approach does a better job of showing individuals within the firm how much they have actually contributed to general overhead and profit.

____ 19. Ideally, a marketing audit should not be necessary because a good manager should continually evaluate the effectiveness of his operation—but, in practice, a marketing audit is probably needed because too many managers are "so close to the trees that they can't see the forest."

Answers to True-False Questions

1. T, p. 575	8. F, p. 590	15. T, p. 596
2. T, p. 576	9. F, p. 590	16. T, p. 597
3. T, p. 580	10. F, p. 590-591	17. F, p. 598
4. T, p. 582	11. T, p. 590	18. F, p. 598
5. F, p. 586	12. T, p. 593	19. T, p. 601
6. T, p. 583	13. F, p. 594	
7. T, p. 586	14. T, p. 590	

Multiple-Choice Questions (Circle the correct response)

1. Total quality management:
    a.   requires that everyone in the organization be concerned with improving quality.
    b.   means more than just using statistical controls to reduce manufacturing defects.
    c.   views the cost of lost customers as an important result of quality problems.
    d.   applies to service producers as well as manufacturers.
    e.   all of the above are correct.

2. Using total quality management to improve the implementation of a marketing program is likely to include:
    a.   the use of Pareto charts to determine the critical path for scheduling marketing activities.
    b.   the use of fishbone diagrams to show which problems are most important.
    c.   an emphasis on treating routine customer problems and unusual ones in the same way--because every problem is equally important.
    d.   training and empowerment of employees to identify and solve customer problems.
    e.   all of the above are correct.

3. According to the "80/20 rule":
    a.   marketing accounts for 80 percent of the consumer's dollar.
    b.   only 20 out of every 100 firms use formal marketing control programs.
    c.   about 20 percent of a typical firm's customers are unprofitable to serve.
    d.   even though a firm might be showing a profit, 80 percent of its business might be coming from only 20 percent of its products or customers.
    e.   none of the above is correct.

4. A marketing manager who wants to analyze his firm's sales should be aware that:
    a.   sales invoice files contain little useful information.
    b.   the best way to analyze sales data is according to geographic regions.
    c.   sales analysis involves a detailed breakdown of a company's sales forecasts.
    d.   sales analysis may not be possible unless he has made arrangements for collecting the necessary data.
    e.   a manager can never have too much data.

5. Performance analysis differs from sales analysis in that performance analysis involves:
    a.   detailed breakdowns of a company's sales records.
    b.   analyzing only the performance of sales representatives.
    c.   comparing performance against standards--looking for exceptions or variations.
    d.   analyzing only people--not products or territories.
    e.   budgeting for marketing expenditures based on contribution margins.

6. If Salesperson X had a performance index of 80 and Salesperson Y had a performance index of 120, then:
    a.   Salesperson X may be having some problems and his sales performance should be investigated.
    b.   the two would average out to 100--and this would suggest that "all is well."
    c.   Salesperson X's performance should be investigated as a guide to improving everyone's performance.
    d.   Salesperson Y probably should be fired.

e.   Salesperson Y obviously had higher sales than Salesperson X.

7.   Which of the following statements best describes the "iceberg principle"?
      a.   Problems in one area may be offset by good performances in other areas--and thus the problems may not be visible on the surface.
      b.   Ten percent of the items in inventory usually account for 80 percent of the sales.
      c.   Within a company's sales force there are usually one or two sales reps who don't carry their weight.
      d.   Many sales reps do not make their quotas because they ignore certain clients.
      e.   Airfreight is less risky than shipping by boat.

8.   If one were using the "full-cost" approach to marketing cost analysis, then allocating fixed costs based on sales volume would:
      a.   make some customers appear more profitable than they actually are.
      b.   not be done--because only variable costs would be analyzed.
      c.   make some products appear less profitable than they actually are.
      d.   decrease the profitability of the whole business.
      e.   Both a and c are true statements.

9.   Which of the following statements about the contribution-margin approach is *false?*
      a.   It is concerned with the amount contributed by an item or group of items toward covering fixed costs.
      b.   This approach suggests that it is not necessary to consider all costs in all situations.
      c.   Top management almost always finds this approach more useful than full-cost analysis.
      d.   This approach frequently leads to data that suggest a different decision than might be indicated by the full-cost approach.
      e.   It focuses on controllable costs--rather than on total costs.

10.   Which of the following statements about a "marketing audit" is *true?*
      a.   A marketing audit should be conducted only when some crisis arises.
      b.   It probably should be conducted by someone inside the marketing department who is familiar with the whole program.
      c.   A marketing audit should evaluate the company's whole marketing program-not just some parts of it.
      d.   A marketing audit should be handled by the specialist most familiar with each of the marketing plans in the program.
      e.   All of the above are true statements.

Answers to Multiple-Choice Questions

1. e, p. 580   5. c, p. 591   9. c, p. 598
2. d, p. 580   6. a, p. 592-593   10. c, p. 601
3. d, p. 590   7. a, p. 596
4. d, p. 590   8. e, p. 597

Additional Questions to Test Your Understanding (Fill in the blanks)

1. Briefly explain why fast feedback regarding marketing strategies and their implementation is important to marketing managers.

   _____

   _____

   _____

   _____

   _____

2. List and describe two TQM techniques to analyze customer complaints and to figure out why things go wrong?

   a. _____

   _____

   _____

   _____

   b. _____

   _____

   _____

   _____

3. What four basic questions must a marketing manager answer in order to make better implementation and strategy decisions?

   a. _____

   b. _____

   c. _____

   d. _____

4. List and briefly describe the two basic approaches to allocating marketing costs.

   a. _____

   _____

   _____

   _____

b. _____

_____

_____

_____

Answers to Additional Questions

1. Marketing managers who get fast feedback on their decisions can often take advantage of it to develop a competitive advantage. They can quickly fine-tune a smooth running implementation to make it work even better. If there are potential problems, they can often spot them early and keep them from turning into big problems. (p. 576,)

2.

a. A Pareto chart is used to show a frequency distribution for different types of customer complaints. This chart is a graph that shows the number of times the cause of a problem occurs. If the causes of problems are ordered from most frequent to least frequent, than organizations can set priorities. (p. 582, Exhibit 19-2)

b. A Fishbone diagram is used to figure out why things go wrong and to help solve problems. This diagram is a visual aid that helps organize cause and effect relationships to problems or "things that have gone wrong." (p. 577, Exhibit 19-3)

3.

a. Which products' sales are highest and why?
b. Which products are profitable?
c. What is selling where?
d. How much is the marketing process costing?
(p. 588)

4.

a. The full-cost approach in which all costs are allocated to products, customers, or other categories. Even fixed costs and common costs are allocated in some way. (p. 597)
b. The contribution-margin cost approach in which all costs are not allocated in all situations. This approach focuses attention on variable costs rather than on total costs. Total costs may include some fixed costs that do not change in the short run and can safely be ignored, or some common costs that are more difficult to allocate. (p. 598)

Exercise 19-1

Total quality management

Introduction

Marketing strategy planning is important to the success of every firm. Yet, a firm that doesn't do a good job implementing its strategy is likely to find itself losing customers and profits.

Many firms are finding that *total quality management* can help them not just with reducing defects in production but also in implementing all aspects of a marketing program. As discussed in the text, total quality management approaches can be adapted to firms of any size and for all classes of products.

There are many technical details on how to use statistical techniques as part of a total quality management process. In the text, you get an introduction to a few of these--fishbone diagrams and Pareto charts. However, even more than the techniques is the basic philosophy that motivates quality management. In that regard, learning about and understanding the basic ideas and concepts (see pages 580-587) of quality management is an important first step to using the approaches.

The purpose of this exercise is to give you practice analyzing different marketing problems from a total quality management perspective.

Assignment

In each of the following situations, a firm is having difficulty in reliably satisfying customer needs. In each situation, identify the most important problem (or problems) and make recommendations for how the firm can improve the implementation of its marketing plan. Be specific in relating your diagnosis and recommendations to the quality management concepts and techniques discussed in the text. The first question is answered for you as an example.

1. Provincial Bank is interested in shifting its emphasis from commercial lending to lending to consumers--especially in the area of residential mortgages. The bank has the "back office" capacity to handle the business and, with interests rates coming down, there is growing demand for new mortgages. Provincial's ad agency developed an effective series of radio and TV ads, and the bank president was pleased to learn that the new thrust seemed to be working. At the end of two months, mortgage applications were up 300 percent over the same period the year before. It wasn't long, however, before there were signs of trouble. Several customers complained about the slow turnaround time for loan approvals and the problems the delays had caused them. When the president checked on the matter, she found that there were many such cases--and she was even more surprised to find that the number of loans actually completed had decreased relative to the previous year. When she asked the head of the loan-processing group for an explanation, he said "It's no one single bottleneck. Sometimes the appraisal is late coming in. Other times there's some problem with the credit report or customers haven't completed the forms correctly. Sometimes the title search process holds us up on some detail. So, it's hard to say." The bank president said, "Well, I'm not happy about it. We'll just have to work harder until we can catch up. In the meantime, I hope it doesn't hurt our reputation."

    a)   Problem: *Neither the head of the loan-processing group nor the president are coming to grips with the problem. They are not actively looking for ways to make continuous improvements. To make real improvements and do a better job of meeting customer needs, they will need to sort out the causes and effects for the things that have gone wrong (the delays in processing.) Some of the delays are interrelated because parts of the process depend on completion of work by other people--the applicants, title company, and appraisers.*

    b)   Solution: *Provincial can begin to get a handle on the delays by developing a simple fishbone diagram to understand which parts of the system are causing delays. Then after some simple data collection, a Pareto Chart would help to identify which problems should be attacked first--for example, improving the application forms so consumers don't have trouble filling them out, and developing closer coordination with the appraisers and title insurance companies. Satisfying the customer is--or at least should be--important to them too.*

2. Excel Skates, Inc. manufactures recreational roller skates. Its new in-line design has turned out to be much more popular than expected--and demand far exceeds production capacity. The only glitch is that there have been some problems with the wheels on some of the skates; after a short period of use, the bearings in the wheel break and skates don't roll properly. The chief of production wants to change to a new assembly procedure that will eliminate the problem altogether, but he acknowledges that it will reduce output somewhat. The sales manager doesn't think that makes sense, however, because "the problem isn't very common, and it will be cheaper and easier to fix any problem skates under warranty."

    a)   Problem:

    b)   Solution:

3. The University Cashier's office is open from 8 until 5 every day and students can come to pay their tuition and fees, take care of campus parking tickets, get a bus pass, sign up to rent a dorm room, and handle just about everything else that involves money. There are two service windows that work on a "first come, first serve" basis and most of the time students only need to wait in line a few minutes to get help. However, sometimes there are long delays. As one student recently complained, "All I wanted to do was pay a fine for a lost library book, and it took nearly an hour because the computer had accidentally unenrolled the guy in front of me--and they couldn't get it straight. The line at the other window wasn't moving either--they couldn't figure out how much to refund a student who had to drop out of school because of an accident. There must have been 20 people behind me in the line. "

    a)   Problem:

    b)   Solution:

4. Lake Winnipeg is a well known summer camp for girls. Many campers return year after year and most of the promotion is handled by direct-mail responses to word-of-mouth referrals. The camp has a unique lake location and special boating facilities, and its superior reputation means that each year the camp has. a waiting list. The camp has been owned by Wade Leastmoon's family for three generations. Prices at Lake Winnipeg have always been set by the Leastmoon family by "what seems fair," and there has never been any customer resistance to price raises. This summer Mr. Leastmoon has received two notes and one phone call from parents complaining that the college and high-school age counselors don't seem quite as involved with the campers. When asked for specifics, parents find it hard to define their complaints, but one notes: "Nowadays, they all seem to bring cars with them to Lake Winnipeg, and as soon as they have time off, they're out of there." When Mr. Leastmoon asked the head counselor, Deborah Rabin, about the parents' complaint, Raffin responded, "That's true. A lot of them have boyfriends back in the city and they're commuting back to see them every chance they get. I guess we've just got a bad crop this year. Next year we'll get a better group of counselors--and be back to the old Lake Winnipeg!"

    a) Problem:

    b) Solution:

5. SportRover Automobile Co. has a reputation for producing elegant--but notoriously unreliable--sports sedans. One writer in the automotive press suggested that there was nothing finer than a Sunday afternoon spin in a SportRover--as long as you could afford a "chase car" to follow behind with a mechanic and spare parts. In the face of aggressive new competition from Japanese and German manufacturers of luxury sedans, SportRover has been losing market share. To counter this trend, Dennis Safari, SportRover's director of marketing, announces to a convention of SportRover dealers that the marketing mix will be adjusted. "For the new model year, leather upholstery and lambswool carpets will no longer be extra-cost options, but instead will be included in the base price of the car. We have also increased the horse power of the engine and made a number of other changes that will make it clear to customers that we have improved the quality of our cars."

    a) Problem:

    b) Solution:

6. Katie Dalton's objective is to build a profitable chain of bookstores, so she's pleased that a literary critic for a local paper has written a very favourable review of the selection of books in her first store. However, while Katie was out to lunch a young woman approached the checkout counter at the store and told the sales clerk, "I don't have my receipt with me, but I bought this book here yesterday and, as you can see, one whole section is just blank pages. I've checked the shelf and the other two copies have the same problem. I'd like my money back." The clerk replied, "I'm very sorry for the problem, but it's store policy that only the manager can approve a refund without a receipt--and she's on her lunch break. Can you come back in a couple of hours?" The irritated customer replied, "I came here on my lunch break just to get this straight." The clerk responds, "I really regret the inconvenience. Would it be helpful if I had the manager call you when she comes back?"

a) Problem:

b) Solution:

Question for Discussion

If a firm has really adopted the marketing concept, why should it need to worry about having some sort of total quality management program?

Exercise 19-2

Sales and performance analysis

Introduction

This exercise shows how sales analysis and performance analysis might be used to help plan and control marketing programs. *Sales analysis* begins with a detailed breakdown of the company's sales records and can take many forms--since there is no one best way to analyze sales data. As outlined in the text, any one of several sales breakdowns may be appropriate--depending on the nature of the company, its products, and which strategies are being evaluated.

Performance analysis seeks exceptions or variations from planned performance. In contrast to simple sales analysis--where facts and figures are merely listed--performance analysis involves the use of predetermined standards against which actual results are compared. Here, the purpose is to determine where--and why--performance was better or worse than expected.

Sales analysis and performance analysis can be useful in pinpointing operating problems which may require corrective action--or in identifying areas in which the company may be performing exceptionally well. Such analyses will *not* reveal *what* is causing a given problem--nor will they provide a *solution* to the problem. This requires sound management judgment--both in interpreting the data and in developing solutions. By using sales and performance analyses, however, marketing managers can rely on factual evidence--rather than guesswork--when problems do arise--and thereby improve the quality of their decision making. Better yet, by continually auditing their marketing programs--by analysis of well-chosen data--they may be able to anticipate problems and take action *before* they become serious.

Assignment

Assume you are the marketing manager for a small manufacturer of electrical products. Your company's products are sold by five sales reps--each serving a separate territory--who earn a straight commission of 10 percent of sales. The company's accountant has just given you the data shown on the next page describing last year's sales. Actual sales were less than expected, so you decide to analyze the data further to help you decide what to do.

TABLE 19-2a

Sales Territory	Sales Quota	Actual Sales	Total Calls	Total Orders	Total Customers
A	960,000	480,000	1,200	360	420
B	600,000	600,000	1,320	780	300
C	720,000	360,000	480	300	240
D	900,000	1,080,000	1,560	1,200	480
E	360,000	540,000	720	360	120
Total	$3,540,000	$3,060,000	5,280	3,000	1,560

1. a) Calculate a *sales performance index* for each sales territory. Show your work. One answer is provided as an example:

Territory A:

Territory B:

Territory C:

Territory D: ($1,080,000/900,000) X 100 = 120.0

Territory E:

b) What do the performance indexes indicate about the relative selling performance of each salesperson? One answer is provided as an example.

Territory A:

Territory B:

Territory C:

Territory D: This salesperson's actual sales were much higher than expected for some reason. We should try to find out why.

Territory E:

2. Some additional sales analysis would be desirable to help you decide why the sales reps performed as they did. Therefore, using the data in Table 19-2, make the necessary calculations to complete the following table. Some answers have been provided as a check on your work.

TABLE 19-2b

Sales Territory	Order/Call Ratio	Average Sale per Order	Average Sale per Customer	Sales Commission
A	30.0			
B				$2,000
C			$36,000	
D		$900		
E				
Average for All Territories	56.8			

3. On the basis of your sales and performance analyses, what do you conclude about the sales performance of each salesperson? What factors would you want to investigate further before taking any corrective action?

Territory A:

Territory B:

Territory C:

Territory D:

Territory E:

Question for Discussion

Does the above analysis suggest any specific management action that was not clearly indicated by a review of Table 19-2a? How does this illustrate the "iceberg principle"?

Exercise 19-3

Marketing Cost Analysis for Controlling Marketing Plans and Programs

Introduction

This exercise shows the importance of marketing cost analysis in controlling marketing plans and programs. Our focus will be on analyzing the profitability of different *customers*--but marketing cost analysis could also be used to determine the profitability of different *products*. (Try it!)

The first step in marketing cost analysis is to reclassify all the dollar cost entries in the natural accounts into functional cost accounts. This has already been done for you in this exercise--to simplify your work. The next step is to reallocate the functional costs to those customers (or products) for which the expenditures were made. Here, careful judgment is required--because although no single basis of allocation is "correct," in some cases one may be better (i.e., make more sense) than others. Further, the basis of allocation selected can have a very significant effect on the profitability of a customer (or product).

Assignment

1.   Using the data in Tables 19-3a and 19-3b, calculate profit and loss statements for each of three customers. Show your answers in Table 19-3c. Where you must make allocations of costs to products or customers, indicate under "Comments" the basis of allocation you selected and why. (Review pages 596-600, See the example on pages 597-600 of the text for suggestions.)

TABLE 19-2a
Sales by Product

Product	Cost/Unit	Selling Price per Unit	Number of Units Sold	Items/Unit	Items Packaged
A	6	12	10,000	3	30,000
B	10	17	6,000	2	12,000
C	$11	$22	5,000	1	5,000

TABLE 19-2b
Sales by Customer

Customer	Number of Sales Calls	Number of Orders	A	B	C
			Number of Units of Each Product Ordered		
1	20	10	4,000	1,000	500
2	25	20	3,500	3,000	2,000
3	15	10	2,500	2,000	2,500
Total	60	40	10,000	6,000	5,000

Other expenses from functional cost accounts:

Sales salaries	$48,000
Clerical expenses (order and billing)	12,000
Advertising	33,000
Packaging expenses	11,750
Administrative expenses	36,000

Comments:

TABLE 19-2c
Profit and Loss Statement by Customer

	Customer 1	Customer 2	Customer 3	Whole Company
Net Sales:				
Product A:	_____	_____	_____	_____
Product B:	_____	_____	_____	_____
Product C:	_____	_____	_____	_____
Total Sales	_____	_____	_____	_____
Cost of Sales				
Product A:	_____	_____	_____	_____
Product B:	_____	_____	_____	_____
Product C:	_____	_____	_____	_____
Total Cost of Sales	_____	_____	_____	_____
Gross Margin	_____	_____	_____	_____
Expenses:				
Sales Salaries	_____	_____	_____	_____
Clerical Expenses	_____	_____	_____	_____
Advertising	_____	_____	_____	_____
Packaging Expense:				
Product A	_____	_____	_____	_____
Product B	_____	_____	_____	_____
Product C	_____	_____	_____	_____
TOTAL EXPENSE	_____	_____	_____	_____
Net Profit (or loss)	_____	_____	_____	_____

2.   What do you conclude from your analysis? Should any of the customers be dropped? Why or why not? What factors must you consider in answering this question?

Question for Discussion

Which of the two basic approaches to cost analysis--full cost or contribution margin--was used in the above exercise? Would your conclusions have been different if the other approach had been used? If so, which approach is "correct"?

Exercise 19-4

Marketing cost analysis

This exercise is based on computer-aided problem --Marketing Cost Analysis. A complete description of the problem appears on page 603 of Wong/Shapiro, 11th edition.

Tapco's marketing manager is considering changing the price of one or both products. He has decided to use the spreadsheet to analyze his idea more carefully.

1. At present, Tapco is selling 5,000 units of Product A for $10.00 each and 4,000 units of Product B for $6.00 each. Based on the full-cost approach, what is Product A's allocated administrative expense and allocated advertising expense? How much profit does Product A contribute to the company?

    Administrative expense-Product A $ _____

    Advertising expense-Product A $ _____

    Net profit or loss-Product A $ _____

2. The marketing manager is considering raising the price of Product A to $12.00. He estimates that the quantity demanded will be only 3,725 at $12.00--but he is not certain how that will affect profits from Product A. Given his price and quantity estimates, use the full-cost approach column of the spreadsheet to compute the following information for this situation (a price increase).

    Administrative expense-Product A $ _____

    Advertising expense-Product A $ _____

    Net profit or loss-Product A $ _____

3.   Based on these two analyses (1 and 2 above), is it a good idea to increase the price of Product A to $12.00? Briefly, explain your answer.

_____

_____

_____

_____

_____

4.   Now, evaluate the same pricing change using the contribution-margin approach. What happens to the contribution margin for Product A at the higher price and lower quantity?

Contribution margin with 5,000 units at $10 each $ _____

Contribution margin with 3,725 units at $12.00 $ _____

5.   Based on the change in the contribution margin, is it a good idea to increase the price of Product A to $12.00? Briefly, explain your answer.

_____

_____

_____

_____

_____

6.   Briefly explain why the effect of the price increase appears to be attractive using the full-cost approach--but unattractive using the contribution-margin approach. Be specific. (Be sure to consider Tapco's total profitability before answering.)

_____

_____

_____

_____

_____

_____

7.   Based on this analysis, Tapco's marketing manager decided not to increase the price of Product A. However, he is also considering lowering the price of Product B to $5.50--because he thinks that the lower price will stimulate increased unit sales. However, he is not certain exactly how much the quantity sold would increase. What (minimum) quantity should Tapco expect to sell to make a price reduction on Product B a good idea?

a minimum of _____ units of Product B at $5.50 each

Appendix A

Marketing "YOU INC."— Preparing a Personal Marketing Plan*

Chapter Summary

- **Understand the process of preparing a personal marketing plan.**

    A personal marketing plan is crucial if you want to achieve career success. A personal marketing plan helps you understand and organize a systematic approach, which determines (1) your unique selling proposition and (2) competitive advantage to the right target employer, at the right income or price, (3) with the right blend of tools to promote your individual skills, education, and experience.

    Exhibit A-1 on page 607 sets out the components of a personal marketing plan.

- **Know how to identify personal payoffs and values, establish priorities, and construct a personal mission statement.**

    Every person has different ways to measure personal success. In order for you to achieve career success and fulfillment, you must define what success means to you. This depends on your values, payoffs and priorities, which can only be determined through an honest self-appraisal that includes the following:

    1. Identifying your own wants, needs, values, dreams, strengths, and weaknesses.
    2. Judging the "fit" of your unique skills and resources against the often uncontrollable environmental variables.
    3. Establishing and keeping focused on your most critical life priorities.

    The next step is to create a mission statement, which sets boundaries on what is done. It also sets the tone for the overall direction and coordination of efforts and resources. A personal mission statement expresses both your vision and your values. It suggests how you will take action on them. (See Exhibit A-4, p. 610)

- **Know how to develop and write specific career goals.**

    Goals are the practical side of vision. A goal must be written and include a deadline. You can set goals in two different ways, either by using a "top-down approach" which means by breaking your long-term vision into more manageable steps or you can use a "bottom-up approach" and execute small steps to explore your long-term dream.

    Be "SMART" - (1) Specific, (2) Measurable, (3) Attainable, (4) Realistic, and (5) True, so that your goals are actionable. (See Exhibit A-5 for an explanation of each of the terms, p. 612)

- **Know how to prepare a personal and industry situation (S.W.O.T.) analysis.**

  A *S.W.O.T. analysis* is a technique designed to identify strengths, weaknesses, opportunities, and threats and ensure that internal and external variables are consistent.

  Think of strengths and weaknesses in terms of internal or personal aspects, and opportunities and threats in terms of external, environmental conditions. Exhibit A–6 on page 613 outlines questions you need to ask yourself when conducting a S.W.O.T. analysis.

  Exhibit A-7 on page 615 outlines topics associated with your external environment. An internal analysis tries to answer these three questions (1) What you want, (2) What you have, (3) The results you have achieved to date. Exhibit A-8 on page 616 sets out a framework for an internal analysis.

  Exhibit A–9 on page 617 presents a model to relate your wants and dreams to eight life categories; (1) family, (2) career, (3) home, (4) social, (5) financial, (6) educational, (7) health, and (8) personal development interests.

- **Know how to identify and evaluate alternative career strategies.**

  Remember that a personal strategy is like a business strategy. It sets out the method(s) of achieving a goal. It allocates resources such as time, money and energy. It also recognizes that there are many different alternatives that can achieve the same goals, but with different payoffs.

  The alternative you should first take action on should be the one that is the easiest to implement in terms of avoiding obstacles and minimizing costs and risks. One way to evaluate each alternative is to use the "CORP" shown in Exhibit A-11, on page 620.

  The next step is to plan and execute a personal marketing mix to make sure that your personal resources and objectives match the external environment. This involves defining your target market and adapting each the 4 Ps to maximize appeal to the market. Exhibit A-10 on page 619, shows how the 4Ps may be adapted. Then, you must set an objective, design a strategy and develop a plan for each of the 4Ps.

- **Know how to prepare an action plan.**

  Action plans are the heart of accomplishing your goals and ultimately your vision. The plan of action worksheet in Exhibit A–12 on page 622 provides a format for summarizing the necessary information into a plan of action. An action plan consists of tactics with deadlines (the specific detailed action steps needed to carry out your strategy) that are scheduled (which comes first, etc.)

  Finally, you should prepare a contingency plan to take into account the "What ifs", such as a downturn in the economy, or a new industry created from a new technology. A contingency plan recognizes that no forecast is 100 percent accurate. It prepares you to be aware of and adjust to early warning signals that things may be moving off course.

Exercise A-1

A Personal S.W.O.T. Analysis

Introduction

This exercise will help you understand the personal S.W.O.T. process and at the same time help you develop an inventory of your skills and an awareness of the external environments.

The first part of the exercise will feature a list of questions and tasks. Remember to be as honest as you can. Before starting this exercise, you may want to take the online quiz at http://www.careerkey.org/ to give you some insight.

Finally, you will be asked to pick out the important ideas and answers and summarize them. As an option, you can share the summary with a partner and ask them for comments.

1. *Strengths* – these are advantages that you have and can give you a competitive advantage. Strengths are what you will emphasize when you market yourself.

   a. *What is my present position?* - Draw a line representing your life. On the appropriate spots, mark the date you were born and the current date. In the area to the left of the current date, indicate key successes, disappointments, and life happenings that reflect milestones in your life and that have contributed to where you are today.

   b. What am I good at? – This could be in terms of education, interpersonal skills, job related skills, etc.

c. What major resources/expertise do I have? What you have is your own unique personal attributes and experiences. Your "tools" for self-analysis include your prioritized values list, an unbiased assessment of your strengths and weaknesses, and information regarding your interests, likes, and dislikes. In addition, consider such factors as health and energy level as well as education and experience.

2. *Weaknesses* – These are things that you will have to address and build up. They are areas of potential weakness, when it comes to your job, school and personal life. For example, you may need a 3.0 average, but unless you work on your study habits (a weakness) you will never achieve this.

a. What are the major problems I face?

b. What am I poor at doing?

c.   What major resources/expertise deficiencies do I have? What you have is your own unique personal attributes and experiences. Your "tools" for self-analysis include your prioritized values list, an unbiased assessment of your strengths and weaknesses, and information regarding your interests, likes, and dislikes. In addition, consider such factors as health and energy level as well as education and experience.

3. *Opportunities* – (See Exhibit A-7 on page 615) Choose a target market with the best potential of employment, and then research individual companies to establish a contact list for your job search. Research employment trends, turnover, and promotion opportunities. How would you describe the climate and culture of your listed companies? To start you may want to visit this site for information on some of the different types of careers, http://www.careerccc.org/careerdirections/.

a.   What favourable environmental trends exist?

b.   How is my industry of choice developing?

c.   In what areas could I achieve success?

4. *Threats* - Research your competition. Consider graduation rates in your academic program or specialty and labour market conditions, as well as the skills, resources, strategies, strengths, and weaknesses of other people vying for the same positions. How will you differentiate yourself?

    a. What unfortunate environmental trends exist?

    b. How are my competitors developing?

    c. Where is my performance likely to suffer?

Discussion Question

Share your S.W.O.T. analysis with a partner. Consider their answers and whether they give you some additional insights into your answers.

Exercise A-2

Discovering What is Important to you

Introduction

This practical exercise relies on the pp. 609 to 612. It depends on two things; (1) your understanding of the concepts in the text and how they apply to you, and (2) How well you are able to reflect (to reflect means to critically think about your actions, thoughts, etc.) on your past, present and future.

Personal success demands that we lead from strengths and minimize weaknesses. A self-analysis enables you to do this by examining past and current objectives, resources, and results.

In this exercise, you will be examining your Objectives, which is built upon your dreams, values, likes/dislikes, and your wants/needs/goals. (See page Exhibit A-8 p. 616) This includes a consideration of your values, a review of your wants and needs.

You will also be asked to prioritize, which means to put in order of importance. This ordered list should always be considered a work in progress that is always changing.

Part A – What Do You Want

1. *Dreams* – List in order of importance to you, your most important dreams. The dictionary defines a dream in this context as a strongly desired goal or purpose. Remember these are your dreams, there is no correct answer for the number of dreams you should have. It changes over time. The hard part is to establish priorities.

   a. _____

   b. _____

   c. _____

   d. _____

   e. _____

2. *Values* - Values are attitudes and beliefs that form the foundation of our personal ethics. Values relate to consequences—what you want to happen—and your conduct—how you will behave to accomplish what you want. Referring to Exhibit A-3 on page 609, list the values that you feel most closely reflect your core values.

_____

_____

_____

_____

_____

3. Likes/dislikes – Do you like to work with people or would you rather work alone? Do you hate mathematics, but love international business management? Do you prefer to read a book or would you rather play tennis? Each of these questions addresses some like or dislike in various parts of your life. They are not the only questions you could possibly ask. For each of the following categories write down three questions that address likes and dislikes. After you have finished all the questions, go back and try to answer them in the space provided.

b. Your Personal Life (family, friends, hobbies, etc.)

i) _____

_____

ii) _____

_____

iii) _____

_____

c. Your Education (subjects, theory Vs. practice, etc.)

i) _____

_____

ii) _____

_____

iii) _____

_____

d. Your Job(s) (not challenging, does not fit my interests, compensation is inadequate, etc.)

i) _____

_____

ii) _____

_____

iii) _____

_____

4. Decision criteria/priorities – What criteria are you going to use to determine what is more important. You are probably going to use your likes/dislikes, values and dreams, but there are others, which are a function of the time and investment needed to achieve some goal. This does not mean that you are going to forget about those goals that are too costly or take too much time; instead, you may decide to do something else first. Criteria can be in terms of salary; they can also be in terms of job satisfaction or personal satisfaction. Review the answers you have given and now try to set out some criteria that you can use to filter your goals and establish some priorities.

_____

_____

_____

_____

_____

_____

_____

_____

_____

_____

_____

5. Wants/needs/goals – Recall what wants and needs mean. Needs are the basic forces that motivate a person to do something. Wants are needs that are learned over time. We can use the PSSP hierarchy of needs in Exhibit 6-3, on page 151 of the text to help you think about four different types of needs; (1), personal (2), social, (3) safety, and (4) physiological.

a. Personal

Needs/Wants_____

_____

_____

_____

b. Social

Needs/Wants_____

_____

_____

_____

c. Safety

Needs/Wants_____

_____

_____

_____

d. Physiological

Needs/Wants_____

_____

_____

_____

Part B - Establishing Objectives and Setting Priorities

Review the answers you have written down in the part a of this exercise. Objectives are what you want to achieve at some point in the future. Try to think of a single overall objective that may involve a series of intermediary steps. As an example, you may want to earn an MBA, but first you get at least a 3.0 average in your undergraduate studies. The intermediate steps are your action plan, but the overall goal – an MBA is your objective.

Understand that each of the objectives you identify is related to all of your other objectives. As an example, earning an MBA may be crucial to getting the job you really want.

Finally, review Exhibit A-5, Making Goals S.M.A.R.T.on page 612, to help you develop realistic measurable and achievable goals. Now answer the questions.

1. What is your overall career objective at this time?

2. What is your overall educational objective?

3. What is your overall personal objective?

4. Are there any other objectives?

5. How do each of the objectives relate to one another. Which objective needs to be realized first in order to realize another objective? In other words, is one dependent on another?

    a. Arrange the objectives in order.

        i)   _____

        ii)   _____

        iii)   _____

        iv)   _____

        v)   _____

        vi)   _____

        vii)   _____

        viii)   _____

        ix)   _____

        x)   _____

    b. Arrange the objectives in terms of the resources, time and energy they will require.

        i)   _____

        ii)   _____

        iii)   _____

        iv)   _____

        v)   _____

        vi)   _____

        vii)   _____

        viii)   _____

        ix)   _____

        x)   _____

c. Arrange the objectives in terms of their importance to you.

i) _____

ii) _____

iii) _____

iv) _____

v) _____

vi) _____

vii) _____

viii) _____

ix) _____

x) _____

Discussion Question

How do your objectives and goals compare to the other students in the class. Remember there are no wrong answers, only what is best for you. However, a discussion with your peers can help reveal other areas for you to reflect upon.

Appendix B

Economics fundamentals

Chapter Summary

- **Understand the "law of diminishing demand."**
  This means that as you increase the price of a product, people will tend to buy fewer of that product. The opposite is also true. If you decrease the price of a product people will tend to buy more of that product.

- **Understand demand and supply curves and how they set the size of a market and its price level.**
  The demand and supply curve graphs the relationship between price and the quantity of a product demanded. (See Exhibit B-2) The price is shown on the vertical axis and the quantity on the horizontal axis. The demand curve is usually down sloping, since in most cases demand decreases as the price increases. The demand curve is specific to some market over a specified time period.

  The supply curve is a "What if" graph that shows the amount of product that will be supplied to the market at a given price. Supply curves generally slope upwards, because companies are willing to supply more of a product at a higher price than at a lower price. In contrast to the demand curve, an extremely steep or vertical supply curve is inelastic, while a flatter curve is elastic.

  The point where the demand and supply curves intersect is called the "equilibrium point, because demand equals supply.

- **Know about elasticity of demand and supply.**
  Elastic demand means that some or all of demand curve has a steeper slope and that total revenue will decrease as the price is raised. Inelastic demand means that the slope of some or all of the demand curve is flatter, and that total revenue will increase as prices increase. (See Exhibit B-5)

- **Know why demand elasticity can be affected by availability of substitutes.**
  A substitute is a product that may be used or bought instead of another product, such as buying a grapefruit instead of an orange. As a rule the more "good" substitutes there are for a product, the more elastic the demand is.

- **Know the different kinds of competitive situations and understand why they are important to marketing managers.**
  There are four different types of competitive market situations - pure competition, oligopoly, monopolistic competition, and monopoly. The text discusses only the first three because a monopoly is very rare. Each type of competitive situation has different characteristics that are important for the marketing manager. (See Exhibit B-11)

Important Terms

law of diminishing demand, p. 626
demand curve, p. 627
inelastic demand, p. 629
elastic demand, p. 629
substitutes, p. 630
supply curve, p. 632
inelastic supply, p. 633

elastic supply, p. 634
equilibrium point, p. 634
consumer surplus, p. 634
pure competition, p. 635
oligopoly, p. 636
monopolistic competition, p. 637

True-False Questions

____ 1. Economists usually assume that customers evaluate a given set of alternatives in terms of whether they will make them feel better (or worse) or in some way improve (or change) their situation.

____ 2. "The law of diminishing demand" says that if the price of a product is raised, a greater quantity will be demanded--and if the price of a product is lowered, a smaller quantity will be demanded.

____ 3. A demand schedule may indicate that as prices go lower, the total unit sales increase, but the total revenue decreases.

____ 4. A demand curve is a graph of the relationship between price and quantity demanded in a market.

____ 5. Most demand curves slope upward.

____ 6. Unitary elasticity of demand means that total revenue remains the same when prices change, regardless of whether price is increased or decreased.

____ 7. If total revenue would decrease if price were raised, then demand is said to be elastic.

____ 8. If total revenue would increase if price were lowered, then demand is said to be inelastic.

____ 9. A demand curve must be entirely elastic or inelastic; it cannot be both.

____ 10. Whether a product has an elastic or inelastic demand depends on many factors including the availability of substitutes, the importance of the item in the customer's budget, and the urgency of the customer's need in relation to other needs.

____ 11. When only a small number of good "substitutes" are available, demand tends to be quite inelastic.

____ 12. A supply curve shows the quantity of products that will be offered at various possible prices by all suppliers together.

___ 13. An extremely steep or almost vertical supply curve is called elastic because the quantity supplied would not change much if the price were raised.

___ 14. The intersection of demand and supply determines the size of a market and the market price.

___ 15. A market is at the equilibrium point if the quantity and the price that sellers are willing to offer are equal to the quantity and the price that buyers are willing to accept.

___ 16. "Consumer surplus" is the difference between the value of a purchase and the price the consumer has to pay.

___ 17. In pure competition, both the industry demand curve and the individual firm's demand curve are horizontal.

___ 18. Except for oligopolies, most markets tend to become more competitive--that is, move toward pure competition.

___ 19. Oligopoly situations develop when a market has a few sellers of essentially homogeneous products and a fairly elastic industry demand curve.

___ 20. In oligopoly situations, individual firms are faced with a "kinked" demand curve.

___ 21. In monopolistic competition, there is only one seller and that seller has complete control over the price of its unique product.

Answers to True-False Questions

1. T, p. 626	8. F, p. 630	15. T, p. 634
2. F, p. 626	9. F, p. 630	16. T, p. 634
3. T, p. 627	10. T, p. 631	17. F, p. 635
4. T, p. 627	11. T, p. 631	18. T, p. 636
5. F, p. 627	12. T, p. 632	19. F, p. 636
6. T, p. 630	13. F, p. 634	20. T, p. 636
7. T, p. 630	14. T, p. 634	21. F, p. 637

Multiple-Choice Questions (Circle the correct response)

1.   The "law of diminishing demand" says that:
    a.   if the price of a product were lowered, a greater quantity would be demanded.
    b.   if the price of a product were raised, a greater quantity would be demanded.
    c.   the demand for any product will tend to decline over time.
    d.   if the price of a product were lowered, a smaller quantity would be demanded.
    e.   the more of a product a person buys, the less utility that particular product offers him.

2.   A demand curve:
    a.   is generally up-sloping from left to right.
    b.   is formed by plotting the points from a supply schedule.
    c.   shows what quantities would be demanded by potential customers at various possible prices.
    d.   shows how total revenue increases as prices decrease.
    e.   All of the above are true statements.

3.   If a firm's total revenue increases when the price of its product is reduced from $15 to $10, the demand for this product is:
    a.   elastic.
    b.   inelastic.
    c.   unitary elastic.
    d.   cannot be determined without looking at the demand curve.

4.   Study the following demand schedule:

PRICE	QUANTITY DEMANDED	TOTAL REVENUE
$500	1,000	$500,000
400	2,000	800,000
300	3,000	900,000
200	4,000	800,000
100	5,000	500,000

This demand schedule shows that the demand for this product is:
    a.   elastic.
    b.   inelastic.
    c.   unitary elastic.
    d.   both elastic and inelastic.
    e.   This demand schedule cannot be correct because it violates the "law of diminishing demand."

5.   The elasticity of demand for a particular product does *not* depend upon:
    a.   the availability of substitutes.
    b.   the importance of the item in the customer's budget.
    c.   the urgency of the customer's need.
    d.   how much it costs to produce the product.
    e.   All of the above affect the elasticity of demand.

6.   Which of the following products would have the most *inelastic* demand for most potential customers?
       a.   A home computer
       b.   A vacation trip to France
       c.   A one-pound package of salt
       d.   A pair of designer jeans
       e.   A "Big Mac" hamburger

7.   A supply curve:
       a.   is generally flatter than its supply schedule.
       b.   is not affected by production costs.
       c.   is generally up-sloping from left to right.
       d.   is a picture of the quantities of goods that would be demanded at various possible prices.
       e.   All of the above are true statements.

8.   Which of the following statements about elasticity of supply is *true?*
       a.   If a product's demand curve is elastic, then its supply curve also must be elastic.
       b.   A product's elasticity of supply determines its elasticity of demand.
       c.   In the short run, the supply curve for most agricultural products is highly elastic.
       d.   In the long run, the supply curve for most products is highly inelastic.
       e.   None of the above statements are true.

9.   Which of the following statements about demand and supply interaction is *true?*
       a.   Demand is the sole determiner of price.
       b.   A market is said to be in equilibrium when the elasticity of demand equals the elasticity of supply.
       c.   The interaction of supply and demand determines the size of the market and the market price.
       d.   For a market to be in equilibrium, the price and quantity that buyers are willing to accept must be greater than the price and quantity that suppliers are willing to offer.
       e.   All of the above statements are true.

10.   Given a situation where there is elastic demand and elastic supply, an *increase* in the quantity suppliers are willing to supply at all possible prices will:
       a.   decrease price, but not change quantity demanded.
       b.   increase price and decrease quantity demanded.
       c.   lower price and increase quantity demanded.
       d.   increase price and increase quantity demanded.

11.   The term "consumer surplus" means that:
       a.   consumers never get their money's worth in any transaction.
       b.   there are more needs than there are products to satisfy them.
       c.   consumers do not consume all the products they buy.
       d.   some consumers would be willing to pay more than the market equilibrium price if they had to.
       e.   there are more consumers than there are producers.

12.   Which of the following is *not* a factor affecting competition?
       a.   the number of the firm's competitors.

b.   the uniqueness of the firm's marketing mix.

c.   the size of the firm's competitors.

d.   the elasticity of the firm's demand curve.

e.   All of the above are factors that do affect competition.

13.   In which of the following situations would an individual firm be most likely to face a flat demand curve?

     a.   Oligopoly

     b.   Pure competition

     c.   Monopoly

     d.   Monopolistic competition

     e.   None of the above--demand is always downward sloping.

14.   Oligopoly situations are generally characterized by:

     a.   essentially heterogeneous products.

     b.   relatively few sellers, or a few large firms and perhaps many smaller firms.

     c.   fairly elastic industry demand.

     d.   a and b above--but not c.

     e.   All of the above.

15.   In an oligopoly situation:

     a.   an individual firm's demand is inelastic above the "kink" and elastic below the kink.

     b.   the market price is usually somewhere above the "kink."

     c.   price wars usually increase profits for all competitors.

     d.   price fluctuations may occur despite the kinked demand curve faced by each firm.

     e.   All of the above are true statements.

16.   A particular market is characterized by different (heterogeneous) products in the eyes of some customers and sellers who feel they do face some competition. This product-market is an example of:

     a.   oligopoly.

     b.   monopoly.

     c.   monopolistic competition.

     d.   pure competition.

     e.   It could be any of the above.

17.   Which of the following statements about the competitive environment is *true'*

     a.   The industry demand curve in a pure competition situation is horizontal

     b.   Monopolistic competition is characterized by down sloping demand curves due to the lack of any substitute products.

     c.   In a pure competition situation, an individual firm is faced with a very inelastic demand curve.

     d.   Since a monopolistic competitor has a down sloping demand curve just like a pure monopolist, it has some control over its price.

     e.   All of the above are true statements.

Answers to Multiple-Choice Questions

1. a, p. 626   7. c, p. 632   13. b, p. 637

Exercise B-1

Estimating and using demand elasticity

Introduction

"Demand elasticity" is a very useful concept for analyzing the nature of demand and competition in markets. As explained in Appendix B in the text, demand elasticity can be defined in terms of what happens to total revenue when the price of a product is lowered.

   a.   If total revenue would increase if the price were lowered, then demand is said to be *elastic*

   b.   If total revenue would decrease if the price were lowered, then demand is said to be *inelastic.*

   c.   If total revenue would stay the same if the price were lowered, then we have a special case called *unitary elasticity of demand.*

Different products have different demand elasticities because of factors such as the availability of substitutes, the importance of the item in the customer's budget, and the urgency of the customer's need in relation to other needs.

The elasticity of a firm's demand curve is extremely important to a marketing strategy planner. It provides a short hand description of the nature of competition and demand facing a firm--often suggesting necessary changes in strategies. For example, a firm with a highly elastic demand curve might have many competitors and would have very little control over the price it could charge for its product. In this case, perhaps the firm should plan a new strategy--one aimed at a different target market with fewer competitors and less elastic demand.

Assignment

This exercise has three parts and is designed to increase your understanding of demand elasticity. The first part focuses on the relationship of demand elasticity to changes in total revenue. The second part shows how demand elasticity can vary in different market situations. The third part shows how product and price are related through demand elasticity.

1.   Demand elasticity was defined above in terms of what happens to total revenue when price is lowered. Now complete the following table--showing what happens to total revenue (TR) when price is *raised* instead of lowered.

	Elastic demand	Inelastic demand	Unitary elasticity of demand
Price lowered	TR increases	TR decreases	TR remains the same
Price raised	_____	_____	_____

2. Figure B-1 shows three demand curves--each with a different degree of elasticity. Each of the demand curves represents *one* of the following situations:

    a) The demand for airline fuel during a holiday season.
    b) The demand for an individual farmer's blueberry crop.
    c) The demand for one firm's "quality" CD player.

In the space provided, state which of the three situations each demand curve most likely represents. Then briefly explain each answer in terms of the factors that can cause demand elasticity to vary in different market situations.

FIGURE B-1

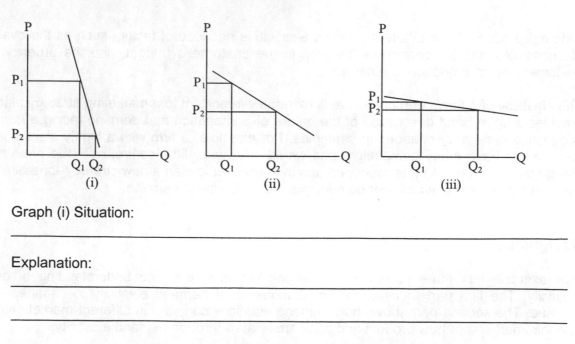

Graph (i) Situation:

_____

Explanation:

_____

_____

_____

Graph (ii) Situation: _____

Explanation: _____

_____

_____

Graph (iii) Situation: _____

Explanation: _____

_____

_____

3.   Read the following paragraph and then answer questions (a) through (c).

Centrex Instruments Plus, Inc. produces and sells quality control instruments that are used by industrial firms to control the production process. The firm's management is seeking a larger share of the market. Thus, its objective for the coming year is to increase both its dollar sales volume and its market share for the instruments--which are currently priced at $1,600. Centrex's estimated demand curve for the next year is shown in Figure B-2.

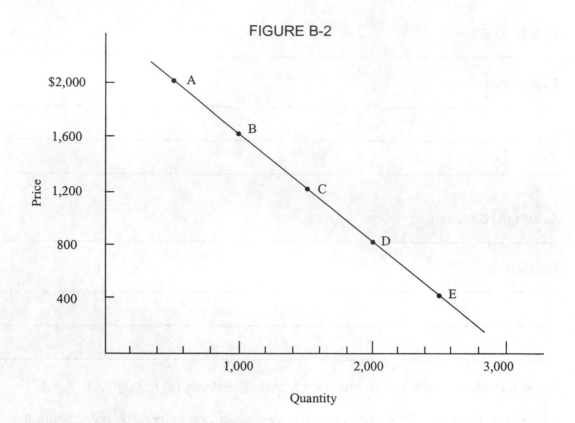

FIGURE B-2

a)   Use Figure B-2 to complete the following table:

Demand Schedule of Centrex's Quality Control Instruments

Points on Graph	Price per unit	Quantity Demanded per unit	Total Revenue per year
A	$2,000	500	$1,000,000
B	1,600	_____	_____
C	1,200	_____	_____
D	800	_____	_____
E	400	_____	_____

b) Looking at Centrex's demand curve and demand schedule, would you describe the demand for the firm's instruments as (a) elastic, (b) inelastic, (c) unitary elastic, or (d) both elastic and inelastic? Explain your answer.

_____

_____

_____

c)   As president of Centrex, you have called a meeting of top management to discuss the firm's pricing for the coming year. After explaining the purpose of the meeting, you have asked for comments and suggestions.

"If we want to increase our dollar sales revenue, then we must raise our selling price," suggest your finance manager.

"That may increase our sales revenue," replies your production manager, "but if we want to capture a larger share of the market, then the only answer is to increase our production to its maximum level--while maintaining our current price."

"Nonsense," yells your sales manager, "the obvious thing to do is cut our price as low as possible."

Since you have to make the decision, explain how you would resolve the conflicting advice of your department managers. Then state what price Centrex should charge to increase sales revenue on the instruments *and* capture a larger share of the market by selling more units.

Question for Discussion

Consider the three market situations in Question 2. If a firm's demand curve is elastic, does the demand curve for the industry also have to be elastic? What if the firm's demand curve is inelastic?

Exercise B-2

Analyzing the competitive environment

Introduction

Marketing managers do not always enjoy a full range of alternatives when planning a marketing mix. Their choices may be limited--or largely determined--by the nature of the competitive environment.

For example, a firm might be able to use almost any marketing mix in a *pure monopoly* situation, while a firm's mix might be entirely determined by market forces in *a pure competition* situation. In an *oligopoly* situation, a firm would have some control over its marketing mix, but it might find it difficult to differentiate its product and any price-cutting could lead to a "price-war." Of course, most firms find themselves in a *monopolistic competition* situation where their control over their marketing mix can range from a lot to a little--depending on how competitive the monopolistic competition is.

It is not always easy to identify the nature of a firm's competitive environment. In general, one must consider many factors--besides just the number and size of competitors. Other factors that should be considered include: (a) the similarity of competing products and marketing mixes--as seen by the target customers, (b) barriers to entry for new firms, and (c) seller concentration--(i.e., the extent to which a few large sellers control the bulk of industry sales).

Assignment

This exercise will give you some practice in analyzing the competitive environment. Read the following cases carefully and for each of them:

a)   Indicate the nature of the competitive environment, taking into consideration the probable target market.

Use the following terms to identify the nature of competition: pure competition, monopolistic competition, monopoly, and oligopoly.

Note: The term "monopolistic competition" can be used to describe situations ranging from near-monopoly to almost pure competition. Try to distinguish between "moderately competitive monopolistic competition" situations and those that may be "extremely" or only "slightly" competitive--by labeling the latter as either "monopolistic competition approaching pure monopoly" or "monopolistic competition approaching pure competition."

b) Briefly explain your answer, taking into account the various factors, which were discussed above.

The first case has been answered for you as an example.

1. Crossroads Truck Stop is a combination gasoline station-restaurant-motel that caters to long-distance truck drivers. It is located at the intersection of two major highways near a city of about 150,000 people. There are no other truck stops in the immediate area.

   a) Nature of competition: *Monopolistic competition approaching pure monopoly.*

   b) Explanation: *Although Crossroads Truck Stop probably gets a large share of the long-distance truckers' business, it does not have a pure monopoly because truckers can go into the city or on to the next truck stop. Further, there is nothing to prevent a potential competitor from locating nearby--that may very well happen if Crossroads is enjoying unusually high profits.*

2. Mont Tremblant Ski Area is one of 6 ski resorts in one part of the Laurentians in Quebec, one of the most popular ski destinations in eastern Canada. All six resorts set their base price for a one-day ticket in advance of the season--with the different resorts settling on about the same "going rate" that most skiers are prepared to pay. When Quebec prices are too high, destination skiers can choose BC, the Eastern Townships, or New England resorts for their vacations. Like destination skiers, day skiers (who drive from Montreal and other towns for a day of skiing without purchasing lodging) are attracted by each area's unique trails, terrain, and facilities. Depending on the snowfall and the level of bookings by destination skiers, the number of special "deals" and promotions offered by the ski areas can be quite large.

   a) Nature of competition:

   _____

   b) Explanation:

   _____

   _____

   _____

   _____

   _____

   _____

3. Delightfully Clean specializes in dry cleaning of clothing and other household items--as well as operating a shirt laundry. It operates a central processing plant and 10 conveniently located branches where dry cleaning can be dropped off and picked up a day or two later. This company is located in a city of 400,000 where there are about 80 other dry cleaners (some of whom also have multiple-outlet operations). All these cleaners charge approximately the same "low" prices for basically the same services--because a steady influx of new dry cleaners has tended to keep prices at a fairly low level. Further, some firms have not been able to attract enough business to cover their rising labour costs and have been forced out of business.

    a) Nature of competition:

    _____

    b) Explanation:

    _____

    _____

    _____

    _____

    _____

4. Racket World, Inc. operates the only privately-owned indoor racket ball court facility in Saskatoon, Saskatchewan--a western city with a population of 215,000. It runs a full program of racket ball lessons, tournaments, and public play. It is also the "sponsor" of local "high school racket ball"--trading practice time for a share of the gate. Its only "indoor" competition is from university courts--which are only five kilometres away. The university athletic department does not run competing programs--because its primary role is to serve the students and intramural teams. However, it does have a large amount of "extra time" and regularly sells blocks of time to groups (for example, businessmen who come to town for conferences at local hotels). The athletic department usually charges such groups prices that are below Racket World's prices (by 10-40 percent) and probably way below its variable costs of operating the facility.

    a) Nature of competition:

    _____

    b) Explanation:

    _____

    _____

    _____

    _____

5. The Ottawa metropolitan area is supplied by five regional manufacturers of bricks. The bricks are used in constructing homes and buildings as well as for other purposes (decorative walls, patios). Three of these firms account for more than 80 percent of all the bricks sold in the area. The bricks are purchased either in standardized sizes or according to buyer specifications, and all five firms charge almost identical prices. When bricks are in short supply, a few buyers have purchased some bricks from other firms located outside the region, but high transportation costs make this an extremely expensive alternative. Two manufacturers have announced plans to boost their production capacity, and all five manufacturers have announced price increases of at least six percent for the coming year.

a) Nature of competition:

_____

b) Explanation:

_____

_____

_____

_____

_____

6. The trend toward cholesterol-free diets has been a problem for Gina Hutchinson, who owns a chicken farm in southern Ontario. Like thousands of other chicken farmers in Canada, Hutchinson produces the eggs that end up on the breakfast tables of Canada, that are used by restaurants in preparing meals, and that are used in producing a variety of packaged foods. Hutchinson's chicken flock has always been a very small portion of the 50,000,000 egg-laying hens in Canada. However, like most other egg producers, she has had to decrease the size of her flock in recent years as consumer demand for eggs has declined.

a) Nature of competition:

_____

b) Explanation:

_____

_____

_____

_____

_____

_____

Question for Discussion

Have the firms described in the above cases achieved any "competitive advantage" over their competitors? If not, what steps might they take in the future to achieve some competitive advantage?

Appendix C

Marketing arithmetic

Chapter Summary

- **Understand the components of an operating statement (profit and loss statement).**
  An operating statement is a simple summary of the financial results of a company'soperations over a specified period of time. The main purpose of the operating statement is to determine the net profit figure and present data to support that figure. Although the time period may vary there are only three basic components (1) *Sales*, (2) *Costs*, (3) *Profit*. (See Exhibit C-1, p. C2)

- **Know how to compute the stockturn rate.**
  The Stockturn rate is a measure of the number of times the average inventory is sold during a year. There are three different methods for computing a stockturn rate:

    1. Cost of sales/Average inventory at cost

    2. Net sales/ Average inventory at selling price

    3. Sales in units/ Average inventory in units

- **Understand how operating ratios can help analyze a business.**
  Operating ratios compare various figures on the operating statement to net sales (gross sales minus returns and allowances) These *operating ratios* can than be compared to earlier periods and to other companies in the same sector.

- **Understand how to calculate markups and markdowns.**
  A *markup* is the dollar amount added to the cost of sales to get the selling price. There are two types of approaches to markup: (1) a *markup* on cost, and (2) a *markup* on selling price.
  A *markdown* is a retail price reduction required because customers will not buy some item at the originally marked-up price. Markdowns are most often a product of business errors – too much of a particular item was bought, too high a markup and so on. The markdown ratio is not calculated using the operating statement. It is calculated using the actual prices of products and the dollar value of the markdown.

  $$\text{Markdown \%} = \frac{\text{\$ Markdowns} + \text{\$ Allowances}}{\text{\$ Net sales}} \times 100$$

- **Understand how to calculate return on investment (ROI) and return on assets (ROA).**
  The *return on investment* (ROI) is the ratio of net profit (after taxes) to the investment used to make the net profit, multiplied by 100 to get rid of decimals. Investment is the

amount of resources expressed in dollars that is invested in a company or in a specific project. The value of the investment can be found on the balance sheet.

Return on assets (ROA) is the ratio of net profit (after taxes) to the assets used to make the net profit—times 100.

Both ROI and ROA measures are trying to get at the same thing—how effectively the company is using resources.

Important Terms

operating statement, p. 644
gross sales, p. 644
return, p. 644
allowance, p. 644
net sales, p. 644
cost of sales, p. 644
gross margin (gross profit), p. 644
expenses, p. 644
net profit, p. 644

purchase discount, p. 645
stockturn rate, p. 645
operating ratios, p. 646
markup, p. 646
markdown ratio, p. 648
markdown, p. 648
return on investment (ROI), p. 648
balance sheet, p. 648
return on assets (ROA), p. 649

True-False Questions

___ 1.   An operating statement is a simple summary of the financial results of a company's operation over a specified period of time.

___ 2.   The three basic components of an operating statement are sales, costs, and return on investment.

___ 3.   Net sales equals gross sales minus returns and allowances.

___ 4.   The "cost of sales" is the total value (at cost) of the sales during the operating period.

___ 5.   Gross margin (or gross profit) equals net sales minus operating expenses.

___ 6.   Net profit equals net sales minus the cost of sales minus operating expenses.

___ 7.   To calculate the net profit accurately, purchase discounts and freight charges should be added to the cost of sales.

___ 8.   Expenses do not include the cost of sales.

___ 9.   The stockturn rate is a measure of how long it takes a certain inventory of goods to be sold.

___ 10. Stockturn rate may be calculated as the cost of sales divided by the average inventory at cost.

___ 11. The various components of an operating statement should always be expressed in absolute numbers rather than in percentages.

___ 12. If a store takes a 50-cent markup on a certain product, then its net profit for that item is also 50 cents.

___ 13. A 25 percent markup on cost equals a 20 percent markup on selling price.

___ 14. A markdown ratio equals dollar markdowns divided by net sales; returns and allowances are not included.

___ 15. Markdowns are generally shown on a firm's operating statement.

___ 16. Return on investment is not shown on the firm's operating statement.

___ 17. To increase return on investment, a firm *must* increase sales.

___ 18. Although return on investment is calculated in the same way as return on assets, the two ratios are trying to show different things about the company's use of resources.

1. T, p. 644	7. F, p. 644-645	13. T, p. 646
2. F, p. 644	8. T, p. 644	14. F, p. 648
3. T, p. 644	9. F, p. 645	15. F, p. 648
4. T, p. 644	10. T, p. 645	16. T, p. 648
5. F, p. 644	11. F, p. 645	17. F, p. 648
6. T, p. 644	12. F, p. 646	18. F, p. 648-649

Multiple-Choice Questions (Circle the correct response)

1. The primary purpose of the operating statement is:
   a. to determine which products or customers are most profitable.
   b. to determine the net profit figure for the company.
   c. to present data to support the net profit figure.
   d. to indicate the source of the firm's assets.
   e. both b and c above.

2. The essential components of an operating statement are:
   a. gross sales, gross margin, and net profit.
   b. net sales, cost of sales, and profit or loss.
   c. sales, costs, and profit or loss.
   d. gross sales, gross margin, expenses, and net profit.
   e. sales, markdowns, and ROI.

3. Which of the following statements is *true*?
   a. "Gross sales" is equal to revenue actually received and kept.
   b. "Cost of sales" means the cost value of goods on hand at any given time.
   c. Expenses are included in the "Cost of sales" section of the operating statement.
   d. "Gross margin" less the "Cost of sales" equals "Net profit."
   e. None of the above statements is true.

4. Given the following data for the OnTarget Company for the year l99X, calculate OnTarget's net profit.

Gross sales	$157,000
Returns	3,000
Allowances	4,000
Purchases	60,000
Beginning inventory	50,000
Freight-in	3,000
Cost of sales	100,000
Expenses	30,000

   a. $10,000
   b. $12,000
   c. $17,000
   d. $20,000
   e. $27,000

5. Which of the following statements is *false*?
   a. Stockturn rate equals cost of sales divided by average inventory at cost.
   b. Stockturn rate equals gross sales divided by average inventory at selling price.
   c. Stockturn rate equals net sales minus gross margin divided by average inventory at cost.
   d. Stockturn rate equals sales in units divided by average inventory in units.
   e. Stockturn rate equals net sales divided by average inventory at selling price.

Use the following data to answer questions 6 and 7.

Gross sales	$1,020,000
Markdowns	50,000
Cost of sales	50%
Beginning inventory	150,000
Returns and allowances	20,000
Expenses	30%
Purchases	400,000

6.   Calculate the net profit (or loss) for the firm described above.
      a. $150,000
      b. $190,000
      c. $204,000
      d. $200,000
      e.   Cannot be determined without more information.

7.   Assume that the average stockturn rate for this industry is 4. How does this firm
      compare to its competitors?
      a.   The firm has an above-average turnover rate.
      b.   The firm has a below-average turnover rate.
      c.   The firm has an average turnover rate.
      d.   Cannot be determined.

Use the following data from a company's last accounting period to answer questions 8-10.

Sales returns	$ 10,000	
Sales allowances	15,000	
Expenses		25 %
Closing inventory at cost	50,000	
Markdowns	45,000	
Freight-in	5,000	
Purchases	150,000	
Net profit	30,000	10%

8.   The cost of sales is:
      a. $225,000
      b. $105,000
      c. $145,000
      d. $195,000
      e. $ 75,000

9.   The stockturn rate is:
      a.   6.0
      b.   3.9
      c.   4.3
      d.   2.8
      e.   1.5

10. The markdown ratio is:
    a. 20 percent
    b. 11 2/3 percent
    c. 18 1/3 percent
    d. 10 percent
    e. 15 percent

11. Josie's Florist Shop uses a traditional markup of 25 percent for all of its long-stem roses. If a rose costs her $6, what should Josie *add* to this cost to determine her selling price?
    a. $1.50
    b. 33 1/3 percent of $6.00
    c. 125 percent of $6.00
    d. $3.00
    e. 25 percent of $6.00

12. Knowledge of departmental markdown ratios for a given period would be useful in:
    a. preparing an operating statement for that period.
    b. determining the value of goods on hand.
    c. measuring the efficiency of the various retail departments.
    d. computing the stockturn rate for that period.
    e. All of the above.

13. To increase its return on investment (ROI), a firm could:
    a. increase its profit margin.
    b. increase its sales.
    c. decrease its investment.
    d. increase its leveraging.
    e. All of the above.

14. *Given the following information, calculate the FirstChoice Company's ROI.*

Net sales	$1,000,000
Gross margin	200,000
Markdowns	200,000
Assets	300,000
Net profit (after taxes)	10,000
Owner's investment	100,000

    a. 3.3 percent
    b. 1,000.0 percent
    c. 10.0 percent
    d. 2.5 percent
    e. 5.0 percent

15. In Question 14, the FirstChoice Company's ROA was:
    a. 3.3 percent.
    b. 2.5 percent.
    c. 30.0 percent.
    d. 150.0 percent.
    e. Some negative number--because the assets were larger than the owners' investment.

Answers to Multiple-Choice Questions

1. e, p. 644
2. c, p. 644
3. e, p. 644
4. d, p. 644
5. b, p. 645

6. d, p. 645
7. a, p. 645
8. d, p. 644
9. d, p. 648
10. a, p. 648

11. b, p. 646
12. c, p. 648
13. e, p. 648
14. c, p. 648
15. a, p. 649

Exercise C-1

Marketing arithmetic

Introduction

A firm's financial records contain much useful information for a marketing manager. An effective marketing manager will make regular use of them in his planning. This exercise is designed to improve your understanding of the operating statement and the information it contains.

Assignment

Answer each of the following questions about the financial records of FastTrack Corporation.

1.   Complete FastTrack's operating statement (on the next page) by filling in the blank lines and then use the information in the financial statement to answer the following questions.

2.   Calculate the stockturn rate (using cost figures).

3.   Calculate the following operating ratios. (Round each answer to one decimal place.)

     a)   Net sales   100%

     b)   Cost of sales   _____

     c)   Gross margin   _____

     d)   Expenses   _____

     e)   Net profit   _____

FASTTRACK CORPORATION
Operating Statement
For the Year Ending December 31, 200X

Gross sales			$62,000
Less: Returns and allowances			a) _____
Net sales			58,000
Cost of sales			
Beginning inventory at cost		$12,000	
Purchases at billed cost	$26,000		
Less: Purchase discounts	3,000		
Purchases at net cost	b) _____		
Plus freight-in	3,000		
Net cost of delivered purchases		c) _____	
Cost of goods available for sale		d) _____	
Less: Ending inventory at cost.		8,000	
Cost of sales			e) _____
Gross margin (gross profit)			f) _____
Expenses			
Selling expense			
Sales salaries	7,000		
Advertising expense	2,200		
Delivery expense	3,300		
Total selling expenses		g) _____	
Administrative expense			
Office salaries	$ 3,800		
Office supplies	900		
Miscellaneous	1,300		
Total admin. expense		h) _____	
General expense			
Rent expense	1,100		
Miscellaneous	100		
Total general expense		i) _____	
Total expense			j) _____
Net profit from operation			k) _____

Question for Discussion

What additional financial information would help the marketing manager of FastTrack Corporation to improve his operation?